1980

CHURCH MUSIC

CHURCH MUSIC

Musical and Hymnological
Developments in Western
Christianity

by Russel N. Squire

THE BETHANY PRESS

ST. LOUIS, MISSOURI

Second printing, 1968

Distributed by Thomas C. Lothian, Melbourne, Australia, and Auckland, New Zealand, and by The G. R. Welch Company, Toronto, Ontario, Canada. All other foreign distribution by Feffer and Simons, Inc., New York, New York.

To my mother
Jean Crookstone Muirhead Squire

PREFACE

This short history of church music is planned to be helpful for ministers, church musicians, and students. From experience in teaching a course in religious music to undergraduate and graduate students preparing for positions in church work, the author has found that available introductory information is too scattered for practical use. Often the material on church music is pointed to the peculiar needs of a certain religious sect and not planned to be helpful also to the general student of religion.

Therefore, this volume represents an effort to compile concisely from various sources an authentic account of church music, extending from ancient times to the present. This work includes consideration of the music of the ancient Hebrews, the early Christians, the Western medieval Christians and the European reformers; it treats on the influx of all this activity on the North American continent, including review of the church music of most recent times in the United States.

That use has been freely made of the work of writers in the field will, of course, be apparent to all. Endeavor has been made, however to acknowledge all such writings, and failure to do so is an unintentional oversight. It is the plan of this book to present the material of each chapter palatably in short sections under suitable headings. Of course, highly technical material occasionally has had to be included; such material should not be ignored. However, its inclusion has always been carefully and separately introduced. Of special value is the distribution, throughout the book, of music representative of the historical periods and places. Also included are a bibliography and a complete concordance of musical subjects and terms referred to in the Bible.

Of invaluable use (thus allowing for more easy synthesizing and briefing on my part of résumés for these notes on the history of

7

church music into a consecutive account) were the many pertinent references in Edward Dickinson: *Music in the History of the Western Church;* Charles Winfred Douglas: *Church Music in History and Practice;* Leonard Ellinwood: *The History of American Church Music;* John Tasker Howard: *Our American Music;* Paul Henry Lang: *Music in Western Civilization;* Gustave Reese: *Music in the Middle Ages;* William L. Sumner: *The Organ;* Albert Edward Bailey: *The Gospel in Hymns;* and Gustave Fredric Soderlund: *Examples of Gregorian Chant and Works by Orlandus Lassus and Giovanni Pierluigi Palestrina.*

I am grateful to Rabbi Wiesel of Los Angeles for reading and helping with the chapter on Hebrew music; to my younger son, William Cassius, for the many drawings which he kindly prepared; to William Green, Professor of Latin, University of California, for aid in the ancient writings; to William D. Foley of Los Angeles for suggestions about the sections on Anglican Music; and to Father Walsh of Los Angeles for valued attention to the references to Roman Catholic music.

I am deeply appreciative of the kindness of W. W. Norton and Company, Inc., 101 Fifth Avenue, New York, in allowing me to quote from Gustave Reese, *Music in the Middle Ages,* pp. 62, 66, and 105; of Appleton-Century-Crofts, Inc., 101 Fifth Avenue, New York, in allowing me to reprint from Ferguson, D. N., *A History of Musical Thought* (Second edition) 1948, p. 13.

Of course, I am indebted to many friends who have read the material and helped invaluably in preparation of the manuscript; to Professor Herman Wilson of the Department of English of Lubbock College; and Mrs. Pamela Willetts Gordon of the Department of Manuscripts of the British Museum, who has been of inestimable good service not only in searching out source materials but in providing helpful suggestions.

R.N.S.

CONTENTS

CHAPTER ONE   HEBREW MUSIC   13

Primitive Origins; Early Hebrew Music; Hebrew Institutional Music; The Music of Solomon's Temple; Music
of the Temple and Synagogue

CHAPTER TWO   EARLY CHRISTIAN MUSIC   29

Grecian Background; Theoretical Considerations in
Greek Music; Greek Spiritual Meanings; The Apostolic
Period; The Early Postapostolic Period; Instrumental
Music in the Early Postapostolic Period; Traditional In-
fluence in the Period

CHAPTER THREE   MEDIEVAL MUSIC   51

The Premedieval Period; Eastern Chant; Ambrosian and
Gregorian Chant; Later Periods of Medieval Chant;
The Liturgy; The Service of Worship; The Hymns of
the Medieval Period; The Roman Liturgy—Its Prin-
ciples; Beginnings of Multivoiced Music; Beginnings of
Modern Music Notation and Theory; Choral Music in
the Medieval Period; Ars-Nova—Fourteenth Century;
The Fifteenth and Sixteenth Centuries; The Venetian
School; Flemish Influence; The Counter Reformation
as Part of the Roman Catholic Reform; Palestrina; The
Opera; Secular Music; Additional Musical Forms and
Devices

CHAPTER FOUR   MUSIC IN THE REFORMATION   112

The Hymnody of Luther; Religious Art Music; Oratorio; Johann Sebastian Bach; Equal Temperament; The Hymnody of Calvin and Watts; Methodist Hymnody; Music in the Church of England; A Note on Baroque Music; A Note on Classic Music; A Note on Romantic Music; Folk Backgrounds among the English-Speaking People

CHAPTER FIVE   THE ORGAN   172

Ancient Beginnings; The Hydraulic Organ; The Pneumatic Organ; The Organ of the Middle Ages; The Winchester Organ; The Organ as a Factor in Worship; The Organ in England and Germany; The Organ in France and the Low Countries; The Positive; The Portative; Landini and the Organetto; Developments in the Keyboard; The Regal; The Organ's Effects upon Music Composition; Development of the Pedal; Choral Music and the Organ; Acoustical Considerations; The Organ of the Sixteenth through the Eighteenth Centuries; The Organ in Britain; The Organ from the Eighteenth Century; England; The Organ in the New World; The Organ Today

CHAPTER SIX   RELIGIOUS MUSIC IN THE
              UNITED STATES OF AMERICA   211

Spanish Background; Colonial Days; Quaker, Mennonite, Moravian, and Other Influences; French Background; The Church of England; Important Musical Personages; Artistic Religious Music in the United States in the Latter Nineteenth Century; The Gospel Song; White and Negro Spirituals; The Rise of the "Shaped-Note" Singing School; Religious Music Today in the United States

CONCORDANCE 261

APPENDIX I 267

APPENDIX II 269

BIBLIOGRAPHY 287

INDEX 295

ILLUSTRATIONS

Ancient Instruments . 24-27

Greek Tetrachords 30

The Inscription of Seikilos 33

Ancient Instruments 44

Ambrosian Hymn 56

"Hosanna Filio David" 59

Simple and Florid Plainsong 70

Parallel and Freer Organum 73

Medieval Modal Patterns 76

"Hymn to St. John the Baptist" 79

Guidonian Hand; Table of Neumes 80

"Ave Verum Corpus," Josquin des Prez 89

"Benedictus," Orlandus Lassus 96

"Ein feste Burg," Luther 118

"Come, Let Us Join Our Cheerful Songs" 133

"Jesus, Lover of My Soul" 137

"Old Hundredth" 169

"Was frag ich nach der Welt"   170

A 14th-Century Organ   184

"Coronation"   222

"Watchman, Tell Us of the Night"   244

"Mary, Don't You Weep"   248

"We Praise Thee, O God"   250

"Sweet By and By" (shaped notes)   252

CHAPTER ONE

HEBREW MUSIC

PRIMITIVE ORIGINS

The origin of music is historically obscure, yet it seems fairly certain that early music possessed a utilitarian purpose above that of merely pleasing the ear and that it was connected with poetic recitation and dancing, usually in ceremonies associated with death, birth, puberty, mating, and religion. Much of the music of all primitive peoples that can be observed today springs from such important experiences of life.

It may be that instruments, rather than the voice, were first used for making music; for all of the instrument families of today can be traced to early times. The earliest ones were the percussion instruments. From among these, in tribal use, there was gradually developed the large drum made of a hollowed log with animal hide drawn over the ends. From this crude beginning there eventually evolved the snare drum, bass drum, kettle drum, and other modern percussion equipment.

Among early string instruments were the lyre and the zither. These were frameworks with three or more strings drawn across a shallow sound-box. Later were developed the harp, violin, and combinations of string and percussion instruments such as clavichord, harpsichord, and piano.

Among early wind horns were both reed and reedless instruments. They were the forerunners of the present-day clarinets, bassoons, cornets, trombones, and so on. An instrument that might be called a hydraulic pipe organ was invented by Ctesibius of Alexandria in the third century B.C. It attained to great favor in Imperial Rome but later became so associated with pagan debauchery that it was excluded from religious ceremony.

EARLY HEBREW MUSIC

Music is mentioned frequently in Old Testament writings, and is thus shown to be an early activity of the Hebrews. Pretentious instrumental and vocal music, for secular as well as sacred purposes, was a popular part of the Hebrew life. At first, the music was informal and spontaneous, expressive of the exuberance of an emotional people, but later, during the time of the prophets, it was consciously developed and systematized, so that it took on, although clumsily, the characteristics of an art form. The earliest Hebrew music served primarily functional rather than artistic purposes, that is, the music was not carefully composed but rather improvised, born spontaneously out of the experience and excitement of great occasions.

The song that the people sang, along with Moses and Miriam, in celebration of Israel's delivery through the Red Sea is perhaps the earliest religious song of Hebrew record (Exodus 15:1-21). It was a spontaneous musical outburst of great proportions. Spontaneity of composition was evidenced also in the much earlier secular song of Lamech:

Lamech said to his wives:
"Adah and Zillah, hear my voice;
          you wives of Lamech, hearken to what I say:
I have slain a man for wounding me,
          a young man for striking me.
If Cain is avenged sevenfold,
          truly Lamech seventy-sevenfold."—Genesis 4:23-24.

Of interest, in connection with the introduction of Lamech's song, is the statement that Lamech's son, Jubal, was the father of all such as handle the harp and organ, i.e., lyre and pipe (Genesis 4: 21). The tambourine and lyre were well known: "Why did you flee secretly, and cheat me, and did not tell me, so that I might have sent you away with mirth and songs, with tambourine[1] and lyre?"—Genesis 31:27.

The song of Miriam, extemporaneous as it was, indicates that it must have been customary to have such kinds of music activity. The fact that musical instruments are referred to in the passage and that the songs rendered were sung by groups rather than by one individual, indicates that organized music was in existence during the Egyptian bondage (Exodus 15:20-21). That this is true is borne out further in the instance of Moses' return from the Mount during the Exodus when he found the people singing to the golden calf which they had fashioned to be their god (Exodus 32:18).

HEBREW INSTITUTIONAL MUSIC

Hebrew sacred music was the "spontaneous outflow of the religious nature"; this is evidenced in the song of Deborah and Barak, one of the important later songs showing the greatness of Hebrew improvisation. (See Judges, chapter 5.) Such informal improvisations are still common among Eastern peoples, even as far west as Italy. Something similar among the bards and among the originators of the English ballad was common. Frequently, such spontaneous outbursts have been witnessed among the Southern Negroes of the United States.

Out of the earlier spontaneity there evolved, first, musical systematization and, much later, ritualistic and institutional regulation. The Old Testament indicates clearly that even as late as Moses there were no required forms of music in the practice of worship—unless such occasions as the Feast of Trumpets are considered worship services (Numbers 29:1). No official delegation of singers is to be found among the officers of the tabernacle although mention is made of "skilled workers" for the tabernacle. In Numbers 21:27, reference is made to ballad singers.

Although it seems very clear that Moses did not *institute* a

---

[1]The tambourine was a small drum without the jingling bell-like attachments associated with today's tambourine.

musical portion in worship, it has been a tradition that he wrote
Psalm 90, which came to be the nucleus for the subsequent collection known as the "Psalms of David." That Moses was educated
musically is supported by Philo, who wrote that in addition to being well trained in arithmetic and geometry, Moses was well trained
in the art of music.[2] Moses no doubt had every opportunity to learn
about contemporary music while he was a member of Pharoah's
household.

The Hebrews finally came to inaugurate procedures for giving
certain people special training for music activities, especially in the
later periods of the temple. Although this seems very doubtful, it
has been thought by some that training musicians was a chief
purpose of the "schools of the prophets" after the time of David,
who is credited generally with having played the greatest part in
developing Hebrew song. It was he who was supposed to have
formulated musical services for the temple worship, although it
was his son Solomon who introduced them into the newly completed temple after the properties which David had dedicated for
temple use had been moved to the new location there (1 Chronicles
15:16-23; 1 Chronicles 25; 2 Chronicles 5:1; 7:1-7).

After the founding of the temple, music and sacrifice were in-
separable parts of the temple worship and the name of David stood
for the newer, more formal musical contributions that were to be
the special trust of the Levites. However, it is not to be supposed
that all the Psalms of David were actually the creation of his mind.
In addition to the refining influence of Egypt that came to Israel's
music through Moses along with the later contributions of David,
there was a considerable modification of Israel's music by the
Assyrian, Babylonian, and other oriental associations. Psalm 137
would seem to bear out this point of view.

With all the growth and change that evolved, however, it is not
likely that the Old Testament music of the Jews was ever pleasant
to the ear, or refined. It is quite certain that ancient Hebrew singing was not tuneful; it perhaps was not unlike present-day chanting
or cantillation.

---

[2]Philo (Judaeus). *Vita Mosis.* Book I, p. 5. Translation—Yonge, C. D. *The Works of
Philo Judaeus* (London: Henry G. Bohn, York Street, Covent Garden, 1885), p. 6.

Instruments among the ancient Hebrews were used mostly for the purpose of marking rhythms such as were necessary for occasions of exotic dancing combined with formless expostulation in song,[3] or for occasions when it would be pleasing to set an accompanying rhythm to a solo cantillation such as David might have sung before Saul. If instruments were used to sound tunes, it must have been in instances of experimentation or casual practice. It is generally believed that any semblance of melody in Hebrew music would be accidental, as occasioned in the rise and fall of pitch when demanded by the sense of the language. Since there was no Hebrew system of music notation, the tune, if there had been one, would have been unharmonized and at the mercy of the talent, the caprice, and the memory of the singer. It is safe to conclude that ancient Hebrew cantillations carried no such meaning as do present-day formally patterned melodies.

In addition to the rhythmic accompaniment to song afforded on occasion by the instruments, there were occasions, such as in a "call to worship," when trumpets or similar instruments were used as today in a fanfare preceding an announcement, or as a church bell striking the hours. There were also the occasions when the whole power of all the instruments was used in order to give color and spirit to an assemblage such as might be given in a modern festivity with hand clapping, shouting, whistling, and blaring of horns.

THE MUSIC OF SOLOMON'S TEMPLE

During the reign of David when music came to its important and vital place in Hebrew life, it became the practice to appoint Levites by the thousands for musical service. (1 Chronicles 9:33; chapters 15, 16, 23, and 25.) The Hebrews made the positions of both priests and musicians hereditary in the tribe of Levi. Per-

---

[3]An interesting commentary on Hebrew religious expression of the day is suggested in the reference to David's shouting and nearly naked dancing before the ark (2 Samuel 6: 14-23).

This reference from Samuel provides a clue to the contemporary music which often, in the earlier periods referred to in the Old Testament, was described as noisy (Exodus 32: 17-19); the passages in the very late Books of Chronicles which parallel references in the earlier Books of Samuel are often colored by contemporary circumstances, thus ascribing more advanced qualities to the period than authentic history would permit. Accordingly the advancements ascribed in Chronicles to both the music of David and that of the first temple were perhaps not actually achieved at that earlier time; more likely they were descriptive of the music of Zerubbabel's time and later.

haps this plan was adopted from the Egyptians, who had the custom of dividing their people into tribes, confining each profession to one family. At any rate, in temple time, only those of the families of priests or Levites performed in the musical service of the LORD.

With the building of the temple by Solomon about 968 B.C., the musical activity in worship was carried on essentially as David had planned (2 Chronicles, chapters 5 and 7). Large instrumental groups and singing groups performed in many of the temple ceremonies. Although there is no complete knowledge of the specific functions of the music in Solomon's temple, it is believed that song had as sure a place in temple worship as did sacrifice, except in times of calamity. It is known, for example, that the Levites sang, unaccompanied, a different Psalm each day. Of course today, since there is no temple, the priest does not sacrifice nor does the Levite sing, but what is thought to be the same songs are performed still by the orthodox Jew in his morning prayer. It is of special interest to note that women singers are thought never to have participated in the temple worship; references to women's singing in the Old Testament are always to occasions of singing other than in temple services.

Solomon, like his father, was fond of poetry and music (1 Kings 4:32; Ecclesiastes 2:8). Thus it is thought that he also was an author of some of the Psalms. Under Solomon, it is suspected that the music services were made even more elaborate than David had suggested (2 Chronicles 8:14; Josephus: Lib. 33, Cap. 4). Under Solomon, certainly, the music traditions were firmly established; and for years after Solomon, music continued its vital part in Hebrew life. Singers and trumpeters contributed to all phases of life, even to the winning of battles (2 Chronicles 13:12; 20:19-21).

There is no doubt that the music of the temple was at first a sincere effort to worship God effectively and acceptably. However, the emphasis, rather than continuing Godward, defected more and more manward until Amos told that God was displeased with his people

who sing idle songs to the sound of the harp,
        and like David invent for themselves instruments of music.
                                                    —Amos 6:5

Moffatt words it:

crooning to the music of the lute,
composing airs like David himself.[4]

And again:

Even though you offer me your burnt offerings and cereal
offerings,
        I will not accept them,
and the peace offerings of your fatted beasts
        I will not look upon.
Take away from me the noise of your songs;
        to the melody of your harps I will not listen.
                                            —Amos 5:22-23;

According to Moffatt:

you offer me your gifts? I will not take them;
you offer fatted cattle? I will not look at them.
No more of your hymns for me!
I will not listen to your lutes.

It is not to be supposed that Amos in these passages was understood by his people to be disparaging David's contributions to
temple worship or that he believed them to be unacceptable to the
LORD.[5] Rather it is to be concluded that God, through Amos, was
being portrayed as showing his displeasure toward the men, priests,
and musicians of the city of Zion who had forgotten the reasons
for worship and who were "not grieved over the ruin of Joseph!"
Indeed, the LORD approved the dedication ceremonies of the
temple (2 Chronicles, chapters 5 and 7, particularly 7:3) and if
there had been disapproval by the LORD of David's musical activi-

---

[4]From *The Bible: A New Translation,* by James Moffatt. Copyright 1922, 1935 and
1950 by Harper & Brothers. Used by permission.

[5]Throughout Christian history there have arisen conflicts over whether or not to employ instrumental music in a worship or religious connection. This passage from Amos has
been used by the "anti-instrumentalists" to indicate that "Jehovah is displeased with instrumental music in worship." Adam Clarke (1762?-1832), a respected Methodist authority, in his *Commentary,* developed this view to infinitely detailed proportions.

ties, such censure must have been toward activities other than those through which he instituted temple music.

The decadence of Hebrew music in the time between Abijah and Jehoiakim (900-600 B.C.) was due to a decline in religious consecration, to continued participation in wars, and to intercourse with other nations. Sporadic attempts were made to re-establish the old glory of their former worship, but in succeeding periods the number of officers and musicians of the temple was decreased until, at the end of the eighth century B.C., in the time of Hezekiah, even the menial workers of the Levites had to help the priests perform the sacrificial duties (2 Chronicles, chapter 29). For a period the priesthood had been restricted to the sons of Aaron of the tribe of the Levites.

Soon the Hebrew nation was pillaged by the Babylonians (586 B.C) ; and during the seventy years of Babylonian captivity there was not very much musical activity:

> By the waters of Babylon,
>> there we sat down and wept,
>> when we remembered Zion.
> On the willows there
>> we hung our lyres.
> For there our captors
>> required of us songs,
> and our tormentors, mirth, saying,
>> "Sing us one of the songs of Zion!"
>
> How shall we sing the LORD's song
>> in a foreign land?
> If I forget you, O Jerusalem,
>> let my right hand wither!
>>>>> —Psalm 137:1-5

MUSIC OF THE TEMPLE AND SYNAGOGUE
(from Babylon to Christ)

Between the time of the destruction of Solomon's temple in 586 B.C. by Nebuchadnezzar when the surviving Hebrews were carried off to the seventy years' captivity in Babylon, and the time of the apostles under Christ, the Hebrew music continued as a closely connected part of the Hebrew institutions of the period. But with their grief at the temple's destruction and the ark's loss, and with their realization that their sorry lot was due to their having mocked "the messengers of God," the captives were in no state to worship the LORD grandiosely with song and music (2 Chronicles 36:16).

It was probably during this period of the Babylonian exile that the synagogue, another institution of Jewish religious life, was founded. It still exists.

It is believed that the synagogue, in the beginning as now, served the Jews' public worship needs in the lands far from the temple. Even after the return of the Jews, the synagogue served as a community gathering place where they could worship less formally than in the temple. It was a place where, in a true community spirit of oneness, the Jews "could bare their hearts to the LORD in sincere communion with God." To the Jews who had been torn from their homes, stripped of their possessions, taken from their friends and relatives, and enslaved by their captors, the synagogue was a source of comfort which by making possible their continued communion with the LORD, was a present salvation to them.

Upon the Hebrews' liberation from Babylon, a second temple known as Zerubbabel's temple was erected about 516 B.C. It was not as splendid as Solomon's temple, and the ark, not having been found, was missing from its Holy of Holies. This second temple was followed by still a third, Herod's temple, which in reality was merely an enlarging and enriching of the second temple, for Zerubbabel's temple had not been destroyed, although about 168 B.C. it was desecrated and pillaged. The renewed temple of Herod stood from 19 B.C. to A.D. 70, when it was finally destroyed by the Romans in their capture of Jerusalem.

After the return from the Babylonian captivity, the synagogue was maintained along with the temple of Zerubbabel; it served as a place for community lawmaking, as well as for worship. Perhaps it was in the synagogue that the work of Nehemiah and Ezra was consummated and that the Old Testament canon was finally established. Certainly the synagogue was an accepted institution in the time of Christ and the apostles, for before and after the institution of the church the followers of Jesus worshiped and prayed in the synagogues of Jerusalem. Up to the time of the destruction of Herod's temple, there were many synagogues throughout Jerusalem; the *Mishnah* mentions that one of them was in the very precincts of the temple (Yomah VII:1; Sotah VII:7, 8).

Although from early synagogue times until long after the time of Christ there was a similarity between the music of the temple and of the synagogue; that of the synagogue was always restricted to pure singing, i.e., instrumentally unaccompanied. It was confined to the intoning or singing which had to do with reading, teaching, and praying—in the manner of cantillation. Rabbi Joshua ben Hananiah, a member of the Temple Levitical Choir, at the close of the first century wrote that the choral singers, "in a body" went from the orchestra by the altar of the temple to the synagogue, thus participating in both services. Singing by the assembled people (the women perhaps did not sing) was carried on in congregational style. The rabbis and cantors led the exercises. It is important to remember that the Hebrew language as written, contained no punctuation; thus the language depended upon the reader to divide the phrases and sentences. When publicly read, the readers indicated the phrases by chanting in the singing manner known as cantillation.

Although the music of the synagogue was restricted to "pure singing," there is an instrument, usually referred to in connection with synagogue activity, known as the shofar, a trumpetlike instrument fashioned out of an animal's horn such as a ram's horn. It is thought to be the only surviving instrument of ancient times; it was employed as a trumpet for battle or to usher in the day of atonement in the year of Jubilation (Leviticus 25:8-10) and for other specific celebrations. However, its use in such ceremonies is not to be construed as use in worship services. The author has visited synagogues which even today do not use any musical instruments as part of their worship services.

From the time of the return from Babylon (516 B.C.) to the time of the Maccabees[6] (141 B.C.—34 B.C.), the Hebrews were attacked

---

[6]The period of the Hasmoneans: the period of history referred to in the books, I and II Maccabees, extended from *c.* 175 B.C.—*c.* 135 B.C. Antigonus, last of the Hasmoneans was executed by Mark Antony in 37 B.C.

and plundered, first by the Egyptians and then by the Syrians. The Maccabees, hampered by inner strife among their own people, were unable to re-establish the Hebrew nation. Thus, finally, the Jews were brought under Roman domination when Pompey was called to Jerusalem to quell the disorders there (63 B.C.).

In 40 B.C., driven from Palestine by those who would make Antigonus king, Herod journeyed, or escaped, to Rome and inveigled the Roman Senate with Octavian and Mark Antony to elevate him to the nominal position, "king of Judaea." Under Herod, in this new role, there began a period of political conniving and crime that is utterly revolting. To appease the Roman ruler, public games after the pagan or Grecian manner were instituted and musicians were employed to perform in them, although since the games were detested by the followers of Mosaic law, it is generally thought that Jewish musicians did not participate. Indeed, the feeling which probably existed among the earnest Jewish musicians against the licentious behavior of Herod, perhaps accounts for the Christians' attitude toward music in a later period.[7] It is not to be inferred that Herod's distasteful reign was resisted by the Jews, for they regarded it as a "mysterious and obnoxious" evidence of the Lord's displeasure, and accepted it as the will of God. While Herod observed the law outwardly and publicly and the Jews accepted him, nevertheless, they had a saying that "it was better to be Herod's *swine* than a *son* of Herod."

In the Book of *Job* (although the time of its writing is unknown) a fine descriptive source of the contemporary Hebrew music is given. In Job, music among the Hebrews was regarded as a respected art (Job 21:11-12).

> "They send forth their little ones like a flock,
>   and their children dance.
> They sing to the tambourine and the lyre,
>   and rejoice to the sound of the pipe."

There is an interesting relationship between the account of a funeral service found in Matthew 9:23 and another in Job 30:31

---

[7]See pp. 28, 41, 46.

Hebrew timbrel

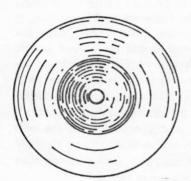

Egyptian cymbals

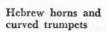

Hebrew horns and
curved trumpets

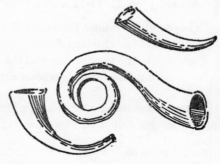

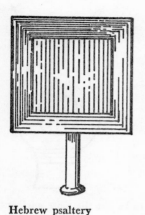

Hebrew psaltery

Hebrew straight trumpet
and pipe

Egyptian hand harp thought to resemble the Hebrew sackbut (sambuke). "Sackbut" and "sambuke" are often interchanged ambiguously. As used in Daniel 3:5, King James Version, "sackbut" indicates "bagpipe." However, as derived out of later Spanish usage, it refers to the forerunner of the "trombone." But again, "sackbut" is often a mistranslation of an Arabic word more accurately to be translated "sambuke," which at once may be understood to refer to an ancient, harplike instrument as shown, or to a bagpipe or even to a hurdy-gurdy.

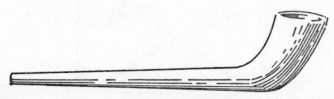

Modern Hebrew shophar not unlike the ancient shophar since to this day it, like the ancient one, is made from a ram's horn, then straightened by heating. This instrument was used in a manner much like a modern bugle, that is, to call groups together or to announce the time of ceremonial events

25

 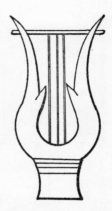

Two Hebrew lyres or cithara (kithara) thought to be like the more ancient Hebrew kinnor

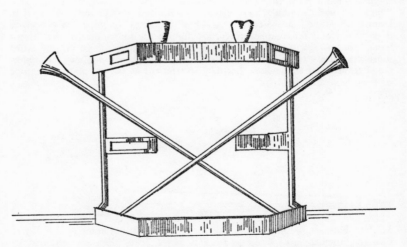

Two ancient Hebrew trumpets as found depicted on the Arch of Titus, showing the table for the shew bread

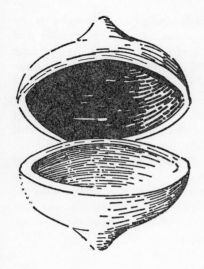

Pair of Hebrew cymbals

indicating the probable use of music for funerals in the times of both of these writings:

"My lyre is turned to mourning,
       and my pipe to the voice of those who weep."

Thus, music for funerals was one of the important requirements in the time of Jacob and Joseph and in the time of Christ. According to the *Talmud,* "The poorest among the Israelites should never at the funeral of a wife engage less than two flutes and one mourner" (Chethubbeth. 4. section 6. *apud* Spencer). In the Matthew reference, it is of interest to note that Jesus on his visit to the ruler's house on the occasion of the daughter's death was met with flute players and noise (Matthew 9:23). This was in a Jewish situation. On other occasions where the tone was Grecian in character such as in the Pauline references in Ephesians and Colossians, instead of tumult the descriptive term is "melody" or "singing." This indicates, as will be noted later, the vast difference existing between Jewish and Grecian music, even of the same period.

From all that has been found about Hebrew music, it may be concluded that it is very ancient; that it was used secularly as well as religiously; and that in some of the religious ceremonies its use was on the most elaborate scale, although its organization and systematization did not occur until after the Exodus. At the time of Christ, music was used in Herod's temple along much the same lines as in Solomon's temple. However, there was no such kind of musical service (except pure singing) in the synagogue, probably for the reason that the synagogue served, in a way, as a reminder to the people, of their former falling away from God and consequent exile in Babylon. Since the Hebrew people looked with disfavor upon Herod's support of the pagan games and the accompanying musical exercises, some think that the attitude of the Greeks, the Jews, and the early Christians toward certain restrictions in religious music and abstinence from musical instruments was provoked partly by their distaste for the public games of the Romans, and subsequent avoidance of "fleshly references."[8]

---

[8]The author has found phonograph recordings very useful in his teaching work. Catalogues of recorded titles are in a continuous process of change. Each month some are dropped from the available list; on the other hand an ever-increasing number of choice recordings of the very rare works are being made available. For available listings, consult your local record shop.

The volumes of THE HISTORY OF MUSIC IN SOUND, RCA Victor: Oxford University Press, are of great value. From these may be selected representative illustrations of each chapter:

Vol.	1:	Ancient and Oriental Music	LM 6057 -1, -2
Vol.	2:	Early Medieval Music up to 1300	LM 6015 -1, -2
Vol.	3:	Ars Nova and Renaissance	LM 6016 -1, -2
Vol.	4:	The Age of Humanism	LM 6029 -1, -2
Vol.	5:	Opera and Church Music	LM 6030 -1, -2
Vol.	6:	The Growth of International Music	LM 6031 -1, -2
Vol.	7:	The Symphonic Outlook	LM 6137 -1, -2
Vol.	8:	The Age of Beethoven (1790-1830)	LM 6146 -1, -2, -3
Vol.	9:	Romanticism (1830-1890)	LM 6153 -1, -2
Vol.	10:	Modern Music (1890-1950)	LM 6092 -1, -2

CHAPTER TWO

EARLY CHRISTIAN MUSIC

GRECIAN BACKGROUND

It was in the latter part of the time of Zerubbabel's temple that the period of classic antiquity embracing the Golden Age of Greece flourished. In it there were illustrious names: Pythagoras, Praxiteles, Plato, Aristotle, Socrates, Aristoxenus, and many more. It was in the Greek culture, largely based upon the foundation of the Golden Age, that Christianity found its most fertile soil.

To be a person of learning in ancient Greece, one had to be well-founded in drama, music, natural and political science, and athletics. "Music" in that ancient time was in a general way inclusive of mathematics, acoustics, astronomy, poetry, and what today is known as music. Greek poetry was probably always sung, as were the Hebrew psalms. In fact, with both the Hebrews and Greeks, poetry and music were in a sense synonymous.

In this period, developments in music such as are known today were nonexistent. Instrumental accompaniment was undeveloped and used mainly, when it was used, for sounding rhythms or for introducing by one or two strokes on the lyre the rhythmic mood of the selection to be performed. However, instrumental music played alone was well known and widely used, especially on the occasions of the public games and the pagan festivities. The use of a one-stringed instrument by Pythagoras (582 B.C.—*c*. 497 B.C.) in his study of the physics of sound was a contributing factor to the development of the instrumental art. Melodic performance on an instrument paralleling at an octave the melody of the singer (called "magadizing") was sometimes practiced, although this was perhaps more often possible when done by two singers performing in unison octaves. As already indicated, subordinated rhythmic stroking on a soft-voiced instrument was perhaps the usual extent of instrumental accompaniment. To the Greek, what he had to sing was to be sung artistically and lyrically in a rhythmic form that took its pattern from the poetic demands of the words. In this latter respect Greek music was similar to the Hebrew; it was different, however, from the Hebrew in that the Greeks had a system of music notation and scales, or modes.

THEORETICAL CONSIDERATIONS IN GREEK MUSIC

The Greek scale was at first a tetrachord (series of four notes or tones) in one of perhaps three possible forms.

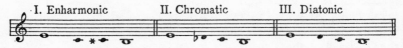

* represents a quarter-tone, approximately between C and B.[1]

The black notes are the "movable" notes between E and B; this is not dissimilar to usage in our own diatonic scales:

In B major, we have C♯ and D♯ between B and E.

In B minor, C♯ and D.

In E minor.

In C major

———————
[1]Reprinted from D. N. Ferguson: *A History of Musical Thought* (2nd ed.; New York: Appleton-Century-Crofts, Inc., 1948), p. 13. Ferguson gives a clear general account of the subject of Greek scales.

By experiments with different methods of combining tetrachords (conjunctive and adjunctive building of one to another) a scheme of alternately joining by both methods was finally chosen.[2]

Example:
    The *aeolian* theory of disjunctive (∧) and conjunctive (◠) extension illustrated.

The tones of identification of the tetrachords as shown are "e" and "a." Through an involved analysis it can be shown that "a" is the prominent tone in the finally established two-tetrachord scale. The "a" thus found to be prominent was called the *mese* by the ancient Greek. Roughly, the Greek "mese" may be likened to today's "middle C"—that is in reference to their both being fixed positions. The Greek melodic range of about one octave could be started anywhere on the total scale line. From this it can be seen that the *mese* might be near the top, or the middle, or the bottom of the melodic range of any specific song.

GREEK SPIRITUAL MEANINGS

The Greek was sensitive about the arrangement regarding the relative location of the *mese*. If it were high in the melodic line, the melody portrayed to him a character of excitement; if medium, a character of virility; if low, a character of sensuousness or idleness. The relative location of the *mese*, which was emphasized in the melody by being frequently sounded, gave to the music its emotional and spiritual meaning. The process of determining what the psychological import of the music should be was related to a Greek concept of meaning called *ethos*.

It must be remembered that with the Greek, poetry and music were *one*. In his interpretation of verse he always employed the musical possibilities of singing, using the tetrachord combination with the *mese* so placed as to suggest accurately the mood of his text and thus fulfill the requirement of his *ethos* concept.

[2]*Ibid.*, p. 14.

These processes were, of course, not all invented at once.[3] It is thought that various cities and communities each contributed their bit to the final codification of Greek music.

In interpretations of poetry, it should be mentioned that before the Alexandrian invasions, the rhythm of the poetry-music was a literary-based rhythm usable because of the distinctive nature of the Greek language. After the invasions, however, the pure Grecian style was so modified by other civilizations and cultures that eventually an accent rhythm, that is, a measured rhythm, was used entirely.

Comparisons between Hebrew and Greek music are interesting. Hebrew music, considered for the moment as a vehicle detached from the words, was, in general, cultural but nonaesthetic; that is it was used to serve a social and religious purpose. Greek music was perhaps no more moving than the Hebrew and was used also as a cultural force, but in addition it was of artistic design manifesting careful, discriminating planning upon the part of the composers. Greek music was more lyrical, artistically more satisfying than the Hebrew. The Greek continually held before himself the aim of apprehending beauty. Greek musical theory was more advanced, being based upon an elaborate system of composition and notation. The artistic sensitivity of the Greek composer demanded that his creative work manifest a unity of thought, organization, and content. In a religious expression, such as the *Hymn to Apollo,* every factor permitted to remain in the song was made to contribute to the central purpose of singing worshipfully to Apollo. Thus, through unity, order, and balanced portions, were the concepts of beauty and *ethos* satisfied.

THE APOSTOLIC PERIOD

The music that Jesus knew as a man on earth was mainly, no doubt, the Jewish music of the temple and the synagogue. Historians consider that in the apostolic period[4] the church was much

---

[3]Cecil Grey did not agree altogether with this account of music in classic antiquity, because he did not place credence in the hypotheses that music is probably an evolutional development. Grey, *History of Music* (New York: A. A. Knopf, 1928) frequently presents very interesting points of view.

[4]The apostolic period extended from the death of Jesus to about A.D. 100.

like the synagogue and that the music of the church was much like
that of the synagogue.

The Inscription of Seikilos[5] (2nd C.B.C.)

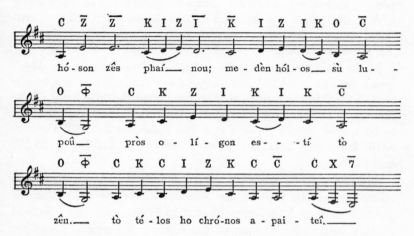

While the New Testament writers included no books of songs
or poetry as did those of the Old Testament, it is known, nevertheless, that the Psalms of the Old Testament were held in high and
important esteem in the lives of the early Christians. However, because of the mistaken notion that music was not given an important
place in the New Testament, many later religious groups have
shunned, neglected, or prohibited music as a Christian exercise. In
an effort to account for the apparent lack of musical reference in
the New Testament, church musicians have come recently to think
that the earliest Christians regarded the Psalms of the Old Testament as so complete and of such a deeply moving, spiritual nature
that they felt no need for additional expression of such kind.

Astonishingly enough, however, upon investigation, the New
Testament has many references which indicate that music was used

[5] On a tombstone in memory of his wife, Euterpe; the words translated, "So long as
you live, be bright– be not overly distressed. Life is but brief– time demands fulfill
ment." Capital letters indicate pitches; dash– indicates equivalent of our ♩, that is,
two pulsations; double dash, three pulsations (♩.).

freely by the early Christians. In 1 Corinthians 14:26, one reads, "What then, brethren? When you come together, each one has a hymn. . . ." Of course in this passage the question arises as to whether Paul referred to an Old Testament psalm. The "psalms" in Ephesians 5:19 and in Colossians 3:16 remove all doubt as to what is meant, for here Paul names different kinds of songs along with psalms; thus, it is believed that in the early days of the Jerusalem church the word "psalm" probably referred to the Old Testament collection.[6]

In the New Testament there are many references to music which give a hint as to what kinds of music were known in the apostolic period. And from these it may be concluded that the early Christians wrote original hymns. Fragments of these hymns are thought to be quoted in the Pauline epistles: Ephesians 5:14; 1 Timothy 3:16; 2 Timothy 2:11; and in Revelation 4:11; 5:9-13; 11:15-18; and 15:3-4.

In Luke 1:46-55 there is a record of Mary's song, spontaneously offered, when she learned that she was to become the mother of Jesus. This song is strikingly similar to Hannah's song, 1 Samuel 2:1-10, sung upon learning of the coming of her son. These are commonly spoken of, respectively, as the New Testament and the Old Testament, "Magnificats."

Again, in Luke 1:68-79, there is record of the prophesying song of Zechariah which he sang at the naming of his son, John. Zechariah's song is spoken of in the Latin as the "Benedictus." Another "Benedictus" is the song recorded in Matthew 21:9.

Simeon's song, sung upon seeing the Christ child, is recorded in Luke 2:29-32. Simeon's song is known as the "Nunc Dimittis." Also in Luke (2:14) is found the angelic song, "Gloria in Excelsis Deo." And in Acts 4:24 is recorded the song of the disciples upon the return of Peter and John from trial before the council.

---

[6]The membership of one orthodox Calvinistic church, according to one of its clergymen, believes today that only the Old Testament Psalms should be used by Christians in their worship. This same church group believes that the reference to "psalms, hymns, and spiritual songs," of Ephesians 5:19, is an ambiguous one due to questionable translation. However, there are others who believe that in this passage "psalms" refer to the Old Testament songs, "hymns" to songs of praise to God or Christ, and "spiritual songs" to other kinds of sacred songs such as specially composed songs of teaching and mutual exhortation about man's duty to God and Christ. There are still others who wonder if psalms, even as used in the apostolic period, did not refer to sacred songs in general.

Toward the end of the century, the Christians' music perhaps took on in many regions the character of the Grecian music, although still retaining the quality of spontaneity found in the old Hebrew cantillations. Those who sang or spoke at public occasions were perhaps often met with immediate responsive song from the assembled group. Their hymns and poems, in accordance with the manner of the period, were of course unmetrical.

The "speaking with tongues" referred to by Paul in 1 Corinthians, chapter 14, is usually known as "glossolalia" and was not unrelated to the spirit of singing. Dickinson agrees that this "speaking with tongues" was a kind of textless vocal outpouring such as can be traced to very ancient times.[7]

The early Christians apparently were fervent in singing: "Is any merry? Let him sing psalms" (James 5:13, KJV).

It should not be forgotten that Paul's exhortations in reference to music, found in Ephesians and Colossians, were addressed to those who were influenced by Grecian thinking, and to apprehend their writer's intention in these passages one must be acquainted with the culture of the people to whom they were addressed.[8] Similarly, in order to apprehend the fullness of the reference, James 5:13, one has to recognize its Hebrew roots. "Let those who are merry sing psalms" is an expression aptly fitting to the Hebrews, for to them the psalms were an essential part of the musical literature. Paul's reference to "psalms, hymns [or odes], and spiritual songs," indicates the influence upon him of the synthesis arising out of the folk nature of Hebrew music and the art basis of Grecian music.[9]

---

[7]In his *History of the Christian Church,* Volume I, section 24, Schaff discusses the subject of "glossolalia" fully.

[8]It is necessary to make clear that while one can be very confident that the apostolic and early postapostolic Christians were much influenced by their relationships with Hebrew and Grecian cultures, not much is known about the actual or specific relationships. Interpretations or conclusions about the early Christian periods in terms of today's mores (and disregarding the contemporary orientation) are likely to be inaccurate. One reference to interpretations of contemporary culture might be cited: the reason for the Puritans' not using musical instruments is different from that of the early Christians. The Puritans did not use musical instruments in worship because of their belief that the early Christians did not. However, that could not be the same reason for which the early Christians abstained from instrumental usages (if they did). It is a common thing for persons to give the reasons of their own age as being the reasons of an age gone by, for some specific practice or attitude which both ages *seem* to hold in common.

[9]Note, also, 1 Corinthians 14:7-8, 15.

W. J. Conybeare and J. S. Howson indicate their belief that Ephesians 5:19 was addressed to Greeks and to the Greek-influenced Gentiles who had become Christians:

Throughout the whole passage there is a contrast implied between the Heathen and the Christian practice, q.d. *When you meet, let your enjoyment consist, not in fulness of wine, but fulness of the Spirit; let your songs be, not the drinking-songs of heathen feasts, but psalms and hymns; and their accompaniment, not the music of the lyre, but the melody of the heart; while you sing them to the praise, not of Bacchus or Venus, but of the Lord Jesus Christ.*[10]

Incidentally, it should be noted that the passages: Ephesians 5:19, Colossians 3:16, and James 5:13, along with those in Corinthians and Romans, should not be considered as references pertaining exclusively to the appointed services of the church or of a local congregation. While reference to such specific services may be included, the passages actually are general exhortations in a musical connection referring to day-to-day conduct of Christians.

THE EARLY POSTAPOSTOLIC PERIOD

By early postapostolic period is meant that period starting from the time when the last of the apostles died to the time roughly a century after the death of Ambrose of Milan (340-397), that is, from about A.D. 100 to about A.D. 476.

By this time Christianity had spread throughout the world. With its decentralization from Jerusalem and its spread throughout all of the greater Mediterranean regions there came a mixing of Hebrew, Grecian, Roman, and barbarian cultures. Any local congregation that had persons in it from these several cultures was faced with a severe problem of assimilation. The consecration and zeal which, characteristic of the race, would mark the spontaneous singing of the Hebrew Christians would not be altogether to the liking of the Greek Christians whose music characteristically evidenced great care in composition and rendition. Also, the music

---

[10]Conybeare and Howson, *Life and Epistles of St. Paul,* p. 775.

of the Romans, although patterned after that of the Greeks yet of less intrinsic worth, would give rise to some trying moments as it was offered in a worship meeting of a mixed group of Christians. Of course, the problem of assimilation in assemblies of mixed cultures probably existed in the earlier time of the apostles themselves.

In 1 Corinthians, chapter 14, such an inference seems plausible. In this chapter Paul suggests: "All things should be done decently and in order." Also he asks: "If therefore the whole church assembles and all speak in tongues, and outsiders or unbelievers enter, will they not say that you are mad? . . . What then, brethren? When you come together, each one has a hymn, a lesson, a revelation, a tongue, or an interpretation."

There can be no doubt that the music of the period just after the time of the apostles took on a tone which evidenced an admixture of all the cultures. Burney wrote, "Music is said by some of the fathers to have drawn the Gentiles frequently into the church through mere curiosity; who liked its ceremonies so well, that they were baptized before their departure."[11] Such persons when added to the local congregation inevitably would modify the tone of the services of that congregation.

It is not believed, however, that any special kind of music was invented by the second- and third-century Christians for the praising of God, or that any peculiar Christian process of music was inaugurated. Justin Martyr wrote, in his *Apology,* about A.D. 139, that the Christians proved their gratefulness to God by, among other things, celebrating his praises with hymns.[12] It is not unlikely that the Christians adopted for their own use the music of their times, including, no doubt, much that was suitable from the pagan literature. Especially would this be so among groups composed of many converted pagans. Origen, in his writing against Celsus (Celsus was one who had treated the Christians as barbarians), said that the Greeks prayed in Greek, the Romans in Latin, that

---

[11]Charles Burney, *General History of Music,* Vol. 2, p. 7.
[12]Justin Martyr, "First Apology for the Christians," *Ante-Nicene Fathers,* Vol. I, p. 166.

all people in the language of their country celebrated and sang the praises of God to the utmost of their power.[13]

Clement of Alexandria, who died about A.D. 220, said in reference to church music:

> Behold the might of the new song! It has made men out of stone, men out of beasts. Those, moreover, that were as dead, not being partakers of the true life, have come to life again, simply by becoming listeners to this song. It also composed the universe into melodious order, and tuned the discord of the elements to harmonious arrangement, so that the whole might become harmony. It let loose the fluid ocean, and yet has prevented it from encroaching on the land. The earth, again, which had been in a state of commotion, it has established, and fixed the sea as its boundary. The violence of fire it has softened by the atmosphere, as the Dorian is blended with the Lydian strain; and the harsh cold of the air it has moderated by the embrace of fire, harmoniously arranging these the extreme tones of the universe. And this deathless strain,—the support of the whole and the harmony of all,—reaching from the centre to the circumference, and from the extremities to the central part, has harmonized this universal frame of things, not according to the Thracian music, which is like that invented by Jubal, but according to the paternal counsel of God, which fired the zeal of David. And He who is of David, and yet before him, the Word of God, despising the lyre and harp, which are but lifeless instruments, and having tuned by the Holy Spirit the universe, and especially man,—who, composed of body and soul, is a universe in miniature,—makes melody to God on this instrument of many tones; and to this instrument—I mean man—he sings accordant: "For thou art my harp, and pipe, and temple."—a harp for harmony—a pipe by reason of the Spirit—a temple by reason of the word; so that the first may sound, the second breathe, the third contain the Lord. And David the king, the harper whom we mentioned a little above, who exhorted to the truth and dissuaded from idols, was so far from celebrating demons in songs, that in reality they were driven away by his music. Thus, when Saul was plagued with a demon, he cured him by merely playing. A beautiful breathing instrument of music the Lord made man, after His own image. And He Himself also, surely, who is the supramundane Wisdom, the celestial Word, is the all-harmonious, melodious, holy instrument of God. What, then, does this instrument—the Word of God, the Lord, the New Song—desire? To open the eyes of the blind,

---

[13]Origen, *Ante-Nicene Fathers*, Vol. IV, p. 653.

and unstop the ears of the deaf, and to lead the lame or the erring to righteousness, to exhibit God to the foolish, to put a stop to corruption, to conquer death, to reconcile disobedient children to their father. The instrument of God loves mankind.[14]

In this quotation from Clement, the influence of the Greek philosophers who had given to music a symbolic, allegorical meaning is obvious. It was under such Greek influence that the "church fathers," as they are frequently called, also came to regard music as a symbolic medium. Thus, from Clement of Alexandria to Eusebius (c. 260—c. 339) there was an increasing turn toward musical and philosophic symbolism leading to ever-greater divergence between oriental and occidental practice in religious music.

Actually there is little specific knowledge about the nature of the music of the early Christians in the apostolic and postapostolic periods. There is the often-mentioned finding of a Christian hymn of seeming Greek character dating from the third century which was discovered at Oxyrhynchos. A quotation from Burney is helpful:

That some part of the sacred music of the Apostles and their immediate successors, in Palestine and the adjacent countries, may have been such as was used by the Hebrews, particularly in chanting the psalms, is probable; but it is no less probable that the music of the hymns which were first received in the church, wherever Paganism had prevailed, resembled that which had for many ages been used in the temple worship of the Greeks and Romans. Of this, the versification of those hymns affords an indisputable proof, as it by no means resembles that of the psalms, or of any other Hebrew poetry.[15]

Philo (c. 20 B.C.-c. A.D. 54) in De Vita Contemplativa, telling of the Therapeutae, a very strict, severe sect, also told of their music and made special reference to their use of antiphonal singing; and Pliny the Younger, in his letter (No. 96) to Trajan[16] in A.D. 111-

---

[14]Clement of Alexandria, "Exhortation to the Heathen," Ante-Nicene Fathers, Vol. II, p. 172.

[15]Burney, op. cit.

[16]Encyclopaedia Britannica, Fourteenth Edition, Vol. 18, p. 79, " . . . they had been wont to meet together on a fixed day before daybreak and to repeat among themselves in turn a hymn to Christ as to a god and to bind themselves by an oath. . . ." (It has seemed useful to provide in this volume the references that can be found conveniently.)

113 (?), confirmed the Christians' use in Bithynia of antiphonal singing. It is interesting that antiphonal singing may have been of two quite different sorts: (1) the Greek style of singing in octaves (magadizing) or (2) the later style of singing alternately group to group, or solist to group, which may have been what Paul referred to in Ephesians 5:19.

Christian singing up through the periods of Constantine (272-337), Ambrose of Milan and as late as Gregory the Great (c. 540-604) was of three kinds: (1) solemn reading of the Gospels in accordance with a formal established mode of cantillation (described in the section on Hebrew music), (2) psalm and hymn singing, ranging from cantillation to a lyrically well-developed, artistic song, and (3) the ecstatic and embellished intoning of one word, "Alleluia."

Because it is thought that during the earliest 200-year period, the Christians' music was not systematized, it is inferred that their music wore the respective colors of the communities in which they lived. But by the third century, the increase of conversions among the pagans led the Christians to organize and authorize certain forms for the music in order to prevent undesirable pagan and worldly associations among the established Christians. With the increase of scholarly men among the Christian writers and the establishment of state tolerance by Constantine, the way was set for large, spacious churches, and a consequent serious organizing and codifying of suitable music.

With this codification (immediately after Constantine) the ritualistic service and the beginnings of the liturgical music of the medieval period arose, out of which sprang the Ambrosian chant, the Gregorian chant, the plainsong and the types of music classified as organum. As the codification became more complete, singing by congregations was more and more limited and the office of singing and performing music was given over to the clergy and to those especially appointed. In the time of Eusebius there had already developed a systematizing and planning of song that depended upon support from the entire congregation. Spontaneity of responsive singing was becoming less frequent.

Eusebius described this period:

. . . And there was one energy of the Divine Spirit pervading all the members, and one soul in all, and the same eagerness of faith, and one hymn from all in praise of the Deity. Yea, and perfect services were conducted by the prelates, the sacred rites being solemnized, and the majestic institutions of the Church observed, here with the singing of psalms and with the reading of the words committed to us by God, and there with the performance of divine and mystic services; and the mysterious symbols of the Saviour's passion were dispensed. At the same time people of every age, both male and female, with all the power of the mind gave honor unto God, the author of their benefits, in prayers and thanksgiving, with a joyful mind and soul. And every one of the bishops present, each to the best of his ability, delivered panegyric orations, adding luster to the assembly.[17]

INSTRUMENTAL MUSIC IN THE EARLY POSTAPOSTOLIC PERIOD

The history of religious music in Christendom is marked with deep dissensions over the employment of "musical instruments in worship." Many students doubt that instrumental music was employed in church services before the time of Constantine. Such doubts seem reasonable, not only because the early church was patterned after the synagogue, which avoided instrumental music in the religious service, but also because the Christian converts of the period, subject to persecution as they were, could scarcely have risked the establishing of instrumental playing and thus the promiscuous publicizing of their services. It is to be remembered also that the Jews avoided the appearances of association with pagan customs such as Herod, to their disappointment, had encouraged when he endeavored to court Roman favor. Also, with the temple's final destruction A.D. 70 the glory of its music was left unsounded. Religiously, only the music of the synagogue was known to the Jews after that time. Several hundred years later, however, after the time of Constantine, with Christianity given the status of a "national" religion, instruments were used freely on the occasions of the great festivals. Such gala use of instruments was in

---

[17]Eusebius, *Nicene and Post-Nicene Fathers*, Series II, Vol. I, Book X, Chap. III, p. 370.

keeping with the old temple tradition of the Hebrews; and Greeks, too, had always used instruments as rhythmic accompaniment to their psalms or their religious rites. In fact, it may have been that a third cycle of intemperate violating of appropriateness and good taste in the period just after Constantine (the first was in the time of Amos; the next in that of Herod) led quickly to a complete abstinence from instrumental usage in the early medieval period, that is, from about the fourth century on.

Thus, "whatever evidence is forthcoming, is to the effect that the early Christians did not use musical instruments. Various causes would operate. . . . But at a later period, after the disruption of the empire, and the re-organization of Society, such causes not existing to any extent, the feeling against instruments ceased to exist. . . ."[18] As has been observed by many, the "proofs" for and against early admission of musical instruments to Christian religious service have been numerous.

From Clement of Alexandria we read,

We no longer employ the ancient psaltery, and trumpet, and timbrel, and flute, which those expert in war and contemners of the fear of God were wont to make use of also in the choruses at their festive assemblies; that by such strains they might raise their dejected minds. But let our genial feeling in drinking be twofold, in accordance with the law. For if "thou shalt love the Lord thy God," and then "thy neighbour," let its first manifestation be towards God in thanksgiving and psalmody, and the second toward our neighbour in decorous fellowship. For says the apostle, "Let the Word of the Lord dwell in you richly."[A] And this Word suits and conforms Himself to seasons, to persons, to places.

In the present instance He is a guest with us. For the apostle adds again, "Teaching and admonishing one another in all wisdom, in psalms, and hymns, and spiritual songs, singing with grace in your heart to God." And again, "Whatsoever ye do in word or deed, do all in the name of the Lord Jesus, giving thanks to God and His Father." This is our thankful revelry. And even if you wish to sing and play to the harp or lyre, there is no blame.[B] Thou shalt imitate the righteous Hebrew king in his thanksgiving to God. "Rejoice in the Lord, ye righteous; praise is comely to the upright,"[C] says the prophecy. "Confess to the Lord on the harp; play to Him on the psaltery of ten strings. Sing to Him a new

---

[18]William Smith, *A Dictionary of Christian Antiquities* (London: John Murray, Albemarle Street, 1880), "Music."

song." And does not the ten-stringed psaltery indicate the Word Jesus, who is manifested by the element of the decad? And as it is befitting, before partaking of food, that we should bless the Creator of all; so also in drinking it is suitable to praise Him on partaking of his creatures.[D] For the psalm is a melodious and sober blessing. The apostle calls the psalm "a spiritual song."[E][19]

A Col. iii: 16.
B [Here instrumental music is allowed.]
C Ps. xxxiii: 1-3.
D (Even the heathen had such forms. The Christian grace before and after meat is here recognized as a matter of course. 1 Tim. iv: 3, 4.)
E Eph. v: 19; Col. iii: 16.

Instruments, however, seem not to have had admission indiscriminately in the early ages of the church; the Harp and Psaltery only, as the most grave and majestic instruments of the time, were preferred to all others. Neither Jews nor Gentiles were imitated in the use of Tabrets and Cymbals in the Temple service. The priests of Bacchus and Cybele, in their public processions and celebrations of religious rites, had rendered these instruments so odious to the Christians, that all the Fathers were very severe and peremptory in prohibiting their use.[20]

The leaders of Hebrew and Grecian thought made a profound impact on the early Christians. Among such persons who, in addition to the Hebrews, influenced the early postapostolic Christians were Plato (427-347 B.C.) and Aristotle (384-322 B.C.); later there were Plotinus (A.D. 204-270), and Porphyry (A.D. 233-304). Also there were Gaudentios (2nd century A.D.), Mesomedes of Crete (c. A.D. 130), Micomachos (2nd century A.D.), and Ptolemy of Alexandria (2nd century A.D.).

Plotinus, like Plato and Aristotle, believing that music was important as a moral influence, concluded that Beauty leads one to contemplation or apprehension of Good. Thus to him music had the magical power of leading one to the Evil or to the Good. Porphyry, a pupil of Plotinus, following in the steps of his teacher,

[19]Clement of Alexandria, "The Instructor," *Ante-Nicene Fathers*, Vol. II, p. 249.

[20]Burney, *op. cit.*, Vol. 2, p. 27. pp. 426-427. Churchmen who oppose instrumental music in church services have often held that the word *psallo*, since it is translated specifically as "sing," thus indicates that the musical exercises of the "New Testament Christians" were purely and entirely vocal.
The Greek word, *psallo*, often translated, "sing," is found in Romans 15: 9; 1 Corinthians 14: 15; Ephesians 5: 19; and James 5: 13. See Appendix I, p. 267.

developed the view into an extreme asceticism wherein he completely opposed music, dramatic spectacles, and the dances on the ground that all of these were sensuous and to be likened to horse races. Proclus (A.D. 411-485), a Neoplatonist, was much in agreement with Porphyry, but he saw in music an involved allegorical and symbolistic system which led him to ascribe to music magical potentialities that could help one apprehend the divine. He, too, disapproved of music of the stage.

Philo, who represented the school of Hellenistic Judaism, is also thought by many to have exerted great influence upon the early postapostolic Christians. Writing at some length on the subject, he contended that music, along with all art and science, is not an end in itself, but rather, a means of building one's philosophy.

If the Christians of the early postapostolic period were touched by the views of such non-Christian thinkers, it seems logical that they were disturbed also by other influential forces in non-Christian culture. It may be that the austerity and the asceticism of the music of the apostolic and early postapostolic periods can be accounted for partly by the Christians' eagerness to avoid

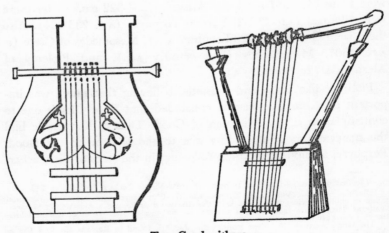

Two Greek cithara

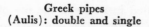

Greek pipes
(Aulis): double and single

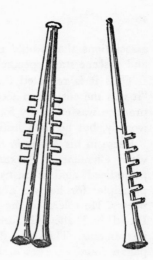

Greek pipes of Pan

Greek tympanon. Information about early Hebrew and Greek instruments is often obscure. No actual Hebrew instruments (or even pictures of them) of the pre-Christian era have been found. And the word descriptions often seem ambiguous or contradictory. In the reference to the Greek tympanon (timpanum, referring to timpanic membrane of the ear), the name refers to a drumlike instrument as shown. Yet in medieval centuries the name referred to string instruments played percussively—like the dulcimer.

Thus, word descriptions may not be faithful, as we understand them, to the periods of ancient time as the people then understood and used them.

45

associations that would echo the sounds of the pagan festivities and obscene stage spectacles.

Thus it is reported that among the Christians at Alexandria, "it was the custom to accompany the singing with the flute, which practice was expressly forbidden by Clement of Alexandria as too worldly, but he then instituted in its stead the use of the harp."[21]

Reese in his *Music in the Middle Ages* expresses much the same view. Clement of Alexandria, Reese says, was not likely to be prejudiced against instruments for the sake of some abstract principle; for he was a cultivated man, interested in music and poetry. He tolerated the lyre and the kithara, only because King David had allegedly used them, and he disapproved of other instruments. This was doubtless due to his fear of associating pagan festal excesses and stage vulgarities with Christianity.

Because of the Grecian propensity for seeing in music a symbolism of the transcendent, and because of the increasing acceptance of Grecian philosophy by the later postapostolic Christians, it is easy to understand why Eusebius, even more than Clement, could absolutely disapprove of instruments, even the kithara:

We sing God's praise with living psaltery. . . . For more pleasant and dear to God than any instrument is the harmony of the whole Christian people. . . . Our cithara is the whole body, by whose movement and action the soul sings a fitting hymn to God, and our ten-stringed psaltery is the veneration of the Holy Ghost by the five senses of the body and the five virtues of the spirit.[22]

Athanasius (297?-373) also held for the symbolic nature of musical instruments as a Christian utility.

An interesting observation to be found in McClintock and Strong's *Cyclopedia* states:

. . . It is strange indeed that neither Ambrose (340-397), nor Basil 328?-379), nor Chrysostom (347?-407) in the noble encomiums which they severally pronounce upon music, make any mention of instrumental

[21]McClintock and Strong, *Biblical, Theological and Ecclesiastical Cyclopedia.* Subject: Music.

[22]Eusebius. Translation from Migne, Jacques Paul. *Patrologiae curses completus.* Series Graeca. 166 volumes. Series Latina. 221 volumes. Volume 221 contains an index to writings on music. This reference: Vol. 23. Graeca. p. 1171.

English translation by permission from *Music in the Middle Ages,* by Gustave Reese (New York: W. W. Norton and Company, 1940), p. 62.

music. Basil, indeed (*Hom.* IV, vol. 1, p. 33), expressly condemns it as ministering only to the depraved passions of men, and must have led to this condemnation because some had gone astray and borrowed the practice from the heathen.[23]

Thus a strong case could be made for the view that instruments were cautiously and sensitively used in the earlier Christian period, i.e., second century, as indicated by Clement, but later were more and more sparingly used until in the fourth century they were completely banned. There is reason to wonder if the usually conceded abstinence from use of instruments in the early period was perhaps only partial since they were undoubtedly used somewhat in the second century. There is reasonableness in the speculation that instrumental music was avoided because of (1) the adverse associative circumstances in paganism; (2) the tradition in the synagogue; (3) the early Christians' lack of proficiency upon instruments; (4) their feeling that instrumental performance on any elaborate scale would be impossible, unnecessary anyhow, and likely for social reasons to be out of Christian character; and (5) the very nature of the musical idiom of the day which made instruments for sacred usage practicable only for striking an occasional pitch and setting a rhythm—rarely, if ever, for sounding a tune or providing harmony.

Basil succeeded Eusebius as bishop of Caesarea, and the liturgy that he wrote is still used in the Eastern church. He defended the singing of psalms antiphonally and responsorially, claiming that they were sung in this manner by the Egyptians, the Libyans, Arabians, Palestinians, Phoenicians, Syrians, and Thebans. Basil wrote that the psalms of his time possessed attractive melodies which were sung in order that youths and children surrendering to the pleasures of the music, might in addition be enlightened in their souls and minds.

Augustine wrote that he feared music appealed strongly to him because of the esthetic pleasure it afforded rather than because of the sacredness of its words.

Augustine, Jerome, Ambrose, and Chrysostom all spoke of the deep effects of singing and of its value in propagating the faith.

---

[23]Based on quotation from Coleman, Lyman. *The Apostolical and Primitive Church.* Philadelphia: Lippincott, Grambo and Co., 1853, p. 371.

But these persons all had an aversion to musical instruments, due perhaps to the ascetic convictions that had grown up in their hearts under the Grecian philosophic influences hitherto spoken of, and to their fear of esthetic experiences of a nature susceptible of being associated with the vulgar festivities of the pagans.

More extreme than Clement's writing is that of Jerome (340?-420) in which he suggested to Laeta how to rear her daughter: "Let her be deaf to the sound of the organ, and not know even the uses of the pipe, the lyre, and the cithara."[24]

Theodoret (386?-457?), bishop of Cyrrhus, spoke of a type of antiphonal psalm singing at a monastery of his time in which there lived both Greeks and Syrians. Each group present repeated in their own language the verses of their song. He also tells that the hymns were accompanied by hand clapping and dance movements.

Thus music, at least vocal if not instrumental, was widely used in the first four centuries of the Christian period; although that it was not universally used is attested to in a translation given by Reese of the words of Pambo (317-367), an Egyptian abbot. From Pambo's words it is clear that music of no kind, not even singing, could meet his approval:

Woe is upon us, O son, for the days are come in which monks shall relinquish the wholesome food given by the Holy Ghost, and seek after words and tunes. What repentance, what tears proceed from hymns? What repentance can there be in a monk who, whether situated in the church or in his cell, lifts up his voice like a bull?[25]

TRADITIONAL INFLUENCE IN THE PERIOD

Because many of the pagan Greeks engaged in the most vulgar kinds of activities, many of the thoughtful Greeks had, by the time just preceding Christ, developed stringent codes of propriety bordering on asceticism in order to prevent association with the

[24]Jerome, *Nicene and Post-Nicene Fathers*, Series II, Vol. 6, p. 193.
[25]Pambo. To be found in Martin Gerbert, *Scriptures Ecclesiastici de Musica*, Vol. 1, p. 3. English translation by permission from Reese, *op. cit.*, p. 66.

carnalities. The early Christians were influenced, then, not only by the Jews' antipathy for degrading associations as experienced under Herod in his encouragement of pagan festivity but also by the Greeks' asceticism as evidenced in their opposition to the debauchery of the dramatic and orgiastic festivals of the period.

The very nature of temple worship, ritualistic as it was, was controlled by the priests and was not of a kind that permitted general participation by the Jews except in definitely prescribed ways. It prevented, at least theoretically, the development in the temple of a degrading worship activity such as might be likened to the Greek and pagan debauches.

In the synagogue, however, the activities, being more communal and informal, were in continual danger of being influenced and degraded by untoward externals. In order to avoid such decline in the synagogue worship, a rigid self-regulation was practiced. Such regulation, which obtains to this very day among the orthodox Jews, was necessary (1) to prevent innovations that might be associated with the pagan carnalities, and (2) to perpetuate the spiritual nature of the Jews' attitude which grew out of their traditional eagerness to serve God seriously and thus not have him turn his face from them again.

Like the Jews of the synagogue, the early Christians were also communally joined and likewise eager to avoid carnal associations. In fact, the early Jewish Christians were in reality much the same people that they had been before as members of the synagogue. To them the church was just a fulfillment of the prophecies, just the long-awaited phase of living to which they had looked forward.

It was not until they lost favor with those brother Jews who refused to accept Christ and until they suffered the cultural inroads made by the converted Greeks and other Gentiles that the realization they were no longer a part of the synagogue struck these early Christians. Even so, for many years they carried on a type of worship that was similar in numerous ways to that of the synagogue.

It is not to be supposed, however, because of the similarities held at first between the church of Christ and the synagogue, that the early Christians, especially after Greek additions, continued for long to hold themselves bound strictly by Jewish custom or by the regulations of the synagogue. Thus the apostles decreed at Jerusalem, upon Paul's request, that circumcision should no longer be required of Gentiles (Acts 15:22-29). The freedom in musical custom may also be surmised from the writings of the second century. The practices of the synagogue, however much they influenced the early Christians, were never legally binding upon the church.

CHAPTER THREE

MEDIEVAL MUSIC

THE PREMEDIEVAL PERIOD

In the medieval period, which extended from the fall of Rome to the Renaissance in the fourteenth century, several events affecting musical development took place. There was the final establishment of the liturgy; and also the establishment of two centers of church government in Byzantium and Rome and the consequent founding of the Eastern Orthodox Church and the Roman Catholic Church. More directly affecting music, there was also a general experimentation with different forms of musical composition; later, there was the formulation of music notation, and subsequent improvement in music composition. Finally, toward the end of this period, there was the gradual abandoning of the strict liturgical conformance which had been demanded from the seventh century on. This resulted in the freedom of artistic musical composition that came to characterize the Renaissance. Of course all these processes, appearing at different times in the medieval period, were themselves influenced by events in the previous centuries of the earlier Christian period.

Among the earlier influential events reflected in the music and culture of medieval Christianity, were (1) the persecution that came to bear upon the early Christians, (2) the rise of Grecian asceticism that in the second and third centuries came increasingly to affect the Christians, and (3) of course, the heritage from the Jewish synagogue which continuously influenced the Christians from the start. The poverty of the Christians, coupled with the circumstances restricting them so often to private and secret meetings, added to their desperate need just to increase their numerical strength. This produced a kind of music completely unlike the musical expression of the modern period.

Musically, the early Christians confined themselves to a kind of cantillation or chanting, sometimes carefully prepared for special occasions and at other times spontaneously sung. The Christian cantillations, a Jewish heritage, soon took on Grecian characteristics as evidenced in the early lyrical chantings. It is very likely that as often as they were sung together by the entire assemblage, the cantillations of the various congregations were done antiphonally and responsorially both by designated individuals and by groups.

Instrumental music as it is known today was nonexistent. The instrumental music of the day was of such kind that it could have done scarcely anything to improve the musical services of Christians. Its use could have been only that of beating out rhythms, of announcing hours of services, of occasionally sounding weird melodies which would most likely be meaningless for the early Christians. Whether the Greek word *psallo* permitted the use of instruments, precluded the use of instruments, or had no bearing on use, nonuse, or disuse of instruments has been discussed at great length by countless theologians.

The observation so frequently encountered that instruments were not used in formal and public church worship in early centuries has been a basis for generations of important groups of church thinkers to conclude that instrumental music should not be a part of Christian worship. Interpretations at this point, however, should be carefully made. Accompanied by dangers of persecution as they would be, formal and public church meetings such as are known today could perhaps occur only irregularly before the time of Constantine; as already noted, the use of instruments such as in the temple would jeopardize the Christians' security. There is another factor that can lead to inaccurate historical conclusions. References asserting that something or other did not occur in the church until this or that time can often be misunderstood. Such references often allude to the *official* use of formal, ritualistic, liturgical church programs of either the Eastern or Western Catholic communions. For example, statements that "dancing did not occur in the church until the twelfth century" are based on the fact that it may not previously have been accepted officially by the Western Catholic clergy for a place in their prescribed service. Such a statement is no warrant for the belief that dancing for religious service was not practiced for many centuries although not officially recognized by "the church" for a place in the liturgy.

Of course, the growing influence of asceticism during the early centuries and the eagerness to avoid sensualism developed to such an extent that Basil, Jerome, Eusebius, *et al.* wrote strongly against the use of instruments both in public church worship and in private life. It was opposition like this that led later to the dropping of instruments from the conservative rendition of the medieval Roman chant.

The Church Fathers were greatly influenced by their non-Christian contemporaries and their attitude toward music was, perhaps, in part a passing reaction. If the writings of the Church Fathers give no analytical descriptions of the music itself, they do testify, along with other literary sources, as to the attitude of the early Christians toward music, and occasionally provide some hint as to some possible reasons for the directions taken by Christian chant as it developed.

EASTERN CHANT

It would be completely inaccurate to regard the music of the earlier medieval church as being a liturgically prescribed single kind of chanting that had a universal sameness throughout the civilized world of the time. Geographical distinctions and different emphases on varied music activities arose, to color the liturgical development from Ambrose, through Gregory, to the separation of the Eastern and Western churches. Also there was the development of Western music notation. The complex processes involved in these are often overlooked.

With the spread of Christianity, many different kinds of people and racial groups were touched. Because interested people of the United States (and of Britain) have frequently been interested in only those particular aspects of history which have affected them, they often have been given to erroneous interpretations resulting from overgeneralized references to medieval history. For instance, the details of the history of the Eastern church music usually have been disregarded, and historical philosophy in the United States has grown mainly and immediately out of the thinking of such categories as the Roman Catholic, the Lutheran, the Calvinistic, or the Wesleyan reformations or their counteractions. This partiality resulting from an unawareness of the historical ramifications of their subject has frequently led church-music students into dissensions through the centuries that, to the disinterested, must seem trivial; it has supported inadequate views of the psychology and philosophy of music for worship and religious service.

Although the church music of the medieval period may be simply described as "Christian chant," it is important to remember that Christian chant probably embodied folk-song elements of the various scattered communities in which it was found. Thus, while Greek and Hebrew influences in the realms of liturgy, philosophy, and literary creation apparently did affect, in an important way, the chants of the Roman church, they were not the only influences.

Of great importance was a category of music in the medieval period known as Syrian chant, an early representative writer of which was Ephraem, who died A.D. 373. Additionally, there was Byzantine chant, a category of music that has not been studied intensively until recently for the reason that Byzantine civilization itself has mistakenly been considered decadent. Recently, however, the notion has been projected that in all probability the European Renaissance sprang out of the migration westward of cultured Byzantine fugitives from military conquest. Thus, it is believed, Byzantine music came to influence the Balkan Cultures. Romanos, of the sixth century, and Sergios, of the seventh, are the important music writers of the Byzantine period.

There were also categories known as Armenian, Coptic, and Ethiopian chant. Out of these three basic categories stemmed the medieval and contemporary Russian chant, as well as the Ambrosian, and Spanish chant (sometimes called Visigothic or Mozarabic chant).

Investigators have hoped that in searching for the histories of these categories some original compositions of the early apostolic period might be uncovered. More information about the several categories of eastern chant[1] would not only be invaluable as a source of knowledge about the peoples of the time and their religious views, but might also provide a clear and detailed picture of the actual musical usage in the first Christian century.

AMBROSIAN AND GREGORIAN CHANT

How much Ambrose and Gregory had to do with codifying the chant types named after them is not known. Perhaps Gregory had very little to do with it. Of all the many types in the regions of Europe, North Africa, and Asia Minor, Ambrosian and Gregorian were the two types that influenced the Roman Church most.

Ambrose, bishop of Milan, introduced the Syrian manner of singing to keep up the spirits of his constituents at the time of his struggle with the Empress Justina, who was the mother of the boy-Emperor Valentinian. Ambrose regarded a hymn as a song of praise to the Lord.

Four hymns, *Aeterne rerum conditor, Deus Creator omnium, Iam surgit hora tertia,* and *Veni redemptor gentium,* are considered to be authentic Ambrosian hymn-texts. Very little is known of the melodies that were used originally as settings for the texts, but it is generally assumed that the rhythm of the melody followed that of the text.

Augustine, who was baptized by Ambrose, and who therefore would be familiar with the music of Ambrose, provides a clue as to the rhythmic structure of the music. According to Augustine the

---

[1]More information than is included here is available in very palatable form in Reese, *History of Music,* also in Erwin Esser Nemmers, *Twenty Centuries of Catholic Church Music* (Milwaukee: The Bruce Publishing Co., 1949); and Manfred Bukofzer, *Studies in Medieval and Renaissance Music.* (New York: W. W. Norton and Co., 1950.)

iambic foot was the equivalent of today's quarter note and half note in a three-part measure.

The following example is interesting[2]:

Ambrosian Hymn: *Aeterne rerum Conditor*

All such songs during this period were sung in unison or by a single voice, without accompaniment by instrument. The use of these Ambrosian hymns spread throughout Europe. Later the church writers ornamented the Ambrosian melodies with involved embellishment called *melisma*. Recently efforts have been made to eradicate all that appears to be of ornamental nature in order to find what might have been the original melodies.

Ambrose adopted for Western use another custom of long standing among the Jews and the communicants of the Eastern church,

[2]This example adapted from Dreves, Guido Maria, *Aurelius Ambrosius*, Freiburg: Herder, 1893.

namely that of antiphonal or responsive singing. This practice was officially adopted by Celestine I (Pope, 422-432) of Rome.[3] In time, all the music of Milan and environs which had been codified into the Milanese liturgy,[4] came to be known as "Ambrosian chant," although none of it is traceable to Ambrose himself.

Ambrosian chant and Gregorian chant influenced one another in the latter centuries of the first millennium. It is thought by some that the famous melody for the Gregorian hymn, *Veni Creator Spiritus,* may have been the music for the earlier Ambrosian hymn, *Hic est dies versus Dei.*

Ambrosian and Gregorian music are often quite similar, although when the Ambrosian music is ornate, it is likely to be much more ornate than Gregorian, and if simple, much more so. This is clearly seen in comparing the Ambrosian and Gregorian psalm tones (the recitative patterns in which the text of a psalm may be chanted).

In the simple Ambrosian psalm tones, earlier than Gregorian, there are only the single tones on which to recite the text of each verse, with a simple cadence included upon which to end each psalm verse. In the Gregorian, however, the psalm tones are made up of three parts for each verse of the psalm: (1) the intonation upon which each verse text is begun, (2) the reciting tone, and (3) a final cadence with which each verse is ended.[5]

The Ambrosian liturgy is very old, much older than the earliest surviving collection in the British Museum which dates from the twelfth century.

In the British Museum manuscript there is an interesting use of musical rhyme (the name given to melodic patterns possessing a motif recurring at the ends of some or all of the phrases in the melody). In the *Aeterne rerum conditor* note the bracketed patterns.

---

[3]Persons who conclude that the "official" adoption by Celestine I marks the inauguration of antiphonal singing into Christian worship err. Antiphonal singing was practiced continuously for centuries before A.D. 442. (See p. 39.)

[4]The liturgy, a set form of public worship in the services of the church, was designed to prevent heretical speaking, praying, or singing; thus in it certain prescribed patterns of service had to be adhered to by the communicants under the order of the bishop.

[5]For further reference see pp. 70, 71, 143, 144.

Ambrosian chant was popular throughout northern Italy, and was used at Monte Cassino until Pope Stephen IX (1057-58) ordered it abandoned for Gregorian chant. Even as late as the fourteenth century it was used together with Gregorian chant in some churches, although in this later period it was never as widely used as the Gregorian. Whether the decline in the use of Ambrosian chant was because of its "formlessness" or its less pretentious structure is, of course, unknown.

LATER PERIODS OF MEDIEVAL CHANT

In addition to Ambrosian chant, the precursor of the Roman or Gregorian chant, there were the Mozarabic and Gallican chants. These four were the great chant liturgies of the Western church.

The Gallican chant flourished among the Franks until the eighth century, when Charlemagne ordered that the Roman chant be used in its place. There is little information about the nature of Gallican chant since it, except for a few manuscripts which remain today, had nearly disappeared before even early music notation (neumes) had been established.

Mozarabic chant flourished in southern Spain to a later date. More is known about it because manuscripts of this early Spanish chant are available. The Mozarabic chant began to develop in the latter part of the fifth century and by the end of the sixth century, three centers of progressive Mozarabic composition—Seville, Saragossa, and Toledo—had arisen. As evidence of the direction in which composition for the Mozarabic school was moving, it is of interest that the Council of Toledo had to prohibit dancing during divine service; further, in 599, St. Leander is spoken of as having made several "pieces to sweet sound"; and several bishops of these towns are alluded to as having written chants for the divine service.

With the coming of the eighth century and conquest of Spain by the Moors, mention of Mozarabic chant became less frequent. However, it continued to flourish both in the conquered lands and in the free lands of Spain until the eleventh century when the "super-stition of Toledo" was finally noted by the Roman authorities and suppressed. Up to that time, in the free lands, while only Roman chant was to be used, there had been some tolerance of the use of Mozarabic chant. Even after 1085, when Toledo was recaptured from the Moors, Mozarabic chant was occasionally allowed, although Roman chant was generally required. Of course, what was officially acceptable in the liturgy of the church was set up by directives from Rome.

Because of striking similarities among the four Western chants it is thought that they were commonly rooted in a single earlier idiom. It is thought that the Gregorian or Roman chant stemmed out of the earlier Greco-Roman and Hebrew music by way, partly at least, of Ambrosian chant. Also, there are the striking similarities

Hosanna Filio David (GREGORIAN)
and Epitaph of Seikilos (GREEK)

between such music as the Kyrie, in mode III, (Processionarium, Rome, 1894, p. 36) and an ancient Babylonian Jewish Pentateuch Melody used as a setting for Exodus 12:21.[6] Again this ancient descent is borne out in the similarities between the *Epitaph* of Seikilos and the Gregorian Antiphon *Hosanna filio David.*

The Gregorian chant finally came to be the favored music of the Roman church. And consequently, it has been felt that the Gregorian chants must be kept inviolate in their authentic form. For instance, the melody *Justus ut palma* in 219 manuscripts dating from the ninth to the eleventh century is found to be extraordinarily uniform. Gregorian chant probably was codified in the seventh century, and thus chants of that date or earlier are very likely recoverable in the form which they had in the seventh century.

THE LITURGY

The efforts to integrate the Hellenistic and Christian culture after Clement of Alexandria have already been noted. Connected with this period and already mentioned, the Oxyrhynchos hymn not only provides evidences of the nature of Hellenistic odes after Hadrian but also betrays strong secular relationships. This hymn and two others also to be found in text in the *Apostolic Confessions* were perhaps used in the manner of folk songs—accompanied by hand clapping and dance movements. This is of interest because by the middle of the third century there followed a trend toward *Biblicism* which would allow only for the use of hymns from the Bible. Extrabiblical hymns if allowed would already have had to have been well established in the "liturgy." Actually the liturgy, as such, had its beginnings in the fourth century, although an incipient liturgical organization seems to be alluded to in Justin's *Apology* (paragraph 61) of A.D. 150. In Justin's plan there were:

1. Readings from the Old and New Testaments
2. A sermon by the president
3. Prayer

---

[6]Reese, *op. cit.,* p. 144. Reese took his information from Idelsohn: Idelsohn, A. Z. *Parallelen zwischen gregorianischen und hebraisch-orientalisches Gesangweisen. Zeitschrift für Musikwissenschaft,* 1922, IV, p. 515.

4. "Kiss of Peace"
5. The offering of bread and wine
6. Prayer of Thanksgiving
7. Communion

The Biblicism referred to above led quickly to its own decline—because of its narrowness, exclusiveness, and detachment from popular acceptance. Thus in a short time there arose the popular use of folklike hymnody. This came into high favor with heretical thinkers and thus the Council of Laodicea felt moved to restate (in its 59th *canon*) the old biblicistic restrictions. These were again soon relaxed and by the end of the fourth century, extrabiblical song was again flourishing.

The liturgy of the Roman church is divided into the Mass and the Daily Hours of Divine Service. The word texts for the first are in the Missal, the word texts for the second, in the Breviary. The music for the Mass is contained in the Graduale while that for the Hour Service is in the Antiphonale.

The Mass is divided into the Ordinary and the Proper. The Ordinary is made up of those parts whose words texts do not change; the Proper, of those parts whose words texts change with the season, the saint being commemorated, or the group of saints, martyrs, evangelists being celebrated. This latter part pertaining to group commemoration is called the Common of the Saints.

In the Mass, then, there are, (1) the Ordinary, consisting of the Kyrie, the Gloria, the Credo, the Sanctus, including the Benedictus, and Agnus Dei; and (2) the Proper, consisting of the Proper of the Season, the Proper of the Saints, and the Common of the Saints.

A collection known as the *Kyriale* contains the music of the Ordinary (also found in the *Graduale*); and a collection known as the *Vesperale* contains music of the vespers (also found in the Antiphonary). The full service for Holy Week is found in the *Officium Maioris Hebdomadae*. Also, in the *Liber Usualis,* the most complete modern chant collection, the music for both the Mass and the Hour Service are found.

The reason for a liturgy is plain to be seen—to maintain the order of the "faith" as defined by the church leaders. Abuses by church leaders usually bring about revolt upon the part of the people. And abuses by the people usually follow, thus leading to a new codifying of a new or renewed liturgy by those who rise up to leadership.

Democracy, sometimes viewed as synonymous with the "right to one's own opinions," is often so striven for that, when achieved, the people forget that their opinions, no matter how indicative of their "rights," may still evidence marks of immaturity, or fallacious belief. In democracy one has not only the "right to be wrong" but also the *responsibility to accord oneself with the Truth*—as one can apprehend it.

THE SERVICE OF WORSHIP

As mentioned elsewhere, the music of the early church was improvisitory. Tertullian spoke of this characteristic of Christian prayer and music and referred to the ecstatic states commonly attained by the worshipers.

Worship leaders were at first chosen from the educated laymen, much as the Cantor of the Jewish synagogue had been chosen. No doubt many former cantors became the new Christian "lectors." A considerable number would be needed in any one week to perform the necessary reading and song services in even a moderately sized church. There is an interesting story connected with the name of that important body of song of the medieval church still known as the *Graduale*. This name sprang up out of the practice of having the lector stand on the steps at the foot of the *ambo,* a large reading pulpit. The steps were known as the *gradus*. Thus the "step songs" sung by the lector, who in time came to be one of the minor ordained officials, were called the *Graduale*.

It is of interest that the following music dates back to the seventh century or earlier:

(1) All the Proper of the Season
(2) All the Common of the Saints
(3) The *Requiem Mass* (except the Kyrie, *Dies Irae*)
(4) The Kyrie, Gloria XV, Mass XVIII, Credo I, from the Ordinary

(5) Almost all the chant sections for 47 feasts, from the Proper of the Saints.[7]

The history of the development of the liturgy probably begins about 350 with the institution of a singing school in Rome and the later introduction of antiphonal chanting into the Mass by Celestine I, although it had already been used in the Hour Service and, as previously noted, perhaps had been used more casually for centuries. Antiphonal chanting would seem to have been dependent upon a body of trained singers. At any rate, it seems clear that by the beginning of the seventh century some sort of codification of the Roman chant had taken place.

A Frankish Monk (in Migne CXXXVII, 1347) tells (in questionable fashion) of the growth of liturgical musical services. According to his account Damasus I (366-384) introduced the liturgical service of Jerusalem into the Roman church. Whatever the truth about these details is, it undoubtedly was the tendency of medieval music to move from a rather flexible and fluid state to a stable and rigid form. Thus Gregorian chant still is the main body of Roman plainsong.

It is not to be overlooked that perhaps, in the very earliest days of Christianity, the fixed services of the synagogue were in some measure adopted by the Christians. Since definite formulas for melodies are to be found in the synagogue chants, it is possible that particular melodies were related to certain word texts.

Whatever the processes toward Gregorian codification were, it is probable that Gregory the Great was not entirely responsible for the codification. At best, he was perhaps an editor and compiler, although certain artistic portrayals show him as a musician. One picture shows him listening as a dove sings into his ear. And he may have written some music, for the medieval writers considered him to be a musician and the author of the Roman chant. They believed that he received his melodies by inspiration of the Holy Ghost and that he added the four plagal tones to the four authentic tones allegedly given to the church by Ambrose.

Certain it is that the Gregorian chants came to be the liturgical base, the authorized and principal music, of all the Western churches.

---

[7]For information about Roman liturgy see Adrian Fortescue, *The Ceremonies of the Roman Rite Described*, 5th edition, 1934.

THE HYMNS OF THE MEDIEVAL PERIOD

With the close of the apostolic age, there was a transition from the democratic homogeneity of the earlier Christians to the hierarchical institutionalism of the Western popes and the Eastern patriarchs. In this transition, as already noted, was formulated an elaborate system of rites and ceremonies into which the music of the church was fitted. The laity shared less and less in the singing portions of worship, finally leaving this function to a chorus made up of the minor clergy. Thus the congregation which had previously provided informal group singing, often spontaneously, finally retired from active musical participation. A highly organized body of chants, for every part of the service, became nearly the entirety of worship music; and so it remained for a thousand years. This transition in respect to the music, partially the result of church leaders' attempts to prevent heresy and confusion, was completed by the fourth century. The thirteenth canon of the Council of Laodicea (fourth century) says that in addition to the appointed singers who mount the *ambo* and sing from the book, no others shall sing in the church.

However, the transfer of the office of song from the laity to the clergy involved no cessation of the producing of hymns for general and popular use. It was only in the liturgical music that the people had no part. As ceremonies and festivals increased in number, hymns and lyric songs for private and social edification were written. These were used in processions, at dedications, and other celebrations. It is unfortunate that most of this earlier Christian music is lost. There are available only one or two lyrics, some early Eastern hymns adopted by the Western church, and some song fragments. Clement of Alexandria is credited with a song in praise of the *Logos*.

The Eastern hymns are of Syrian and Greek origin, and furnish a great body of early Christian literature. Of the Syrian poets, the most celebrated are Ephraem (d. 373) and Synesius (b. 375). Ephraem, a poet, churchman, and religious commentator, lived in Nisibis from the time of his birth in the early fourth century until the fall of the city to the Persians in 363. Many of his writings are available although not in his original Syriac. Translations into

Greek, Armenian, Coptic, Aratic, and Ethiopic, exist. Ephraem's commentaries on Genesis, Exodus, the New Testament Gospels and the Pauline Epistles are important. Seventy-two of his hymns, written after 350, are known. They deal with Christ's birth, his manifestations to the Gentiles, the next life, and subjects such as "free will" and opposition to heresy and skepticism. His hymns were loved by the Syrian church and are still sung by the Maronite Christians. The Syrian school, dying out in the fifth century, was supplanted by the Greek.[8]

But before the rise of the Greek hymn there appeared a number of great, unmetrical hymns which are beloved alike by Eastern, Western, and Protestant faiths. These hymns are anonymous. Among them are the *Gloria Patri* and the *Gloria in excelsis,* the *Ter Sanctus* (cherubic hymn heard by Isaiah), and the *Te Deum.* Adopted by the Eastern church there were the *Magnificat* (thanksgiving of man) and the *Benedicite* (from *The Song of the Three Children*). There also appeared the *Kyrie eleison,* sung responsively by the people in the liturgies of *St. Mark* and *St. James.* These hymns date from before the fourth century.[9]

Beginning in the time of the great anonymous hymns mentioned above and continuing for centuries, there was the great epoch of the Greek hymns. J. M. Neale[10] divided the epoch into three periods:

1. Formation of a distinctive poetry which threw off the bonds of classical structure, this period extending from the fourth century to A.D. 726.

2. Perfection of the Greek hymn, 726-820.

3. Decadence, marked by a self-conscious effort to be showy, entertaining, bombastic, 820-1400.

---

[8]Reference has already been made to this period and the persons in it in the section on "Eastern Chant."

[9]It must be made clear that "hymns" whenever and wherever used in literary or musical writings always refers to word-texts and never to the tunes or music that may have served as a vehicle for the singing of the hymns: "chant," and "psalmtones," a specific kind of chant, usually refers to the music and the words, although often to the music alone; in casual and inaccurate everyday usage, "hymns," for many people, has come to refer to the music.

[10]Church people owe a great debt to J. M. Neale, who translated many of the ancient hymns into English; Neale's translations are found in almost any hymnal published in England or the United States.

The centers of Greek hymnody were Sicily, Constantinople, and Jerusalem. John of Damascus and his foster-brother Cosmos who were monks at Mar Saba Monastery, near Jerusalem, were the two greatest of the Greek Christian poets.

In contrast to the earlier anonymous hymns that manifested a spirit of tranquility, the Greek hymns reflected the bitter struggles of the iconoclastic[11] war. These hymns showed a consciousness of guilt and personal sin; they magnified perils and the temptations; they expressed a fearfulness in looking toward judgment. In the later period (tenth or eleventh centuries) the Roman church adopted into its liturgy many of these hymns along with those of Hilary, Augustine, Ambrose, and Gregory.

But with the separation of the Eastern and the Western churches over the iconoclastic struggles there came upon the Eastern church a softening, a spiritual decay, an effeminacy, a formalism, a stagnation, and a bigotry that stopped the growth of the Eastern music. But in the Western church this was not the case. From the beginning, the growth and developing vigor of the Western music kept pace with the resolving of the Roman Empire's tempestuous inner struggles, from which evolved the feudal system and the centralized doctrinal systems of the papacy.

In the medieval church there arose an exclusively vocal music which rejected the support of instruments of music; it was characterized by a melodic quality that broke with the earlier metrical music of classical prosodic measure; it possessed a distinctive sacred style that in no way resembled secular music. The church avoided the peril of introducing an alien drama into the holy rites, exercising instead the nobler power of creating an atmosphere in which there was no worldly custom or worldly association.

THE ROMAN LITURGY—ITS PRINCIPLES

The music of the Roman Church has always evidenced the skillful and thoughtful use of psychological and aesthetic processes.

In analyzing the influence of these processes over the different cultures, one comes to recognize the Church's appeal to people's

---

[11]Reaching its peak in the eighth and ninth centuries, the iconoclastic struggle was a dissension over use of "images" in the church edifices and as a part of worship.

universal sensitivity to beauty, grandeur, and mystery, as embraced in sound and form.

The Roman Church has built great buildings, made use of paintings and fine sculptures of the masters, and devised a ritual carefully varied and enriched, integrating all these in a way that heightens their effect and seizes upon the perceptive imaginations of the people.

The Roman Church's worship is founded in the mystery of the Real Presence as exemplified in the teaching that the bread and wine of the communion are the actual body and blood of Christ.

Symbolism, artistic decoration, and portrayal are the very natural products of the spirit and genius of the Roman Church which recognizes that for most men, mystery and spiritual influences have to come as something definite, tangible, and concrete. The Roman Church, therefore, has translated numbers of its ideas into physical representations in order to make them efficiently operative. Thus, because its leaders have made extensive use of symbols and images, the Roman Catholic Church has often undeservedly incurred the charge of idolatry.

The Roman liturgy is a development contributed to by many individuals from the different ages. With the earliest Christians, set prayers were used and the "eucharist" or "thanksgiving" soon became the center of the developing liturgy. As a final, logical outcome of the liturgical growth, specific prayers, Scripture lessons, hymns, and responses were welded into a set program. The resultant liturgy has been referred to as a glorious religious poem or as a great church prayer. The liturgy (a heritage mainly made up of contributions from the Eastern church's first four centuries) at the end of the sixth century had been completely adopted and Latinized by the Roman church. It thus has come to be the voice of the church and, to devout Roman Catholics, it takes on the significance of scriptural inspiration.

The Mass is the Roman church's most solemn rite, representing the chief sacrifice of the clergy and laity as they join together in this occasion which includes the eucharistic "sacrament." It is a lavish portrayal revolving about and centered in the Last Supper of Christ with his disciples; it embodies and fulfills the perpetual injunction

68 CHURCH MUSIC

laid by the Master upon his disciples. (Matthew 26:20-30; Mark 14:17-26; Luke 22:14-23; John 13:20-35.)

The entire ceremony of the Mass, always an enigma to the uninstructed, is never vain or repetitious. All parts of the rite are embraced in a unity of consecration:

1. Upon the priest's entrance he says: "In the name of the Father, and of the Son, and of the Holy Spirit, Amen."
2. He then recites Psalm 42 (Psalm 43 in the King James Version).
3. He then confesses sin and prays for forgiveness.
4. He then speaks a few brief prayers, which are followed by responses.
5. He then chants the Introit (a short Scripture reading, usually from a psalm).
6. The choir sings *Kyrie eleison, Christe eleison.*
7. The choir sings *Gloria in excelsis Deo.*
8. The Collects (short prayers appropriate to the day) imploring God's blessing are spoken.
9. The Epistle, a psalm verse called the Graduale; or the Alleluia or Tractus, which also is usually a psalm verse followed on some occasions by a hymn called the Sequence, occurs.
10. Next comes the recital of the appointed Gospel.
11. The sermon (if there is to be one) comes after the Gospel.
12. The choir next sings the *Credo.* The *Credo* used today dates from 589 in Spain, and from 1014 in the Roman liturgy. It actually dates from its establishment in Constantinople in 381.[12]
13. After a sentence from a psalm the Offertory occurs.
14. Then comes the Oblation of the Host (preparation of bread and wine with prayers and ceremonials).
15. An ascription of thanksgiving and praise is then offered. This is called the Preface; it varies with the season, but the ascription always closes with the *Sanctus* and *Benedictus,* sung by the choir.
16. The Canon of the Mass now opens. It consists of prayers that the holy sacrifice may be acceptable and that it may

[12]Again, it is important to remember that the words of the *Credo* are those that date from 381. Nothing is known of the early tunes used as settings for the ancient text.

redound to the benefit of those present. After the priest pronounces Christ's words, the cup and the bread become subjects of the deepest adoration.

17. In the midst of the prayers which follow the consecration of the *host* and the *chalice,* the choir sings the *Agnus Dei.* The priest then communicates and those of the congregation who have been suitably purified by confession and absolution receive the wafer.

18. The postcommunion consisting of prayers for protection and grace, of dismissal and benediction, and the reading of the first fourteen verses of the first chapter of the Gospel of John closes the service.

Included during the service of the Mass, and during the prayers, responses, and chants, are a number of ceremonial actions such as crossings, and changing of robes. To the uninitiated, much of the ceremonial may, of course, seem meaningless. Even to the people who are Roman Catholics it is not necessary that the fullness of the rites be clear. It is considered that the rites are being performed by the clergy for the people. To be sure, the people should lend themselves fully to co-operating with the priest in faith and sympathy, and to abandoning themselves completely in the "contemplation of the adorable mystery."

But the Mass, a prayer of the church at large, might in a sense be construed as coming not so much from the congregation as from the clergy for the congregation. Theoretically it is not necessary that the laity be present. Private masses for individuals are in keeping with the discipline of the Roman church.[13]

BEGINNINGS OF MULTIVOICED MUSIC

In the music of the Roman church there are three main categories: (1) the unison chant, already treated, which was essentially the only music of the Western church from the fall of Rome to

[13]For further reading on the topic see these subjects: creed, eucharist, liturgy, mass, missal, as treated in the following publications:

Catholic Encyclopedia (New York: The Encyclopedia Press, Inc., 1913).

Encyclopedia Britannica (New York: The Encyclopedia Britannica, Inc., 1937).

Dictionary of Music and Musicians (New York: The Macmillan Company, 1954). Fifth Edition, Eric Blom, editor.

Nikolaus Gihr, *Dies Irae;* also, *Holy Sacrifice of the Mass* (St. Louis: B. Herder Book Co., 1927).

1100; (2) unaccompanied choral music, a development of music in the eleventh century which reached its peak in the sixteenth century; (3) mixed solo and choral music accompanied by instruments which arose after the sixteenth century.

In the early Gregorian chants or plainsong,[14] there is found the link that connects Christian religion with ancient religion. The plainsong provides even today an ideal sacred music. Indeed there are churchmen today who would have all modern harmonized music abandoned and the old plainsong restored to every part of church service. Such an ideal betrays, of course, a spirit which is ascetic and monastic and not likely to prevail generally.

However, the medieval chant represents a high attainment in musical artistry, even though it was a kind of music that was always

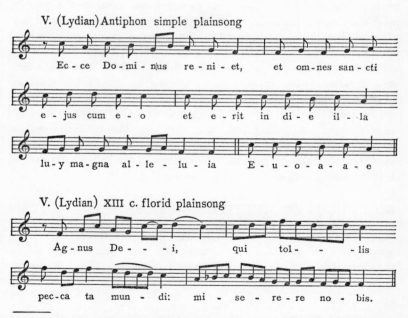

V. (Lydian) Antiphon simple plainsong

Ec - ce Do - mi - nus re - ni - et, et om - nes san - cti

e - jus cum e - o et e - rit in di - e il - la

lu - y ma - gna al - le - lu - ia E - u - o - a - a - e

V. (Lydian) XIII c. florid plainsong

Ag - nus De - - - i, qui tol - - - lis

pec - ca ta mun - di: mi - se - re - re no - bis.

---

[14]Plainsong is a name frequently encountered, referring to the unison chant melodies of the church; the term refers to chants in general rather than to Gregorian chant or Ambrosian chant, *etc.*; the term may sometimes seem to be ambiguously used, as in "Gregorian chant or plainsong"; Gregorian chant and Gregorian plainsong would be the same thing.

unfreed, subservient to the text, the ritual, and the liturgical purpose. In general, there are two kinds of plainsong: *simple* and *florid*. In the first, one usually finds each tone (rarely more than two tones) of the chant paired with a single syllable of the word text.

It is to be remembered that the form of the chants, however florid (or melismatic), was always authentically in keeping with the soberness of the worship text to be chanted; unrelated or meaningless artificiality was not a mark of the Gregorian plainsong.[15] The musical structure based on the unison concept of melody, which characterized the first millennium of the Christian era, began to give way to a new form in the tenth or eleventh century. A manuscript of the tenth century tells of a kind of performance in which the singers instead of singing in unison sang in parallel melodic lines a fifth and an octave or a fourth and an octave apart. The manuscript goes on to tell that a second voice might accompany the first voice in direct parallel or in oblique progression or even in contrary progression. Strictly speaking, these early stages of part writing or singing called *organum* or *diaphony* were not kinds of part writing at all but were, rather, combinations of unisons. It was not until the respective voices of a composition took on independent character of their own and progressed in a way that gave emphasis to their individuality that part writing can be said to have begun.[16]

The *sequence* is an interesting musical device that was introduced into the singing of the plain chants. From the ninth century on, florid improvisations were interpolated and spontaneously sung by the chanters as embellishments of the chant. This ornamenting by the singer was called "troping." Sequences were tropes that were learned and remembered and that became traditional integral ornamentations of the chant. In order to make learning them easier for the performers, rhythmic arrangements of the words were composed which became the additional text for the patterned trope or

---

[15]It must be noted again that the term "plainsong" embraces not only Gregorian or Roman chant but all the other types of chant; however, Gregorian chant, as previously indicated, came to be the most generally accepted kind of musical expression in the medieval church as supported by the authorities in Rome.

[16]For examples of parallel and freer organum, see p. 73.

sequence for certain chants. The Council of Trent (1545-63) authorized for use in liturgy, patterned formalized tropes or sequences: *Victimae paschali,* for Easter; *Veni sancte Spiritus,* for Pentecost; *Lauda Sion Salvatorem,* for Corpus Christi, and the *Dies irae, dies illa* for Requiem Mass.

The sequence as an incipient "piece" of music, rhythmically and regularly fashioned in order to facilitate its being performed from memory in an established traditional manner, is regarded as a forerunner of the "dance forms," and also as a device out of which grew the liturgical dramas and the later miracle and mystery plays.

For those especially interested in the subject of medieval forms, particularly the thirteenth-century forms that ushered in the Renaissance, investigation of the *conductus*[17] and the *motetus* is also important.

Out of the use of organum or diaphony there arose *discant.* Discant in its early stages was merely an unordered mixture of parallel and nonparallel successive octaves, fifths, fourths, and occasionally thirds. Long progressions of fifths and fourths eventually came to be avoided as of unsatisfactory sound. Later came the principle of contrary motion which is the key factor in modern harmony and composition. In the medieval period, however, no sense of chordal or "tonal"[18] characteristics existed. Thus, before

---

[17]The *conductus* was a "piece" of music deriving from plainsong, popular song, and organum. Its tenor voice might be a melody originally composed for the piece, or a selected melody from another source (most likely not a plainsong). Different word texts were chosen for each of the parts (1) the tenor melody, (2) the organum effect found in the duplum melody above the tenor, accompanied (3) by a third line of music functioning as diaphony either to the duplum or the tenor melody. Usually the texts were those used earlier with the melodies which were selected now to be combined in the conductus; sometimes not all the parts had texts. The different texts served as means (later) of sounding the melodies in their distinct rhythms, the text meanings themselves being regarded as unimportant. The earlier polyphonic conductus was composed note against note; later, more freedom in composing the voices developed. This was a beginning in the composing of "abstract" or "pure" music for its own sake, making use of musical sounds in free formal design to interest the performer and listener without any textual or conceptual reference. Modern instrumental music is of such kind.

A very careful study is required of one interested in these topics (*conductus and motetus*) to distinguish between them and thus to identify them in their peculiar characteristics. The motet, in its incipiency (9th century) shows a development not unlike that of the melismatic *alleluias* into the sequences. Different from the conductus which had strong secular implications, the motet was a development of plainsong, and probably always employed sacred liturgical texts. The basis of the early 13th-century motet perhaps was a two-voice simple (note against note) sacred conductus with the same rhythm and words in each voice now augmented by a new tenor voice of different, perhaps slower, rhythm, using a new text. Often the different texts of the motet were paraphrases of each other so that greater freedom in rhythm was possible; also the religious teachers of the time liked the notion of giving extended variety to the same religious idea through this device of paraphrasing.

[18]Here "tonal" describes the quality which exists when a grouping of tones, as in a scale or melodic figure, seems to center round about a specific tone as in the affinity the tones of the major mode have for the anchor tone or final *do.*

Parallel organum with doublings:

Organum doubled at the 8va above

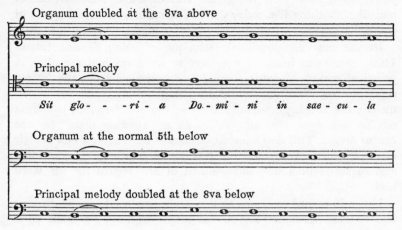

Principal melody

Sit glo - - - ri - a Do - - mi - ni in sae - cu - la

Organum at the normal 5th below

Principal melody doubled at the 8va below

Freer organum (without the possible doublings indicated)

Principal melody

1. Rex coe - li Do - mi - ne ma - ris un - di - so - ni
2. Ti - ta - nis ni - ti - di squa - li - di - que so - li

Free organum

3. Te hu - mi - les fa - mu - li mo - du - lis ve - ne - ran - do pi - is
4. Se iu - be - as fla - gi - tant va - re - is li - be - ra - re ma - lis

(adapted from Musica Enchiriadis)

the seventeenth century, multivoiced or polyphonic music was composed on a basis that recognized melodies and combinations of melodies. Nothing like today's use of harmony, or blocking out of chordal progressions from which melodies might evolve, was known.

In the new compositional technique of using discant (about 1100) there was included no effort to write original melodies. A principal melody *(cantus firmus)* was borrowed from the known repertoire of the day, usually an old plainsong, and the second melody for accompaniment, known as the *counterpoint,* usually a secular folk tune, was adapted to fit as "running mate" for the *cantus firmus.* This development of discant ushered in a new artistic concept which encouraged the practice of handling musical tones and melodies in a way independent of any regard for the word text.

Usage in regard to words as they were employed for the discants was of two divisions. The words might be used for both parts together or the words of the liturgical office for which the discant was written might be used only with the *cantus firmus,* while the words of the secular folk song from which the counterpoint was taken might continue as the text for the second melody.

By the twelfth century, the monks who interested themselves in music composition began writing in three parts. This kind of more advanced part-writing necessitated the original invention of melodies (excepting the *cantus firmus,* which was always a borrowed tune), for it was impossible to find three melodies already written that would fit together unless almost completely overhauled, adapted, and rewritten. Thus later composition of discant brought about the experimenting that ushered in the period of the great choral renaissance composition of the Roman Church, the music of which reached its highest advancement in the sixteenth century.

BEGINNINGS OF MODERN MUSIC NOTATION AND THEORY

There is no conclusive evidence as to the existence of a system of music notation before the seventh century. The early clergymen, providing melodies for their texts, transmitted their melodies with only the aid of their ears and their memories. It may have been that they used signs for memory aids. It is known that there were special orders of monks whose sole duty it was to preserve, sing, transmit, and teach religious melodies.

The music of the Middle Ages was based upon a diatonic or modal system of tonality. It was quite different from today's music, which is based mostly upon two transposable major and minor modes. In today's system, each major or minor scale respectively embraces the same patterned succession of whole steps and half steps as any of its fellows. The establishment of the present system dates from no earlier than the seventeenth century.

The medieval system included twelve (theoretically, fourteen) "modes" or keys. These are known as the ecclesiastical or Gregorian modes. They are divided into two classes, authentic and plagal. Each authentic mode is a scale extending from its keynote or final to the tone an octave above. Each such scale may be likened to the tones represented by the white keys of the piano. The first authentic mode begins on a tone represented by the piano's D, the second by its E, and so on.

Every authentic mode is related to a plagal mode. The plagal mode is formed by taking the last four tones of the authentic mode, transposing them to the lower octave, and following those four tones by the first five tones of the authentic. It will be noted that as a consequence of these procedures the final in the authentic mode is the first tone of the scale and the one an octave higher is the last tone of the scale. In the plagal mode the final is sounded only once in the scale pattern, being the fourth tone of the scale pattern. (In the examples on page 76, the finals are indicated as solid notes with stems.)

The modal patterns were established and used long before the invention of modern music notation. They may be transcribed into convenient modern notation as represented by the white keys of the piano.

It will be noted that the modes on the final B♮ are not used. However, by utilizing the tone that is represented by B♭ it was possible to "run" these twelve modes again through a range five tones lower. Thus parallel fifths in same mode for a discant could be contrived. (Dorian I starting on G.)

The first four authentic modes are, according to tradition, the creation of Ambrose; the first four plagal, that of Gregory. These traditions are not historically founded, so far as is known now. The Greek names for the medieval modes give rise to the hypothesis that they evolved out of the ancient Greek scale system. However, they are different from the Greek modes because the medieval scholars did not understand many of the technicalities involved in the Greek modes. While the medieval scholars may have thought that they were using the Greek modes accurately, they actually were not.[19]

Although the modes were well established in the medieval church and although the chants based upon them were soon definitely marked out in the "office" books, it must be remarked that the medieval chanter held it as his privilege to add to the melody whatever embellishment he might invent upon the impulse of the moment. This right was also claimed up to very recent date by Italian opera singers; the florid Italian style in the opera is only the

Medieval Modal Patterns

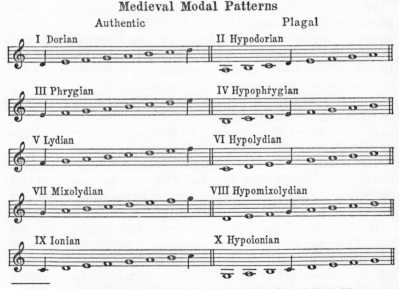

[19]Grey op. cit., and Warren Dwight Allen in his Philosophies of Music History provide important information here; both raise dissident voices against the traditional treatment of this subject by musical historians. For an enlightening discussion, see Nemmers, op. cit., p. 63.

perpetuation of the practice generally prevalent in the medieval church. Such practice of free and spontaneous embellishment, often making the melody nearly unrecognizable, may date from antiquity. It is a modern idea that tones should be sung as indicated by the notation. Even in Handel's time and after, free embellishment was introduced into such things as "I know that my Redeemer liveth." In fact, throughout history the artistic merit of singers frequently has been judged by their ability to invent florid embellishment which went beyond the received notation.

From this background developed music notation. In the music notation of the early medieval period specific pitches could be shown only approximately. The method of this early medieval notation was a heritage from the Orient, using a system of marks, *neumes,*[20] a Greek term used in this notation method. In translation, *neume* means *sign.*[21] In the medieval church these neumes or signs were put above the words to be sung. They showed in a general way, the direction in which the melody went, i.e., its rise and fall. When the clear and exact system of notation in use by the classic Greeks is remembered, one can scarcely understand how such a primitive system as that of the neumes could have been the system of medieval church notation. Certain it is that the knowledge of the Greek system was lost, for Isidore of Seville wrote that if music "is not retained in man's memory, it is lost, for it cannot be written down."

Neumic notation was dependent upon oral tradition. The singers, singing by memory, watched the gestures of the song leader or precentor, who took his directions from the neumic indications above his text.

It was not until the addition of lines, which developed into the modern staff occurred that the neumes became anything more than "an auxiliary to aid the memory," as Hucbald (*c.* 840-939), codifier of the *organum* in the tenth century, said.

It was Guido d'Arezzo, an eleventh-century Benedictine monk of Pomposa, who gave impetus to codifying modern musical nota-

---

[20]See table of neumes, p. 80.

[21]*Neuma* indicates a group of notes sung on the last syllable of a text until the breath is expended; pneuma refers to the breath, which in turn in religious usage was a reference to the *spirit;* in the New Testament, when a "sign" was asked of Jesus, what was asked for was an evidencing of the working of the Spirit.

tion. That is, Guido is credited by history with the invention of modern music notation. But actually much of what Guido introduced or "invented" was known or had been known by other cultures of various historical periods. Even in the very time of Guido others might have had much to do with the formulating and codifying of music notation in the Roman church. But just as Gregory often is credited with the composition of Gregorian music, so Guido is often credited with the invention of music notation and of solmization.[22]

As a starting point, Guido (c. 980-1050) used as elements of his notation the one or two lines already somewhat abiguously used with the neumes. Guido used four lines marking them with clefs which indicated exact pitches, thus putting an end to the possibility of ambiguity in indicating pitches.

Guido, who invented his system in Pomposa, so incurred the disapproval of his jealous colleagues of the clergy, when he made his boast that his pupils could learn in five months what formerly had taken ten years, that he was compelled to flee to Arezzo. From there his fame spread. It is said that Pope John XIX invited him to Rome to demonstrate his system. Guido handed to the Pope an *antiphonale* written in his new notation. ". . . after explaining the rules to the pontiff, the latter, to his great astonishment, was able to sing a melody unknown to him, without the slightest mistake."[23]

Guido in establishing his hexatonic system of solmization used the hymn to St. John the Baptist, a six-line hymn. In the music as Guido contrived it, the first syllable of each line sounded on a pitch a diatonic step higher than the preceding.

Thus came about the solfeggio names applied diatonically: *ut, re, mi, fa, sol, la,* first identified in terms of modern notation in Guido's hexachord. Note that there are only six tones in Guido's scale and that these are transposable to the various tone levels. It is readily seen in examination of the modes that the *leading tone,* our *ti,* was not used by the churchmen of the medieval period. *Si* (suggested by the initials of *S*ancte *J*ohannes or *I*oannes), later

---

[22]Solmization has to do with the tone names *ut* (later *do*), *re, mi, fa, sol, la.*
[23]*Micrologus,* Prologue, in Gerbert, II, p. rr A.

replaced by *ti,* was first used in the seventeenth century, at which time *ut* was replaced by *do* (*do* is taken from the first two letters of the Latin *Domine*). Between each two syllables, except mi-fa, a half step, there was the interval of a whole step, just as today. Except in France where *ut* is still used, the syllable *do,* for sake of euphony, has been substituted.

Hymn to St. John the Baptist
(Text by Paul the Deacon, c. 770)

In addition to his "invention" of notation and solmization, Guido is credited with inventing the Guidonian "hand." By use of a representation of the left hand, a certain degree of the staff being ascribed to each joint of the fingers, it was possible, by holding up his left hand and pointing to the proper finger joints, for the precentor to indicate to his singers what notes they should sing and when. One need not be reminded that music copy was scarce in the days before printing.

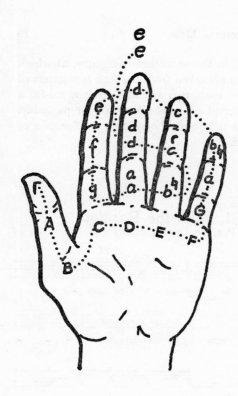

Guidonian hand

Table of Neumes

Name	Sign	Possible example of Equivalent	Name	Sign	Possible example of Equivalent
Virga (Acute accent)	⁊		Scandicus (2 grave and 1 acute)	⟋	
Punctum (Grave accent)	⌃		Climacus (Acute and 2 grave)	⌐	
Clivis (Acute and grave)	7		Torculus (Gravè, acute, and grave)	⌒	
Podatus (Grave and acute)	♩		Porrectus (Acute, grave, and acute)	N	
			Quilisma (Tremolo)	⌇	

CHORAL MUSIC IN THE MEDIEVAL PERIOD

The period from the twelfth through the fifteenth centuries is marked for compositional and intellectual experimenting in the writing of choral music.

With growing skill in handling parallel and contrary motion among the several voices, the term "discant" gave way to the term "counterpoint." But an old plainsong or popular tune, never a newly composed melody, was still the *cantus firmus,* to be accompanied by other melodies designed to integrate themselves with the given melody.

In the early discant, the melodies sounded note against note; later the subservient parts sounded several decorative tones against single sustained tones of the *cantus firmus.* Thirds and sixths, and resolving dissonances were utilized as compositional devices. Consecutive fifths were avoided. Development and experimentation along these lines went on through the thirteenth and the fourteenth centuries. This period was not a period noted for artistic musical development but rather for scientific musical progress. Thus, impetus was given to the early *polyphonic* music. The *cantus firmus* or the *teneo* (*tenere*—to hold) was sounded in the range of the present-day *tenor* voice. Even today, tenor parts in certain kinds of male voice arrangements are often called the "lead voice," although by the sixteenth century, confining the "lead part" to the tenor was in general discontinued.

The desirability for developing an artistic, beautiful music, nicely proportioned with suitable variation and regularity in design, soon made itself felt. One device for achieving such interesting quality in choral composition was that of *imitation.* The "round," the "canon," the "fugue" are examples which utilized the device rather obviously. And today in the modern, more subtle, musical forms, *imitation* and *repetition* are still very important compositional elements.

Since the newer composition could no longer be served by the ancient neumic signs, the notation of Hucbald and Guido had to be modified and elaborated in order to make possible the notating and the fitting together of the intricate melodies. Not only did the pitches upon which the melodies were built demand indication but so also did the rhythm of the several melodies, long notes against cascades of short notes, and so forth. While the experimentations in notational development were hazardous, often ineffectual (they are sometimes still a source of despair to the musical student), they apparently were a delight to the "ingenious monkish intellect" of the monastics. Composition under their influence came to resemble algebraic calculation more than free art, and symbolic representations of trinity and unity, of the perfect and the imperfect, were embraced in the monks' efforts at musical notation. Consequently the growth of music as an art was tedious.

In the medieval choral music, as in the earlier liturgical chanting, and also in the later Italian opera, the singers did not restrict themselves to singing the written music. They were quite eager to extemporize adornments for the given melodies. Not unlike present-day singers of a certain amateurish status who know little about the artistic demands of song, the medieval singers, as Jean Cotton of the eleventh century put it, were to be compared with drunken men. Others, such as 14th-century Jacques de Liége and Oelred, the twelfth-century Scottish abbot of Riverby, even John XXII, also have told of the offensiveness of some of the contemporary singers' style.

Such abuses, however, were not general. Instead, the effort, in a spirit of consecration, was to enrich the church service through improved music. Consequently, later church music rose to a level of excellence that is still unrivaled. The powerful princes of Europe themselves aided in its development. Robert of France in the eleventh century, and Louis IV, both devout rulers, and even those princes who were crafty, heartless rulers, co-operated in making the music, mathematical as it was, a thing that showed continuing improvement toward artistic ends.

The greatest confluence of fine writers occurred between 1400 and 1500 in Northern France, Belgium, and Holland, thus gaining for their period the appellation, "age of the Netherlanders." To be sure, this school is noted mainly for its technical genius and accomplishment, every imaginable device of intricacy being employed by its composers: multiplicity of parts, rhythmic complications, puzzling variations in rapid sequence. But even while these composers reveled in writing to outdo their contemporaries, often suiting their music to the eye and the intellect rather than to the ear and the feelings, there were numberless instances when, manifesting an encouraging emotional sensitivity, they wrote music, complicated for us today, to be sure (but easy for the persons of that day), which touched, and in all periods since, has touched devout hearts deeply.

ARS NOVA—FOURTEENTH CENTURY

With the opening of the fourteenth century, sweeping changes in religious, social, literary, and musical outlook had begun. What at first might have seemed trivial can now be seen to be deeply symptomatic, namely, the revolt against the use of Latin as an international language. Dante, Boccaccio, and Chaucer wrote in their mother tongues, thus introducing what was later to become a challenge to the church's dominance through her use of the Latin as a mark of her international influence.

Another evidence of change was in the music of France and Italy. In France there was Guillaume de Machaut (b. Rheims, c. 1300-d. 1377) who wrote his polyphonic songs in two and three voices on secular, romantic, and love themes. The influence of a treatise by Philippe de Vitry, written about 1325, over the thinking of Machaut is clear. This work, *Ars Nova,* confirms the musical and spiritual changes in France, as does the music of Machaut which was characterized by great rhythmic freedom making use of duple and triple measure, and the more consonant effects of harmonic thirds and sixths.

In Italy there was Francesco Landini (1325-1397) (referred to in the chapter on Organ) who wrote also in romantic forms such as those found in France, except that Landini introduced the new, distinctive madrigal (not to be confused with the madrigal of a much later period, however). He developed also the *caccia* (in English, the catch; in French, the *chace*), a hunting song featuring the polyphonic canon.

Characteristic of the fourteenth century, was the dignifying of secular enterprise. Up to the thirteenth century, more is known in general of sacred music, because of the careful and devout protection of sacred music by the church and the monastery. And except for the music of the troubadours, trouvères, and the minnesingers, most medieval secular music has been lost, because it had no great institutions to preserve it. What secular music was preserved came from the knightly and royal minstrelsy, or else from the preserved sacred music into which secular melodies were introduced for the sake of the new polyphonic elaboration and development. Of course, the secular music of the troubadours, trouvères, and minnesingers, was produced partly as a result of the impact of the Crusades upon European cultures.

But in the fourteenth century, secular song began to take on new stature. Its text was not in Latin, but in the vernacular. Its tune was now in the highest voice, and none of its parts was derived from the sacred chants. Secular music brought to the fourteenth century the age of the *Ars Nova,* while sacred music was still tied to the traditional and authoritative chant. However, the new secularization had its inevitable effect upon sacred music. Machaut himself composed a complete polyphonic setting of the Ordinary of the Mass. Interestingly enough, his Mass was preceded by that of another writer which because of its ancientness of style was mistakenly ascribed to the thirteenth century by Charles E. Henri de Coussemaker (b. Bailleul, 1805-d. Bourbourg, 1876) in his *La Messe du XIIIᵉ siècle,* published in 1861.

The new rhythmic freedom gave new flexibility to the contemporary handling of chant motifs in the new sacred composition. Duple, triple, and syncopated rhythms were all utilized in the new sacred melody.

But there must always have been tension between sacred and secular enterprise. A quotation from Basil (329?-379) in *Hexaemeron* IV, I, is of interest:

> There are towns where one can enjoy all sorts of histrionic spectacles from morning to night. And, we must admit, the more people hear lascivious and pernicious songs, which raise in their souls impure and voluptuous desires, the more they want to hear.

Thus, perhaps, Pope John XXII, of the fourteenth century, in his decrees about music, was meeting an age-old problem when he noted that the grandeur of the old music of the Gothic art was in decline and that the church composers of the *Ars Nova* were modeling after the secular music of the day. Although John's decree (1324-25) warned the followers of the "new tendency," innovations nevertheless infiltrated the music of the church. And the *ars antiqua*, the great and grand *organa* of Perotinus (b.?, d. Paris, ?), gave way to the *ars nova*. However, the music of the newer style maintained for the most part the dignity that the church prized so highly in its liturgy.[24]

THE FIFTEENTH AND SIXTEENTH CENTURIES

The first half of the fifteenth century continued in the same general direction as had the fourteenth. Now it can be seen that the 150 years (1300-1450) comprised a bridge between the medieval ages and the full-blown Renaissance.

Among the composers of the first half of the fifteenth century, three stand out: John Dunstable of England (b. ?-d. London, 1453), Gilles Binchois (b. Belgium, *c.* 1400-d. France, 1460), and Guillaume Dufay (b. Belgium, *c.* 1398-d. France, 1474).

Many manuscripts of Dunstable's works have been found on the Continent. No doubt this is because Dunstable was stationed in France during his part of the Hundred Years War which required that England maintain a large force there. The work of Binchois and Dufay was done mostly in the Court of Burgundy in Dijon.

Following the legacy from Machaut, Guillaume Dufay, traditionally regarded as the leading musical figure of the Burgundian School, did not overlook the development of the accompanied polyphonic song in secular usage; and, along with the rest of his generation, he contributed to the rising interest in polyphonic settings for the five parts of the Ordinary of the Mass. The old Gregorian melodies were adapted to this new music. And for those parts of the Mass which are changeable (*Proprium Missae:* Proper of the Mass), new life was brought to what had been a stagnant liturgic form since the days of organum.

---

[24]For further reading:

Adams, Henry, *Mont-Saint-Michel and Chartres.* Boston: Houghton Mifflin Co., 1904. Provides insights into medieval thought and an account of medieval art.

Strunk, Oliver. *Source Readings in Music History.* New York: W. W. Norton and Co., 1950. Contains the *Ars Nova.*

As Dufay followed de Machaut, so Dufay was followed by his pupil Johannes Ockeghem (b. c. 1425-30 in Flanders-d. 1495 in Tours). Dufay was followed also by Okeghem's pupils (Josquin des Près was one of these) and contemporaries: Jacob Obrecht (c. 1430-1505), Gaspar van Weerbecke (b. Oudenarde, c. 1440-d. Rome, 1514) and Antoine Busnois (b. ?-d. Bruges, 1492).

Ockeghem developed his secular music, as influenced by the Burgundian School, along lines that soon diverged from those of his religious music. In his church music, he maintained remarkable polyphonic balance, making use of both full and divided choirs. He observed the ecclesiastical tonalities carefully, and followed his texts sensitively, in noble, dignified musical language evidencing the purest of musical ideals, all in keeping with the highest liturgical requirements. Some have regarded Ockeghem as the greatest church musician of all time—but one cannot thus ignore his pupil Josquin des Près (b. Hinaut?, c. 1450-d. Condè, 1521) who, as Boyden describes him, "is comparable to Leonardo and Raphael." Nor can one ignore the Gabrielis, or Orlandus Lassus, or Byrd, or Palestrina, or Bach—about all of whom more will be said later.

Mention was made above of the divergence between Ockeghem's secular music and sacred. Because of the opprobrium that is usually heaped upon such practice as indicative of the deterioration of the spiritual feeling of the day, it should again be noted that the secular melodies were mostly used in modified situations and forms. As Láng has pointed out, they would be recognizable in their secular reference only by the most erudite of musical scholars, and such recognition would lead some observers to feel that the melodies had been enobled by their being judged worthy of a place in which to exalt the spiritual ideal.

The cultural importance of the Renaissance is partly to be apprehended through the music of men of the period such as Josquin des Près, a pupil of Ockeghem. Among the most important contributions of Josquin were those which modified the subsequent compositional ideas—even though there were numbers of composers to follow who, unaware of Josquin's worth, paid their allegiances to Ockeghem, not recognizing the genius of his great pupil. But it is interesting that Luther, himself no mean musician, recognized the superb qualities in Josquin. He saw that Josquin des Près evidenced keen musical and artistic insights. To Josquin, the subtleties of contrapuntal composition were contrived, not for their own sake, but to serve as a means of significant expression. Because so many church musicians of the day did not see with such perception, this age of music has been frequently disparaged, but not always deservedly.

Refinements in the compostion of the latter half of the fifteenth century which were given impetus by Josquin des Près were chiefly in reference to "equalizing" the voices. Earlier, the melody selected for a *cantus firmus* was added to by countermelodies. Later, along with the countermelody (descant) which was added to the "tenor" voice, a third voice, the "contratenor" voice, was also added to fill out and augment the resonance. Each of these voices in the period before Josquin des Près was almost always treated individualistically, sometimes each voice having its own set of words. But after 1450, it was a chief aim to use the same text for each voice; and to have each voice imitate the other instead of going its own independent way. Now, in this new treatment, and in order to add resonance and sonority, more than the usual three voices in the new imitative style could be indulged. However, such use of additional voices called for greater attention to harmonic combinations. Thus in the later fifteenth century, there were introduced what has proved to be incipient chordal progressions. Such harmonic portions of a composition provided interesting contrasts with the canonic portions in the purely imitative polyphonic sections. Use of only one text plus the musical contrasts between "chordal" and canonic sections led to careful choosing of one or the other to serve as the better vehicle for the differing moods in the text. Thus the new composition of this period possessed the ingredients of modern musical design: the canonic, imitative portion; the older traditional polyphonic style for another portion; and the new chordal treatment for a third kind of part. Now it was possible to choose certain kinds of musical groupings as settings for the textual parts. These groupings presented a kind of "through composed" design—not usually possessed of any repetitions of parts—that gained unity from the text itself and from the imitative portions in the polyphonic treatment. The *Ave Maria* of Josquin des Près furnishes a most excellent example of the new compositional style. It is included as number 19, in Parrish and Ohl.[25]

The introduction of the new music of Josquin des Près is said to have led directly to the establishing of the *a cappella* ideal. But it is well to note here that *a cappella* references have been much misunderstood. Many historians have in error assumed that the localized ideal of Rome (unaccompanied vocal music was and is required in the Sistine Chapel) was a general practice and requirement of the Roman Catholic Church. However, the German scholar, Arnold Schering, emphasized that even with Josquin's music, it was played on the organ with only one voice being sung by voices. No doubt the current view that *a cappella* music is purely vocal music came partly through imaginative traditions which arose in reference to Palestrina of the sixteenth century. Palestrina's successes at Rome have served to exalt him to a place of almost universal reverence. Many have come to look upon his musical achievements in the Sistine Chapel as fairly representing the ideal of church musicians everywhere. Actually, Palestrina as well as other church musicians of his day often used instruments to "double" the various choral parts. It was not until the latter part of the sixteenth century that the instrumental parts which heretofore had been identical with the vocal were specially indicated with the term *concerto* or *concertato*. *A cappella* (in the mode of the chapel) has come in our time to mean "instrumentally unaccompanied music" partly also as an aftermath of the Cromwellian revolt in England and again partly because tradition has led us to believe that this was the manner in which church music was rendered in the glorious age of church choral music. It is true that in *a cappella* usage, when instruments were employed, they did not usually play parts other than those which could be sung.

THE VENETIAN SCHOOL

Adriaan Willaert (b. *c*. 1480-90-d. 1562), founder of the Venetian School, enjoyed an influence throughout Venice equal to that of Ockeghem in France, or of Josquin des Près in Ferrara, Milan, and Rome as well as in the various regions of France. Willaert's

---

[25]*Masterpieces of Music before 1750* (New York: W. W. Norton and Co., 1951).

Ave, Verum Corpus

Josquin de Près
c. 1450-1521

contribution to musical literature was the madrigal (quite unlike that of Landino of the 14th century). Here in the Venetian madrigal a most sensitive effort was made to require the musical interest to serve as a complement to the text.

Willaert composed extraordinary motets for antiphonal choirs, and also music for independent instrumental usage. The two organs in St. Mark's attest to the brilliance of the music to be furnished by the choirs—opposite to each other in the apses of the nave.

Many of the developments of the Renaissance have sometimes been credited to the Venetian School—but this is not correct as may already have been surmised through the references to the work of Josquin des Près. Such musical enterprises as the antiphonal choirs, for example, have a long history. However their new rise to spectacular glory was the work of the Venetian School as started by Willaert. He had countless numbers of pupils, Italian and Flemish. Among the Netherlanders who had come to Italy were Jachet Buus (b. Belgium, ?-d. Vienna, 1565); Jachet de Berchem (b. Berchem, ?-d. Ferrara, 1580), a Flemish organist of Ferrara; and Cypriano de Rore (1516-1565).

FLEMISH INFLUENCE

The influence of the Flemish musicians which had held sway came slowly to be modified by the revitalized music of Italy. The Italian music profited by and continued to use the compositional devices from the North, but with a renewed emphasis upon text. Now the contrapuntal and polyphonic devices were subjugated to the import of the word texts. With this change, already set in motion by des Près, the era of *a cappella* music in what might be called the Italo-Flemish style was now established.

Having its impetus out of the North where the technical skills of many-voiced writing were gloriously consummated, and its impulse out of the humanistic sensitivities of the South, there came a music characterized by an elaborately complex polyphonic treatment but warmly interpreting the ideas for which the music was a vehicle. The working toward this new achievement had been the interest of all the great composers from Josquin, Willaert, the Gabrielis, and to Monteverdi yet to come. This is not to imply the overlooking of Lassus and Palestrina, also to come, whose participation in this era was so much a part of it but yet so distinctive.

It was the disciples of Josquin, who did the most to bring on the glory of the *a cappella* period. One of his pupils, Adrien Petit Coclico (b. Hinault *c.* 1500-d. Copenhagen, *c.* 1563) who had become a Protestant, in 1552 first published works in the new style entitled *Musica Reservata*. This style perhaps through its interesting name indicated a protest against the unreserved extravagances of the older Flemish style; perhaps also it implied that it was the special reservation of those sensitive souls who could discern the subtle values not to be revealed in the mechanics of musical notation but in the warmth of skillful interpretation springing out of personal insight.

THE COUNTER REFORMATION AS PART OF THE
ROMAN CATHOLIC REFORM

The Roman Catholic Reformation was very different from the Protestant, and earlier. It had taken upon itself a similar task, however, that of attacking corruption in the Roman clergy in order to strengthen Christian piety and resoluteness. Many later efforts to integrate the forces of Luther's Reformation with the Roman Reformation were attempted—long after 1521—but, as can be seen now, by 1521 the divergence was irreparable. That the two faiths were violently divergent was clear to all with the onslaught of the Thirty Years War (1618-1648). The Roman Catholic Reform which had been increasingly active toward the end of the fifteenth century was supplanted by the Roman Catholic Counter Reformation which occurred finally when it was obvious that the Protestants were making inordinate gains to the peril of the Roman Church. It is a misunderstanding, however, to assume that the Protestants brought about the reforms that finally were accomplished in the Roman Catholic Church. It is true that the abuses against which Luther had protested were in many ways corrected by the close of the sixteenth century—but through the processes of the Roman Catholic Counter Reformation. However, it must be remembered that the efforts in the fifteenth century of the older Roman Catholic Reform had worked for a restoring of pure Christian living, and had actually achieved the revival of the mysticism and asceticism which had characterized the Roman Church centuries before. This achievement, nevertheless, had had little effect upon the papal court and the secular-minded clergy. Thus the finality of a new kind of establishment, Protestantism, moved the earlier somewhat unsuccessful Roman Catholic Reform toward the more effective devices of the Counter Reformation.

Developments and changes in musical usage are of course related to the reformative struggles. As already indicated, the rise of *musica reservata* really began with Josquin des Près, extended into Spain with Gombert, and found its firm entrenchment in Italy with Willaert and those who followed. There were, of course, many important church musicians during the sixteenth century who were

part of the new musical spirit of the Counter Reformation.
Among these were:

Jacob Arcadelt (Flemish)—born about 1514; died in Paris,
about 1570.

Jacob Clemens (Flemish)—born in Ypres, c. 1500; died, Dixmude,
c. 1556.

Thomas Crecquillon (Flemish)—born near Ghent; died at
Béthune, 1557.

Cypriano de Rore (Flemish)—born in Antwerp or Mechelen,
1516, died in Parma, 1565.

Ludwig Senfl (German), a Catholic, but one of Luther's favorite
composers—born in Zurich or Basel about 1492; died in
Munich, 1555.

Claude de Sermisy (French)—1490—Paris, 1562.

Antonio de Cabezón (Spanish)—born near Burgos, 1510; died
in Madrid, 1566.

Cristóbal Morales (Spanish)—born in Seville, about 1500; died
in Malaga, 1553.

Maintaining the Netherland tradition in the German regions
were:

Jacques de Kerle—b. Ypres, c. 1531-d. Prague, 1591.

Johannes de Clève—b. ? Cleves, 1529-d. Augsburg, 1582.

Jacob Regnart—b. ? Douai, c. 1540-d. Vienna, 1599.

Francois Sale—dates uncertain, died Prague, 1599; member of
the Imperial Court Choir, Prague, 1593; composer of masses
and motets.

The leadership in Roman Catholic church music was centered
in the papal control at Rome. And the Roman music of this
period was influenced by the tempestuous changes of the Counter
Reformation. Two great musical names, Philippe de Monte (b.
Mechelen, 1521-d. Prague, 1603) and Roland de Lassus (c. 1532-
1594) are of this period and of the Roman-centered development.
Lassus (de là-dessus) Italianized his name to Orlando di Lasso. It
was in de Monte and di Lasso that the height of the musical
development springing out of Dufay, the Burgundian, was reached.

In 1534 Paul III became Pope, and Ignatius Loyola with six companions took their vows establishing the Jesuit Order—not actually to combat the Protestant Reformation, but as a fulfillment of the changes that had been materializing with the ascendency of those heads of the church who were bringing about the older Roman Catholic Reform.

In 1545 the Council of Trent was convened to codify the gains of the Catholic Reform under Paul III. The Jesuits as chief supporters of the Papacy, through encouraging obedience to the Pope and through establishing educational centers, had been able to gain back for the Roman Catholics the southern parts of the Low Countries, parts of Germany, and all of Bohemia, Austria, Poland, and Hungary. This resulted in permanent animus from the Protestant world.

When Pius IV continued the Council of Trent to deliberate on the liturgy and music, complaints about the music touched upon the neglect of the word texts, disrespectful attitudes of the singers, the secular spirit, and the overabundance of musical instruments in the service. During this convocation, expressions came from some who would do away with polyphonic music altogether— while others staunchly supported it. Reports about the Council of Trent have been romantically colored by subsequent generations. Actually, it was the recommendation of the twenty-second session that the service of worship should include only those elements in keeping with the dignity of the service. Actually, views as to what kinds of music were to be advocated had already been pretty well clarified in earlier sessions of the Council, for Otto, Cardinal Truchsess, Bishop of Augsburg, had commissioned his choirmaster, Jacobus de Kerle, to write suitable music for the meetings of the Council. Kerle's music was in such good taste, making use of both homophonic and polyphonic devices, and was so admired by all who heard it, that it was commended by all. Thus it was Kerle and not Palestrina (to be treated later) who was the "Saviour of Church Music"—if anyone at the Council of Trent should be so described.

The often-repeated statement that the Council of Trent forbade use of *chanson* tunes for *cantus firmi* is without foundation. Instead, the practice was continued, although Palestrina and others

Benedictus

Orlandus Lassus
1520–1594

of his contemporaries no longer would name the *chanson* serving as a *cantus firmus* but would merely indicate it as *sine nomine*.

Lassus, composer of 2,000 works of music ranging from secular, often mischievous, pieces to his glorious masses, could project himself as a German writer of part songs, as a lovesick Italian, or as a delicately sensitive Frenchman composing his *chanson*. His masses were not always as exquisite as those of Palestrina, not as tender, perhaps, but in his motets, he knew no peer. Lasso sprang from the heritage of two centuries of music and he stands as a culminating synthesis of all that was beautiful in them. "This," as Làng puts it, "the history of music has since experienced but once again in the art of Mozart."

Thus by the middle of the sixteenth century, choral composition reached a level of artistic and consecrated attainment that has never been surpassed. It was the climax of a short but glorious age of great, moving choral music.

One more great name of this age needs to be introduced—that of a man who wrote sincerely, devoutly, majestically, and in greatest purity: Palestrina. As already noted, there were numbers of men who occasionally have written with as sublime power as he, but, like the name of Moses in his age, or of David in his, Palestrina's name above all others, has stood for the best in sixteenth-century choral writing.

PALESTRINA

From the thirteenth century on, leading to the climax of choral attainment in the sixteenth century, in addition to names already noted such as those of Josquin des Près, Orlandus Lassus, Adrian Willaert, and others, there were Giovanni Croce (b. near Venice, *c.* 1557-d. 1609) whose church music is noted chiefly for its employment of double antiphonal choirs. Remarkable also was Croce's considerable influence over English composers of the day such as Thomas Morley (1557-1603) who is known to many for his *Plaine and Easie Introduction to Practicall Musicke* (1597). Morley had been a pupil of William Byrd who in partnership with Thomas Tallis (b. Leicestershire, *c.* 1505 ?-d. Greenwich, 1585) had held an exclusive printing license under royal appointment. Morley succeeded to the printing license after Byrd and Tallis died.

Thomas Tallis held several important musical posts such as at Waltham Abbey. Here he perhaps was known to Henry VIII since the king frequented this place before the disfranchising of the

Roman Catholic places of worship. Later, Tallis was given the post in the Chapel Royal which position he held for forty years. Tallis composed a great and numerous list of church pieces including many motets and anthems.

In addition to Croce of the Venetian School, the two Gabrielis should be noted: Andrea and Giovanni. Giovanni (b. Venice, 1557-d. 1612) was a nephew of Andrea (1520-1586) who had studied under Willaert. For a time (1575-1579), Giovanni was an assistant to Orlandus Lassus at Munich. Later he was appointed "second organist" at St. Mark's in Venice. This was in 1584 when his uncle, Andrea, was appointed to be "first organist." In 1586 when Andrea died, the nephew, Giovanni, succeeded to the post of first organist, a post he held until his death. During his service at St. Mark's, Giovanni published many of his uncle's works along with his own. Giovanni had many distinguished pupils, among them the great Heinrich Schütz. Even today, Giovanni's contributions are hardly assessable. He was the first to achieve good balance between chorus and instrumental group in joint musical presentation. He contributed the idea of doubling voice and instruments in octaves, and giving to instruments independent parts. His compositional ideas were given extension and fulfillment in the works of men like Monteverdi, Schütz, Praetorius, Hassler, Frescobaldi, and Sweelinck. Several of these latter personages are discussed in the chapter on history of the Organ.

Certainly, the work of Claude Goudimel (b. Besançon, c. 1510-d. Lyons, 1572) should not be overlooked. In his early years Goudimel was a Roman Catholic, but by 1557 he was living and associating with the Huguenots in Metz. The last music that he composed for the Roman Catholic service, a *Magnificat* and four masses, appeared in 1557 and 1558. It is of especial interest that in 1551 he produced a book of *Psalms in the form of Motets*. These were used evidently by both Catholics and Huguenots, for a time, in their religious services. Goudimel perhaps only selected the tunes and then harmonized them, usually placing the melody in the tenor voice. He was killed in the massacre of the Huguenots at Lyons.

Of all the great figures, Palestrina is the one which has come to represent the highest choral attainment. Legendary fancifulness has ascribed to him the credit for being "the saviour of church music."

The story back of this, mostly imaginative, tells that the Council of Trent was about to ban all polyphonic music as being too lascivious, but that Palestrina, regarding the Council's attitude as dangerous and regrettable, wrote his famed *Mass of Pope Marcellus,* and by its austerity, purity, grace, and devotion saved polyphonic choral music for the church, the Cardinals being so impressed by its rendition that they no longer felt that antagonism toward such music was valid. The story serves mainly to point up that a need for musical improvement was felt.

The abuses felt in the choral music of the day stemmed from the custom of borrowing the themes and words from secular tunes (perhaps some of which were no more than ditties) for use as *cantus firmus.* Consequently, on many occasions the songs of the church when composed by less responsible musicians may have betrayed an unseemly artificiality. The chief complaint, even so, was not against the secularizing tone of borrowed *cantus firmus,* since such borrowing, though often in poor taste, was done with good intention and therefore not considered sacrilegious; the chief complaint was against the rhythmic interferences of the intricately interwoven parts or voices leading to such garbling of the word text that its meaning could not be grasped by the hearers.

There have always been, in all periods, groups who oppose any kind of sacred music which seems to carry within its style an artistic element. At the Council of Trent (1545-1563) no doubt such persons had a voice.

Palestrina, actually Giovanni Pierluigi, was born in 1525 or 1526 and died in 1594. He was buried in St. Peter's at Rome, in one of the side chapels where his coffin is marked with the words, "Prince of Music."

He apprenticed in Santa Maria Maggiore in Rome, and then went back to the town of his birth where he became choirmaster and organist. The Bishop of Palestrina, Cardinal Giulio del Monte, became Pope Julius III; and Pierluigi, called *da Palestrina,* the name by which he is always known, was made *magister puerorum* (teacher of the boys) in the Cappella Giulia at St. Peter's.

Upon the succession of another Pope, Paul IV, Palestrina was dismissed (because he was married) from the Choir of the Sistine Chapel of which he had also been a member under Julius III.

Because a subsequent appointment to St. John's provided him too meager support, Palestrina took a posiiton at the church of his apprenticeship, Santa Maria Maggiore, where he stayed until 1571. At this time he again went to the Cappella Giulia, now as its leader, a position he held until his death.

Pope Sixtus tried to have him made a member of the Sistine Chapel, but again because of his marriage he was prevented by the authority of the Clergy. However, he was awarded the title of Master of Composition *(maestro compositore)*.

Honor and offices were heaped upon him because of the remarkable liturgic quality of his music that so fitted in with the earlier rulings of the Council of Trent. Nearly all of Palestrina's composition was for the church, a very few madrigals representing his entire secular output.

Palestrina's "Mass of Pope Marcellus" while unsurpassed by any of his other works, was perhaps equaled many times. It does not represent a "new music" or a new style, but rather in purity, chastity, and technical subtlety, it represents one of the mountain peaks in the age of choral music—an age which began at least as early as the fourteenth century.

All the while that this musical development was going on, there was, as already indicated, a rising sensuality, an emotional indulgence, a luxurious debauchery among many of the potentates of the church and state, and there was a corresponding decadence in the faith of many of the churchmen. But this widespread moral degeneracy which resulted in the Lutheran, the Calvinistic, and the Anglican revolts, did not pervade all of the Catholic constituency. The earlier Roman Catholic Reform and the Counter Reformation attest to this. It is to be remembered, then, that the high attainment of the music of the Palestrinian era reflected the *better forces* in the Roman Catholic movement.

There were two kinds of choral composition in the Palestrinian era: (1) the continued intricate and complicated, but beautiful and satisfying style of the motets and the larger forms, and (2) a "familiar style," much simpler, often note against note which seems to anticipate the later processes of *harmony*.[26] Since the older music was conceived melodically rather than harmonically, and the interweaving of several melodies as they each moved mostly degreewise, were temperately consonant or dissonant, with no "harmonic system" such as used today, the medieval harmony sometimes seems vague. And since it was without a "chromatic" or "dominant" feeling for a pivotal, final, tone of rest, it is sometimes monotonous to the modern ear.

In the more simple or "familiar style" *(stile famigliare)* the haunting anticipations of tonic and dominant stemmed perhaps from the popular music with which the important composers of the fifteenth and sixteenth centuries were familiar. Dickinson appraised this simple style as strangely tender and gracious, the forerunner of what is "sweetest" in the modern Latin and English hymn tunes. Including no chromaticism it reached the ultimate in serenity, suggesting the "confidence and response of spirit" which is the essence of soulful devotion.

During the tranquil period of Palestrina and the "Roman School," a more dynamic, more vigorously moving religious choral composition, casting a shadow toward the new *harmonic* system, was being produced, as already noted, in the Venetian school.

---

[26]In comparing Palestrina's incipient harmonic style with today's harmonic idiom, there is an important difference however which must be noted: Because the writers of the sixteenth century mostly took as pitches with which to work only the diatonic tones equivalent to those of the white keys on the piano, with a B♭ thrown in, they did not have in their compositions the fluidity that is found in modern harmony. Tonic and dominant feelings so easily given in "modulatory" progressions in today's harmony were impossible in the sixteenth century. For instance, III, VI, II, V, I as a dominant progression in today's C tonality would not likely have been thought of in the medieval idiom and if it had been, it could have been permitted only on white keys, although avoiding the B♮ in III and V, the B being considered as desirable. Today each chord can be chromatically altered to give it modulatory dominant quality if desired, e.g., III♭, VI♭, II♯, V, I or, more brilliant still, III♯$_6\atop5$, VI$_7$, II♯$_6\atop5$, I$_6\atop4$, V$_7$, I. But, as just mentioned, since "dominant chromatic" progressions were unthought of, actually impossible, then, even a medieval succession of unaltered III, VI, II, V, I, would be unlikely unless by accident.

As in their painting, where one sees color and contrast emphasized, so in the Venetians' music, one sees the contrasts of dissonance and consonance, modulatory anticipation, and all the
other forerunners of today's music. The Roman music was more
serene, perhaps more mature; the Venetian, more frontierlike,
though in technical achievement not inferior to the Roman music,
was more dynamic, often making startling use of the musical color
of instrumental combinations.

Shortly after his death, Palestrina came to be looked upon as a
mysterious figure; he was held in awe by many, and subsequently
became an almost legendary character.

No doubt, Palestrina's music possessed an otherworldliness, and
a universality which kept it apart from the immediacies of local
interpretive idioms. Làng has compared him with Dante who spoke
of man in hell, paradise, and purgatory—but not on earth. Palestrina for many has represented the ultimate in the new Roman
Catholic religiosity. Church music, among many Roman Catholics,
is regarded as having closed with him.

Giuseppi Baini (1775-1844) romantically contributed to the
establishing of the "prince of music" with his biography of Palestrina, issued in 1828. And in Germany, a Heidelberg lawyer, Justus
Thibaut (1774-1840) who developed a consuming interest in *a
cappella* music of the sixteenth century, extended the Palestrina
romance. Contemporary with Palestrina and recognized as an important musical figure in Rome was Giovanni Nanini (b. Tivoli,
c. 1545—d. Rome, 1607). Nanini was the first Italian to found a
public school of music in Rome. In this work he was associated with
Palestrina. He composed many splendid motets and his six-voice
motet, *Hodie nobis coelorum rex* is still sung every Christmas morning in the Sistine Chapel.

It is important to recognize that many who have professed
adulation for the name of Palestrina have actually been acquainted
with very few of his works. One must be wary of certain spurious
works that are not Palestrina's at all, but the work of Marc
Antonio Ingegneri (b. Verona, *c.* 1545—d. Cremona, 1592), teacher
of Monteverdi. *O Bone Jesu* is one of these.

That Palestrina was well acquainted with the musical advances
in Venice is very clear, although he steadfastly restricted himself

to the modal church style based on diatonic progressions. That his musical acquaintance was wide is also attested by his use of *chanson* melody in "l'Homme Armé Mass" which he composed long after the Council of Trent. Indeed, within the framework of what he felt appropriate to church music, Palestrina vitalized his music by appropriating what he would from other schools of composition, both those of the past and of the contemporary.

But his music evidenced an understanding of and reflection of the spirit of the Roman Catholic Reformation. His music depicted the new Reformation mood of meditation, mystery, awe, and elation which were characteristics of the new Roman Catholic religious outlook. Thus his music established the *new church style*. The *a cappella* idiom of the Roman church was not of the Venetian school but of the Roman school of Palestrina. However, this should not be taken to mean that his music was always done without instrumental music accompaniment, nor was that of Lassus so restricted either.

It should be remarked that while romantic tradition had it that Palestrina's music possessed no earthly reference, was spirituality altogether disembodied as it were, the truth is that his works glow with passionate feeling, exultation, sorrow, jubilation, and all the other ranges of emotional color that human beings call upon for their best artistic revelation.

A study of the sixteenth-century music gives rise to many philosophic theories about religion and art. In the religious connection, art has never been considered as existing for its own sake, but rather for the service and glory of God and man. Religious art always has been a means of teaching. Accordingly, church tradition has always hampered art when art showed signs of following after a goal other than the needs of man as he endeavors to strengthen his relationship with God.

It has been noted[27] that when artists attain to a certain success, becoming self-conscious about their personal technical skill, they break away and go beyond the traditional creativity of their particular church age. The "purest stage" in church art is rarely the maturest stage in the development of the art itself; rather, it is an

---

[27]Dickinson, Edward, *Music in the Western Church* (New York: Charles Scribner's Sons, 1902), pp. 176-178.

"adolescent period" in the particular art's development so far as ultimate artistic advancement goes. Nevertheless, one should not be doubtful of the sincerity of religious artists who are endeavoring to move beyond this adolescent stage. For the religious artistic techniques, church artistic styles, and secular artistic attainments do not obliterate each other, but rather are different stages of advancement in a consummate whole.

Church art is often the precursor of the secular art to come, and due to the slowness of change in church tradition, the older church art is likely to continue on even after the consequent secular advance has suggested the beginning of a new trend in church art. In church art, then, there is always a tension between the height of its artistic attainment just passing and the adolescence of the new artistic stage just beginning to make itself felt in an oncoming different church art. Church styles and secular styles thus are often the same techniques at different stages of growth. So medieval polyphonic music, however wonderful, could not hold the center of the stage for long. A devotional experience, not unlike "spiritual trance," which was all that the old music could suggest or provide, was only a part of what the new mentality regarded as desirable in worship.

Even as the sixteenth-century choral music was at its glorious best, further developments in the art of music began to appear in the worship program of "the church": solo singing was displacing the chorus; modern harmonic flexibility was eclipsing the older modality; homophonic music was replacing the polyphonic; independent instrumental accompaniments and interludes and pieces were supplanting the older *a cappella* ideal of the Roman school.

The music for the Roman Catholic medieval mass was quite unlike the music of the mass today. The choral music of the sixteenth century, while it lasted on even into the eighteenth century, was in its latter years supplanted by a new style of church music. Polyphonic music, as we shall find, gave way to homophonic music, which embodied a new compositional design that resulted from a balanced succession of structural "parts."

In those periods of history in which one finds some certain development in a particular category of advanced level (such as in the sixteenth-century polyphonic music of the Roman school) one may fail to recognize that such a period, even so, is only one of transition. It is always true, however, that the church artist, developing his skills in a certain idiom as he serves his church's needs, soon finds that his artistic curiosity demands he also interest himself in the processes of everyday secular living.

Because it has usually been true that the traditions of the church have held the artist from expressing himself in those advanced processes which he enjoys in his other than religious insights, it has consequently been a common mistake among some to suppose, for example, that the sixteenth-century *a cappella*[28] music was exclusively church-style music. However, in its day, such music was employed artistically for all the purposes to which its serenity, its objectivity, and its impersonal character fitted it. In addition, though, even while its use was being continued, exercise in other kinds of music marking the secular excursions of an advancing artistic culture was becoming increasingly vigorous. One can thus account for the change in the music of the postmedieval church as the old medieval polyphonic music was displaced; for as secular art succeeded in its endeavor to give more effective expression to the words, many began to wonder why such advances should be ignored by church music.

Thus, in the seventeenth century occurred the development of solo singing which was given priority over choral singing. The tonality of major and minor transposing scales displaced Gregorian modality. Homophonic composition, that is, harmonized melody, displaced the contrapuntal many-voiced or polyphonic music. Accompanied music became more and more elaborate. Instrumental music arose as an art in itself, and, divorced from word texts altogether, it was able to satisfy the needs of aesthetic abstraction. Consequently, in the Roman church, the *a cappella* contrapuntal chorus, a "stately monument," faded over the horizon along with the culture and the philosophy of the Middle Ages.

It was seventeenth-century inventiveness and the development of the opera, the ballet, and "pure" instrumental music that

---

[28]*A cappella* music until recently was thought by many to refer to all church music of the medieval period up through the sixteenth century with the further belief that all such church music was purely vocal with no instrumental connections. It is known now that even Palestrina accompanied his own choral music.

brought about the disappearing of the medieval polyphonic choral music.

THE OPERA

It is perhaps not so that opera has any connection with the classic Greek drama. Yet similarities between these exist. It was Peri (b. Rome, 1561—d. Florence, 1633) and Caccini (b. Rome, c. 1545—d. Florence, 1618), and others, who during a period of about nine years starting in 1580 in the home of Giovanni Bardi, Conte di Vernio (b. Florence, 1534—d. Rome, 1612) met to explore the nature of Greek drama, and who really inspired the opera composition which has come to influence us most. The roots of opera are much deeper than is supposed, however, and the history of opera must be taken back much further than the opening of the seventeenth century.

The creation of opera, a new art form, is, of course, the greatest contribution of the seventeenth century to music. But it was nevertheless a part of a continuum having roots in the church drama of the tenth century. The Easter Sepulchre Play, centuries before, had been performed in all the great church centers of Europe. It made use of music, costumes, and other properties. As early as 980, in Winchester, dramatization of the theme of the Easter Mass took place. By the end of the thirteenth century, many settings of New Testament and Old Testament events were dramatized— always with singing.

Eventually these performances outgrew the facilities of even the great cathedrals. Consequently, in many places the music drama of the church took place in secular surroundings.

In their attempt to reach the ideal achieved by the ancient Greeks, the "Camerata" (as those who frequented Bardi's house are called) discovered new kinds of musical expression which changed music's direction in innumerable ways.

Of this group, Caccini, a celebrated singer, wrote a considerable number of songs made up of a single line of melody accompanied by the simplest kind of bass. This monodic style was in striking contrast to the commonly heard polyphonic richness of the older music. The new music came as a result of a new attempt to achieve *natural* expressiveness through the medium of musical declamation. The new monodic style was a characteristic product of the baroque period (seventeenth century)—itself a passionate, restless, searching period, often placing its emphasis on the pleasurable, the flamboyant, the grandiose: the baroque spirit was one which no longer permitted the overlooking of the real feelings of human beings.

The new opera composers earnestly attempted to support the dramatic import of the words of their text with music that was intimately and integrally related. To this end, as is especially notable in the work of Monteverdi (b. Cremona, 1567—d. Venice, 1643), instruments for an orchestra were developed. Out of all the ferment, grew the ballet, the chamber instrumental group, the instrumental solo, and the symphony orchestra yet to come. All these had their effect upon the music of the church: there arose the sacred cantata, the oratorio; and the developments in the organ and in organ music turned in new directions.

One of the ideals of the "Camerata," as we have seen, was to free music as an art from the fetters of arbitrary compositional rules and let it act freely as a vehicle for poetic and serious prose expression. Since Italy was a musical land, as soon as the traditional musical rules had been so happily relaxed, the musical minds saw that music had unique functions important to the edifying of the human consciousness, in addition to those of acting as a poetic vehicle. Recognizing the new musical powers, composers saw the possibility of entering "all the recesses of the soul"; of giving voice to all the human emotions.

It is not to be supposed that significant, profound improvements were made in this new era. Far from it. Imitators, persons of superficial talent, persons lacking in insight, outnumbered those who, though popularly submerged in musical flamboyancy, actually made the contributions which moved music forward. Because of its many artistic inadequacies, many see only a shallowness in the seventeenth-century secular music whose changes have so profoundly and beneficently affected our modern age through the opera, the music drama and ballet, the instrumental ensemble and orchestra, the oratorio, cantata, communal anthem, and hymn.

The Roman Catholic church musicians of the time were also aesthetically sensitive artists and they did not overlook the opportunity, the challenge, indeed the obligation to take to themselves the benefits of the contemporary musical findings. However, as was inevitable, among the musically artistic clergymen who were not religiously sensitive, there arose (and still exists) an intermixing of church, religious, artistic, and secular factors that brought about, in too many instances, the formation of a conglomerate which, because of its lack of character, has hindered the fruition of the church's musical enterprise into authentic religious service. The purity, the austerity, the virginity that characterized the best of the older Roman or medieval music (which, to be sure, is still performed), is no longer embraced as the ideal in the newer Roman music.

While one can hope for a restoration of the *quality* of the older music, one should not urge that the complete diet of religious music be taken from an older idiom which may, because of its intrinsic genuineness, still prove to be artistically and culturally arresting. A purist or an ascetic who urges adoption of the old and the ignoring of the new, unwittingly urges worship of an anachronism and unwittingly neglects the opportunity to commune intelligently with those who still find living in the present to be provoking and stimulating.

SECULAR MUSIC

In the Middle Ages there were the jongleurs in France and gaukler in Germany who traveled from place to place as minstrel entertainers. They were not so much composers or poets as they were performers. Their chief importance in musical history was their keeping alive a large body of secular music which otherwise would have been lost, since the medieval church was not officially interested in such music. The secular music is an important reservoir to which historians go today for information about the culture of the Middle Ages.

There is another important group of minstrels who were restricted to Northern and Southern France. These were the trouvères and troubadours. They, in contrast to the jongleurs and the gaukler, were persons of rank. The troubadours, flourishing in Southern France, mainly in Provence, during the periods of the eleventh, twelfth, and thirteenth centuries, left about 264 preserved melodies and some 2,600 poems. Some leading troubadours were: Bernard de Ventadour (d. 1195), Bertrand de Born (b. *c.* 1140—d. *c.* 1215), Giraut de Bornelh (d. *c.* 1220), Giraut Riquier (d. 1292), Marcabru de la Gascogne (d. *c.* 1150), and Guillaume de Aquitaine (1070-1127).

The trouvères, who roamed Northern France (the period of their growth paralleling the period just somewhat later than that of the troubadours), have left about 1,400 preserved melodies and perhaps 4,000 poems. Important names in this group are: Adam de la Halle (b. *c.* 1230—d. *c.* 1287), Blondel de Nesle (b. *c.* 1150— d. *c.* 1200), Conon de Béthune (d. 1224) and Thibaut IV, King of Navarre (b. Troyes, 1201—d. Pamplona, 1253).

The songs which these groups sang fall into types, such as love songs, songs of satire, laments for occasions of community mourning, pastorales, spinning songs, songs celebrating deeds of heroic accomplishment, et cetera. These songs were mostly melodies which had about an octave range. While sometimes based on the church modes, these songs usually exhibit tendencies toward what are the present-day major and minor modes. The songs were usually rhythmic in character.

In Germany during the twelfth and thirteenth centuries, perhaps as an outgrowth of the movement of the troubadours in France, there arose a group, mostly of noble birth, known as the Minnesingers. The term *minne* meant "love." The minnesingers took as subjects for their lyrics, beauty and love. The music of these persons was not unlike the music of the troubadours and the trouvères. They sometimes employed the older church modes; they employed duple and triple rhythmic meter for their songs; and they gave themselves to singing much the same kind of material as did their French colleagues. Important names in this group are those of: Walther von der Vogelweide, Germany's first important lyric poet (b. *c.* 1170—d. *c.* 1230), Neidhart von Reuenthal (*c.* 1180-1240), Heinrich von Meissen, known as Frauenlob (d. 1318), Hugo von Montfort (1357-1423), and Heinrich von Morungen (14th century).

Later, during the fourteenth through the sixteenth centuries, there arose groups known as the *Meistersinger*. These persons were guildsmen of the worker class and thus distinguished from the aristocratic minnesinger. However, like the minnesinger, they gave themselves to the cultivation of music and poetry. In the music of the meistersinger one finds evidence of a growing body of rules about how to write music. Certain standard melodies were used over and over again for various purposes as accompaniment to different song texts. Many times, of course, the music of the meistersinger is marked by crudeness and lack of inspiration.

During this same period there was an important artistic development in secular music in the British Isles, although there is not much actual material which dates from before the fifteenth century. Performing in this period were minstrels known as "scops" (resident minstrels) and others known as "gleemen" (traveling minstrels) who gave to their communities the recitation of lengthy song texts to accompaniment on the harp. One name is left as representative of this middle English period, that of St. Godric (d. 1170).[29]

ADDITIONAL MUSICAL FORMS AND DEVICES

A fanciful story may refer to a compositional item of the latter period of the medieval church: the device known as false bass *(faux bourdon)*. Because there had been frequent introductions of popular tunes into the sacred writing for church use, by the fourteenth century abuses had become so extensive that Pope John XXII issued a decree forbidding the use of "discant" as a musical device in church service. In this edict, issued in 1322? 4? 5? at Avignon, he outlined that above the principal melody *(cantus firmus)*, consonances of the octave or the fifth or the fourth might be used, but only if the integrity of the chant tune itself were still maintained. The tale goes that as an evasion of this edict a melody a sixth below the chant tune and an organum a fifth above the accompanying low melody *(cantus firmus)* were introduced. This introduction of the interval of a sixth may have been a violation of the edict, although it was not specifically forbidden, and perhaps was condoned because it gave smoothness to the accompani-

---

[29]See *A Literary History of England,* Baugh, ed. (New York: Appleton-Century-Crofts, Inc., 1948), p. 120.

ment and may have seemed also to be a complement to the consonances such as the octave, the fifth, and the fourth. The subterfuge then came in the performance of the music, when by taking the lowest notes and having the sopranos sing them an octave higher there was gained a new effect that, after all, achieved the artistic effect (originally forbidden) of a high discant over the chant tune. This was the very thing which the edict had opposed. The term "false bass" has been given to the procedure.[30] In earlier periods many writers had entertained a fear that music would introduce a secular tone into religious service; for instance in the twelfth century, John of Salisbury (*c*. 1115-1180) said, "Music defiles the service of religion. For the admiring simple souls of the congregation are of necessity depraved—by the riot of the wantoning voice, by its ostentation, and by its womanish affectations in the mincing of notes and sentences. . . ." Or again, in a statement by Jacques de Liége (14th century), one reads, "Oh, if those of the olden time who were skilled in music could hear such discanters, what would they say—what would they do?"[31]

---

[30]Actually the progressions in *faux bourdon* varied, there being at least two methods, one, in England, the other, on the continent. The *cantus firmus* could be in the lowest voice, the tone a sixth below being transposed to a third or tenth above, with the usual fifth above the *cantus firmus* now fitting in between. Or, the *cantus firmus* could be in the highest voice with the sixth below remaining in position; between these the voice normally a fifth above the *cantus firmus* could sound by being transposed down an octave. Or, a singer could improvise an inner voice to fit between the high *cantus firmus* and the low voice a sixth away.

[31]*Speculum Musicae*. Often ascribed, formerly, to Jean de Muris, author of *Ars Novae Musicae*. Investigation of these writings of Jean de Muris indicated a new spirit of experimentalism in music not consistent with the writings of the *Speculum* and thus led to the finding that it was de Liége who wrote the views often quoted from *Speculum Musicae*.

CHAPTER FOUR

MUSIC
IN THE REFORMATION

THE HYMNODY OF LUTHER

While in many ways the music of the Lutheran Reformation resembled the music of the Roman church by which it was influenced, it possessed also many distinctive qualities. The Lutheran music was based primarily on the *hymn,* designed to be sung by congregations, while the Roman Catholic music had been based on the liturgic music for special music offices which had evolved out of the Gregorian chant. Since the Catholic church had always kept its office of music separate from the laity, congregational singing had never been encouraged. But with the Reformation, the entire membership of the Protestant church was regarded as a priesthood. Each member had direct access to the Father, through Jesus. Thus, in Protestantism, the office of song and, in fact, all the offices of worship, were taken back to the congregation, while in the Catholic churches the music was still the responsibility of and supplied by the clergy. Congregational responsibility for the music in Protestantism accounts for the introduction of popular song into the religious services. Congregational action gave opportunity for any individuals in the various groups to express themselves creatively; it gave encouragement also to the militant group spirit of the people as they consciously served God directly as their hearts and knowledge guided. An important distinction between Protestant and Catholic church music is found in the Protestant church's use of the vernacular or local language, while the Roman church nearly always performed its music in Latin. Lutheran hymnody is of special importance because of its departure from nearly a thousand years of clerical control of the musical religious service.

Many have erroneously regarded Luther (1483-1546) as the *creative* genius who gave to the common people a body of songs for expressing their religious convictions. However, before the Reformation, there was in existence in Germany a great body of popular religious songs. These had been sung by the Roman Catholic people at other times than in the formal services of the church. It is perhaps most nearly correct then to conclude that Luther took the old musical forms which had been so well known by the people and gave to them a new spirit that captured the interest of the people.

Many hundred religious lyrics had been created in the years between 868 and 1518,[1] although before the ninth century, popular church song in Germany had confined itself mostly to the exclaiming of *Kyrie eleison, Christe eleison.* On almost every occasion, at burials, on pilgrimages, even on the march into battle, these exclamations were voiced ecstatically. Later, under the influence of the rise of chivalry and the exalting of women, songs about the Virgin Mary began to burst forth from the people. In this pre-Reformation period, the poets of the court, influencing both the clergy and the common people alike, aroused in the Germans a fervent love for singing at religious service. Among these there were certain men of unorthodox belief, out of favor with the church, who wrote hymns having great influence upon the people. The clergy, trying to counteract this practice, also composed hymns for the people to sing which would express the orthodox beliefs. Thus by the fourteenth century, a great wealth of popular songs created by numerous peoples, including the mystics and also those

---

[1]Wackernagel. *Das deutsche Kirchenlied von der ältesten Zeit bis zu Anfang des XVII Jahrhunderts.* Vol. II. Wackernagel, in this second volume of his work, has collected over 1,400 religious songs in the German tongue representing the period from the ninth century to the Reformation.

religious fanatics, the Flagellants, was added to the popular religious music of Germany.

After the fourteenth century it became customary to take the secular tunes of the people and use them as settings for religious poems. As a result, love songs and drinking songs, with a few changes in the words, could be made acceptable as religious songs. By the fifteenth century, popular religious song was flourishing in Germany to a degree that had been hardly surpassed even in the first two centuries of early Christianity.

It was out of such a background that Luther took his music, adapted it to the purposes of the Reformation and gave it to the people. Another influential factor of the pre-Reformation period affecting the Lutheran Reformation, was the custom of church teachers' use of songs to teach their peculiar doctrines which often were conflicting, inaccurate, or contrary to the teaching of Jesus and the apostles. For instance, some of the songs of the period represented the church as being the controller of the Son who did the bidding of the church. Many later critics, of course, have looked upon such a state of religious propaganda in song in the Roman church as being altogether bad. However, removing the objectionable material still leaves a residue of rich and pure song literature which equals and in some cases perhaps even surpasses in quality and spirit what the early Reformers were able to create. It is partly from this store of pre-Reformation German music that Luther and others[2] of his time took their hymnody.

Martin Luther (b. Eisleben, 1483—d. 1546) was highly respectful of Josquin des Près because he saw in him not merely a competence in musicianly craft but a sensitivity for the things of the spirit. While Luther was interested in music for the common man in the vernacular tongue, he recognized that ordinary, earthbound music will lead only to decline. Thus Luther never followed the strictures of Calvin who banished all which might seem to be a

---

[2]Using the chorale tunes as *cantus firmi*, numerous German composers of this period constructed chorallieder which were performed specially in the worship services by the choir; these were more elaborate than the harmonized chorale but not so complex as the German motets which were not unlike the Roman motets. Important German composers for the Lutheran church of the period were: Johannes Eccard (1553-1611), Hans Leo Hassler (1564-1612), Ludwig Senfl (dates uncertain), Johann Walther (1496-1570), and others. In addition, helping in the development of the hymnody for congregational use were J. R. Ahle, Johann Crüger, Andreas Hammerschmidt, and many, many more.

reference to "the popish." Luther never subscribed to the austere and severe phases of the unaccompanied community singing of the Calvinists and the Puritans.

Calvin's distrust in music was partly based in the fears already found in Augustine and Gregory the Great, but he carried his fears to unusual lengths. Even today, the development of music where Luther's influence grew is considerable; but the contrast is woeful in those parts of England, Scotland, and Wales, Germany, and Switzerland, where Calvin's influence was strong. Calvin subjugated music to a point further than even Zwingli attempted.

Contrary to the belief of some, the Roman Catholic church had not been opposed to congregational singing during the centuries but had always been strict about prohibiting the singing of songs in the vernacular language for any part of the eucharistic service. In less important offices of the service, hymns in the vernacular were permitted. It was the case, however, that congregational singing had only a minor part in the formal service of the Roman church. With Luther and the Reformation this attitude by the Roman church was of course neutralized, and congregational singing in the vernacular for all parts of religious worship came into being.

It was not Luther's purpose to destroy the traditional worship of the people, but rather to purify and to reform the worship. To this end Luther outlined a liturgical program of singing for the newly reformed Germany. The order of service that Luther gave to his people follows: (1) Hymn, or a German psalm by the people, (2) *Kyrie eleison,* (3) Collect, (4) Epistle, (5) Hymn by the congregation, (6) Gospel, (7) German statement of the Creed, "Wir glauben all' an einem Gott," sung by the people, (8) Sermon, (9) Lord's Prayer, (10) Exhortation preliminary to the Sacrament, (11) Description and Explanation of the significance of the Sacramental Institution, (12) Distribution of the Bread, (13) Singing by the people of the German Sanctus or "Jesus Christus unser Heiland," (14) Distribution of the Wine, (15) Singing of *Agnus Dei,* a German hymn, or the German Sanctus, (16) Collect, giving thanks, (17) Closing Benediction.

Luther's background as a priest in the Roman church was, of course, an important influence upon him all his life. He envisioned

116   CHURCH MUSIC

the evangelistical idea of a militant Protestantism, and toward this end, supported the emphasis upon community or congregational singing of religious song, but he called upon the resources of all the hymn literature of Christendom for his material. Thus he gave to the world the *Ein' feste Burg* (Psalm 46) and the *Aus tiefer Noth schrei ich zu dir* (Psalm 130). Luther in his association with excellent and consecrated musicians was able to adapt the old Latin hymns to Germanic evangelical religious use. He actually encouraged the performance of the complete Latin Masses in the German service, only insisting that the sermon in German be introduced immediately after the *Credo*.

The Protestant music of Germany and the Roman Catholic music had different meanings, each in their place, but they sounded the same. It was not until the seventeenth century that a music distinctively Protestant appeared.

In 1524 the first hymn collection for the new Reformation was published by Johann Walther. Subsequently, many songbook revisions began to appear. In these collections there are at least thirty-six text arrangements or adaptations by Luther himself; it is thought that perhaps five of these are completely original. It is of interest that in 1551, the collection showed 78 German and 47 Latin songs thus indicating that unlike some of his fanatical colleagues, Luther did not urge an intemperate kind of separation from the traditions of Roman Christendom. Luther's authorship of some of the Lutheran chorales and hymns has been doubted. It was claimed by Baeumker that Luther wrote no tunes, only word text adaptations and that when Luther's songs were spoken of it was the word texts that were meant. There has always been, however, the tradition that Luther composed the tune for "Ein' feste Burg" although its form has seemed to some to be that of an early Gregorian chant.[3] There are available, in Luther's own handwriting, a number of musical compositions: a motetlike piece by Luther in four-part writing, *Non moriar sed vivam,* was published by Breitkopf and Hartel, Leipzig, in 1917. This composition was used in a play, *Lazarus,* by Joachim Gräff, one of the

---

[3]The first line of Luther's tune interestingly enough is found as a bass line in a Latin motet published in Johann Walther's *Chor-Gesangbuch* of 1524.

poets whom Luther knew. Luther had friendly relations and correspondence with the notable sixteenth century musicians, Agricola, Senfl, Walther, and many others.

Among the important texts which may be in large part original creations of Luther is the famous "Ein' feste Burg." This song has been called the embodiment of the spirit of Protestantism and the Reformation. The new hymnody of the Reformation was in accord with the new teaching, thus enabling the people through repeated singing to grow more deeply aware of the principles of their faith. One doctrinal principle continuously emphasized in this music was that salvation is not dependent upon the works of man but upon the merits of Jesus, who shed his blood for man's salvation.

As will be noted later, herein lies one of the differences between Luther and Calvin. Melancthon, the philosopher of the German Reformation, declared that where the *cultus dei* failed to permeate the complete man and his life, where the music of the church ceased to be heard, there would set in a breaking down of the sacred teachings.

But the *application* of the old music to the *new* evangelism made the difference. In the Roman view, the Gregorian music was objective and universal, detached from personal influences that might tend to modify it and thus interrupt its transporting man to higher contemplations. In the Protestants' modification and re-use of the ages-old traditional music of Christendom, the need for personal and immediate response in accordance with immediate faith gave the clue to the dominant musical thought of the German Reformation—a principle of spiritual considerations as opposed to that of a sacramental service.

It was the German or Lutheran Reformation that set in motion the wheels of sixteenth-century French Protestantism. Francois I recognizing that the new movement could be a menace to the Crown at first was tolerant of the German Reformation. His sister Margaret was a leading protector of the Protestants. However persecution did grow as Protestantism grew, becoming in a short time a sufficiently well-organized group to meet in Paris as a Synod in 1559. Interestingly enough this synod of "Huguenots" subscribed to the views of Calvin and to the presbyterian system of government. Calvin had fled to Geneva in the earlier persecutions of the French

Ein feste Burg

"Der XXXXVI Psalm"

Luther, c. 1529   Luther, c. 1529

Ein' fest - e Burg ist un - ser Gott, Ein' gute Wehr'
Er hilft uns frei aus al - ler Noth, Die uns jetzt

und Waf - - -fen.
hat be - trof - - -fen.   Der alt' böse Feind,___

___ Mit Ernst er's jetzt meint, Gross' Macht und viel List,

Sein grau-sam Rü-stung ist, Auf Erd' ist nicht sein's Gleich - en.

Tr. F. H. Hedge, 1853   J. S. Bach, c. 1717

A might - y for - tress is our God, A
Our help - er He, a - mid the flood Of

bul - wark nev - er fail - - ing,
mor - tal ill pre - vail - - ing;

For still our an - cient foe seeks to

work us woe, His craft and pow - er great and armed with

cru - el hate, On earth is not his e - - qual.

"Lutherans," and because the Huguenots did become a threat to the Crown, they were then persecuted viciously. So much so that Pope Paul III remonstrated with Francois I on his treatment of the Protestants.

In connection with Luther and his immediate followers, of interest today, equal to that of the word texts and their implications, is the musical usage evidenced in the tunes. As already mentioned, the tunes of Luther and his contemporaries were taken in large part from the Latin music of the Catholic church, partly from the German songs of the period before the Reformation, and from secular folk songs. At first the tunes for the hymns were unharmonized and were sung by the congregation after having been learned by rote. Later, the songs were "harmonized" in contrapuntal style. The congregation still sang the tunes but the harmony was sung by a specially trained group of people who knew how to sing artistically and how to read music. This gave rise to the employing of a choir to assist the congregation as it sang the melody in unison. By 1600, however, the services of the choir were augmented, then displaced, by the use of an organ to play the harmonies while the congregation sang the tune.

In the centuries since the Reformation, the traditional singing of the chorales has been maintained, but the original militant spirit has softened. On occasion, there are efforts to restore the old ideals of the Lutheran hymnody. But as yet there have been no significant signs of a restoration of the vigorous congregational song such as arose in the early days of the Lutheran Reformation.

RELIGIOUS ART MUSIC—THE ORATORIO AND THE CANTATA

With the transformations brought about by the German Protestant music in the seventeenth century and later, comparable changes were taking place at the same time in the Roman Catholic music. As has always been the history of changes in religious music, the old order was displaced by a new kind of music which could more completely express the new cultural demands provoked by the advances in secular music. In the German Reformation three important kinds of religious music were in use at the beginning of the seventeenth century: (1) the chorale, (2) the motet, and (3) the music for organ. At the same time there were in existence the Italian recitative and aria which had been contributed by the developments in opera. These operatic contributions were products of the new developments in harmony, tonality, and formal structure. As a result of increased experience with the Italian operatic forms, there developed in Germany an interest that led to the creation of the German cantata and the Passion music. Consequently, the seventeenth century "German reformed music" took on a form and style and tone that evolved out of five sources: the chorale, the motet, the organ music, the operatic recitative, and the operatic aria. Unfortunately, this development in the music was often marked by an ostentatious concert style which betrayed a decadence into formalism and unseemly provincialism. This artificiality continued as a partial factor in the music of the German church through the seventeenth and eighteenth centuries. The loss of the original spirit of the German Reformation, evidenced in the great patriotic hymns of faith, was thus threatened when the choirs began to sing buoyant melodies accompanied thinly in the manner of the Italian music.

Perhaps it was the work of only a few, like Praetorius, Schütz, and others, who, preserving the most lofty ideals made it possible that out of ominous decadence there arose the *cantatas* and the *passions* of Johann Sebastian Bach.

ORATORIO

Any discussion of the German cantata to come should be in light of the development of the oratorio. An oratorio may be described as a sacred dramatic poem set to music for nonliturgical religious service. The oratorio includes choral and solo singing accompanied by orchestra, or organ, and is frequently presented in the concert hall rather than in the church. The oratorio today does not require or make use of stage scenery or stage movement. It has roots in the liturgical music drama. With the gradual discontinuing of the liturgical music drama, partly due to its dependence upon secular connections, the oratorio (and opera) came into being.

It is remarkable that in 1600, Peri's opera *Euridice* was produced in Florence; and in Rome, the same year, but ten months earlier, Cavalieri's large scale, allegorical oratorio, *La Rappresentazióne di' Anima e di Córpo* was produced.

Such events as the canonizing of great church servants were celebrated by the production of oratorios. A piece commemorating the canonizing of Ignatius Loyola, set to music by Loreto Vittori (b. Spoleto, Jan. 16, 1604, d. Rome, April 23 or 27, 1670), is notable.

Important in the development of the oratorio was Carissimi who also gave himself to the composing of sacred cantatas. Carissimi (b. nr. Rome, 1605—d. Rome, 1674) wrote a considerable number of oratorios about characters in the Old Testament. His *Jeptha* is notably beautiful and religiously effective.

Carissimi's pupil, Alessandro Scarlatti (b. Palermo, 1660—d. Naples, 1725), who composed some 500 sacred cantatas, as well as excelling in the composing of opera, was also a leader in the development of the oratorio. In his oratorios, one finds systematic, formal design. Scarlatti would take the simple but important speeches in the story of the oratorio and set them to orderly rhythmic sequence, thus giving them greater intensity and effectiveness. Up to now, it had been usual to present the speeches freely in recitative. Scarlatti employed the recitative mainly for the connecting language of the narrative. Thus his oratorios were musically and dramatically effective and enjoyable. They served as models to other composers for a century to come.

Oratorio had its artistic beginnings in Italy at the same time as opera. And thus oratorio has been much influenced by the developments in opera. The deep religious spirit of Italian sixteenth-century music began to dissipate, however, with opera's development, and similarly oratorio in Italy failed to maintain continuing support of the religious spirit which had characterized the earlier church music. The oratorio influence became mixed with the German music which developed in the Passion celebrations. It was out of this mixture that there sprang the modern oratorio.

In the Palestrinian tradition there followed Tomás Luis de Victoria (b. Avilac 1548—d. Madrid, 1611), William Byrd (b. Lincolnshire, 1543—d. Essex, 1623), and Orlando Gibbons (b. Oxford, 1583—d. Canterbury, 1625), and, finally, Heinrich Schütz (b. Kostrich, Saxony, 1585—d. Dresden 1672). Schütz, it is to be remembered, had studied with Gabrieli in Venice. From Schütz to Elgar (b. Worcester, 1857—d. 1934) a deep religious spirit continued to characterize the oratorio. But in Italy, after Cavalieri, to the time of Rossini (b. Pesaro, 1792—d. nr. Paris, 1868), with few exceptions, oratorio was mainly pleasurable rather than deeply religious.

As has already been indicated, the continuity from the important Italian music of the 16th century to that of the German Schütz, was by way of the great Giovanni Gabrieli of Venice to whom Schütz went to study. While Gabrieli wrote no oratorios himself, he represents an integrating of the musical sensitivity of the Netherlanders and the older Italians themselves, with the newer technics being developed by the operatic composers. Thus in his own six oratorios, Schütz (actually the only "descendant" of Gabrieli—although not Italian) carried on the spirit of Gabrieli. Among Schütz' six oratorios were four "Passions" each according to a different one of the Four Gospels.

The sole musical and artistic aim of Schütz was to present the subjects of his oratorios faithfully—he dispensed with such things as glamor, and anything else that would detract from the dignity of his creation.

More and more, as the German oratorio developed, reliance upon the chorale tune displaced the older use of plainsong. To anticipate a later period, it should be remarked that the German interest in the oratorio, and in the cantata, had great influence over Johann Sebastian Bach to come.

Immediately after Schütz, there followed the great musician Keiser, born just one year after Schütz' death. Reinhard Keiser (b. nr. Weissenfels, 1674—d. Hamburg, 1739) is one of the un-recognized composers who should not much longer be overlooked. Immediately preceding Bach there were Schütz; Buxtehude, of Danish birth (b. Helsingborg, 1637—d. Lübeck, 1707) ; and Keiser. Of these three, Keiser still goes almost unnoticed. Of course, Bach, himself, has only recently, comparatively speaking, come into his own.

At this point some special attention should be given to the cantata. Cantatas are often difficult to distinguish from oratorios. They are usually smaller in dimension than the oratorio although not always shorter in time of presentation. They very frequently treat upon secular subjects—although toward the close of the seventeenth century, the rise of the sacred cantata, especially the German sacred cantata is important. Bach wrote nearly 300 sacred cantatas for performance in his church services. Carissimi wrote a multitude of beautiful sacred cantatas which were to have early and great influence on the German cantatas which came to be so important in the German protestant service. The German cantata almost from the beginning was characterized by the harmonized chorale tune for its musical foundation rather than the Latin plainsong which was used in the Italian cantata.

As mentioned previously, it is not always easy to distinguish the cantata from the oratorio. Both had their beginnings in Italy. But at first, the cantata was performed by a single singer, accompanied by a few chords struck upon some single instrument. There was no dramatic action. Later, in the seventeenth century when the German Protestant church took up this form, it was given the extension that finally developed the cantata into a large musical work.

This later cantata, which can be likened to the anthem of the Church of England, usually began with an instrumental introduction followed by a chorus singing in harmony some text taken from the Bible; then came one or two vocal solos accompanied by an instrument followed by the singing of a closing chorale. Toward the end of the eighteenth century, the cantata also included the recitative and the Italian aria form as part of its structure.

We have already indicated that in the early stages of the Passion music the work of Heinrich Schütz is important, and that in his creations the characters of Bible history and the Gospel story were portrayed accurately and literally from the Scripture. Later, the dramatic scheme of the Passion music was extended to include participation by the congregation in singing appropriate chorales which fitted into the development of the play. Shortly, this participation by the congregation in the Passion play brought about the inclusion of the whole procedure into the *regular* church service. Thus, in the Protestant service there occurred something comparable to the liturgic program of the Roman church, from which the

German church had earlier departed. Later, the congregational singing was again discontinued and the chorales of the cantata were sung by a choir. And once again the congregation took its place purely as a spectator in the group. In this uneven period, between Heinrich Schütz and J. S. Bach, the musical quality varied in *cycles* ranging from the grossly inartistic to some of the most sublime.

In Hamburg, in the early seventeenth century, opera, often not very good opera, was flourishing, and its influence over the religious music grew; it even came to pass that in some presentations of the Passion play the scriptural text was abandoned and poems of inferior literary value were introduced. When this happened of course the Passion music deteriorated into something quite inadequate and disgraceful. It must be said to the credit of the German church that these inferior Passion plays of degraded type made very little use of the religious chorale or organ music. Actually, they should hold only a place of reference in the history of German church music.

The epitome of achievement yet to come in German church music was the contribution of Johann Sebastian Bach.

JOHANN SEBASTIAN BACH (1685-1750)

The name of Bach is the greatest in Protestant church music. There are many music critics who think his name is greatest in all the history of music, religious or secular. The Bach family was musically important during six generations, Johann Sebastian being of the fifth. There were thirty-seven people in the Bach family, all of whom held important musical positions. Bach was a deeply devout Lutheran. He was absorbed in his religion as much as Palestrina was in his. Bach separated himself from nearly all else in the world giving himself to music and to the service of the church. He believed that the whole business of music is pleasant recreation and the glorification of God.

Bach's music for the church may be divided into two classes— organ music and vocal music. His organ music is heard everywhere, on the concert stage, and in the public services of Roman Catholic and Protestant churches throughout Europe and America;

the use of his organ music is increasing as the years go by. In the course of time, because of the contribution by Bach in the field of organ music, the serious, profound organ solo has come to be a constituent part of the service in the German Protestant church. The German church's organ music has remained completely untouched by later tendencies in contemporary secular music. Bach's church music was always deeply intellectual, majestic, overwhelming in its vigor of forward movement. His organ music fairly represents the ultimate in musical writing.

Of course, a form of instrumental music had existed in the German Protestant church before the time of Bach. With the development of organ playing in the early seventeenth century, organists had begun to take up chorale tunes as a basis for *improvising* at public performances, for the ability to improvise was an important requirement. In the featured voluntary musical services, it would be most unusual for an organist to play contemporary work by other people or even any of his own former writings. As a documentary record of what his power at improvisation must have been, Bach's writing of 130 choral preludes provides an indication. His more than 295 cantatas vary in length of performance from twenty minutes to over an hour. The multitudinous treatments of the themes from the German chorales manifest, in these cantatas, a genius that is unsurpassed. In addition to the cantatas and chorale preludes and a great wealth of music for secular use, Bach wrote five Passions. Only the Passion of St. John and the Passion of St. Matthew have come down to us. The St. Matthew is the more famous. It is this work which has made the name of Bach familiar throughout the world. In it, Bach gave to the world the best means for making communicable the mysticism of the German religious mind.

EQUAL TEMPERAMENT

With the rise of instrumental writing, interest had arisen in the color contrasts that were possible by modulating to nearby "tonalities." Consequent to the establishment of a feeling for definite tonality, the need for a system of equal temperament was recognized by all, because it was apparent to all that modulating to remoter "keys" would provide for and make possible more vivid contrast in musical composition. The scales or modes up to this time had been so tuned in relation to their basic "final" that the pitches in each specific "scale" or "mode" were peculiar to that scale and not readily usable in another scale of different tonality.[4] That is, for example, "F" founded in the tonality of "C" and giving the quality of "fa" was not the same pitch as "F" founded in the tonality of A♭ and giving the quality of "la." It was later considered that the variations between, for example, the different "F's," were so slight that they could all be compromised somewhat and thus the same "F" could do for all keys. Up to the time of devising a successful equal temperament F♯ and G♭ were not the same pitch. The modern development of music on keyboard instruments could never have been possible without equal temperament. Equal temperament refers to the dividing of the octave as nearly as possible into twelve equal half steps. Although originally the modes or scales had not progressed by exact half steps, it was believed that no ears would be offended if the successions of varyingly intervaled tones were now slightly modulated so as to proceed by exact half steps. This would enable one to modulate to any tonality, since with the new system all related tones could be in the same half-step pattern. Equal temperament permits free moving from any tonality to any other tonality, using the same given range of pitches.

Today, then, music generally is written in such a manner that it can be played on a piano.[5] Even the *a cappella* choruses, unless they are made up of *very sensitive* members that have trained diligently in the processes of pure temperament, find that they can sing acceptably to the accompaniment of piano, at least for the purpose of rehearsal. (The pseudopurists of course decry such degradation.) The result of all this is that in equal temperament, one never

---

[4]Interestingly enough, the "nearest" tonalities are those at a fourth or a fifth; the remotest, those at only a second or third. Discrepancies in tonal tendencies in closely related tonalities are easier to listen to than those of remote tonalities. A succession of tones, purely and perfectly tuned to the key of C can be tolerated in the key of F, or G, but not nearly so well in the key of D or E. However, only slight modification of a pitch is necessary to make it tolerable in any or all keys, thus enabling it to serve as any tone in the solfeggio range.

[5]Every serious piano student sooner or later has worked on Bach's *Well-Tempered Clavier*, a collection of 48 preludes and fugues composed by Bach to demonstrate the practicality of equal temperament.

sings or plays quite in perfect tune. But, thanks to compromised tuning, one can sing or play in all or any "keys." The complete "intuneness" of pure temperament accounts for the sweetness and purity of toneblending that of course occurs when one hears an *a cappella* chorus or a string quartet when they produce their music in the ancient temperament. When they do so, it is impossible to accompany them on any fixed pitched instrument such as the piano or the organ. For a long time composers had been experimenting with equal temperament. It was Bach, finally, who in his preludes and fugues for the well-tempered clavier, demonstrated the complete feasibility of "equal temperament."

The *late* development of instrumental music in church connections is thought by many to be due to previous unawareness of the possibilities for *equal temperament*.

THE HYMNODY OF CALVIN AND WATTS

In the sixteenth and seventeenth centuries, contemporary with the developments in German music, there was a development of psalmody among the French and the Netherland peoples which was greatly influenced by the reformer, John Calvin (1509-64). In France, metrical settings of the Psalms were devised by Clement Marot and Theodore Beza. These were as enthusiastically received as were the hymns and chorales of Luther and his successors in Germany. However, these metrical settings of the Psalms were sung to tunes that were nothing more than the popular ditties of the day. As a result, their popularity, while enthusiastic, was less enduring than the popularity of the great sweeping hymns and chorales of Germany. Guillaume Franc, compiled a Psalter which was first published by Calvin[6] at Geneva in 1542. In 1561 there was published another volume by Louis Bourgeois at Lyons. This second volume contained eighty-three dittylike tunes arranged for four,

---

[6]Actually, Calvin was not well disposed toward music. Thus, in all the strongholds of Calvinism where it was not quickly modified by opposing forces, the development of the art of music was stifled; the famine of artistic expression in these places (Scotland, parts of England and Wales, Germany, and Switzerland) still exists. Calvin himself was a sincere individual whose cultural and spiritual contributions are important.

It is of interest that Ambrosius Lobwasser (1515-1585) of Saxony "forced" the psalter of Marot and Beza into German. Although of inferior quality it became the official collection for the "Reformed" churches using the German language. It was used in the British Colonies of North America among the German-speaking people under the control of the Church of Holland.

five, and six voices to which metrical settings of the Psalms were adapted. Later, in 1565, Adrian le Roy printed, at Paris, a complete Psalter. In this book the melodies were set in the manner of motets by Claude Goudimel.[7] Although the collection contained, in general, songs that were too difficult for congregational singing, this last work was again printed in 1607 in Holland. Later, tunes less elaborately arranged were substituted by Claudin le Jeune, who published his collection at Leyden in 1633. During this period the melodies for these songs were usually in the tenor rather than the soprano.

Along with the musical developments in Germany and in France, there was a musical awakening in England. In place of the traditional liturgical and congregational music of the Roman Catholic church, there was an emphasis, in England, upon two kinds of Protestant music: (1) the Protestant music of the church of England, which, in a general way, was not unlike the Roman music, and (2) the Protestant music of the *people*; that is, of the dissenters and the nonconformers, who found little pleasure in the established church. Both in England and in Scotland this large group of dissenters, nonconformists—self-styled reformers—gave to today's musical heritage an important religious music of the people. It was influenced more by the theology of Calvin than by that of Luther. In its present-day extensions it is found in the Methodist, Presbyterian, and Baptist churches of Britain and the other English-speaking peoples, as well as in some smaller church organizations.

In England the first attempt at popular hymnody was the rendering of the Psalms into English verse. A collection of fifty-one psalm settings by Sternhold was published in 1549. In 1562 another collection called *The Whole Booke of Psalmes* was compiled by Thomas Sternhold, John Hopkins, and others. This book was "imprinted" by John Day "with apt notes to sing them withal"; that is, the melodies for the various songs were scored. A year later, John Day reprinted this same book harmonized "in foure partes." These harmonies were contributed by Thomas Tallis, Richard Brimle, William Parsons, Thomas Causton, Edward Hake, and Richard

---

[7]This was the same Goudimel (1510-1572), a Roman Catholic of France, who associated himself with the Huguenots and who composed a book of "psalms in the form of motets." He was killed in the Huguenot massacre in Lyons, France.

Edwards. Probably this was the first collection of hymn tunes harmonized for four voices published in England. In 1579 another collection by William Damon was published. Its harmony is quite acceptable and extremely simple in construction. In 1591 Damon compiled a new collection in which the tune was placed in the "highest part" rather than in the tenor. Six years before this, in 1585, another author, John Cosyn, had published a collection of sixty songs with the tunes printed by Day. These settings were arranged for five and six voices.

Another most important volume of religious song was the *Psalter* printed in 1592 by Thomas Este. This collection, harmonized for four voices, contained important tunes by John Dowland, Edmund Blancks, Edmund Hooper, John Farmer, Richard Allison, George Kirbye, William Cobbold, Edward Johnson, and Giles Farnaby. These composers are generally considered to be the most representative composers of hymns of the period in England. Later, in 1599, a most excellent collection appeared, by Richard Allison. It was "to be sung and plaide upon the Lute, Orpharion, Citterne, or Base Violl, severally or altogether. . . ." But the climactic work was the one published in 1621 which carried the title: *The Whole Booke of Psalmes: with the Hymnes evangelicall, and songs spirituall. Composed into 4 parts by sundry authors, . . . newly corrected and enlarged by Tho: Ravenscroft.* This famous volume had in it German, French, and English tunes arranged for four voices. In addition to Tallis, Dowland, Morley, Bennet, Stubbs, Farnaby, and Ravenscroft himself, fourteen other important musicians of the day are represented in the book. Again, the melody is placed in the tenor. The contrapuntal compositional style, for the most part, is quite acceptable. While the bass and tenor parts move forward "note against note," the treble and the alto manifest a little more variation in harmonic treatment. The effect of such kind of musical composition when the tenor melody is sung by a large group of voices and the harmony added by another group of well-trained voices is very satisfying and highly impressive. The most famous tune in the Ravenscroft collection is John Dowland's setting of the 100th Psalm.

There were several additional publications released at subsequent dates during the sixteenth and seventeenth centuries, but, regrettably, they are marked by a sorrowful deterioration in quality, technical skill, artistic feeling, and sensitivity.

English hymnody did not live long on the high plane of the music in Ravenscroft's *Psalter*. If there had been any hope that the decadence of the English hymnody would be stopped and that there would occur a revival in writing fine English music, this hope was completely destroyed by the Great Rebellion (1640-1660), when the art of England and its books and its literature were destroyed or threatened by the zealous followers of the Puritan Revolution. With all its high purpose the Puritan Restoration did not help to bring life to a deteriorating art, and the later tunes of Hayes, Wainwright, Carey, and Tans'ur were of much less significance than the tunes of their predecessors in English hymnody. In general, the work of many of the very recent hymn writers evidences even greater deterioration.

An important name in English hymnody is that of Isaac Watts. Isaac Watts (1674-1748) was to the English hymnody what Ambrose was to the Latin; what Marot was to the French; and what Luther was to the German. It has been said that Isaac Watts was the first who succeeded in overcoming the prejudices which opposed the introduction of hymns into English public worship. Today it is difficult to realize that such a prejudice ever existed. But so strong was the feeling in England that many a church was split over the proposal. However, the proposal to sing only the psalms, set in metrical version, was not quite so vigorously opposed, thus, again, singing in the post-Reformation Church of England was confined largely to congregational singing of the Psalms. But in a Baptist church (whose minister was Benjamin Keach—this was the same Baptist church which was later served by Spurgeon), after the decision to introduce singing into its worship, there was a sizable minority who left the worship service and met together elsewhere in a "songless sanctuary." In a tract entitled *Truth soberly defended,* published in 1692, Isaac Marlow opposed the introduction of singing into the services of the church. It must be noted again that the objection to singing usually was not an objection to the singing of the Psalms but an objection to the singing of hymns that had been composed in modern time. This was because it was felt that, while the singing of the Psalms was proper, a line had to be drawn about singing and so it was drawn at the introducing of recently composed or "unscriptural" hymns. But there were several collections published during this period, a fact which indicates that hymn singing was allowed in some churches. However, many of the collections were used merely for reading or singing at home. Probably by the close of the seventeenth century the singing of hymns in churches was permitted generally.

When Isaac Watts' hymns began to find their way into favor, many conservative religious people disdainfully called them "Watts' Whims." While Luther's hymns were being sung widely in Germany, Watts' hymns were still fighting their way into some churches— sometimes as much as thirty or forty years later. Those churches that adopted them were suspected of being heretical. A line of one of Dr. Watts' hymns is appropriate, "O what a wretched land is this, that yields us no supplies." It was out of such spiritual and artistic poverty that Watts founded modern English hymnody. His versions of songs and his original hymns were used almost exclusively for years in the nonconformist churches.

The place of Isaac Watts in English hymnody is unique. No other instance in music history gives such recognition to an individual hymn writer, unless it be the Methodist collaborators, Charles and John Wesley, who were highly and popularly respected for their contributions to the people's hymnody.

Watts, for over one hundred years, was the only hymnist of the individual nonconformist churches in England. Thus, while at first his introducing of hymns was resisted, in later times many churches would use no hymns except those written by Watts.

In a way this was somewhat unfortunate because hymns by contemporary hymn writers of importance, such as George Herbert, John Milton, Richard Baxter, and John Mason were lost to many people of the church. Watts, himself, was aware that he had written too many hymns in response to a demand for his work. He wrote over five hundred, many of which, unfortunately, are of inferior type. Watts was reported as saying once that Charles Wesley's hymn "Wrestling Jacob" was worth all that he, Watts, had ever written.

Other contemporary hymnists were Simon Browne (1680-1732), Alexander Pope (1688-1744), and Samuel Wesley, Jr. (1690-1739), the elder brother of John and Charles Wesley. Samuel

Come, Let Us Join Our Cheerful Songs

(Chesterfield)

Isaac Watts

Thomas Hawels

1. Come, let us join our cheer - ful songs With an - gels round the throne; Ten thou - sand thou - sand are their tongues, But all their joys are one.

2. "Wor - thy the Lamb that died," they cry, "To be ex - alt - ed thus;" "Wor - thy the Lamb," our lips re - ply, "For He was slain for us."

3. Let all that dwell a - bove the sky, And air, and earth, and seas, Con - spire to lift Thy glo - ries high, And speak Thine end - less praise!

Wesley, ignoring the Methodist movement started by John and Charles, remained a loyal member of the Church of England until his death. Other writers of the time were John Byrom (1691-1763) and Robert Seagrave (1693-1759).

METHODIST HYMNODY

The United States evangelical "revival meeting" has its roots in the traditions that were largely given impetus by the Methodist church. What Charles and John Wesley did in England can be compared to what Huss did in Bohemia and Luther in Germany. This is true even though neither Charles[8] nor John Wesley had the talent and ability of Luther,[9] who had been a gifted performer upon different musical instruments. John Wesley was limited to playing very simple music upon the flute, and had little formal training in music. But when he entered upon his evangelical work, he recognized the need for having more singing in the congregation. As already indicated, up to his time, hymns had not been sung in church and very few had even been sung in the chapels of the "nonconformists."

However, a new era was at hand. Modern English hymn singing can be dated from 1740, when Charles Wesley wrote and published a collection of hymns under the title *Hymns and Sacred Poems.* Subsequently, many tune books and hymnbooks were produced. Among them was *The Foundery* tune book published in 1742. This book got its name from its being used at the Methodist meeting house in London, which had formerly been a "foundery" for making cannon. Wesley excluded most of the old psalm tunes, admitting only three to his book: the "Old 81st," "Old 112th," and "Old 113th." In place of the many old psalm tunes which he omitted he substituted new psalm tunes.

---

[8]Of important interest is the fact that Charles Wesley's two sons, Charles (1757-1834) and Samuel (1766-1837)), were distinguished musicians, infant prodigies indeed. Samuel Wesley at 18 joined the Roman Catholic church and wrote a mass for Pope Pius VI; in his late years Samuel denied joining the Roman Catholic church. Samuel Wesley, in his time, was England's most distinguished organist. He endeavored ardently to have Johann Sebastian Bach's organ works performed in England. He was present at an organ concert by Mendelssohn and was prevailed upon to play himself upon this occasion just a month before his death.

[9]Zwingli is reported to have been a greater musician than Luther, to have been an expert on some ten musical instruments. Thus Luther was astonished at Zwingli's opposition to music in the church at Zurich where he had the church organs destroyed. It was the latter 19th century before instruments were allowed again in Zwinglian-influenced churches.

Wesley was acquainted with the literature of German chorales because of his connection with the Moravian Brethren with whom he associated on his journey to America and during his visit to the Moravian settlements, in 1738. He seemed to be very appreciative of their tunes and their manner of singing them. It is not surprising, then, that he introduced many of the Moravian songs and tunes into his collection. In 1746 the first book of tunes written expressly for Charles Wesley's hymns made its appearance. It was entitled *Hymns on the Great Festivals, and Other Occasions*. This book was a better printing than *The Foundery* tune book, which had been full of serious errors that prevented its being successful as a business venture. The publication of 1746 was the production of John Frederick Lampe, a successful German composer who in 1725 at twenty-two years of age had settled in England. He had been a renowned bassoon player and a member of the instrumental group which performed for Handel's operas. Lampe had come under the influence of the Wesleys and been converted to their new religious movement. For many years the *Foundery* and the book by Lampe were the two sources of the tunes used by the Methodists. Before long the Methodists became noted for the heartiness and attractiveness of their religious songs. In 1744 Dr. John Scott said, "The Methodists have got some of the most melodious tunes that ever were composed for Church music; there is great harmony in their singing, and it is very enchanting."

Soon, however, the necessity for a new collection of tunes was evident. Thomas Butts, a good musician and friend of the Wesleys, issued a collection entitled *Harmonia Sacra*. This collection was probably the best collection of hymn tunes to be issued during the eighteenth century. It also is one of the best examples from this period of the music engraver's art. In 1761 Charles Wesley published a second tune book described as "Select Hymns with Tunes Annext," and entitled, *Sacred Melody*. He seemed not to have been quite pleased with the previous collection of Thomas Butts. In his preface, he referred to the Butts collection as a book deserving of high commendation but not quite the thing he wanted. He said,

I have been endeavoring for more than twenty years to procure such a book as this. But in vain. Masters of music were above following any direction but their own. And I was determined whoever compiled this, should follow *my* direction; not *mending* our tunes but setting them down neither better nor worse than they were. At length I have prevailed. The following collection contains all the tunes which are in common use amongst us.

His book, *Sacred Melody,* was highly successful, and was published in a second edition in 1765, and in a third in 1770. The two later editions were similar to the first except for the addition of twelve new tunes.

About this time, the latter part of the eighteenth and the early part of the nineteenth century, there began a movement to do away with the florid tunes that had found their way into the churches. The directions found in the preface to some of the copies of *Sacred Melody* are interesting:

1. Learn these *Tunes* before you learn any others; afterward learn as many as you please.

2. Sing them exactly as they are printed here, without altering or mending them at all; and if you have learned to sing them otherwise, unlearn it as soon as you can.

3. Sing *All.* See that you join with the congregation as frequently as you can. Let not a slight degree of weakness or weariness hinder you. If it is a cross to you, take it up, and you will find it a blessing.

4. Sing *lustily* and with a good courage. Beware of singing as if you were half dead, or half asleep; but lift up your voice with strength. Be no more afraid of your voice now, nor more ashamed of its being heard, than when you sung the songs of *Satan.*

5. Sing *modestly.* Do not bawl, so as to be heard above or distinct from the rest of the congregation, that you may not destroy the harmony; but strive to unite your voices together, so as to make one clear melodious sound.

6. Sing *in Time.* Whatever time is sung be sure to keep with it. Do not run before nor stay behind it; but attend close to the leading voices, and move therewith as exactly as you can; and take care not to sing *too slow.* This drawling way naturally steals on all who are lazy; and it is high time to drive it out from among us, and sing all our tunes just as quick as we did at first.

7. Above all sing *spiritually.* Have an eye to God in every word you sing. Aim at pleasing *Him* more than yourself, or any other creature. In order to do this attend strictly to the sense of what you sing, and see that your *Heart* is not carried away with the sound, but offered to God

Jesus, Lover of My Soul

MARTYN. 7. 7. 7. 7. D.
(First Tune)

CHARLES WESLEY, 1707-1788   SIMEON B. MARSH, 1798-1875

In moderate time

1. Je - sus, Lov - er of my soul, Let me to Thy bos - om fly,
2. Oth - er ref - uge have I none; Hangs my help - less soul on Thee;
3. Thou, O Christ, art all I want; More than all in Thee I find;
4. Plen-teous grace with Thee is found, Grace to cov - er all my sin;

While the near - er wa - ters roll, While the tem - pest still is high;
Leave, ah, leave me not a - lone, Still sup - port and com - fort me.
Raise the fall - en, cheer the faint, Heal the sick, and lead the blind.
Let the heal - ing streams a - bound; Make and keep me pure with - in.

Hide me, O my Sav - iour, hide, Till the storm of life is past;
All my trust on Thee is stayed, All my help from Thee I bring;
Just and ho - ly is Thy Name, I am all un - right - eous - ness;
Thou of life the Foun - tain art, Free - ly let me take of Thee;

Safe in - to the ha - ven guide, O re - ceive my soul at last.
Cov - er my de - fense-less head With the shad-ow of Thy wing.
False and full of sin I am, Thou art full of truth and grace.
Spring Thou up with - in my heart, Rise to all e - ter - ni - ty. A - MEN.

The tune, *Martyn,* to which these words of Charles Wesley are traditionally set is inherently and intrinsically of questionable musical value;
the newest hymnals are providing more worthy settings as church groups
are becoming more discerning.

continually; so shall your singing be such as the *Lord* will approve of here, and reward you when He cometh in the clouds of heaven.

Sacred Melody was so named because only the melody for each hymn tune was provided with the words. In 1781 Wesley brought out another edition which was completely harmonized and which he called *Sacred Harmony*. In this collection a few new hymns were added. Among the writers who contributed to Wesley's books were Thomas Olivers and Dr. J. Worgan.

In the Methodist movement, there had been separations among the followers; George Whitefield, one of the preachers who left the Wesleys prepared a hymn book in 1753 called *Divine Musical Miscellany*. In this book were found many first printings of tunes which later made their appearance in the Methodist books. In Whitefield's book were some "dialogue" hymns. At this time, it was fashionable to enter into dialogue singing in some of the congregations and chapels. Men and women would occupy different sides of the chapel and then these hymns, properly arranged, could be sung in dialogue fashion:

> MEN: Tell us, O women, we would know
>   Whither so fast ye move.
> WOMEN: We're called to leave the world below,
>   Are seeking one above.
> CHORUS: Hallelujah.

John Cennick is one of the important hymn writers who wrote songs of this type.

MUSIC IN THE CHURCH OF ENGLAND

Along with the music of the Roman Catholic church, the Lutheran and German Protestant groups; and the Calvinistic music of Switzerland, France, the Netherlands, and Britain; and in addition to the English hymnody of the Independent and Nonconformists' groups of Britain; there was also the music of the Anglican Church. The Church of England is a state church which regards itself as being the Holy Catholic church. It differs from the Roman Catholic church in many ways, but principally, so far as is pertinent here, in its not recognizing the Holy See at Rome as being its ruler; it does not have ecclesiastical fellowship with the Roman Catholic clergy.

In the Anglican church there has not arisen any great musical name such as that of Palestrina in the Roman church or Bach in the German. Even so, the music of the Anglican church has won its important position because for the last 350 years it has maintained a high standard of excellence and also because it has related itself closely to the deep interests of its people.

It is a peculiarity of English ecclesiastical history that there have been in it fervent struggles over doctrine, ritual, and dogma. And methods of expressing themselves musically have concerned the English church people as vitally as have any other theological problems. The struggle between the liturgic and antiliturgic groups; that is, the struggle between clergy and those of the laity opposed to clerical orders and the struggle between Anglicanism and Puritanism, have marked English church history, from the beginning to this day. For one example, there was the struggle as to whether to allow an instrument of music to be used in the church worship. The struggle between Anglicanism and Puritanism, conformist and nonconformist, state and independent groups, has marked itself frequently as being a struggle between the artistic and the utilitarian, "the high and plebeian."

The Reformation in England was different from the Reformation on the European continent. In Germany, France, Switzerland, and the Netherlands, the revolt against the Roman church was carried out by men who came from the ranks of the people. But in England the Reformation, less revolutionary than that on the continent, was a reformation initiated by the King of Britain. With the founding of the Church of England there arose new attitudes in reference to the music of the liturgy which for so long had framed the pattern for established English worship. Because it had not been the mind of the English reformers to build an entirely new kind of church or to separate themselves from the ancient traditional communion which had come to them through the medieval Roman church, the Anglican reformers continued to hold firmly to the traditional concept of ancient, historic, "apostolic" Christianity which had been given to them through the Roman church. They regarded the Anglican church as the logical continuation of the

"Universal Church" which in its Roman phase had become an apostatized church, departing from the pure doctrine of the apostles and thereby destroying her right to make claims upon the faithful. In general, however, the Anglican church continued important parts of the Roman tradition which she considered to be the more admirable of the practices of the Roman church.

Thus, one is not astonished to find that much of the liturgic material of the Anglican people is not to be distinguished in style from that of the Roman. Also, there is emphasis upon many artistic appeals to the senses, such as is seen in the carrying on of ceremony and ritual and in the giving of prominence to vestments, and official and ceremonial dress. The ritual of the Church of England is contained in the one volume known as *The Book of Common Prayer*. The Anglican service is divided into *matins* and *evensong, Holy Communion, confirmation* and *ordination,* and the *occasional* offices. Not very much of this liturgic material is entirely original, a great portion of it having been taken from the historical liturgy of the ages. However, although it is compiled from Roman Catholic sources, Anglican usage has greatly modified and simplified it. Litanies to the saints and the Virgin Mary have been omitted. The "days of the saints" are no longer commemorated. The seven canonical hours are reduced to two. The selections from the Scriptures have been extended so that the Psalms are read in entirety each month, the Old Testament is read once a year and the New Testament, three times in each year. The English language is used in place of the Latin.

In the course of time there have evolved three distinctive modes of worship service in the Church of England: (1) the choral or cathedral mode, (2) the parochial mode, and (3) the mixed mode. In spite of there being three modes of service common to all the congregations of the established Church of England, the necessity for classifying the services has arisen because of the varying talents, potentialities, and abilities of the congregations, some being in underprivileged areas, others in small country parishes, and still others in important richly endowed metropolitan areas. The choral or cathedral service is the one that is used in the important cathedrals, in the royal and college chapels, and in those parish churches where resources of money and talent will permit. In this cathedral mode, all of the service is performed musically, that is, by actual singing or by chanting or intoning. The only exception is in the bringing of the teaching lesson, which is spoken. The essential parts of the choral service may be outlined as follows: (1) the minister, mostly in a monotone, chants the sentences, exhortations, prayers, and collects throughout the service; (2) the minister and choir alternately chant the versicles and responses; (3) the choir, divided, alternately chants the daily psalms and such other pieces as occur in the various offices of the church; (4) the choir sings, in the morning and evening service, the canticles and hymns, either alternately as a chant or in songs of intricate style, like anthems, which are technically identified as "services"; (5) the choir sings the anthem after the third collect; (6) the minister and choir alternately chant the litany; (7) the singers perform the responses after the commandments in the communion service; (8) they then sing in the manner of an anthem the creed (Credo), "Gloria in excelsis," and "Sanctus" in the communion service (the Sanctus has been more recently replaced by a short anthem or hymn); and (9) the singers chant or sing those parts in the "occasional offices" which are specified to be sung.

The second mode, the parochial mode, is the kind of service practiced in the smaller churches where it is impractical to support a choir. Due to the lesser talent, the mode of performance of divine service of the second mode consists in reciting, rather than singing, unaccompanied by any kind of music at all, all the parts of the liturgy. In this mode, metrical versions of the songs are included in the service.

The mixed mode is not quite as simple as the parochial service, although the mixed mode and the parochial are interchangeable at the option of the person in charge. In general, a choir is employed for some portions while the statements of creed, litany, and recitations of responses are carried on in speaking voice. There is no certain law which forbids any congregation to adopt any part or the whole of the choral mode. This is another distinction marking the Anglican church as different from the Roman church. The liberty as to choice of service, not found in the Roman church, perhaps grew out of the Anglican church leaders' eagerness to adjust to the Puritan tendencies which, in the sixteenth and seventeenth centuries, played such an important part in English ecclesiastical history. In the Anglican church a great blow to its music (but not as great as the ascendency of Cromwell's regime about a century later) was struck in the abolition of the daily services of the mass. Searching for other religious resources, the church music composers set about producing music for the "services" as outlined in the Book of Common Prayer. For these services there were three offices: Holy Communion, Morning Prayer, and Evening Prayer. For Communion there were the *Kyrie, Credo, Sanctus,* and the *Gloria* (which was dropped later, in the time of Elizabeth I). For the Morning Prayer there were five canticles: *Venite, Te Deum,* and *Benedictus* (also later dropped by Elizabeth) with two alternatives, the *Benedicite* and *Jubilate.* For the Evening Prayer there were the *Magnificat* and the *Nunc Dimittis* with the alternates, the *Cantate Domino* and the *Deus Miseratur.* Bishop Cramner in a letter to Henry VIII urged that the canticles should be of short service. "The song should not be full of notes, but, as near may be, for every syllable a note so that it may be sung distinctly and devoutly."

Just as with the followers of Calvin who had their own musical ambitions, like Goudimel and Le Jeune, there were English composers who, exercising their imaginations, were able to produce readily acceptable motetlike settings for the canticles. Thus there were composed for the English church the "Great Services."

Important in this new compositional effort was John Merbecke (*c.*1523-*c.*1585), referred to also in the chapter on the organ, who issued in 1550, *The Booke of Common Praier Noted.* This was the first musical setting of the English liturgy as authorized by the Act of Uniformity in 1549. He produced his work after composers' efforts to adapt the Roman Latin masses proved ineffective. As a substitute for the discontinued daily celebrations of the mass which so deeply hurt the established musical offerings of the cathedrals and the collegiate churches, Merbecke sought eagerly for tunes suitable for congregational singing. He chose for this purpose traditional melodies or original music of his own composing in similar style. After Queen Elizabeth issued a new Prayer Book thus making his early work no longer useful, he, instead of composing new music, went along with the growing and prevailing view that church music should be condemned as a "vanity."

As noted elsewhere, the new austerity in reference to church music did not stifle the creativity of men like Byrd and Gibbons who wrote with a skill and a sensitivity scarcely less than that of Palestrina. Their output is mostly distinguished in the realm of secular music however. Among the important church music composers in England of the sixteenth century are Christopher Tye (c. 1500-1572/73) and Thomas Tallis (c. 1505-1585). Not to be overlooked is Robert Whyte (c. 1530-1574). These three devoted themselves to the music of the church. Robert Whyte's works, still in manuscript, are mostly not available for use.

About John Merbecke's (Merbeck, Marbeck) personal life, not much is definitely known. He was a theological writer, and sometime about 1540, was organist at St. George's, Windsor. He was saved from burning at the stake in 1544 for heresy, through intercession of the bishop of Winchester. His famous *Booke of Common Praier Noted* was composed for the First Prayer Book of Edward VI, later superseded as already indicated. His "playne tunes" were a compromise between Latin plainsong and mensural or measured music; they were his attempt to solve the problem of chanting an accentual language in place of the old Latin, a quantitative language. He was not altogether successful, but the quality of his work has been more recently recognized. In 1844 his *Booke* was reprinted. The Eucharist as sung today in the English church is mostly based on his work.

The music of the Anglican church is made up of the chant, the special music of the choir, and the congregational hymn. The English chant differs from the Roman in that, oftentimes, it is rhythmically proportioned into measures, thus giving to the music a formal appearance that makes it steadier of performance. The florid nature of the Gregorian chant has been dropped. The English have invented a chant form known as the double chant: instead of including only one verse of a psalm in two melodic strains of three and four measures, it includes two verses of a psalm, the first verse ending after seven measures on an incomplete cadence. Often, in the double chant, the two verses of the psalm differ musically in sentiment, consequently bringing two altogether unrelated verses into one short musical form; thus there have been, through the years, regular attempts to adapt the Gregorian tones to the English language and to reintroduce the Gregorian system into the Anglican church.

But, because of the very nature of the English language which involves successions of accents and slurrings of its syllables, and because of the traditional English love for music in full rhythmic and tuneful style, it is doubtful whether attempts to adapt the Gregorian music to Anglican use would be very successful or even feasible.

With the publication, in 1560, of John Day's *Certaine Notes Set Forth in Foure and Three Parts to be Sung at the Morning Communion, and Evening Praier,* and the adoption of the vernacular as the spoken language of the church, the choir's singing of the Psalms and Canticles was introduced into the Anglican liturgy or "service." The service, since the sixteenth century, has been the inspiration for the anthemlike compositions that have assumed the dignity of liturgical stature as they have found a place for their performance in the official offering. The Service, as finally consummated, includes the *Venite* (Psalm 95); *Te Deum; Benedicite* (song of the "three children" from the Greek addition to the Book of Daniel); *Benedictus* (Zacharias' song); *Jubilate* (Psalm 100); *Kyrie eleison, Nicene Creed, Sanctus, Bene qui Venit, Agnus Dei, Gloria in Excelsis, Magnificat* (Mary's song), *Cantate Domino* (Psalm 98); *Nunc Dimittis* (Simeon's song) and *Deus Misereatur* (Psalm 67).

The anthem of the Anglican liturgy is usually a short sacred choral piece to be done either accompanied or unaccompanied. It is not unlike the medieval Latin motet of the Roman church. The anthem, although not strictly a part of the ritual, is provided for in the Prayer Book: "In quires and places where they sing here followeth the anthem." The director of the choir is responsible for wisely choosing the kind of anthem to be presented. It is generally understood that the words of the anthem shall be taken either from Scripture or else from the *Book of Common Prayer* although frequent exceptions to this custom are permitted by many Anglicans.

The anthem as successor to the Latin motet, is, as ant-hymn indicates, a kind of music to be used alternately with congregational
hymns. It dates from the seventeenth century. Henry Purcell (1658-
1695), and Handel also, wrote successful anthems, the latter bringing the English anthem to a place of important recognition
throughout Europe. The present-day anthem is a composite of the
Latin motet and the German cantata. It has been affected somewhat by the influences of secular music, just like religious music
of other groups and times. In spite of the heritage from a host of
great writers, critics have seen a disappointing monotony and
lack of creative spirit in the later English anthem; but perhaps
this has not been so much the fault of the English church composers
as of the requirements of the Anglican liturgy and ritual.

In the earliest days the anthems of the Anglican church, like the
Roman motets, were unaccompanied; the use of organs or orchestral instruments was not introduced until about the middle of the
seventeenth century. After the beginning of the eighteenth century,
the anthems were written in a style that *required* instrumental accompaniment. Consequently, the *a cappella* choir disappeared almost
entirely from Anglican usage. With this change the anthem began
to lose its individuality and spirit. The compositions of this period
by Hayes, Boyce, and Crotch, generally considered as respectable
enough, are definitely lacking in inspirational power.

But from just before the middle of the nineteenth century, a
turn in the composition of the anthem took place which promised to
bring the Anglican anthem to a position of new respectability in the
musical world. Among the composers of this period were Bennett,
Hopkins, Barnby, Bridge, Garrett, Goss, Martin, Monk, McKenzie,
Smart, Stainer, Sullivan, and Tours. For a time it seemed that the
works of these men would mark a new spirituality and zeal among
the people of the Anglican church. But this change in the artistic
awareness of the people in the church, coming about partially, at
least, as a result of the general continent-wide heightening of musical interest never did mature sufficiently to emulate the works of
Beethoven, Schubert, Schumann, and other continental classicists
and romanticists of the eighteenth and nineteenth centuries.

A NOTE ON BAROQUE MUSIC

"Baroque" is a term indicating irregularity in form, sometimes even grotesqueness or tastelessness in form. In music, the term refers to that period in its history, the latter sixteenth and the seventeenth century, before it was developed into a unified, well-ordered, and defined formal structure; at least the music of the period lacked the fulfillment in formal completeness that was evidenced in the classic music of the eighteenth century.

Baroque church music of the seventeenth century was involved with a parallel development in instrumental composition after 1600. Much of the baroque religious music was not church music at all, that is, not liturgical, but rather religious music to be performed for special occasions such as in public concerts. In Italy, Pergolesi and Durante; in Germany, Schütz, Buxtehude, and Bach; in England, Purcell, Blow, and Handel are the great representative persons of the period.

In the baroque period there was increased use of instrumental music in the churches. This was directly the result of improved music notation and better developed musical instruments. In some regions it now became common to have instrumental solos as part of the church services. On the record books of St. Mark's in Venice, accounts are to be found over a period of years for salary payments to two violinists. It was a custom in the German Protestant church to play on the organ during the communion service. J. S. Bach played secular tunes on such occasions, this being considered appropriate according to the custom of the day.

Michael Praetorius (b. Kleuzberg, Thuringia, 1571—d. Wolfenbüttel, 1621) was acquainted with both the Roman and the Venetian schools. He produced more than 1,000 settings of chorales for ensembles of all kinds. He, like Johann Walther was an important organizer of church music, but more pertinent to our interest, he is a most important source of information about this period. He described every form of music and every kind of instrument known to him.

Mention has already been made about Heinrich Schütz who went to Venice in 1609 to study with Gabrieli. He was much influenced by the Venetian music and at one time strongly favored the bril-

liant music of that school. However, his faith was of such consecrated kind based trustingly in Bible reading that he was later
moved to write his four Passions making no use of the newer devices whatever. His music was unaccompanied, making no use of
instruments even for the recitatives.

In the late baroque period, the music for the mass in the Roman
Catholic church took on more and more the characteristics of
concert music. In Italy and France this concertlike aspect of
religious music was being encouraged by the great interest in opera.
But in Germany the distress following the terrible Thirty Years
War allowed for only the kind of religious expression that can come
from music created by the people. Many have not recognized that
the congregational church singing of the people led to the rise of
the oratorio and the cantata as much as did the composers' knowledge of opera.

It is also interesting that at this same time in Italy, in the Neapolitan school, there arose anew, an era having its roots in the century
gone Palestrinian type of *a cappella* music. Such men as Caldara and
Fux were giving themselves to the service of fugal music.

Thus the baroque period is marked by a mixing of North with
South, Italian with German, Italian with English, and German
with English cultures. Additionally there were the impressions upon
each other of Roman Catholic and Protestant thinking. Such mix-
ings were not without benefit. The revival of the *a cappella* art in
Germany came through visits by German students to Italy and
from the Italians going to Germany. The introduction of the vocal
aria (from opera influence) into the Italian mass led to the introduction of the vocal aria into the "cantata mass." Solo instrumental
obligatos were also introduced. All in all, the music of the baroque
period, even in the church, was a brilliant thing far removed from
the pure music of Palestrina. Yet these contrasting elements were
made to mix: thus in the Roman Catholic music there were the
stile antico, and the *stile misto* (mixed) when the *stile antico* was
mixed with the *stile moderno.*

The essence of the *a cappella* ideal, however, was mostly not sup-
ported by baroque musicians except by two who are of interest:
Pasquale Pisari (b. Rome, 1725—d. Rome, 1778) and Matteo
Palotta (b. Palermo, 1680—d. Vienna, 1758). These two maintained

the Palestrina feeling although with the addition of instrumental accompaniment. Johann Sebastian Bach himself transcribed Palestrina's *Missa Brevis* to which he introduced an ensemble of cornets, trombone, bass viol, harpsichord, and organ to play the parts also sung by the voices.

Although the Germans did not take to opera as did the Italians, neither did they go back to the "monotonous congregational singing" of the early German Lutheran church; instead they adapted elements from Italian opera leading to the development of the cantatas and Passions which reached their height in the work of Johann Sebastian Bach.

A number of notable Italian musicians settled in England about the last quarter of the seventeenth century. Among these were Giovanni Battista Draghi (b. Rimini, *c.* 1640—d. ?) and Nicola Matteis (b. ?—d. ?), a distinguished violinist. Charles II of England was, like the German princes, jealous of the French Court. Thus Italian coloratura singing, instrumental writing for orchestra and small ensemble, and even imported church music had great influence upon the church music of England. As a result, polyphonic church anthems came to include solo passages in the manner of the opera and Byrd's anthems resembled the German church concertos.

Charles II (1630-1685), eager to have English music emulate what he remembered of the French, re-established the music of the Chapel Royal. To the music post of this chapel, he appointed Captain Henry Cooke as master. Captain Cooke was a military man, but in the minds of many he is held to be perhaps the greatest teacher of singing that England has ever had. Charles II being an admirer of the famed Jean Baptiste Lully (b. Florence, 1639—d. Paris, 1687, the founder of the French opera), chose Pelham Humfrey (1647-1674) of his Chapel Royal and sent him to France to study under the great Lully. When Humfrey came back to England, while evidencing good acquaintance with French style and Lully's techniques, he nevertheless addressed himself to a kind of composition that was distinctly his own and decidedly of English flavor. John Blow (1648/49-1708) and Blow's pupil Henry Purcell also helped to establish a distinctly English style. It is true that Blow fell under much influence from the Italian style, and

Purcell likewise from the French, but these were turned to a kind of composition that justly distinguishes this period in English musical history as glorious. While Purcell was largely a church musician, to many he is known best for his opera *Dido and Aeneas*. Both Blow and Purcell, his pupil, who outdistanced him, were eminently sincere in their musical composition for the church. However, in their own day, they were vigorously criticised by their English contemporaries because their music was so brilliant and dramatic in quality, especially when placed in comparison with the usual stuffy English music.

In Spain, church music during the baroque period was closely tied to Rome. However, like the Netherlander school, the Spanish school of music was also influenced by contacts from other regions and exhibited strong tendencies to move with the new musical feeling. In spite of this, traditional choral polyphony in Spain continued to flourish long after Morales, Guerrero, Fuenllana, and Cabezon were gone. And while Juan Pujol (*c*. 1573-1626) was introducing new music that relied upon folk music for its compositional development instead of the traditional contrapuntal reliance upon a *cantus firmus*, writers like Sebastian Aguilera de Heredia (*c*. 1570-?) and Juan Bautista Comes (1568-1643), and Juan de Esquivel Barahona, were still maintaining the old traditional church style in their composition.

It is of interest that in the Neapolitan school, intimate relations stood between opera and church music. For example, Francesco Durante (1684-1755) was a church musician of distinction, but yet as a teacher of composition he produced a long list of opera composers. And of course many opera composers devoted themselves to composing church music too. Among these were men such as Scarlatti and Hasse who have been mentioned already in connection with the development of the oratorio. Their church music as well as that of others of the time would either be in the *stile antico* or in the new operatic manner.

While Lully is known for his dramatic genius and for developments in connection with the ballet, he produced two noteworthy works in a religious connection, a *Te Deum* and also his *Miserere*. The latter was composed in the last months of his life during his last illness. He had been conducting, and in some way injured his foot with his baton. The report is that the injury became cancerous and led to his death in March about two months after his accident.

A NOTE ON CLASSIC MUSIC

The Classic period in music, 1750-1820, is principally an instrumental and operatic era. From the classic standpoint, the contribution to religious music is not great. The great names of the period are Karl Philipp Emanuel Bach, Haydn, and Mozart; and possibly Beethoven, who marks a transition from the classic to the romantic period.

The classic musical forms in religious connection are (1) the *oratorio* (two incipient forms of which are seen in Philipp Emanuel Bach's *The Resurrection* and *The Israelites in the Wilderness*), mainly represented in Haydn's work, *The Creation* (for general religious use rather than for the church liturgy); (2) the *mass* as musically portrayed in orchestral and choral settings employing soloists; (3) the *Mass* such as the *Requiem Mass* of Mozart and the *Missa Solemnis* of Beethoven; (4) the *motets* and other short anthemlike compositions for choruses and solo voices with various kinds of instrumental accompaniment, such as the *litanies,* the *vespers,* and *antiphons,* and the psalm- and hymn-settings.

This period of "classic music" is of course an involvement of the eighteenth century "Enlightenment." Man, his nature, and his happiness were the most important considerations of the Enlightenment. While the scope of influence of this period is sometimes limited to the Germany of Lessing, Mendelssohn, and others, it is more properly to be extended to include the England of Newton and Locke, and the France of Diderot and Voltaire. Pope's observation that the object of man's seeking and thinking should be man himself is a fair betrayal of the thinking of this period. Such feelings had, of course, serious implications for traditional religious thinking and brought about serious reactions in the areas of religious music.

A product of the Enlightenment was an attack upon intolerance, piety, orthodoxy, and church formalism. This generated as a substitute for the usual vigorous religious militancy, a fervent appreciation for a new kind of godliness partly evidenced in, among other things, the pursuit of the beautiful. Interest in philosophy, science, and ethics, in place of religion, emphasized secular developments. Church music in both England and Germany came more and more to be concert music of high artistic appeal, and less and less a music of the people. It should be remembered that even the music of the great Bach was not the music of the people that earlier Lutheran music had been. Although he remained a devout representative of Protestantism, his music became an art music of lofty, spiritual character. Even the old Latin hymns lost their traditional liturgical character and were now adapted to new religious use. Thus it was that during this period in Protestantism the processes of the liturgy were broken down. The religious unrest and insecurity resulting from the attacks on religious formalism were further aggravated by the continuing attempts on the part of church leaders halfheartedly to maintain the older traditions. Thus in the eighteenth century there was a general deterioration in church music. Because of the great artistic advances in secular music of this period, names of those German church musicians who did try to preserve the integrity of church music are almost lost to view: men such as Johann Ludwig Krebs (b. Buttelstädt, 1713—d. Altenburg, 1780); Johann Peter Kellner (b. Gräfenroda, 1705—d. Gräfenroda, 1772); Franz Vollrath Buttstädt (b. Erfurt, 1735—d. Rotenburg, 1814); and others.

Handel's oratorios, while of serious religious implications, are hardly to be considered as for the service of the church. *Der Tod Jesu* of Karl Heinrich Graun (b. Wahrenbrück, 1701—d. Merseburg, 1759) was premiered in a theatre. And even the oratorios of men like Philipp Emanuel Bach and Johann Schulz (b. Lünenburg, 1747—d. Schwedt, 1800) were secular in tone although maintaining very high musical standards. The new attitudes reflected in the musical works of the time while prompted out of religious considerations were not thought of as coming out of churchly interests.

In the breakdown of Protestant church music, "spiritual songs" supplanted the great music rooted in historical church thought. Congregational singing displaced what formerly had been carefully planned vital music performed by rehearsed specially selected groups. The people's reaction against those artistic advances which had been too detached from their personal interest in their own spiritual participation led unfortunately to a seriously deteriorated musical expression. This breakdown, evidencing itself clearly among the English-speaking people, also occurred on the continent among evangelistical splinter groups, and in the New World. Church services moved in the direction of avoiding the appearance of splendor, becoming, now, simple, "from the heart." Nor is this thing of the eighteenth century done away with today. Church groupings in the United States that have their roots in the Enlightenment, either as a negative force to counteract it or as a sympathetic product of its thinking, still reflect in their music the results of having deprived themselves of the values to be found in the larger historic sweep of great and powerful church music.

It may be observed here that the effects of the Cromwellian revolt in England of course are still to be felt—and even more deeply in the United States than in England. In England the revolt was in a few years, outwardly at least, contained. The good contributions of the Cromwellian interlude were assimilated and its deteriorative effects apparently neutralized. But in the New World, this revolt was transplanted and, detached from the historic counterforces, it flourished, encouraged by the migrations of dissenting peoples who were not always able to rightly divide the meanings of history especially when out from under the curb of contact with countering modes of thinking. It is true that basic sincerity, and an intensity of vision have helped to compensate for a host of cultural deprivations. But nevertheless, in the New World, the deteriorative properties of the Cromwellian Revolt coupled with those of the Enlightenment have been long a-dying; and the positive goods in these two elements of our heritage have often been neglected or set aside in an undiscerning succumbing to what appears to be a beneficent materialism.

At any rate, Protestant church music in the United States in general is at a low ebb.

It is perhaps of small comfort to learn that not all bad effects can be charged to the Puritan revolt, or to the English heritage. The Enlightenment played its peculiar part, and as already indicated, in places other than in England. Of course, the cynical opposition to religious formalism was a natural enough reaction which must be clearly charged against an earlier misguided religious direction as well as against the spirit of the Enlightenment itself. Basic insincerity and tension in the religious fabric of Germany produced out of the Enlightenment a shoddy kind of church music. Friedrich Gottlieb Klopstock (b. 1724—d. 1803) was one who sincerely undertook to rewrite some of the more deteriorated songs which had become an all too regular part of the German Protestant church repertoire. Yet Klopstock's rewriting activity triggered an onslaught from countless would-be poets and composers who did not hesitate to tamper with and remodel any and all music, however great, in order to bring it into line with the times. This was another vandalism produced by the Enlightenment, the effects of which still are felt.

The Roman Catholic church was not so adversely affected by the Enlightenment. Protestant groups had no historical perspective in common, and thus had to work out their procedures along continuously changing lines. The liturgical legacy now overthrown in Protestantism had not been adequately replaced. But the Roman church, however interrupted, could always resume where it had left off. Its processes were only modified slowly and in the light of tradition and historical perspective. Its liturgical principle is in general unchanged regardless of location anywhere in the world.

During the Enlightenment, music for the Roman Catholic church had been making good progress. The church was strong in the South of Europe and in these regions the rise of the opera and the orchestra was also vigorous. The masters of opera and orchestra composition were also masters of the music for the church. Thus the new classic forms of classic music were introduced into the music of the Roman Catholic church. The entire mass was now seen as a classic art form. The *Kyrie* before the *Christe* might now be repeated after the *Christe* in order to establish the three-part (ABA) unity. The *Kyrie* itself might be in sonata allegro form. Other parts of the mass might also be in sonata form or the sections together might be used as parts of a large sonata form to be concluded in a fugue.

In this classic period the texts of the Roman Catholic liturgy were presented in terms of the old ideals of the *a cappella* heritage. The composers employing symphony orchestra as accompaniment, or providing for the solo singing of texts in the manner of the operatic aria, restrained the music in order to have it serve indeed as a vehicle for the historic lofty purposes of the mass, in accordance with the tradition of the Roman church. The choruses were always in polyphonic style, the whole musical setting of the mass was in traditional church style, psychologically speaking—that is, untainted with worldliness, yet *in* the world, making use of all the musical advances of the period. The symphonic polyphonic masses of this classic period reached their height of sensitive religious devotion in the works of Haydn (b. Rohrau, 1732—d. Vienna, 1809) and Mozart (b. Salzburg, 1756—d. Vienna, 1791).

Any concise evaluation of the classic period must not overlook that in some areas of the German Protestant church there was also important growth of church music. Also there were important church composers who attempted to write music that would be useful to both Roman Catholic and Protestant. Joseph Alois Schmittbauer (b. *c.* 1718—d. Carlsruhe, 1809) was one of these. In 1783 he wrote the oratorio, *The Friends at the Grave of the Saviour.*

The ideals of the classic period were extended by men like Beethoven, Cherubini, and Schubert. Unfortunately, due to their excellent example, the composing of masses and religious songs became the fashion among lesser, uninspired, even insincere composers. Thus the Roman Catholic as well as the Protestant world was inundated by a flood of cheap music composed by obscure musicians to be found in every village of Europe. However, casting its towering shadow before. Beethoven's *Missa Solemnis* stands out. This great work, transcending the bounds of the Roman Catholic liturgy, is out of place in the church. Yet it is of such solemn and dignified structure that for many it is difficult to conceive of its being presented elsewhere. This, of course, might also be said of the baroque period Bach's *B Minor Mass*—which is not a mass after all, but, rather, a series of sacred cantatas.

A NOTE ON ROMANTIC MUSIC

The Romantic Period of music's history, 1820-1900, is marked by the growth of (1) individualism, (2) subjectivism, (3) interest in the mystical, the supernatural, the philosophical connections, and (4) a growing consciousness of nationalism among the many peoples. It is of interest that romanticism in music paralleled romanticism in literature.

Among the great names of the period (of which there are a host although many did not interest themselves in significant religious composition) are Ludwig van Beethoven, Hector Berlioz, Anton Bruckner, Gioacchino Antonio Rossini, Giuseppe Verdi, Richard Wagner, Felix Mendelssohn, Franz Schubert, Johannes Brahms, Franz Liszt, and many more.

The music of religious connection was not so much music for worship service in the church as it was for special musical service providing aesthetic experience to members and nonmembers of the church alike. Often this music instead of being presented in the church was presented in the concert hall.

The religious music of the period was mainly choral and oratorio music. There were songs too, such as the famous and popular *Ave Maria* of Schubert.

The rise of romanticism in all art had profound implications. It was not merely an experimental expressiveness born of the earlier classic formulas, rather, it was the consummation of imaginative impulses which had been seeking to *explore* in areas beyond the reach of the classical limitations. And additionally, romanticism was a restatement of the proposition that it is the things of the *heart* and *spirit* which matter most. This was a complete and devastating reversal of the most tenderly regarded beliefs of the Enlightenment.

In its religious references, the romantic movement found sympathetic support from the churches. New emphases of Roman Catholic doctrine were manifest in the new privileges granted the Jesuits in 1814 by Pope Pius VII.[10] The Roman Catholic church engaged again in vigorous attempts to glorify the "verities" and achievements of the past.

The impacts upon one another of *Romanticism, Traditionalism, and the Enlightenment,* contributed a continuous struggle during the entire nineteenth century.

---

[10]The Jesuit order had been abolished in 1773 by Pope Clement XIV in his bull *Dominus ac Redemptor noster.*

Two strains of activity in nineteenth-century romanticism presented themselves in connection with Roman Catholic support.
There was a renewed adulation of the ancient values of earlier
medieval art coupled with a revived awareness that the ancient
devices must be reframed in the contemporary artistic mode if
they would be fruitful. The ancient values must be couched in a
new music, rather than a historic music: in order to reach the
people the music must be in keeping with the spirit of the time.
To this twofold end there occurred in the second quarter of the
nineteenth century a renaissance of the music of Palestrina.

The new tender and reverent, mysterious, warmth for Palestrina
was increased, of course, by the imaginative romanticism of Thibaut
and Baini (already indicated in the section on Palestrina). It was in
Germany especially, under representative composers like Edouard
Grell (1800-1866) and Heinrich Bellermann (1832-1903) that the
very technique and spirit of Palestrina's *a cappella* music was recaptured.

The efforts to restore the historic values, but in a contemporary
idiom, were aided by the new scientific devices of the Enlightenment itself which had kindled an interest in a new kind of
scholarly consciousness.

The two great works of the German, Franz Commer (b. Cologne,
1813—d. Berlin, 1887), *Musica Sacra* and *Collectio Operum
Musicorum Batavorum,* helped to aid historical research in reference to music. Evidence of this new scientific curiosity is seen in
the expansiveness of the work by the Benedictines of Solesmes who,
under Abbot Guéranger, developed interest in Gregorian Chant,
collecting and restoring a great body of plainsong. The Benedictine
restoration and the Palestrinian renaissance were supported and
consolidated by the Cecilian movement. Thus, in the nineteenth
century, a new Roman Catholic church music of international
character but excluding all forms of the more recent contemporary music, was introduced. It preserved for the church music a
distinctive character all its own.

A critical observation may be in order at this point. The absence
of a liturgy in much of Protestantism (which Protestantism often
has been proud to point out) has not always been a blessing. While
the deteriorations that have set in from time to time in both Roman

Catholicism and Protestantism will not allow for saying that the music of one is superior to that of the other, it is true that the basing of its music in history and tradition (only made possible in a well-regulated liturgy) has enabled the Roman Catholic church to revive the good quality of its musical offering after every siege of decline.

The very nature of declines in Protestantism allows for kinds of religious consciousness that amount almost to religious anarchy. Protestant revivals, indeed the feeling of need for revival, are often slow to be set in motion. The feeling that music should be an expression of the people who use it is in keeping with the democratic spirit of Protestantism; but often this spirit is allowed to deteriorate into something less than one of *responsibility*. Protestantism should train itself away from irresponsibility—and, of course, all should recognize that music is not mere self-expression; music is a transcending force for helping in the influence of the human spirit. Tawdry, or inconsequential, or bad music begets a like quality in the whole religious life and expression of the people who produce such music.

How the moorings in the liturgy tend to re-establish the good qualities periodically attained in history after intervening declines is exemplified in the events following the Palestrinian renaissance and the rise of Cecilianism. The Cecilian movement[11] had attempted to reform the plain chant, but had based its efforts on a published work, the *Editio Medicea*. For long years after his death, this work had been regarded as the product of Palestrina himself, and as a genuine Palestrinian restoration of Gregorian Chant. But Palestrina, whose co-operation in such a work had been enlisted by Pope Gregory XIII, had early given up the project (due to certain strong objections from the Spanish hierarchy). The project was eventually completed and published, in 1614, by Felice Anerio 1560?-1614 and Francesco Suriano 1549-1621. However, the work evidences an unclear understanding of plain chant and is blemished with many inaccuracies. In 1889 the first volume of the work of the Benedictines, the *Paléographie Musicale*, was published. Al-

---

[11]The Society of St. Cecilia (Cacilienverein) was formed in Germany in 1867. It was named after St. Cecilia, who, according to some traditions, was martyred in the year 176, in Sicily, under Marcus Aurelius. She is the patron saint of music because tradition has it that she praised God in songs and the performance of instrumental music.

though musicologists are not ready to accept the work of the Benedictines as being altogether authentic, their work has come to be regarded as a correction of the efforts of the Cecilians.

The Cecilians had supported the *a cappella* ideal—although what that ideal was, they did not clearly define. At any rate, directly out of their efforts there arose (as exemplified in the revival of strict modal counterpoint, after Johann Fux [1660-1741] and his *Gradus ad Parnassum*) the adulation of a music that was archaic and dated.

The development of the Romantic period in France and Italy, both secularly and religiously, provided interesting stimulation for the Cecilian movement. This is not to imply that there was any reverence for the German Cecilian ideal in either of these countries, for there was none. But due to inroads of secularization in the churches of Italy and France, Pope Pius IX, in 1868, renewed the *Schola Cantorum* at the Church of St. John the Lateran. Additionally, schools were founded in Milan, Rome, and Venice for the study of church music. The school at Venice was founded by the Patriarch Sarto who was later to become Pope Pius X. In 1882 a meeting for the study of liturgic song was held in Arezzo. And out of this meeting there was established an international society for the improvement of church music.

It had been the custom to make casual use of unrelated or even inappropriate organ accompaniments in the French church service. Consequently, in 1883, Pope Leo XIII regulated the French service by an official decree. The service was further regulated by a pastoral letter from Sarto in 1895. But in 1903 Sarto (Pope Pius X) issued the famous *Motu Proprio*. This was not merely an *official* declaration—it was the work of a musical scholar. The influence of the *Motu Proprio,* an encyclical of twenty-nine points, is perhaps as great and transforming as was the work of Gregory I.

The Cecilians had had greater support in Germany than in the south countries, as already indicated. They had been opposed to "chromatic" church music and to superficial organ accompaniments for the mass. At the same time, the Benedictines were restoring Gregorian music to its historic status. Thus Pope Pius X had found confusion amidst the "music champions" of the church. As the

German Cecilia movement reached France, many French composers interested themselves in the Cecilian standards and in the new *schola cantorum*. However, the French composers were not attracted to the archaic *a cappella* music of the older polyphonic style. But through compromise, Pius X achieved his reform. He set aside the unfortunate *Editio Medicea* upon the expiration of its publishing privilege by Pustet at Ratisbon; he accepted the work of the Benedictines; he supported the renewal of the Palestrina style; he banned theatricals in church music, women in the choir; and he banned instruments, even the organ, except for certain modest places in the service. Boys were reintroduced into the choir, and when instruments were allowed, only wind instruments, as being more nearly of organ quality, were admitted.

In reference to questions that are raised in connection with the work of the Benedictines, it should be noted that their rhythmic constructions and their regulations as to accompaniment are not entirely trusted. Historically, the correct way to perform Gregorian Chant is by unaccompanied singing. Of course it is true that today's familiarity with harmonic and polyphonic considerations in both our vocal and instrumental music makes it almost impossible not to supply privately, even silently, harmonic accompaniments which seem to be implied in the ancient single line chants. From a purely musical standpoint, if accompaniments are to be provided, they would better be provided by persons of musical, religious, and theological insight than by just any casual organist or musician who might happen along. When Pope Pius X urged that no music subsequent to that of Palestrina be permitted in the service, he was ignoring the work of the distinguished musicians who followed Palestrina, and he was in effect negating the work of men like Dunstable, Dufay, Josquin, Lassus, and others who preceded Palestrina; he was overlooking the fact that what he was banning in the dawning of the twentieth century often included work of a quality and philosophy equal to that of the very men of old which he espoused.

In this connection, the work of Berlioz and Liszt is important. Both were Roman Catholics. Liszt was able to transform the qualities of the old music into a modern style of composition that was very appropriate to the Roman liturgy; on the other hand, Berlioz wrote religious music that could have no place in a church service.

Liszt produced, reverently and at the same time masterfully, a new *ars sacra,* but Berlioz seemed to have no feeling nor respect for the liturgy, and no insight into its spiritual meanings. Berlioz was skillful with musical effects, orchestral colors, grandeur, and all-enveloping sound, for their own sake. Thus his religious music, such as his *L'Enfance du Christ* (1854) is not church music.

Liszt however, in his essay, *Church Music of the Future* (1834), urged a renewal of music that would lead men of the church back to appropriate religious awareness. Liszt later entered the service of the church and devoted his life to the advancement of church music. He was an ardent Roman Catholic mystic. In addition to many Masses, Psalms, and Litanies, he wrote two oratorios, *Christus* (1866-1867) and *Saint Elizabeth* (1862). The mystic and spiritual character of these two oratorios make the theater completely inappropriate as a place for their presentation.

A third Roman Catholic of the Romantic period is Richard Wagner (1813-1883). This great man whose life must have been one of continuous inner turbulence is recognized by most, perhaps, for his music drama. He was a poet and a musician. In his later life his musical feeling came to the fore. After *Lohengrin* his music dramas sometimes suffer from long, tedious periods of complete stage inaction while musical outpourings that are nothing short of ecstatic but completely unrelated to dramatic continuity take place. Wagner was much of the time anti-Christian, and yet on occasion he reached the sublime, as Làng points out,[12] in such works as his *Parsifal* which Nietsche regarded impiously as "Christianity arranged for Wagnerians."

After the oratorios of Germany in the baroque period, that is, after the cantatas and oratorios of Johann Sebastian Bach, the development in oratorio, from Handel on, reflected not only the developments in opera but also the musical changes of the artistic and compositional periods which we have been noting; the *classic* and the *romantic.*

---

[12]Much of the point of view as found in appraisals by Paul Henry Làng is adapted in this section. (Làng, Paul Henry. *Music in Western Civilization.* New York: W. W. Norton, Inc., 1941.)

Among the oratorios of the Romantic period which should be noted, are Mendelssohn's *Saint Paul* (1836) and his *Elijah* (1846). At the beginning of the century, more in keeping with the classic than the romantic spirit, Beethoven had written his *Christus am Ölberge* (1800). Also important is Louis Spohr's *The Last Judgment*. In addition to these there were Schumann's *Das Paradies und die Peri* (1844); Hubert Parry's *Job* (1892); Edward Elgar's *The Kingdom* (1906); and John Stainer's *Crucifixion* (1887), this last still enjoying (but surely not much longer) popularity of a remarkable kind.

In the Romantic period, for the Roman church many new settings for the *Ordinary of the Mass* and the *Requiem* were composed. Religious choral music such as Mendelssohn's *Psalms* and his *Lauda Sion;* Brahms' *Deutsches Requiem;* Berlioz' *Te Deum;* Franck's *Les Béatitudes;* and Bruckner's *Mass in F Minor* are representative of the general choral music for religious service that the Romantic period produced. All of these were Roman Catholic except Mendelssohn who was Lutheran.

From 1830 on, then, one might say from the time of Liszt's *Church Music of the Future,* what had been going on in the Protestant areas from the baroque period, now began to have its effects in the Roman Catholic music. Outstanding examples of this new direction in Roman Catholic music are of course seen in Liszt's and Berlioz' works. Berlioz' *L'Enfance du Christ* was perhaps the prime mover. The oratorio had taken hold and become very popular in France after the Napoleonic period. The French oratorio vogue supported instrumental composition rather than vocal or choral. Saint-Saëns composed his Latin *Christmas Oratorio* in 1854. Franck's *Les Béatitudes* is one of the notable examples of the new French school although his lack of skill in handling textual material is apparent. Edgar Tinel (1854-1912) and Pierre Benoît (1834-1901) are also representative of the French spirit. They evidence traces of Wagnerian influence too, but show no understanding of the legacy from Handel. Of course, with the exception of Brahms, all writers in one way or another (not only the French) were influenced at least somewhat by the work of Wagner. The French writers began to introduce theatrical and decorative musical devices which had always been avoided by the Northern Protestants but which had been so characteristic of Southern Roman Catholic music. The most flagrant users of the theatrical were Gounod and Massenet.

In Italy, Verdi, like Scarlatti and Durante before him, demonstrated the intimate connection between the drama of opera and the spirit of church music. His great *Requiem Mass,* completed in 1874 upon the death of Alessandro Manzoni, is memorable.

It is in England, however, that the oratorio has found its home, no doubt due to the Handel legacy. This is true in spite of the fact that through much of the romantic period, there were no distinguished English composers. It is the great English choral tradition that has kept the works of Cowen, Mackenzie, Parry, and Stanford alive. Even Elgar's *Dream of Gerontius* (1900) lacks any powerful statement although the work evidences considerable musical craftsmanship.

Although in England, from the opening of the nineteenth century on, the decline in musical creativity has been clearly apparent, this weakness has not been so severe in church music. Thomas Attwood Walmisley (b. London, 1814—d. Hastings, 1856) and Sir John Goss (1800-1880) were both distinguished church musicians. The decline in English music is generally considered to have been greatest in the third quarter of the century. But after this, a revival occurred, and, in reference to church music, this was the most striking in the work of Sir Charles Hastings Hubert Parry (1848-1918). As already indicated, he was most effective in choral treatment. His oratorios, *Judith, King Saul,* and *Job* are of high order.

By the nineteenth century the vitality of the nonliturgic Protestant music had been lost, yet there was a great quantity of uninspired compositional activity. A host of unimportant composers produced innumerable anthems and even masses for the Protestant services. In the opinions of many, this was a reflection of the loss of purpose, vision, and spirit in Protestantism. Protestant composers were influenced by the sweet, but devitalized music of Franck, Rheinberger, and Bortnyansky. By some composers there was an earnest effort to recapture the historic glories of the church music of old. Such an attempt is apparent in the work of Max Reger (b. Bavaria, 1873—d. Leipzig, 1916) who patterned his music after the baroque Lutheran chorale music. But as has been pointed out by many, sentimentality is not vitality; historism is not creativity! The complexions of church music are the reflections of church thinking and human life. "Without vision, my people perish." This might well be kept in mind for, without dominant purpose, or creativity, church music will be trivial; the churches themselves will be wasted and anemic.

As for Roman Catholic music, in the restrictions contained in Pope Pius X's *Motu Proprio* (in spite of the contributions of that important work), because of its specificity of purpose, there are inherent a lack of vision and historical perspective that have interrupted the musical development set in motion by Liszt and Bruckner. Although these restrictions were relaxed later, even today in the twentieth century, the spirit of the musical service has not yet been rekindled.

FOLK BACKGROUNDS AMONG THE ENGLISH-SPEAKING PEOPLE

It was not long after the establishment of the Church of England that the resistance against it grew to an extent that was even more formidable and bitter than that which had been turned against the Roman Catholics. This resistance against the Anglican church was brought by the Puritans who, accusing the Anglican church of being at least half "papist," intended to revolutionize its ecclesiastical service. The Puritans wished to reduce its form of worship to a complete peasantlike simplicity in keeping with the general trend among the people toward a deeply demonstrative kind of folk-government in religious as well as in political affairs.

The conflict between the Puritan and the Anglican churches had its beginnings under Queen Elizabeth, who controlled it by vigorous repression. But under James I, the Puritan resistance became even more determined, growing to such power as finally to enable it to overthrow the succeeding king, Charles I. For a time Puritanism triumphed.

The Puritan party was principally the party of John Calvin.[13]

---

[13]Upon the death of Edward VI, there came to the throne of England a Roman Catholic queen who was known later as "Bloody Mary." In her reign, religious zealots of whatever Protestant category either escaped to Switzerland and France or were burned at the stake in England. With the coming to the throne of Elizabeth, the English religious people who had fled the country returned, bringing with them the Calvinistic fervor that they had learned on the Continent.

He was the chief source of its doctrine and organization. Calvin was a powerful leader, a fact attested by the adoption of his theological system by an enormous section of the Protestant world. Calvin's doctrine included an asceticism that was assumed by all his loyal followers and which colored the Puritan movement in England. The influences of the movement still affect congregations in both England and North America. The Calvinistic asceticism was a normal outcropping from the Calvinistic doctrine which gave so much importance to the concept of predestination. In this concept it was held, as it had been held from the age of Augustine (and before) that man, a creature of God, was totally depraved, totally unworthy. For some reason, however, God in his good pleasure (according to the dogma) would choose to elevate a few of his depraved creatures to the level of salvation, completely independent of any desire or activity on man's part. Since all men were deemed worthy of death, the Calvinists did not see that there was anything gross or shocking in man's being predestined to everlasting condemnation. Rather, they saw manifested the wonderful grace of God in their doctrine that he would choose, out of generosity and love, to elevate a few to salvation, even though they were unworthy. Since the total depravity of man was seen in fleshly, carnal, bodily manifestations, it followed, in the Calvinistic doctrine, that all things that satisfy any function of the flesh are to be regarded as sinful and evil. As a result, the asceticism that came out of the Calvinistic processes became austere and at times inhuman (at least in the minds of those who were opposed to the Calvinistic doctrine). One can readily understand how easy it was, then, for the Calvinistic Puritan Party to abhor anything that was formal, ceremonious, artistic, pleasing, or entertaining. It was common practice for the members of the Calvinistic party to denounce normal recreational activity as being frivolous, fleshly, and anti-Christ. This Puritan tone affects the membership of all churches in the English-speaking countries, even churches that were opposed to the Calvinistic doctrine. To this day, in England and America, there will be found in every church group some who have certain taboos connected with daily living which find their roots in this vigorous Calvinistic abstinence of the sixteenth, seventeenth, and eighteenth centuries.

In the Puritan movement, no ritual was allowed in the church. The stain-glassed windows found in churches which they took under control, were mostly destroyed. Artistic works such as paintings, ornaments, sculptures, beautifully designed books were thought to be an offense to God and were therefore destroyed. During the short rule of Oliver Cromwell, untold and inestimable harm was done in the destroying of the works of art over which the Puritans got control. Of course, in the churches of the Puritans, no instruments of music and no trained choirs were permitted; in fact, it was only after a struggle that congregational singing of any kind was permitted, and to this day there are certain church groups, influenced by this Calvinistic background, that will permit no singing except the singing of Old Testament Psalms which are metrically translated into English. There are several groups of religious people whose musical activity is confined to general singing of Psalms, short religious songs, and approved hymns.[14]

An interesting collection of religious song material came out of the Puritan movement. (See also sections on Calvin and Watts, and Methodist hymnody of this chapter.) The earliest collection of importance is the *Genevan Psalter*. This Psalter, in a way, was the result of the work of Clement Marot, who was a poet in the court of Francis I of France (see pp. 117; 128). As we have already mentioned, in 1538, Marot, not having any deeply sacred reason, began, for amusement, to translate the Psalms into French, setting them metrically so that they could be sung to popular songs of the day. His songs were found to be a diversion for the dissolute members of the court of Francis I. Each member of the royal family and each of the attendants had his own favorite song which, by its continued use could be likened to a coat of arms, as a distinguishing badge of identification. Prince Henry, whose favorite sport was hunting, had as his favorite Psalm setting, "Like as the

---

[14]In so far as the Anglican church held strictly to its "apostolic" traditions, its music was solely the responsibility of the clergy. In its high services then, there was no congregational singing, just as in the Roman mass. Later, in an effort to appeal to the "people," it introduced the more flexible services (cathedral, parochial, mixed) as already mentioned, pp. 140-142. Singing and, later, use of instrumental music were admitted to the official Anglican service only after considerable controversy, since such "innovations" diverged from the tradition which had come to the Anglicans through their Roman heritage.

hart desireth the water brooks." The king's mistress had as her song the 130th Psalm, "Out of the depths have I cried to thee, O Lord." This practice in the court did not obtain for very long. The theological ministers of the Sorbonne became very suspicious that Marot's songs had some connection with the Protestant revolution (all of these people in the king's court were, of course, Roman Catholics) and so they "sought out" people who responded to this dissolute practice of singing the Psalms, and treated them as heretics.

In 1543 Marot, his life endangered, escaped to Geneva which was Calvin's headquarters. Calvin, who had already made use of thirty-five of Marot's songs, upon Marot's arrival at Geneva, accepted twenty more. After Marot's death in 1544, the remaining Psalms were assigned by Calvin to Theodore de Beza for translation; in 1552 the *Genevan Psalter* was completed as a result of Beza's work. Occasionally, in modern hymnbook collections one finds melodies credited to Guillaume Franc and Louis Bourgeois. Such accrediting is misleading. The tunes of the *Genevan Psalter* are adaptations of popular secular tunes, the composers of which are unknown. The most celebrated of these tunes is the famous setting for the "Doxology" which was used as a setting for Psalm 134, although it is generally called *Old Hundredth,* and ascribed to Bourgeois. At first, these songs were sung in unison without any harmony, but later on, between 1562 and 1565, the melodies were contrapuntally harmonized in four parts, the tune being given to the tenor. This harmonizing of the melody was the work of Claude Goudimel, a Netherlander who was one of the foremost musicians of his day. He was suspected of sympathy with the Huguenot party and so was killed in the massacre of St. Bartholomew's night in 1572.[15]

---

[15]The name "Huguenots" popular from 1560 on, is perhaps a nickname ascribed first to those French Protestants who used to assemble by night at the Gate of King Hugo. Although as early as 1512 there was published by Jacobus Faber a liberating, "protesting" doctrine, in general the French "Protestants" were regarded as "Lutherans." They suffered severe persecution, sometimes by official edict of the government. In 1538 a number of Huguenots fled to Strasbourg and established a church there. Among these, the most important personage, later to become famous, was John Calvin. The Massacre of St. Bartholomew's night, August 24, 1572, was one in a long succession of bloody battles between the Huguenots, "loyal to the crown but fighting for conscience' sake," and the Roman Catholics, fighting for the "Holy League." The Bartholomew night's massacre was instigated by Catherine de Medici, Charles IX, and the Duke d'Anjou. This night's treachery touched off a bloody, nation-wide, purge of Huguenots that was temporarily relieved only by the end of the century. Actually, the present-day respectable relationships of Roman Catholics, Protestants, and government in France, date from 1870, more correctly, from 1905.

In Geneva it was the practice to have an hour appointed each day of the week for a sermon. A bell would ring, the shops would close, conversation and business would be broken off, and the people would gather in the nearest meetinghouse. Upon arrival at the meeting house, the people would take from their pockets their small books of songs with notes, and, in their native speech, sing as a congregation before and after the sermon.

Such were the earliest beginnings of Calvinistic psalmody as supported by the "folkways" of the people. The influence of Calvin and the music which represented his system lived for nearly two centuries in the Reformed Churches of Switzerland, France, and The Netherlands, and the Puritan churches of England, Scotland, and North America. Let it be remarked again that the "liturgy" (which properly was not a liturgy at all) for the singing of the Calvinistic groups was confined to the Psalms alone. This marks a difference from the music of the Lutheran people, who were encouraged to express their religious convictions in hymns of their own spontaneous creation and choice.

The key word to the understanding of the strange power of the Calvinistic system might be *self-denial*. Any appeal to what was interesting or enticing or artistic in worship was considered in this system to be a compromise with "popery." One should keep in mind, before judging the Puritans too harshly, that these people had been subjected to a fierce kind of religious persecution. It was only human that they would feel a deep hatred for the people who had persecuted them, namely, the Roman Catholics. Although the present age is tempted to despise the uncharitable and austere Puritan spirit, especially the Puritans' hatred for the papists, one must remember what their fathers and friends had endured. In similar circumstances, would today's generations deport themselves any differently?

It is remarkable that the Calvinistic system deviated from artistic interest mainly for religious reasons and not altogether for personal reasons. For instance, John Milton was sensitive to the charm of poetry and music and yet was a representative Puritan, too. Of course, in his later years, he also denounced the "levities" of the time.

Asceticism became a mark of the party. To espouse only the simple and the unadorned became a devout religious cause.[16] Oftentimes, although they were seeking to re-establish apostolic simplicity, because of their neglect of the study of history, the Calvinists erred seriously in their purpose: for instance, among the Puritans, only congregational singing was permitted, antiphonal singing being dismissed as a mark of "popery" and a departure from apostolic practice. Actually, a mode of antiphonal singing was the regular practice in the apostolic age, and congregational singing as the Puritans practiced it was a comparatively modern usage.

In upholding their party in its battle against religious imperfection which it considered to be "popish," the Puritans developed their intolerance and bigotry to such an extent that they could hold a clear conscience while abusing violently the rights of others who differed with them. The Puritan, in general, was honest in matters of business and social living, and generous to a fault; but in matters that affected his religion he became bigoted, unsympathetic, and fanatical. In this group there arose opposition to the use of surplice or to reference to the sign of the cross, and to the custom of kneeling at the Lord's Supper. Indeed, Puritan reform came to mean opposition to anything that was practiced by the Roman Catholic or Anglican church. Counteropposition to the Puritan movement from the standpoint of the Anglican church naturally arose.

Notable in the counter-Puritan struggle is the writing of Richard Hooker, who presented a clear penetrating essay defending the practice of ritual as a worship practice for Christians. In his essay he proved the antiquity of antiphonal chanting by means of quotations and documentations from the writings of earlier Christians. On this and other matters, Hooker's fervent appeals for sanity in regard to reading the Scripture were, however, lost upon the Puritans.

Such have been the backgrounds of religious singing among the English-speaking people. As already mentioned, with the coming of Isaac Watts and the Wesleyan movement, the establishment of

---

[16]It is well to note that Puritan austerity was not always evident in secular connections. Gilbert Chase in his *America's Music* (New York: McGraw-Hill, 1955) elaborates on this point. Also, it must be remembered that the Puritan movement was not a revolt of the lower classes; it was peopled by many noblemen. Nor were the Puritans total abstainers from alcoholic beverages.

Old Hundredth[16]

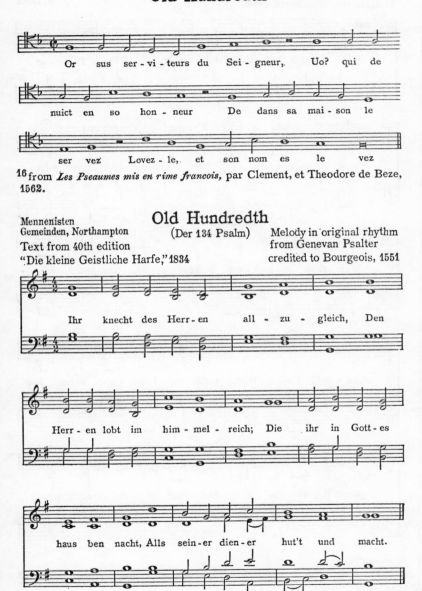

Or sus ser - vi - teurs du Sei - gneur, Uo? qui de

nuict en so hon - neur De dans sa mai - son le

ser vez Lovez - le, et son nom es le vez

[16] from *Les Pseaumes mis en rime francois,* par Clement, et Theodore de Beze, 1562.

Mennénisten
Gemeinden, Northampton
Text from 40th edition
"Die kleine Geistliche Harfe," 1834

Old Hundredth
(Der 134 Psalm)

Melody in original rhythm
from Genevan Psalter
credited to Bourgeois, 1551

Ihr knecht des Herr - en all - zu - gleich, Den

Herr - en lobt im him - mel - reich; Die ihr in Gott - es

haus ben nacht, Alls sein - er dien - er hut't und macht.

Martin Rinkart,[17] 1586–1649
Tr. Catherine Winkworth, 1858

J. S. Bach

All praise and thanks to God The Fa - ther
now be giv - - - en, The Son, and Him who reigns
With them in high - est heav - en, The one e - -
ter - nal God, Whom earth and heav'n a - dore; For
thus it was, is now, And shall be ev - er more.

[17]This hymn, "Nun danket alle Gott," is usually set to Crueger's tune, number 183 in his *Praxis* of 1648. In a few hymnals it is set to this chorale of Bach which closes Cantata 94: "Was frag ich nach der Welt."

the Anglican church as the Church of England with its development of a doctrine opposed to that of Calvin, there came a new era in religious thinking. The music of the new period seen in the Church of England and among the Methodists and other more liberal church groups reflected a new, more invigorating religious tone.

CHAPTER FIVE

THE ORGAN

The history of music for the church is involved with the history
of the organ. Christendom has its groups which either allow or dis-
allow its use in worship—but for twelve centuries, like no other
musical instrument, the organ has had peculiar affinities in musical
and religious thinking. Political, historical, and sociological considerations have regulated the organ's use or disuse in religious connections and as might well be suspected, these considerations have
not always allowed for unmixed religious thinking.

There are two areas of interest to be considered in summarizing
the history of the organ: (1) to report the more important technical developments of the instrument from its earliest beginnings,
and (2) to list the main events of its use including the social out-
comes and attitudes connected with its historical contribution.

ANCIENT BEGINNINGS

Presently available information will not allow one to be exact
about the times and places of the earliest events in the development of the organ. It is certain, however, that the most important
parts of the organ, in primitive form, had been invented long before
Christ.

In its earliest forms, the organ principle was perhaps suggested when men noted that musical tones could be produced by air passing over the end of a hollow tube, such as when wind passes over the broken ends of hollow reeds.

Binding together in a row several reeds of different lengths and then blowing over the ends makes possible the producing of differently pitched tones. By careful choosing of lengths, pitched tones as desired can be exactly provided for, in even such a primitively fashioned contrivance.

Just such an invention, the syrinx, was known to the Hellenic cultures—and no doubt to many cultures preceding. With the Greeks, tradition had it (the writings of Virgil and Lucretius bear this out) that the syrinx was the invention of Pan—hence the name, "Pan's pipes" or "Pandean Pipe." This instrument, like the present-day mouth organ, had to be moved from side to side in order that the person playing it could blow into the proper tubes.

Another very ancient instrument, fashioned out of a small bowl itself fitted with a mouthpiece, and having a number of pipes or reeds "sprouting" out of it, has been known to the Chinese for 5,000 years. The tubes have apertures at their base, which, as they are closed with the fingers, will cause the tube to sound when the bowl is blown into. This instrument is known as the *sheng*.

Eventually an improvement of greatest importance was made: the tubes were rooted at their "feet" in a confined chamber of air; each tube was either operated or else stopped by the fingers, the air in the chamber maintaining pressure to all tubes simultaneously. The bagpipe of today so frequently associated with the Scottish culture has a very old tradition with its beginnings in this very ancient invention.

Farmer[1] includes a description of such an instrument as discovered by him in Arabic manuscripts dating from the eighth and ninth centuries. These Arabic descriptions themselves were based upon Greek writings believed to be of pre-Christian times. The descriptions tell of gigantic bagpipes of twelve tubes fashioned from reeds which were supplied with air from three bags which themselves were kept inflated from a "blast bag" into which four men

[1]Farmer, H. G., *The Organ of the Ancients from Eastern Sources (Hebrew, Syriac and Arabic)*, London: Reeves, 1931, "Sources of Arabian music," p. 59.

seated nearby would blow. In some descriptions of this type of instrument it is mentioned that twelve men would be employed to blow into the blast bag. In these instruments, a stopcock, or a mechanism either to be slid or depressed, served as a valve to actuate each pipe as desired by the performer.

THE HYDRAULIC ORGAN

An ancient instrument, the hydraulus, sometimes spoken of as a "water organ," played a most important part in the development of the modern-day pipe organ. In the early hydraulic organ, each pipe was rooted in a shallow box. Into this box, positioned in such a way as to pass immediately below the end of the rooted pipe, a slide could be moved back and forth. The slide moved in its track with an airtight fit keeping the air in the shallow box from escaping into the pipe just above. A hole in the slide could be moved into position under the pipe so that at the will of the performer the pipe could be actuated by the air passing into it from the box below.

In principle, this invention (credited to Ctesibius who was born about 265 B.C. in Alexandria, during the reign of Ptolemy II) continued to be used up into the eleventh century. Fortunately the history of the hydraulus can be traced clearly. On a medallion of Nero's time, Laurentius, victor in the games, is shown with his hydraulus beside him; on the opposite side, a likeness of Nero is shown. Nero was himself a performer as an amateur on the instrument. Also, the hydraulus is pictured on a medallion of the time of Trajan (98-117); again, in the mosaic dating roughly between A.D. 117 and 138, found at Nemming bei Sierck on the Mosel[2]; and on the Julia Tyrrhenia tomb (2nd, 3rd century); on the Villa Ludovisi fragment (4th century); on the Valentinian medallion (425-455); and on the diptych of Anastasius[3] of Constantinople (517).

---

[2]Moser, H. J. *Geschichte der Deutschen Musik.* Stuttgart: p. 59. This hydraulus possesed 12 pipes.

[3]Anastasius (c. 413-518), an emperor of Rome, reigned prudently and generously. He belonged to the religious party which believed that Christ, in human and spiritual or Godly character, was one. This view, while it did not prevent his being tolerant of differing beliefs, earned for him the animosity of the leaders in the Western church.

A diptych was a folding tablet, often in gold or silver, in which were contained the

Tertullian who died about 222 praised the hydraulus and Publilius Optatianus wrote a poem that was in the shape of a hydraulus.[4] Marcellinus wrote, about 380, that in Nero's day there were contests featuring performances upon the hydraulus. It was regarded by the Romans as the most suitable instrument for use in the large amphitheatres. This may in part account for the Christians' opposition to the instrument when they came into power upon the breaking up of the Empire. Reference already has been made to the Jews' great antipathy for the musical instruments of the Romans and against the flagrant use to which they were put from the time of Herod.

Numerous untrustworthy and imaginative descriptions of the hydraulus have been produced. Even authorities of the ninteenth century have been misled by some of the older descriptions which they discovered. The hydraulus was an instrument in which reservoirs of water were used to maintain even and consistent wind pressure in the air chamber. The air was usually pumped by bellows. There was also an ingenious method for generating air pressure by gravity feed of water from a reservoir through a small water wheel that operated valves to two cylinders which alternately filled with water or air, the air-pressurized cylinder being the source of air for the pipes. After the sixth century, the hydraulus disappeared giving way to the pneumatic organ which was developed with the discovery of a new method for weighting the blast bag.

In the ninth century there was a revival of interest in the hydraulus. To bear this out there is an illustration of the hydraulus shown in the *Utrecht Psalter,* which itself may date from as early as the eighth century.

As the result of an interesting combination of circumstances, this revival of making large organs occurred in the ninth century among the Greeks and the Syrians. This is the more notable because the Syrians are not known to have been interested in such things previously, and the Byzantine Greeks had already adopted

names of the faithful, living or dead. At the eucharistic service, when names were read from the diptych it thus signified that such were to receive the prayers of the church. To be struck out of the dipytch was to be excommunicated. This custom lead to the later processes of canonizing and admitting to sainthood of those especially designated.

[4]Wernsdorf, Poetae Lat. Min., Vol. II, p. 394. The poem includes 26 lines representing the pipes, each a little longer than the former, the last line (for a pipe) being twice as long as the first.

to their own use the pneumatic organ with a weighted blast bag to maintain constant pressure. But the Arabic scholars (who had neither hydraulic nor pneumatic organs) became interested in the ancient Greek writings. They engaged in the translating of the Greek writings on hydrostatics and pneumatics and they studied the works of Archimedes, Apollonius, Philo, and Hero. Of special interest is a writing known as the Muristus document which it is believed may be the actual work of Ctesibius. The Arabs examined this document along with the others and soon were trying their unskilled hands at building organs such as their readings referred to.

Thus from the ninth century on, there are many references to the organ, particularly the hydraulus, as these were constructed for the great Arabian palaces by Greek craftsmen. Many Arabian writings on the organ date from this period. Indeed the development of the hydraulus became almost a craze among the Arabs. Once more it was learned not only how to utilize water to stabilize the air pressure for operating the pipes, but how to use water to generate air pressure.[5] They seemed to prefer this method to that of raising air pressure by means of a bellows. They built organs that could be operated and made to play tunes automatically. To accomplish this, they built contrivances coupled with water wheels having projecting pieces attached to a cylindrical drum. The rotating cylinder with its projections would operate the valves to the pipes in the correct order to sound out the particularly desired musical combinations. In England, as late as the nineteenth century, barrel organs were used to play the psalm tunes automatically.[6]

In contrast to the interest in the hydraulus that sprang up among the Arabs, there was no such revived interest in Western Europe. Knowledge of its construction and of the hydrostatic principle was virtually nonexistent.

---

[5]The reader always must exercise care when coming across the terms "hydraulic organ," "hydraulus," and so on. Writers do not use the terms as consistent references. Some seem to use the term *hydraulic organ* as a reference to the mechanism in which the air pressure is initially generated by water power, and the term *hydraulus* (hydraulic) to the organ in which air pressure is regulated by the weight of water. There is much variation in the usages.

[6]One of these, no longer used in service, is to be seen in Brightling Church, Sussex. Descriptions of how to set barrel organs enabled Arnold Dolmetsch to deduce time values in old musical ornamentations. *See* Dolmetsch, *The Interpretation of the Music of the Seventeenth and Eighteenth Centuries* (London, 1915, 1944).

Actually, knowledge of this phase of the history of the organ has been generally lost to the Western world up to comparatively recent time. However, from the midnineteenth century, written references and pictures referring to the centuries-older hydraulus and organ have become increasingly available.

In 1885 a small baked-clay model of the hydraulus was found in the ruins of Carthage. It dates from the second century.

After 1855, many writings such as those of Rimbault's *The Organ, Its History and Construction* appeared. These were not always trustworthy, however, because they depended on Western writers of the pre-Reformation period whose understanding of the Arabic findings is now known oftentime to have been erroneous.

In 1899 W. Schmidt's authoritative translations of the works of Hero were published.

In 1931 the parts of a third-century hydraulus were discovered at Acquincum near Budapest. On this ancient instrument is the inscription:

Gaius Julius Viatorinus, Decurio of the Colony of Acquincum, Aedile Prefect of the College of Patchworkers, presented as a personal gift to the said College an Organ (Hydraula) in the Consulate of Modestus and Probus.

The location of this instrument was destroyed by fire, but the upper portions of the instrument were carried to a nearby basement for safekeeping where it remained until it was discovered in 1931. Because the lower part of the organ was not removed, all its wooden parts were burned. However, the bronze mechanism (pipes, slides, wind channels, etc.) is well preserved.

THE PNEUMATIC ORGAN

The pneumatic organ using a system of bellows to generate air pressure for the pipes, dates from long before the fourth century before Christ. Probably it was known in Mesopotamia even before it was known to the Greeks. The word, *moshroquitha,* sackbut,[7]

---

[7]*Sackbut,* perhaps more accurately to be translated *sambuke,* probably related not to *trombone,* as often remarked, but to *bagpipe.* See Daniel 3:5 and illustration on p. 25.

found in Daniel 3:5, 7, 10, 15, may have referred to a pneumatic organ.

In the first thousand years of the Christian Era, as such, there apparently was no significant improvement of the organ. As already noted, the organ was introduced into Western Europe from the Greek culture. Between the sixth and ninth centuries, it seems to have been forgotten, but was reintroduced by way of the Arabic cultures.

At any rate, it is clear that the arts of organ building were known to the English by the *first* of the eighth century; in France, organ building was begun in the *middle* of the eighth century.

Charlemagne's father, Pepin, asked of the Byzantine emperor, Constantine Copronymus VI, that he be sent an organ. The Emperor did send an organ to Pepin in France about the year 757. This was a pneumatic organ with lead pipes. The instrument was accompanied en route by Stephanus, a Roman bishop and installed in St. Cornelius at Compiègne. The report is that it was played by an Italian priest who had learned how to play the organ in Constantinople.

Charlemagne later imported an Arabian organ which he had installed in Aachen in 812.

THE ORGAN OF THE MIDDLE AGES

As already indicated, the remarkable organ development under the Greeks and Romans was, after the decline of those cultures, taken up by the peoples of the Middle East. Later, interest in organ advancement trickled back into the West.

By some, the organ was regarded as an aid to Christian worship, by others, as a hindrance.

From the writings in Migne (*Patrologiae cursus completus,* Latin, XXX, 219) one learns that St. Maildulf, who died about 675, and St. Ethelwold, who died about 984, built organs. St. Dunstan (925?-988) is reported to have had great interest in music, both as a performer and builder. His interest included not only the organ, but also the bell chimes, harp, and psaltery.[8] Other

---

[8]Galpin, Francis W., *Old English Instruments of Music.* London: 1910.

mentions of the organ, such as that of the gift of an organ by
Count Elwin in the tenth century to a convent in Ramsey, are
frequent.

In the period of the ninth and tenth centuries, considerable
activity in organ building was going on also in Germany. Numerous source references are available.[9]

THE WINCHESTER ORGAN

Of special interest is the large organ at Winchester which existed
in the tenth century. Interesting description of this organ is the
subject of a poem by Wulstan, a deacon at Winchester who died
about 963. Wulstan dedicated his poem to Bishop Elphege. Perhaps the description of the organ as given in the poem should not
be regarded as reliable. However, the Winchester instrument was
undoubtedly a pneumatic organ, although the type of bellows employed is uncertain.

The Winchester organ was really just a large "mixture stop" of
40 notes and sliders that each connected with ten pipes. Two performers were required to operate this organ. Each performer pre-
sided over a section of diatonic "notes" ranging probably from C
to F but with a B-flat added. Thus all of the old chants could be
performed with these 36 notes. The additional four notes very
likely were "drone pipes," or they may have been included to increase the range of the organ upward. This is not known.

THE ORGAN AS A FACTOR IN WORSHIP

In other chapters, mention has been made of the varying degrees of antipathy that existed toward the organ and other instruments as a part of Christian worship.

In the *Life and Letters of Erasmus*, Chapter VII, there is this
writing:

There was no music in St. Paul's time . . . nowadays . . . men must
leave their work and go to church to listen to worse noises than were

[9]See Gerbert. *Scriptores ecclesiastici de musica sacra potissimum.* Also, note Mahren-
holz. *Die Berechnung der Orgelpfeifenmensuren.* Kassel: 1938.

ever heard in Greek or Roman theatre. Money must be raised to buy organs and train boys to squeal.[10]

George Bernard Shaw in his Preface to *Plays for Puritans* wrote:

I am as fond of fine music and handsome buildings as Milton was, or Cromwell, or Bunyan: but if I found that they were becoming the instruments of a systematic idolatry of sensuousness, I would hold it good statesmanship to blow every cathedral in the world to pieces with dynamite, organ and all, without the least heed to the screams of the art critics and cultured voluptuaries.[11]

Some writers state that the organ was used in the Western church as early as the sixth century. It must be noted, however, that the assertion that Pope Vitalian introduced the organ into the service of the mass in the seventh century is unsupported. It seems very clear that the organ was not used in the mass until the 12th century—although for other services of the church it was increasingly used from much earlier times.

Before the fourth century, after Clement of Alexandria, only the cithara and lyre were permitted, but by the eleventh, the organ was coming to displace all other instruments. Thus by the fourteenth century the organ is described by Guillaume de Machaut as "de tous instruments le roi." While the organ has very early connections in the culture of Byzantium, it should be remembered that here it was used exclusively for secular purposes. Only in the West was it permitted in the services of the church. Johannes Aegidus (In Gerbert, *Scriptores* . . . etc., Vol. II, p. 388) is reported to have declared that in the thirteenth century the organ had displaced all other instruments for service in the mass.

THE ORGAN IN ENGLAND AND GERMANY

From the time of the Winchester organ, information about the organ in England up to the sixteenth century is problematical. Until very late, most of the English organs were of one manual,

---

[10]Erasmus (1466?-1536) was unfortunately reared; his spirit was studiously subjugated in his education for the priesthood. His revolt against this perhaps partly accounts for his eagerness to restore biblical, "apostolic" Christianity in its simplest forms.

[11]Permission to use the excerpt from the Preface to *Three Plays for Puritans*, by George Bernard Shaw, has been granted by The Public Trustee and The Society of Authors, London.

had half a dozen stops and no pedals. However, good information about the German organ is available, thus enabling one to trace the German organ through the Gothic, Renaissance, and Baroque periods. While the references of Praetorius[12] to instruments of early times are not always dependable, his accounts of Gothic period and sixteenth-century organs in Germany are most helpful. Perhaps the most significant organ development occurred in Germany, but large organs were erected in France, the Low Countries, and in Spain, too.

THE ORGAN IN FRANCE AND THE LOW COUNTRIES

In France and the Low Countries, development of the organ from the thirteenth century on, is especially interesting. For information about the organ in France and the Low Countries during the fourteenth and fifteenth centuries, the writing of Henri Arnaut of Zwolle, astrologer to the Duke of Burgundy, is valuable. The building of the "positive" organ started at that time.

THE POSITIVE

A positive was so named to indicate that it was a stationary organ, not readily to be transported or moved. It came to be a chamber organ, and later a single manual of the larger organ, or a special organ to be used for accompanying a choir. A positive is distinguished from a portative organ which is of course easily to be moved, carried, or transported—even by one person while playing it. In the earliest period of the positive, such organs, as in France, for example, possessed up to 36 "notes" of six to eight pipes each.

To add smaller pipes for extending the treble range upward, and larger pipes for the bass was not hard to envision, of course, but no convenient devices for operating the bass pipes had been invented. Since the levers, or keys, or slides to actuate the pipes had to be placed immediately under the "feet" of the pipes, the extensiveness of the mechanical operation of very large pipes that thus had to be spaced widely apart, made their use difficult and even impractical for performance. In the early experimentations with

---

[12]Praetorius, Michael. *De Organographia.* Wolffenbüttel, 1619, Facsimile edition, Kassel, 1939, Vol. II "Syntagma Musicum."

large bass pipes, valves would be placed at the hands of the performers in order to turn them on or off as desired. When the bass pipes would sound, they would sound continually as "drones" until turned off by the performers. Thus one encounters the beginnings of the "drone" bass introduced to undergird the upper voices and to give vital and contrasting interest to the melodies above.

Drone bass, or "pedal point," or "organ point" is employed today as a device of the musical composer. Thus musical composition in this, as in many other instances, is seen to be influenced dramatically by the mechanics of organ building.

Soon there was felt the need to use several keyboards, one to play the drone bass pipes, another to play the melody pipes, and a third to play the smallest treble pipes (*descant:* "away-from-the-tenor," i.e. "melody, pipes"). Development of the keyboard will be briefly touched upon later. Preceding the keyboard, there was a device, a "roller," which permitted moving the levers laterally to play neighboring pipes. Also, a system of ropes and pulleys to be operated by levers pressed by the feet was invented.

The placing of the "descant" pipes in separate enclosures, while the large pipes were positioned in the tops of the organ cases proper, and the main pipes, for the "tenor" or melody, enclosed in the ever enlarged organ cases, was common practice by the end of the fourteenth century. In 1386 such an organ was built in the Cathedral at Rouen. It is said that the organ in the Cathedral at Amiens, in 1429, contained some 2,500 pipes. In the Chateau de Blois, the organ is reported in 1451 to have had 1,400 pipes.

Henri Arnaut wrote that the small positives of the fifteenth century contained up to 636 pipes in the main case, exclusive of the descant, bourdons, and the reeds.

Information about how organs were built and pipes made out of tin and lead, of varying shapes and contours to produce desired variations in tone is to be found in the thorough descriptions by Theophilus[13] and Arnaut.[14]

---

[13]Theophili et Rugeri. *Presbyteri et Monachi Libri III de Diversis Artibus.* Harleian Ms., British Museum. Translation by Robert Hendrie. London: John Murray, 1847.

[14]*Instruments de Musique du XVᵉ Siècle; Les traités d'Henri Arnaut de Zwolle et de divers Anonymes* (d'après le ms. Latin 7295 de la Biblioteque Nationale, Paris), edited by G. LeCerf et E.-B. Labande. Paris: Picard, 1932.

THE PORTATIVE

In addition to the positives there were the truly portative organs with pipes no longer than two feet with tones ranging from the lowest, equivalent approximately to our "middle C." The portative had nine to twelve keys for the diatonic scale (actually, the positive, up to the twelfth century, had no more). By the fourteenth century, both positive and the portative were furnished with the chromatic scale.

The gradual development of the keyboard can be traced by examining pictures of portative organs. By the fifteenth century, the present type of keyboard was established. Even this late, it was often the practice to place the letters of the notes on the keys as had been necessary earlier with the systems of levers and slides.

LANDINI AND THE ORGANETTO

Of interest is the life of an important musician, Francesco Landini, born in Fiesole in 1325. Blind from childhood, he became a heralded performer on the organetto or portative organ, as well as on many other instruments.

His playing and composition were much admired during his lifetime—and was remarked by such greats as Petrarch and Peter, King of Cyprus. About 150 works of Landini remain today. He died in 1397 and was buried in Florence. On his tomb he and his organetto are shown in replica.[15]

DEVELOPMENTS IN THE KEYBOARD

It will be remembered that the pipes of the Winchester organ were actuated by slides. We know that as late as the eleventh century (when Theophilus produced his work on "Divers Arts," including a treatise on the organ) slides were the devices used for admitting wind to the pipes or shutting it off; and that by the end of the eleventh century, the increase in the number of pipes and size of the organ brought about the devising of a system of levers to be pushed down by hand and then returned to place by springs. These

---

[15]For a very complete report on Landini, see L. Ellinwood, "Francesco Landini and his Music." *Musical Quarterly*, Vol. XXII, 1936, p. 190.

levers, forerunners of the keys to be introduced later, were much more efficient and easier of operation than were the close-fitting, airtight slides which were hard and cumbersome and slow to operate because of friction.

In their earliest usage the "keys" were up to five inches wide, nearly two inches thick, and often up to a yard long. In operation they were dropped through the distance of a whole foot. Organists of this time were often spoken of as "beaters." The earliest trustworthy account of a virtual keyboard organ is of the eleventh century organ in Magdeburg. It is reported to have had a range of sixteen notes.

More than one pipe would be connected to the same key: those of the fifth, the octave, and sometimes of the third and the tenth. Thus when a key was depressed all of several pipes would speak at once. A concert in the eleventh century on the organ would continuously be a full-organ concert.

A 14th-century organ

Early in the fourteenth century, a most important advance was made, that of adding F sharp, then later, C sharp, E flat, and next, G sharp. The B flat had already been in use, as in the Winchester organ. All these additional notes were built by Nicholas Faber, a priest, into the Halberstadt organ of 1361 which was notable for having the first chromatic keyboard (of 22 keys). It is also of interest that thirteen years earlier a monk of Thorn, in Poland, had also made an organ of 22 keys.

The Halberstadt organ is important also for its being the first with three manuals so that less than full organ could be sounded if the proper keys in the proper keyboard were struck. But the contrasts between full organ and only one set of pipes must have been severe. Therefore, devices for coupling different keyboards or manuals were invented; and what amounted to building more than one organ to be actuated by the performer through proper choice of correct manuals and couplings was achieved. By the end of the fifteenth century a multitude of mechanical inventions were regularly used.

In increasing the size of the organ to make possible much freer variation in volume and also to provide many gradations and shadings of tone quality, serious difficulties had been encountered. One solution as already seen was the planning of more keyboards. Powerful springs had to be provided to raise the keys and close the pallets (valves) to the pipes. Strong devices to "pull" the stops and hold the desired ones open had to be built. But the new keys were a great improvement over the older system of slides.

THE REGAL

In addition to the positive and the portative, a third kind of small organ, the regal is important in organ history. The regal was a medium small organ, not usually portable. Most frequently it used reed pipes,[16] and was used to keep the "order" of the plainsong. Some have felt that this function gave the instrument its name. This may be true, because "regal" could be a corruption of the Italian *Rigabello,* itself an instrument used in the churches of

---

[16]In reed pipes the wind vibrates a curved brass tongue over the surface of a reed (or shallot). The pitch is dependent upon the length of the vibrating tongue and on the position of the spring wire which modifies the length of the tongue.

Italy prior to the organ. Henry VIII of England, according to the "Inventory of the Guardrobes,"[17] 1547, possessed a number of regals. Others have thought that the instrument after all may have been named the regal from its being presented initially to a king. Regals were frequently used in the sixteenth century by the English nobility. In Scotland, there is still to be seen a large positive *regal* at Blair Atholl Castle. This instrument was made by John Loosemore of Exeter in 1650.[18]

THE ORGAN'S EFFECTS UPON MUSIC COMPOSITION

After 1470 organ advancement was remarkable throughout the continent—in Germany, Burgundy, Flanders, Normandy, Castille, and in the region of the Po, and also in the low country of Austria.

There had taken place the introduction of the pedals with separate pipes; of couplers between the manuals and also to the pedals; the development of stops of complete pitch range and with extensive varieties of tone color. All this was paralleled by the rise of great organ composers and performers.

The work of a priest and musician, Adam Ileborgh, who in 1448, in Stendhall compiled an organ book of very primitive preludes and pieces is interesting. Written in music tablature,[19] it requires performance by pedals. This manuscript is in the Curtis Institute, Philadelphia.

Another person of importance was the blind musician, Conrad Paumann, born in Nuremberg about 1410. In 1452 he produced the *Fundamentum Organisandi*. He also composed elaborations of Gregorian chants and folk tunes. A delightful example is his "Mit ganczen Willen" (With all my heart, I wish you well). Paumann served in the Court of Bavaria, was publicly acclaimed by Frederich III, Duke of Ferrara, and was also knighted by the Pope. He had a number of pupils whom he taught to improvise on liturgical

---

[17]British Museum, Harley, 1419.

[18]See Galpin, *op. cit.*

[19]In tablature notation, there were staves of 4, 5, 6, or 7 lines (with C clearly indicated) upon which the notes (not too unlike our notes today) were placed. For the lower voice however, the *letters* of the desired notes would be given. In Ileborgh's preludes, a double line of bass notes to be played by pedals is indicated.

themes. Some of his work is in the *Buxheimer Orgelbuch*. He was organist at the Frauenkirche, Munich, where he died in 1473. He is buried in the church grounds, and his grave is still marked.[20]

By the end of the fifteenth century, three important names appeared: (1) Heinrich Isaac (1450-1517), (2) Arnold Schlick (*c.* 1445-1516), and (3) Paul Hofhaimer (1459-1537).

Nothing is known of Isaac's early life, but he lived a full and distinguished musical career. His ancestors may have been from Bruges although he was born in Brabant. From 1475 he was a teacher in Firenze (Florence) in the household of Lorenzo de Medici. He came to be known widely as an organist and composer, not only in the churches in the vicinity of Firenze, but as far away as Innsbruck. With the fall in 1494 of Pietro de Medici, a former pupil, Isaac had to leave his service. He accepted a commission as court composer in 1497 at Innsbruck with the Duke of Tyrol. After Pietro's reinstatement in 1512, and the rise of Giovanni (another former pupil) to the papacy, Isaac was re-established in Firenze in 1515 where he died two years later. Isaac's genius and productivity place him among the great musicians and composers. The catalogue of his secular and sacred music is extensive.

Arnold Schlick, about whom more will be mentioned, introduced the playing of chant themes in long tones on the bass while playing a three-part counterpoint on the manuals. This device was very popular for over two centuries; indeed it is still used today as a species of composition and improvisation.

Paul Hofhaimer, born in Radstadt, in the bishopric of Salzburg, was an Austrian composer and organist in the courts of Archduke Sigismund of Tyrol. Later, he served the Emperor Maximillian I. While Hofhaimer traveled with his patrons, his residence was mainly at Innsbruck between 1480 and 1519. In 1515, at St. Stephens, Vienna, he was knighted by King Ladislaus of Hungary. He was admitted also to the nobility by the emperor. Upon the emperor's death, Hofhaimer moved to Salzburg, in 1519, where he served as organist in the Cathedral for the Archbishop. He is

---

[20]Examples of the work of both Ileborgh and Paumann are to be found in Willi Apel's *Masters of the Keyboard*. (Cambridge: Harvard University Press, 1947.)

known chiefly as a composer of simple four-voice German songs, tender and lovely of expression. In Ritter's *Zur Geschichte des Orgelspiels,* page 97, a three-part fantasy on a song, *"On freudt verzer ich manchentag,"* is reproduced. This piece testifies to Hofhaimer's greatness. He was known internationally as an artist; also he produced many distinguished pupils among whom were Ottomar Nachtgall (1487-1537), Hans Kotter (1485-1541), Johannes Buchner (1483-1544?), Bernhard Schmid (1520-1592), Leonhard Kleber (*c.* 1490-1556), and Elias Ammerbach (*c.* 1530-1597).

In the works of Nachtgall, organist at St. Thomas; Kleber, organist at Pforzheim; and Kotter, at Freiburg; incipient forms of harmony began to grow out of their counterpoint. There were also a number of important French composers at this time whose names, unfortunately, are not known.

Two important historical collections memorialize this period. One, published in Venice, 1523, is an early example of printed music, by Marco Antonio Cavazzoni da Bologna. The other is by the musician, Andrea Antico da Mantona, and was published at Rome in 1517.

The *Buxheim Organ Book,* compiled sometime between 1460 and 1475, was discovered in a monastery at Buxheim, near Munich, and taken to the Bavarian State Library in Munich in 1883. It contains many original organ works and songs arranged for organ by such composers as Dunstable, Dufay, Binchois and others. The music is in three voices, the root in each chord being placed in the highest voice in the manner of *faux bourdon.*

It is coming more and more to be recognized that medieval music was good and beautiful in its own right. In some of its earlier forms it may have been experimental but today musicians are learning that what seems to be its strangeness (and often regarded as confirming crude or primitive qualities) is really the mark of its own compositional system—a system in which the major and minor modes were "not a divine institution." The representative music of this earlier period is no less beautiful than that of Palestrina, or Bach, or Brahms. Indeed, today's ear, attuned to the dissonances of contemporary music, will find satisfaction in the music of the medieval period.

DEVELOPMENT OF THE PEDAL

The reader will have noted already frequent reference to the organ pedals. The early history of the pedal clavier, an arrangement of pedals not dissimilar today to that of the manual keyboard, has been obscured in a confusion of traditions. However, it seems clear that pedals to operate a carillon were used at St. Nicholas Church in Brussels by Ludwig van Valbeke of Brabant who died in 1312. The organ at Halberstadt, built by Faber, as already noted, in 1361, had an octave of pedal keys. Because other organs had the large 32-foot pipes, they also, no doubt, used pedals to actuate them. Thus it is probable that the Halberstadt organ was not the only one to make use of a pedal system. In 1468-69 St. Sebald in Nuremberg had installed an organ with an octave of pedals. The builder was Traxdorff of Mainz.

From the earliest use of handles to actuate drone pipes, it was simple to conceive of the large bass pipes of different pitches being used to produce a simple *cantus firmus*. The development of pedals made such performance easier. Thus musical development and mechanical improvement spring out of reciprocating influences.

While the pedals were used in the Low Countries and Germany in the fifteenth century, they were not used in England, and were neglected in Italy although in Italy, pedals were certainly known by the fifteenth century. However, pedals for organs in England were not introduced, so far as records show, until 1720. Of course the religious revolutions in England had a large bearing on the tempo of organ advance there.

CHORAL MUSIC AND THE ORGAN

In Southern Europe, especially in Italy, and in other regions such as those of the Flemish school, where the glorious rise of polyphonic writing and *a cappella* choral literature occurred, the cruder melodic mixture of the medieval organ was not so readily received. But it is interesting to note that, in Northern Germany, where the competencies in singing were not so well developed, there, the organ made the greater advances.

Thus the great peak of polyphonic choral writing occurred principally in Italy in the sixteenth century, while great advances in organ construction and musicianship, in the same century, occurred principally in Germany.

Arnold Schlick published a work in 1511 at Heidelberg which provides information about the large contemporary positive organs of Germany. The single known copy of this work was found in an old house of Saxony.[21]

Additionally, Arnold Schlick wrote a work, *Tabulaturen etlicher Lobegesang,* in 1512.[22] In it he wrote of theoretical considerations touching upon the use of scales and modes.

At this time, the German organs were large and cumbersome. But those in the Netherlands were smaller, making use of keyboards upon which harmonies could be played by the fingers. These were being used on the more moderate-sized positives, and thus made possible advances in the facility of keyboard performance.

ACOUSTICAL CONSIDERATIONS

It has been noted that the medieval organs had no stops as such, but, rather, ranks of pipes all of which "spoke" when their particular key was depressed. Additionally, all the pipes of metal were cylindrical in form and of the same diameter, varying only in length in order to give different pitches. Under the acoustical principles operating in these circumstances, the long pipes producing low pitches, when longer in proportion to their diameter, give a "string" tone of clear distinctness of pitch. The medium-length pipes in the middle of the pitch range produce loud tones of proper pitch; and the short pipes of high pitch (still with the same diameter as the longest pipes) now produce soft, "flute" tones.

In order to achieve similarity of tone quality throughout a scale or range of pitches, the pipes not only must vary in their length but also in the ratio of their diameter to their length.

---

[21]This work is today kept in the Paul Hirsch collection. A 1932 publication and a facsimile have been produced by the Rheingold Press, Mainz, Germany.

[22]In this work, Schlick also pled for a discontinuing of trick ornaments on the organ cases—such as animated figures which moved during performance. As one example of those he pointed out as ridiculous, there was the large figure of a monk (on an organ in a Capucin monastery) which rose up and looked out a window at the audience and then after startling all, disappeared only to repeat the performance. Mechanical devices, seen today on clock towers, such as at Munich and Nuremberg, were found on some organs up to the end of the eighteenth century.

In the earlier medieval organ, then, a single rank of pipes might range from low string tone to high flute tone, and from soft to loud and harsh and back to moderate volume. In the baroque organ, the dimensions of the pipes in any rank were so altered in scale, that is, in ratio of length to diameter and in respect of cylindrical and noncylindrical pipes, that, for example, flute tone could be maintained throughout the entire pitch range—or string tone, etc. Thus the real beginning of meaningful use of organ stops was conceived and brought about.

THE ORGAN OF THE SIXTEENTH THROUGH EIGHTEENTH CENTURIES

The baroque period began in the seventeenth century.

An important French scientist, Marin Mersenne (1588-1648) published a work in 1635, *Harmonie Universelle,* in which he treated on music theory and acoustics (actually anticipating Helmholtz of 225 years later) and also described the instruments of the day. His book, in France, was what Praetorius' book was, in Germany. Mersennes gave specifications making use of mixtures and combinations of stops to produce desired tonal effects.

The organ developed rapidly in France from the beginning of the fourteenth century. But in Italy, as late as the sixteenth century, the organs were still small.[23]

Several generations of the Antegnati family were important in Italian organ building: Bartolomeo Antegnati built organs for the cathedrals in Milan, Como, Cremona, and Mantua. His grandson, Gratiado, was a very capable artist, and in 1580 he replaced the organ at Brescia originally built by his grandfather. Gratiado's son, Costanzo, was a great builder, and also a performer and composer. He produced a work *L'Arte organica,* in 1608, at Brescia.

The Italian organ of this period was usually a one-manual organ with an octave of "pull-downs" for the pedals. It was on such an organ that Frescobaldi (1583-1643) played.

Constanzo Antegnati in his writing also indicated how to com-

---

[23]See Jeppesen, Knud. *Die italienische Orgelmusik am Anfang des Cinquecento.* Copenhagen: Munksgaard, 1943. See also, *The Organ,* Nos. 117, 119 "Notes on the Organ in Italy, by Shewring, Walter.

bine stops in order to achieve varying degrees of quality and brilliance. This was well over 250 years before Helmholtz.[24]

From Praetorius, similar information about the German organs
of the same period may be found.

Among the important organ builders of this period in Germany
were Compenius, Fritsche, and members of the Scherer family; in
France were Jousseline and François des Oliviers. During the
seventeenth century in France, there was a host of builders. Among
these was William Leslie, a Scot, who like others of his countrymen
escaped to France during the religious unrest at home. In France,
Leslie was known as Guillaume Lesselier.

A fine example of a representative northern baroque organ is
the one still in perfect condition, to be found in the chapel at the
Frederiksborg Castle in Denmark, near Copenhagen. It was built
in 1616.

The pedals in better organs of this period often controlled more
stops than the manuals; and synthetic tone building was available
to the pedals as well as to the manuals.

Carrying on in the great tradition of the Scherer family was
Arp Schnitger. He built the great organ at Hamburg in the St.
Jakobi church. This was the church to which Bach had unsuccessfully applied for the position as organist. It was the finest organ
upon which Bach ever played. To study the details of this organ's
specifications is to know something of what Bach had in mind,[25] in
his organ works.

Principal organists and composers from the latter sixteenth and
seventeenth centuries were:

Johann Christopher Bach, 1642-1703, Eisenach
Georg Bohm, 1661-1733 (contemporary with J. S. Bach), Lüneberg
Nikolaus Bruhns, 1665-1697, Lübeck
Dietrich Buxtehude, 1637-1707, Lübeck
Francois Couperin, 1631-1701, Paris

---

[24]Herman Helmholtz (1821-1894), German philosopher and scientist, was successively
professor at Königsberg, Bonn, Heidelberg, and Berlin. He wrote extensively on the
physical sciences. His best-known work was in the physics of sound and acoustics, reported in his *Sensations of Sound*.

[25]Details of construction in a long list of great organs are set forth in Sumner's book,
The Organ. While there are occasional unevennesses in Sumner's book, its assembling
of materials into a single complete volume is invaluable.

Jean François Dandrieu, 1682-1738 (contemporary with J. S.
Bach), Paris

Louis Claude Daquin, 1694-1772 (contemporary with J. S. Bach),
Paris

Johann Kasper Ferd. Fischer, b. c. 1665, d. 1746 (contemporary
with J. S. Bach), Rastatt

Girolamo Frescobaldi, 1583-1643, Rome

Johann Jakob Froberger, 1616-1667, Vienna

Nicholas Gigault, 1625-1707, Paris

Nicolas de Grigny, b. 1671, d. c. 1703, Paris

George F. Handel, 1685-1759 (contemporary of J. S. Bach),
London

Johann Kasper Kerll, 1627-1693, Munich

Vincent Lübeck, 1654-1740 (contemporary of J. S. Bach), Hamburg

Georg Muffat, 1645-1704, Passau

Johann Pachelbel, 1653-1706, Nuremberg, and Erfurt

Bernardo Pasquini, 1637-1710, Rome

Michael Praetorius, 1571-1621, Wolffenbüttel

André Raison, d. c. 1700, Paris

Johann Adam Reinken, 1623-1722, Hamburg

Heinrich Scheidemann, 1595-1663, Hamburg

Samuel Scheidt, 1587-1654, Halle

Jan Pieterzoon Sweelinck, 1562-1621, Amsterdam

Georg Phillip Telemann, 1681-1767 (contemporary with J. S.
Bach), Hamburg

Jean Titelouze, 1563-1633, Rouen

Franz Tunder, 1614-1667, Lübeck

Johann Gottfried Walther, 1684-1748 (contemporary with J. S.
Bach), Weimar

Matthias Weckman, 1619-1674, Hamburg

And of course,

Johann Sebastian Bach, 1685-1750, Eisenach, Weimar, Anhalt-
Cöthen, Leipzig

The beginning of the seventeenth century in Germany was
marked with great organ activity. The large cities of the Hanseatic
League had taken pride in their musical accomplishments and

were jealous of the quality and size of their organs and of the prowess of their organists. But with the onslaught of the Thirty Years' War, organ activity on any important scale ceased. In the second half of the century, activity resumed, but first, new organs had to be built where old ones had been destroyed. All of the old organs of course were in a poor state of repair.

As already indicated, an important name among organ builders of the latter half of the seventeenth century was that of Arp Schnitger. His organs represent the epitome of attainment in the "baroque organ." They were a logical fulfillment of the Praetorius tradition. Schnitger represented the Lutheran spirit at its best.

Schnitger was rivaled by the Silbermann brothers, and also to a lesser extent by Joachim Wagner. The Silbermanns were somewhat affected by the organ building of the South, of France, and other regions. Theirs were more sophisticated than Schnitger's organs, less wholesomely Germanic, perhaps. But the great organs of this latter half of the seventeenth century were the organs known by Johann Sebastian Bach. So far as is known, he had no contact with the organs of Wagner. Wagner began his work in 1720 which is also a date marking the beginning of decline in organ building and design in Germany. This was partly because of the influences from the South, where the purposes of the organs to satisfy religious feeling were somewhat different, perhaps as Sumner suggests, "less contemplative."

While after 1720 there was a decline in the acoustical qualities of the German organ, the kind Bach knew, the organs of this later period seemed greater in attractiveness and richness. However, the rococo and romantic influences of the period led the organ away from its central spiritual purpose, becoming something "sterile and soulless."

Mozart, Haydn, and Beethoven wrote for other media than the organ—for the opera, the symphony, and the chamber music ensemble.

To organists today it may seem a curious thing that the organs of Bach's time had no *swell*. However, the swell was not necessary for the baroque organ with its capability for pyramiding tone dynamics through mutations and mixtures of stops. The swell today is still precarious for rendition of the clear, contrapuntal designs of the music of Bach and other German composers of the period.

In this period it was the custom for new organ installations in the German churches to be tested by organ experts (experts as performers, acousticians, and often as builders). Examiners would be paid to come long distances to "test" a new organ. Bach was one of these who were in great demand.

As Sumner declares,[26] "It is a pity that many modern organs are not inspected by experts who are competent as builders, engineers and acousticians as well as organists."

In relation to the "austerity" of the German organ, two organs of importance in Spain, one at the monastery of Saint Bonaventura in Seville, 1721, and the other in the Cathedral of Seville, 1673, evidenced advances that were to have profound influence upon organ building in England.

The organ of the Cathedral at Seville (there were two organs in this great edifice) was of four manuals, the pipes for one being contained in a "swell box."[27] Additionally, 140 feet above the floor, an echo organ, also enclosed in a swell box was connected to the main organ by a system of "trackers" of 180 feet in length.

The reed and mixture quality of the pipes in the "swell" of this particular organ demonstrated that reed pipes are especially effective in a swell box.

It is of great interest to learn that a French organ builder, Cavaillé-Coll (1811-1899), of whom more will be said, had been inspired by the organs of Northern Spain upon which he had had opportunity to work when a boy. The organs throughout this region of Spain were influenced by the innovations of the organ in the Cathedral at Seville. The Cathedral organ was built in 1668-1673, by Antonio Padro Faleiro, a Portuguese, and later improved by Faustino Carvalho, in 1703. An English organ builder of the nineteenth century, Henry Willis, studied under Cavaillé-Coll, and then in the 1850's built great organs in England, possessing qualities not unlike those of the organ in the Cathedral at Seville.

The organs of the postbaroque period were inspired by the influence of the symphony orchestra in contrast to the German baroque organs which had had no tendencies toward the orchestral kind of development. Nor did the organ music of the baroque period, if it were to be rendered faithfully, lend itself readily to performance upon the postbaroque organ.

Thus, the swell box did not find ready acceptance among the German organ builders. This was because there was no need felt for swell box regulation of dynamics when the volume could be more faithfully regulated stopwise.

Certainly the German failure to adopt the swell box is not to be compared with the British failure to recognize the benefits and possibilities of the pedal organ.

THE ORGAN IN BRITAIN

References have already been made to St. Dunstan, an organ builder, and to St. Ethelwold, who as Abbot of Abingdon built an organ there in 955. It was he who became the Bishop of Winchester in 963. It was the large organ at Winchester which played an important part in the history of the instrument. There may have been other organs like the one at Winchester in tenth- and eleventh-century England but they could scarcely have been typical. Although there is no comprehensive information about organ development in England immediately following the eleventh century, it is pretty clear that the positive and the portative were more in the English mode.

There are good reasons for this. First, English cathedrals were not well adapted to the installation of large organs, and second, the musicians of the English church have traditionally felt greater appreciation for singing than for the music of large organs such as those in the cathedrals on the continent of Europe.

Also, through the centuries antipathies for instruments of music in worship were frequently encountered among particular groups. Among the English-speaking peoples, the opposition to musical instruments in religious service was very clear. This opposition, involved in the Puritan Revolt of the seventeenth century and finally brought to fulfillment under the protectorate of Oliver Cromwell, has had its effects upon religious thinking to this day, even in the

United States. Previously, the English had been pleased enough at the use of a small organ to accompany the psalms, singing, and other exercises of their worship.

In addition to the fact that with the English, the need for the organ was not felt to the extent it was on the Continent, the anti-Catholic feeling was increasing. After the Dissolution of the Monasteries, in 1536, those things that could be construed as association with Roman Catholicism came to be increasingly avoided. Thus, the use of organ in religious service, associated more and more in England with Catholicism was finally completely disallowed after the Puritan Revolt. With the establishment of Puritan control, anything in the Anglican church that seemed tainted with "popery" was purged.

Indeed, for a hundred years or more before the coming of the Commonwealth, especially during the reign of Elizabeth, the Puritans had been contending (most successfully in London and in Cambridge) for religious reform and the eradication of all elements in worship that did not have divine, scriptural, sanction. Because musical instruments had no such sanction, they were an "abomination unto the Lord," that is, in religious usage. Thus even before the Revolt, organs, when permitted at all, had usually been unobtrusive.

However, before and during the early sixteenth century, with feeling not yet running high, there was in England great interest in the organ. Organ building of small instruments for religious service was an important industry. Among the builders of the day there was John ("Father") Howe, the most notable builder in England at the opening of the sixteenth century. He died in 1571, and during his lifetime he built or renewed at least twenty-six organs. Before his death, however, he was reduced to straitened circumstances because organ building by now had come to a standstill, and many fine organs were being dismantled or destroyed. The metal in the pipes was usually sold for scrap.

The organ came into such disrepute that great organists and composers of music for the organ were forgotten. It is only recently that the work of men such as John Redford (1485-1545), organist at St. Paul's Cathedral, has been recognized as in some ways superior to that of such men as Byrd and Bull who lived a century

later and never of course wanted for recognition by their countrymen.

It is not to be concluded that the destroying of the organs and
the desecrating of hallowed shrines was altogether and merely the
work of a radical mob in the early days of Cromwell's regime. As
early as 1552 the organ in St. Paul's stood unused; it was restored
to use for only a short time under the reign of Mary. In 1536
the Lower House had listed organ playing as one of the 84 "Faults
and Abuses of Religion." And in 1550 it was decreed that two
organists in St. George's Chapel, Windsor, should continue to receive their salaries for life, "if they continue in the Colledge, in as
large and ample a manner as if organ playing had still continued
in the Church."

This is the time of John Marbeck (who is thought to perhaps
have been born in Windsor, about 1510, and to have died there
about 1585). Marbeck who distinguished himself as a church
musician, is best known for "The booke of Common Praier noted"
which is dated 1550.[28] In this year he also published a "Concordance of the Bible in English."

In 1563, under Elizabeth, a resolution before the Lower House,
calling for the taking of all organs from places of worship was lost
by only a single vote.

Some organs were allowed to stand, such as in St. Paul's;
Lincoln; Christ's College; and perhaps King's College, Cambridge.

In 1644 Parliament ordered the destruction of all organs, but
ten years later, the organ at Magdalen College was still there.
Gibbon, the famous musician, played on it at that time (according
to diary notes by John Evelyn on July 12, 1654). But later, this
organ was given to Cromwell and set up in Hampton Court. In
1660 it was returned to Oxford; and in 1737 it was installed in
Tewkesbury Abbey. Parts of this organ still remain.

It is interesting that in York Minster, in 1644, the religious exercises including service on the organ were going on apparently un-
disturbed. In *Musick's Monument,* 1676, Thomas Mace reports on
his impressions of the services there during the Civil War and the
siege of York:

---

[28]See the facsimile edition, edited by Eric Hunt, London: Society for the Promotion
of Christian Knowledge, 1939.

Now here you must take notice that they had then a Custom in that Church (which I hear not of in any other Cathedral, which was) that always before the Sermon, the whole Congregation sang a Psalm, together with the Quire and the Organ; And you must also know, that there was then a most Excellent—large—plump—lusty—full-speaking—Organ, which cost (as I am credibly informed) a Thousand Pounds. This Organ I say (when the Psalm was set before the Sermon) being let out, into all its Fulness of Stops, together with the Quire began the Psalm. But when That vast-concording-unity of the whole Congregational Chorus, came (as I may say) Thundering in, even so, as it made the very Ground shake under us: (oh, the unutterable ravishing Soul's delight!) in which I was so transported, and wrapt up into High contemplations that there was no room left in my whole man, viz., Body, Soul, and Spirit, for any thing below Divine and Heavenly Raptures.

The antiorgan feeling among the Puritans mostly pertained to religious usage. Milton owned an organ, Cromwell had a private organist, Hingston by name, in his employ.

The antiorgan feeling was of long standing in Scotland also. In 1633 the Church Session at Holyrood noted that the organ there stood in "the yle, idle, mothing and consuming." It was remarked that it might well be sold "for a tolerable price, and the money given into the poore."[29]

The organ was reintroduced for religious usage in Scotland in the Established Church in 1866; in the United Presbyterian Church, 1872; and in the Free Church, in 1883. (These dates have interesting implications in relation to the "Campbellian Restoration" in America.)

The musical unrest of the sixteenth and seventeenth centuries brought about changes in the lives of organists that were to have considerable effect upon the musical history of several other nations.

Thomas Dallam, born in 1570, built an automatic organ which he delivered to the Sultan, Mohamed III, for Queen Elizabeth, who was eager to secure allies in the Mediterranean area in order to be strong against the Catholic nations. Dallam's account of the fifteen-month trip is interesting.[30]

[29]Dalyell, Sir John Graham. *Musical Memoirs of Scotland.* Edinburgh: T. G. Stevenson, 1849, pp. 126, 129.
[30]See British Museum Additional Ms. 17,480.

Dallam had a son, Robert, also an organ builder, who moved to Brittany in France in 1642 to escape the organ depression of the Commonwealth. Thomas Dallam's only daughter married Thomas Harris to whom was born Renatus Harris, the great organ builder of England at the time when the monarchy was restored.

Later, in 1661, Robert Dallam who had gone to France, returned to England. But his two sons stayed in France where they continued to follow the occupation of organ building.

After the Restoration, there was a general increase in the use of organs, but men equipped to build and repair organs were scarce. Some, like the Dallams and the Harrises returned to England. Additionally, organ builders from other nations migrated to England. One of these, "Father" Bernard Smith, from Germany, distinguished himself as an organ builder in Restoration England. So also did Renatus Harris. There are interesting accounts of the rivalries and successes of "Father" Smith and Renatus Harris.

Father Smith was a member of a literary club which numbered among its members John Locke, John Evelyn, Isaac Newton, Christopher Wren, and others. He was an intimate acquaintance of John Blow and Henry Purcell. His successes were more spectacular than those of Renatus Harris. Smith died in 1710; Harris in 1724.

The details of a contest to win the bid for building the Temple organ is dramatic. Both Smith and Harris installed their organs in the Temple at great personal expense. When, after many, many months, it was decided that Smith's was the better, Harris had to move his. But he installed it eventually in St. Andrews, Holborn. Both these great organs were destroyed in 1940 by fires from the bombardment.

Some technical considerations in reference to the organs of this time may be helpful. It is common to speak of the choir organ. This term is misleading. Originally the term was "chair organ." It referred to what might be the equivalent of the "positive" on the continent. The chair organ was positioned in such a way, with its own manual, as to be readily performed upon by the organist who had only to turn about in his chair to reach the chair organ clavier. It is unfortunate that the chair organ has come to be connected with the notion of a choir. In the modern organ, of course, the choir (corrupted term) manual is before the performer along with all the other manuals, the "great," etc. The English word "chair" itself has interesting connotations including the idea of being a helper or servant. A charwoman is one who serves or helps in a particular kind of assignment. Whether the chair organ derives from its being a helper organ (as it actually was), or an organ that is nearby to the chair of the organist, is of course not clear. At any rate, as Sumner declares, there is no reference to *choir* in the term.

References to the use of a swell box by Spanish and French organ builders have already been made. As early as 1710 Renatus Harris was experimenting with swells in English organs. But he may have been antedated in actual production by another builder. In the *Spectator*, February 8, 1712, the following announcement appeared:

Whereas Messrs. Abraham Jordan have, with their own hands, joynery excepted, made and erected a very large organ in St. Magnus' Church, at the foot of London Bridge, consisting of four sets of keys, one of which is adapted to the art of emitting sounds by swelling the notes, which never was in any organ before; this instrument will be publicly opened on Sunday next, the performance by Mr. John Robinson. The above said Abraham Jordan gives notice to all masters and performers that he will attend every day next week at the said church to accommodate all those gentlemen who shall have the curiosity to hear it.

It has been noted that the pedals of the continental organs, especially those in Germany, were unknown to many of the English. It is remarkable that in 1712 Renatus Harris unsuccessfully endeavored to win a commission to build an organ in St. Paul's which would include six manuals—and a pedal clavier. Yet, more than 150 years later, when Holdich installed a pedal organ in Lichfield Cathedral, the organist, Spofforth, declared that he would not use the pedals.

It seems strange today that even in 1800, the English did not know the music of Bach; and that in 1844, Mendelssohn refused to play an organ concert at the Hanover Square Rooms because the organ did not have German pedals.[31]

---

[31]See footnote, p. 134.

THE ORGAN FROM THE EIGHTEENTH CENTURY

From the time of Bach, there have been developments in the organ, each peculiar to its own country, yet which have had effect upon organ building and organ playing in general.

Both the French and German organs reached their zenith in the eighteenth century. Toward the end of the century, after the death of Bach in 1750, great organs were built over all Europe, but the rise of orchestra and opera furnished new media for musicians' activity. This, coupled with the fact that organs did not inspire new modes of musical composition, helped lead to the decline in organ music although there was a passing revival of organ development beginning roughly in 1830.

This development, lasting only for about two decades, was marked by the fashioning of devices to operate the pallets on the pipes more easily under conditions of greatly increased air pressures to the pipes, and methods of connection to allow for separation of the consoles from the pipe chambers.

By the middle of the nineteenth century the romantic-symphonic music of the period soon brought about further decadence. The organ was recognized not as an instrument in itself, but rather as a mechanical orchestra (the description of the organ in Webster's *Dictionary*, indicates this); consequently, the resources of tonal changes peculiar to the organ were overlooked.

Actually, at the beginning of the nineteenth century, the great organs of Germany and Holland, such as the one at the Church of St. Baron, Haarlem, (completed by Christian Müller in 1738) were regarded only as monuments of past glory.

The organ was more and more being relegated to the functions of accompaniment in the churches. The great musical occasions of old no longer were furnished in the the churches, but rather in the concert hall and auditoriums through the agencies of the opera and the orchestra.

If it had not been for Mendelssohn, who was able both to compose vital music for organ and then to perform it along with the music of Bach, in concerts before the public throughout Germany and also in England, the history of the organ in the nineteenth century would have been inglorious.

This seems the more clear when one views the depths to which organ music fell in France. Many of the fine organs such as those built by Cliquot were repaired after the French Revolution and used in secular celebrations which took place in the churches, now known as "Temples of Reason." At Notre Dame, the organ was used to accompany paganlike orgies.

Even with the restoration of religious emphasis to the churches of France, the fine work such as outlined in *L'Art du facteur d'orgues* by Dom François Bedos in 1770 remained forgotten. Even the music that was performed on the organ for the Roman service was trivial. At the celebration of the eucharist, sarabandes, minuets, and romances, would be played.

Toward the end of the nineteenth century, French organ works by men such as César Franck, Widor, Vierne, and Guilmant evidenced the tendency for organ music once more to rise. It is true that the music of these men was not always appropriate to the organ. But Franck was sensitive to the qualities of the organ; and Guilmant, musician and scholar, through his research did point the way to a finer understanding of the significant work of the earlier French organ builder, François Henri Cliquot (1728-1790) who was in the tradition of the Silbermanns and Schnitger.

The nineteenth century is marked by the name of Aristide Cavaillé-Coll (1811-1899), son of a family of organ builders dating from at least as far back as 1700. Aristide and his father worked to make their organs more expressive. They devised couplers to connect the manuals more easily than before.

Later, the son, on recommendation of Rossini and of teachers at the University of Toulouse went to Paris where he underwent examinations by a leading engineer, Borel. Aristide passed these tests so brilliantly that opportunity to meet physicists and musicians was abundant. He had arrived in Paris in 1833 and made such an impression that within days he was asked to submit plans for an organ to be built for the church at St. Denis. Plans had already been submitted by four leading organ builders, Erard, Abbey, Callinet, and Dallery, and there were only three more days in which to submit plans.

The youthful Aristide Cavaillé-Coll submitted his plans on time. They were complete as to all computations, specifications, and placements; he was awarded the job—after being in Paris only ten days, and at the age of twenty-two.

Aristide at this time assumed the leadership of the organ building firm with the active support of his father and of his brother, Vincent. While building the large organ at St. Denis, the firm completed several smaller ones.

The work of Cavaillé-Coll was to affect music composition for the organ for decades. It was this instrument at St. Denis which was the starting point for the development of the French school of organ playing and composition in the symphonic style (already referred to in connection with Franck, Widor, Guilmant, and others).

Aristide found methods by which to use varied air pressures to fill the ever-varying needs of the divisions of his organs; he also made the couplers from pedals to manuals more easy of operation; and ingeniously employed mutation ranks of pipes to synthesize the orchestral colors.

At this same time, across the channel, a younger contemporary, Henry Willis was also at work developing the full swell of the English organ, so wonderfully demonstrated in the organ at St. Paul's of London. Willis had come under the influence of Cavaillé-Coll and thus incorporated in the organ which he built for the Royal Albert Hall in London, all the features of the "grand" and the "chorus" which he had discovered in Aristide's organ at St. Sulpice, in Paris. This organ, as well as many others by Cavaillé-Coll, such as the one in Notre Dame, are still much as he built them. It has already been mentioned that his work was part of the impetus for the school of composition produced by Franck (1822-1890); Dubois (1837-1924); Gigout (1844-1925); Guilmant (1837-1911); Saint-Saëns (1835-1921); and Widor (1845-1937). However, there are those who feel that Widor never understood the essence of Bach's organ works or of the baroque manner which was so well served by the organs of Arp Schnitger of northern Germany.

This is one of those debatable views that always arise at the point of contact between different schools. The purity and austerity of the German organ requiring technical proficiency of the highest order from the organ performer is, to many, the epitome of musical value. But in the views of the French and English schools, the absence of the *swell* in German usage is a great fault; also, the limitations in tonal variety to be found in the German organ. In turn, the German school would view the fancy stops, the solo stops, and the infinite variety of dramatic and sensational tonal and orchestral colors of the French organ (but lacking the sublimity and solidity of the German) as evidence of poor taste. The French school, of course, is partly the product of the Roman Catholic service in which the organ is an accompanying instrument.

The author has had contact with pupils of Widor and has also been one to feel that Schweitzer could do no wrong. Thus astonishment has arisen when he heard that some of Widor's pupils speak of the bad phrasing in Schweitzer's editing of the organ works of Bach.

ENGLAND

It will be well to recall that from the eleventh century on, in England, the organs had been more modest than those in France, Germany, Italy, or Holland. In the nineteenth century the two largest organs were those in St. Paul's and York Minster.

But a nineteenth-century revival in the Church of England and a growth in civic self-consciousness led to the building of new churches in the growing industrial districts and of new town halls and other public buildings. Needs for new organs and the repair and restoration of old ones grew. Books about how to play the organ sold readily—especially books such as those by Stainer (1840-1901) and Rinck (1770-1846).

Stainer, Henry Smart (1813-1879), George Cooper (1820-1876), and W. T. Best, famous for his performances in St. George's Hall, Liverpool, along with the founding of the College of Organists, were all products of this organ revival in England.

Still, the advance in interest and development of improved organ playing technique lacked musical depth and insight.

Of the fourteen organs exhibited in 1851 at the Crystal Palace in Hyde Park, there were one each from France, Germany, and Italy. Most of the organs exhibited were one- or two-manual instruments without pedals. The organs by Willis and the one by Schulze of Germany were the ones that came to influence the British organ for the rest of the century. The Willis organ had three manuals and seventy stops. The exhibiting of this organ, financed by patrons who loaned Willis the money, led to his being awarded the building of the organ at St. George's, Liverpool. It was for the organist's post here that Willis was influential in having W. T. Best appointed.

On this organ, Willis built a concave pedal clavier with the pedals radially arranged. He got the idea of concaveness from Schulze's organ and the idea of radial arrangement from Samuel Wesley (1810-1876)[32] who was with him when inspecting the German organ at the Crystal Palace.

Another organ builder, Robert Hope-Jones, extended intemperately the direction of tone synthesization which was initially pointed by Cavaillé-Coll. The innovations of Cavaillé-Coll had been from the beginning in danger of being placed in the hands of the musically irresponsible. The work of Robert Hope-Jones consequently had a real and very bad effect upon authentic organ playing.

It is to be remembered that the musical repertoires of English (and American) organists consisted largely of orchestral transcriptions. It had been only with the greatest persistence that the French Guilmant, scholarly musician and musicianly scholar, had been able to induce Cavaillé-Coll to not completely break with the tradition of Cliquot but to include mutation stops in his organs in order to make possible the production of distinctively organ tones for rendition of the great organ music.

The unfortunate developments by Hope-Jones led to theatre organ development such as those of Wurlitzer manufacture in the 1920's. Voices of protest were raised, and, among others, Lt. Col. George Dixon of St. Bees, England, who had studied Willis and Schulze, helped to advance authentic modern organ tone by his writings.

Schweitzer wrote[33] on the inadequacies of the nineteenth-century organ for playing the works of Bach.

---

[32]This is Samuel Sebastian Wesley, son of the great organist, Samuel Wesley and grandson of Charles Wesley; Samuel Sebastian was himself a distinguished organist and church composer.
[33]Schweitzer, Albert. *Duetsche und französiche Orgelbaukunst.*

Guilmant, in his work[34] of editing old French organ music, made available for the modern organ, the music of earlier times.

Pirro, the French musicologist, and others, have stimulated a revival of interest in the classical organ.

And in Germany, Walcker built an instrument at Recklinghausen in 1927, of eighty-eight stops in which he endeavored to incorporate the qualities of the Praetorius and Silbermann organs.

Thus in the latter nineteenth and early twentieth centuries, an improving of the organ and its music along more authentic lines in the light of history was taking place.

THE ORGAN IN THE NEW WORLD

In 1524 a school was founded in Mexico City by a theologian and musician, Padro de Gante. He, of course, made use of the liturgical music of the Roman Church. It is reported[35] that in 1527 he built an organ. There is no reason to doubt that this would be the first organ of the New World. Soon, many churches of Mexico had organs; "Indians" who had studied in the school were the players.

In New England, the settlers were, of course, given largely to the view of the Puritan Revolt in England. The planting of the English Colonies took place in the early seventeenth century during the time which reached fruition with the ordinances of Parliament in 1644. Thus the idea that organs should have no place in Christian worship was firmly transplanted from England to the Colonies.

Of interest is a story of an organ owned by Thomas Brattle (1656-1713), a Harvard graduate, and treasurer of the college from 1693 to his death. Brattle had ordered an organ for private use in his home. A quotation from Brattle's *will* leaving the organ to the Brattle Street Church is revealing:

. . . given and devoted to the praise and glory of God in the said church, if they shall accept thereof, and within a year produce a sober and discreet person that shall play skilfully thereon and make a loud noise; otherwise to the Church of England in this town, on the same terms and conditions; and on their non-acceptance or discontinuation to use it as

---

[34]Guilmant, Alex. *Archives*. Mainz: Schott, 1901.
[35]Braden, C. S. *Religious Aspects of the Conquest of Mexico*. Durham, North Carolina: 1930.

above, unto the College; and on their non-acceptance or discontinuance as before, I give the same to my nephew, Thomas Brattle.

However, not so much as a pitch pipe was acceptable in the Brattle Street Church, so the gift was refused. The King's Chapel accepted the organ and kept it until 1756. From there it went to St. Paul's Church, Newburyport, where it remained until 1830. It was brought and reconstructed by St. John's Church, Portsmouth, New Hampshire, in 1831, for use in a mission. It is still preserved.

The first organ to be *built* in the Colonies appears to be one erected by John Clemm in 1737 for Trinity Church. But twenty-five years later, it was replaced by an organ imported from England.

Numbers of organs installed in American churches were imported from England. Of special interest however is an organ built in 1754 by Thomas Johnson for St. Peter's Episcopal Church. This organ displaced the English importation which was given to St. Michael's Episcopal Church in Marblehead.

In 1790, the old Brattle Street Church in Boston capitulated to the organ party being the first Independent Church in America to admit an organ. So great was the opposition, however, that when the vessel containing the organ arrived below in the harbour, a wealthy gentleman of the parish, who had refused to subscribe towards it, offered to pay into the treasury of the church, for the benefit of the poor, the whole cost of the organ and freight, if it might be thrown overboard below the lighthouse.[36]

The minister, Dr. Thatcher, refused however to be bought off.

In the United States, there has long been an interest in organ playing, even among those church people who do not favor its use "in worship."

Raynor Taylor,[37] came to Baltimore in 1792 where he became known for his organ improvisations. Andrew Law, also referred to in other connections,[38] wrote a book in 1809 on the *Art of Playing the Organ*. Many organists from England, Germany, and other European countries came to the United States to make their homes.

George W. Morgan (1822-1892) was from Gloucester, England. He was America's first concert organist and became famous for his performance on the Tremont Temple organ of Boston. This large

[36]Sumner Salter, "Early Organs in America," *Musical Opinion*. May, 1892.
[37]See p. 233.
[38]See pp. 220, 249, 250.

organ by Hook and Hastings, American builders, possessed four manuals and seventy speaking stops. Representative works of Bach were played on it perhaps for the first time in the United States.

Perhaps no single instance better illustrates the effects of a social point of view of music than the story of the large Walcker organ in Boston's Music Hall.

This organ, a most excellent one, built over a period of at least five years by the German, E. F. Walcker of Ludwigsburg, and then shipped to America created much interest in the United States. Such organ notables as J. Knowles Paine played upon it.

It had been thoroughly tested by the German builders before it was disassembled and shipped to Boston. After many months required to reassemble it, it was first played upon for a private occasion before the committee which had commissioned it, by George W. Morgan. He performed on it, Rossini's *Overture to William Tell*.

This great organ remained popular from 1863 for little more than twenty years. The growing popularity of the Boston Orchestra founded in 1881 regimented against the organ which, after all, seldom had had great organ music as such played upon it. It had been, and still is to too great a degree a custom in America to play orchestral transcriptions arranged for organ, rather than organ music written for organ.

At any rate, this organ originally costing $60,000 was sold in 1884 for $5000 and in 1887 again sold for $1500. Today it is still in the possession of the Aeolian-Skinner Co. in the Methuen Hall where it is played in concerts.

It is interesting that this great organ of German manufacture has had important influence upon American organ building firms such as the Hutchings and Roosevelt, and Hook and Hastings companies. The German organs, it is to be remembered, gave distinctive development to the instrument throughout history. It would have been a different development in America if this large organ had been of English or French manufacture.

While many European influences came to bear on United States organ building such as that of Moller from Denmark, for one instance, the influence of this German organ helped toward the appreciation in the United States of the glories of European organ music. As a result, men such as Holtkamp of Cleveland, Ohio, brought about a considerable relivening of interest in the baroque organ.

Even during a period when perhaps more applications of American ingenuity were being made to improving electric mechanization of the console than to perfecting the acoustic and musical capabilities of the tonal parts of the organ, the interest in the baroque organ, partly through the musicological researches in the United States universities, led to the advances achieved by such men as G. Donald Harrison, an Englishman, formerly a Director of the Willis Company and later, artistic director of the Aeolian-Skinner Company. The Tabernacle organ at Salt Lake City is a Harrison organ.

The largest organ in the world is said to be the one in the Convention Hall at Atlantic City. It occupies eight large spaces in six different locations of the Hall which is capable of seating 41,000 people. The organ utilizes two electric consoles, one of which can be moved about. The one console has seven manuals, the other, five. The organ was designed by Senator Emerson Richards who had made a thorough study of the tonal structures of the fine organs of Europe. The organ was built by Midmer-Losh, Inc. of Long Island. The voicing of this organ was done by Henry Willis, grandson of the famous "Father Willis" of England.

THE ORGAN TODAY

Interest in reestablishing and strengthening the great traditions of the organs of history is high.

A new development has also presented itself: the electric, or electronic, synthetic organ. No doubt this new instrument will be greatly improved. But as yet, it cannot duplicate the fineness and richness and subtleties of tone that can be produced from the pipes of a great organ. Whether this can ever be done will be learned in the future.

In the meantime, the electric, synthetic organ might better be considered a new instrument in itself, and not as a substitute for great pipe organs.[39]

[39]For a description of several electronic or synthetic organs, see William H. Barnes. *The Contemporary American Organ.* New York: J. Fischer and Bro., 1952.

CHAPTER SIX

RELIGIOUS MUSIC IN THE UNITED STATES OF AMERICA

SPANISH BACKGROUND

Religious music in the United States is mostly rooted in the music of Europe. The kinds of music from the Old World, differing according to their Old World moorings and appearing as a kind of patchwork in the New World, began to lose some of their distinguishing marks as the Old World provincialisms were, in the new land, brought into dynamic contact with one another in totally new ways.

The Spanish migrations which occurred after Columbus' discoveries, were during the period of Spain's most glorious economic and artistic achievements. In the sixteenth century the music of the Royal Chapel of Madrid, or of the establishment at Valencia maintained by the Duke of Calabria, or of the Cathedrals at Seville and Toledo, was on a par with any in Europe. Cristóbal Morales, to name one Spanish composer, was as noteworthy as most of the distinguished composers to be found elsewhere on the continent.

In 1524, some few years after Cortéz had come to Mexico, a Father Pedro de Gante established at Texcoco a music school for the training of the natives; three years later, he founded another school in Mexico City where he worked until his death in 1572. Later, other church musicians came from Europe to Mexico City

211

and Lima, thus keeping these places abreast with European developments in music.

In 1556 *The Ordinary of the Mass,* perhaps the first book to be printed in the New World, was produced at Mexico City. Nearly thirty years later, in 1583, a collection of Christian psalms and hymns, known as *Psalmodia Christiana,* was translated into Aztec by Bernardino de Sahagún. By 1604 a number of works had been published in the Spanish colonies, among which were four Passion narratives by the Spanish composer Juan Navarro, published by Diego López Davalos.

An interesting kind of folk music called *alabados,* that is, "Songs of Praise," sprang up in the regions of the New World under Spanish influence. In these songs, translated into the several Indian tongues, the basic tenets of the Roman Catholic faith were set forth.

Also, in addition to the *alabados,* there were religious pageants. One of these, the *Comedia de Adan y Eva,* was performed in 1532 at Mexico City.

Perhaps of greatest importance, so far as future effects on the United States (as yet nonexistent) are concerned, was the establishment of the Franciscan Missions in California by Junípero Serra. The first of the twenty-one California Missions was founded by him at San Diego in 1769. Junípero Serra was also a sensitive musician; he placed emphasis on the plainsong as well as other religious tunes which were subsequently taught to the Indians. Representative of the music of this period is a four-part *Misa de Catluñ* by Padre Narciso Durán (1776-1846) who, in the Mission of San José, in 1813, compiled in manuscript the most complete Mission Music Collection.

After Mexico, in 1822, won its independence from Spain, the support of the missions by the home country was disastrously curtailed, and the conditions worsened in 1834 when the missions under the territorial government were secularized. Now, all the properties of the missions, such as lands, furnishings, and art objects, were taken from their control, often damaged, or lost, by the new and tragically unappreciative authorities. By the time these properties were returned to the missions in 1855 after California came under control by the United States, irreparable losses had been sustained.

However, the influence of Padre Durán was felt long after his death. Robert Louis Stevenson in "Monterey" shows something of the worth of the musical efforts of Padre Durán and his colleagues in the Missions:

Only one day in the year, the day before our Guy Fawkes [November 4]; the *padre* drives over the hill from Monterey; the little sacristy, which is the only covered portion of the church, is filled with seats and decorated for the service; the Indians troop together, their bright dresses contrasting with their dark and melancholy faces; and there, among a crowd of somewhat unsympathetic holiday makers, you may hear God served with perhaps more touching circumstances than in any other temple under heaven. An Indian, stone blind and about eighty years of age, conducts the singing; other Indians compose the choir; yet they have the Gregorian music at their finger ends, and pronounce the Latin so correctly that I could follow the meaning as they sang. The pronunciation was odd and nasal, the singing hurried and staccato. " In saecula saeculo-ho-horum," they went, with a vigorous aspirate to every additional syllable. I have never seen faces more vividly lit up with joy than the faces of these Indian singers. It was to them not only the worship of God, nor an act by which they recalled and commemorated better days, but was besides an exercise of culture, where all they knew of arts and letters was united and expressed. And it made a man's heart sorry for the good fathers of yore, who had taught them to dig and to reap, and to read and to sing, who had given them European mass-books which they will still preserve and study in their cottages, and who had now passed away from all authority and influence in that land—to be succeeded by greedy land-thieves and sacrilegious pistol-shots.[1]

COLONIAL DAYS

In the North American Puritan and Pilgrim colonies, the music was even more crude and less refined than the music of Puritan England. It was about 1640 that the *Bay Psalm Book,*[2] containing no music notation, was compiled for the use of the colonial New

---

[1]Published originally as "the Old Pacific Capital," *Fraser's Magazine,* November, 1880.
[2]John Eliot, "Apostle to the Indians," who had helped in preparing the *Bay Psalm Book,* prepared the texts metrically in 1661, for use in the Algonquin tongue. This was included with his Indian Bible. Thus, as in Florida and California, the love for Psalm singing by the Indians was again demonstrated. In 1687 Increase Mather reported that "the whole congregation of Indians praise God with singing."

Englanders. This book was the first of any kind to be published in the English colonies of North America; and by 1762 it had gone through twenty-seven editions in America, and twenty in England. Interest for *new* tunes to be used for the Psalms of this book was dormant. The worshipers sang the words to the tunes as they remembered them, handed down from generation to generation. If "Old Hundredth" *(Doxology)* was sung by one hundred assembled people, there would sound at once, it has been said, virtually one hundred different tunes.

It is to be remembered that the Pilgrims who came to Plymouth in 1620 (and who should not be confused with the Puritans) had brought with them the *Ainsworth Psalter* published in Amsterdam in 1612. This book differed from the *Bay Psalm Book* that followed in that it included tunes learned from the Dutch while the Pilgrims had lived in Holland (actually nineteen of the thirty-nine tunes were Dutch). The "Ainsworth," used in the New World until 1692 (without the "lining out" by the precentor) was further distinguished in that it supported a much higher standard of music than obtained elsewhere in the English colonies. The "old" Sternhold and Hopkins *Psalter* of England had been brought to the New World by Sir Francis Drake, and also, in 1607, by the Jamestown settlers who used it with the musical settings of Thomas Este, compiled in 1592 (in the time of Palestrina).

The Massachusetts Bay Colony, established in 1628, used the *Ravenscroft* tune book[3] which had been published in 1621.

To even the most conservative church musician today, the attitude of the Puritans toward church music is unbelievably limited. The metrical versifications of the Psalms were sung to a very limited number of designated tunes. It is reported that some believed it sacrilegious even to practice the tunes or speak the texts. Sometimes the tunes were practiced but with words other than the Psalm texts. Some regarded the tunes so sacred that whenever they were heard, and under whatever circumstances, the auditors would stand, assuming a most dignified and reverent demeanor, the men with hats removed.

---

[3]William Paul Stroud, *The Ravenscroft Psalter (1621): The Tunes, with a Background on Thomas Ravenscroft and Psalm Singing in His Time.* (A dissertation for the Doctor of Musical Art degree). Los Angeles: The University of Southern California, 1959. This is an interesting and profitable study.

An old manuscript of 1647 by the Reverend John Cotton is interesting because it reflects an attitude toward singing and some of the problems of those days:

Singing of Psalmes a Gospel Ordinance; or a Treatise wherein are handled these foure particulars:

1. Touching the duty it selfe.
   . . . Singing of Psalmes with a lively voyce, is an holy Duty of God's Worship now in the dayes of the New Testament.
2. Touching the Matter to be Sung.
   . . . We hold and believe:
   1. That not only the Psalmes of David, but any other spirituall Songs recorded in Scripture, may lawfully be sung in Christian Churches. . . .
   2. We grant also, that any private Christian, who hath a gift to frame a spirituall Song, may both frame it, and sing it privately. . . . Nor do we forbid the private use of an Instrument of Musick therewithall.
      Neither doe we deny but that in the publique thanksgivings of the Church, if the Lord should furnish any of the members of the Church with a spirituall gift to compose a Psalme upon any speciall occasion, he may lawfully be allowed to sing it before the Church, and the rest hearing it, and approving it, may goe along with him in Spirit, and say Amen to it.
3. Touching the Singers.
   1. Whether one be to sing for all, the rest joyning onely in Spirit, and saying, Amen; or the whole congregation?
   2. Whether women, as well as men; or men alone?
   3. Whether carnall men and Pagans may be permitted to sing with us, or Christians alone, and Church members?
4. Touching the Manner of Singing.
   . . . It will be a necessary helpe, that the wordes of the Psalme be openly read before hand, line after line, or two lines together, so that they who want either books or skill to reade, may know what is to be sung, and joyne with the rest in the dutie of singing.

By the time of the American Revolution the practice of "lining out" the psalms was beginning to disappear. John Cotton in his pamphlet had pointed out that where all "have bookes and can reade, or else can say the Psalmes by heart," there would be no need for reading each line. Of course it is doubtful if the Plymouth colonists (Pilgrims) had ever made use of "lining out." Deacons who could sing a proper tone of correct pitch and who could musically intone the words line by line preceding the congregation's following in echo were scarce. Thus there was ever-increasing willingness to permit the use of choirs to improve the musical services—but not without occasional pitiable struggle. The record indicates that in 1779, the town of Worcester, having its peculiar concern with music, voted:

That the singers sit in the front seats in the gallery, and that those gentlemen who have hitherto sat in the front seats in the gallery have a right to sit in the front and second seat below, and that said singers have said seat appropriated to said use. Voted, that said singers be requested to take said seats and carry on the singing in public worship. Voted, that the mode of singing in the congregation here, be without reading the psalms line by line to be sung.

The Sabbath succeeding the adoption of these votes, after the hymn had been read by the minister, the aged and venerable Deacon Chamberlain, unwilling to desert the custom of his fathers, rose and read the first line according to the usual practice. The singers, prepared to carry the alteration into effect, proceeded without pausing at the conclusion. The white-haired officer of the church, with the full power of his voice read on, until the lower notes of the collected body overpowered the attempt to resist the progress of improvement, and the deacon, deeply mortified at the triumph of musical reformation, seized his hat, and retired from the meeting house in tears. His conduct was censured by the church, and he was for a time deprived of its communion, for absenting himself from the public services of the Sabbath.[4]

Of interest is the restraint of the First Presbyterian Church of Mendham, New Jersey, where, in 1791, it was voted "to sing half the time without reading."

The results of restrictions of musical usage by the churches, such as allowing the singing only of metrical Psalm tunes were not only limiting but perhaps psychologically damaging. Interest in producing new music was further stifled by the awareness that there were already a sufficient number of tunes for the singing of the metrical Psalm text arrangements. Because Puritan Psalmody was dependent upon oral tradition, and the music itself was pro-

[4]George Hood, *A History of Music in New England*, Boston: Wilkins, Carter and Co., 1846, pp. 183-184.

duced by those of the most meagre musical sensitivity, the Psalm tune repertoire dwindled continuously so that by the early eighteenth century the congregations could sing only a small proportion of what congregations a hundred years earlier had been able to do.

It is to be noted that this deteriorating musical situation was not peculiar to the American Colonies; it was characteristic also of the same kinds of religious groups in England, Scotland, and elsewhere. The paucity of musical expression in all these similar church constituencies was the result of a religious philosophy. While the philosophy had many redeeming qualities, musically, it was very damaging—not only to the cause of music, but to the quality of religious faith for generations to come. And, of course, this delimiting of musical expression, however often it was claimed to be in accord with the effort to emulate apostolic musical practice, actually had very little in common with church musical practice of the apostolic period.

Musical expression is not a pastime that can be engaged in or discontinued, like overeating. Musical exercise, like any kind of artistic comunication, is a serious human outlet for expression and fulfillment. Musical expression is one of the potentials that distinguishes the human being from his resemblances in the animal world. The limited musical fare of the Puritans may have been sufficient for those in their group who were tongue-tied, dumbfounded, and esthetically unaware—but for the rest of their number, it must have left a painful void, midst a vegetablelike mentality which stultified sensitivity and thus made the religious feelings partial, inadequate, and distorted, preventing, more than necessary, the development of *whole* spiritual beings—for this to happen among the religiously consecrated is of course only tragedy.

George Hood reports the struggle which lasted into the eighteenth century over whether Christians should learn to sing their music correctly and whether they should learn to read notes. He tells that even well-informed persons of the colonists' days raised objections to such kinds of musical advancement. The objections seem trifling today, but they were serious and important to the early settlers. Reading music and singing correctly were nearly as devilish as witchcraft. The usual Puritan objections as indicated below are to be found, approximately as given, in many writings of the period:

1. That it was a new way; an unknown tongue.
2. That it was not so melodious as the usual way.
3. That there were so many tunes, one could never learn them.
4. That the new way made disturbances in churches, grieved good men, exasperated them and caused them to behave disorderly.
5. That it was Quakerish and popish and introductive of instrumental music.
6. That it was a needless way, forbears getting to Heaven without it.
7. That the names of the notes were bawdy, yea blasphemous.
8. That it was a contrivance to get money.
9. That it was only young upstarts, some of them lewd and loose persons who fall in with this way.
10. That it required too much time to learn it, made the young disorderly, and kept them from the proper influence of the family. . . .

The controversies such as indicated above were taking place in the early eighteenth century. They were generated by the fears which some church leaders felt because of the successful efforts at establishing "regular singing," that is, singing "by note." In a pamphlet of 1720, *Utile Dulci; or Joco-Serious Dialogue,* concerning "Regular Singing," a Reverend Thomas Symmes treated on the objections in a satirical manner purposed to destroy the opposition with ridicule:

". . . if the Papists sing a better Tune, or with a better Air, than we do, I'd as soon imitate them . . . the Quakers don't Sing at all, and I should be out of the noise . . . ; the Papists sing much better . . . such as are not willing to be at the Cost of a Bell, to call the People together, . . . will never be so extravagant as to buy Organs, and pay an artist for playing on 'em."

In the early eighteenth century two interesting writings appeared. One, by John Tufts, in 1712, was entitled, *A very plain and easy introduction to the whole Art of Singing of Psalm Tunes.* Some have wondered if this work was suggested by Thomas Morley's *Plaine and Easie Introduction* of 1597. It is believed that Tufts' was the first book of music instruction to be published in the colonies. The other work was a book by Thomas Walter of Roxbury, Massachusetts, *The Grounds and Rules of Musick explained.* This book was published in Boston in 1721 at James Franklin's Printing Press, where, at this very time, Benjamin Franklin was an apprentice.

An increased number of Psalm tunes was available in the eighteenth century, leading to an increase in the number of song books available to the churches. Isaac Watts' *Hymns and Psalms of David Imitated* was well known to the more advanced churches. Watts kept in touch with the colonies, carrying on regular correspondence with different religious leaders, such as Cotton Mather. Benjamin Franklin published Watts' *Psalms* in 1729. Although this work turned out to be slow of acceptance, it seems clear that by 1740 it had caught the interest of the American colonists.

In 1735, representing the Church of England, John and Charles Wesley came to Georgia. Having met some Moravian followers while on ship, they brought with them to Georgia the Moravian Count Zinzendorf's *Gesang-Buch der Gemeine in Herrnhut* which their new acquaintances had given to them. The Wesleys also had with them some hymnals of Watts. The first in a long series of hymnals was published by John Wesley during his three-year stay in Georgia, through the printing services of Lewis Timothy. And for this publication, Wesley was brought before the Grand Jury of Savannah for introducing unauthorized and uninspected compositions of the Psalms and hymns into the church "and service at the altar."

Under Jonathan Edwards (1703-1758), the Great Awakening in religious thought occurred in the colonies. The evangelism of George Whitefield and others followed; and the introducing of choirs and improved singing was a consequence of this new religious vitality. Thus new songbooks were needed. The first of the improved books for musical service was one published in Philadelphia in 1762 by James Lyon. He included some half dozen songs of his own in this new compilation entitled: *Urania: or A Choice Collection of Psalm-Tunes, Anthems, and Hymns, from the most approved authors.* . . . A year later, Francis Hopkinson brought out a *Collection of Hymn Tunes.* At the turn of the century, a considerable number of such collections had been published in the seaboard cities of the colonies.

During the eighteenth century, the increasing ferment in the religious life, evidenced partly by changes in the musical usage of the churches, gave rise to the singing school. The singing school came into being in order to improve the singing in the churches. From the diary accounts of Samuel Sewall[5] it is known that as early as 1721 there was a singing school in Boston; and that in 1741 the Moravian Brethren had established schools in Bethlehem, Pennsylvania. By 1750 there were schools not only in the large cities such as Boston, New York, and Philadelphia, but in many other places. The early singing schools were merely regular group meetings, usually in the evening, where the assembly studied choral singing and the rudiments of music. The *sol-fa* syllables were used as the basis of instruction.

The singing school carried on well into the latter nineteenth century, although toward the end, the original characteristics of the school were largely lost. The Worcester Musical Convention, started in 1858, was an outcropping of the earlier singing school. After the *War Between the States* there arose a later development of the singing school, the "community festival." By 1876 most characteristics of the singing school were lost although, of course, even today there are places where church singing schools are supported.

Out of the early singing schools are to be traced at least two important developments: (1) the enormous popularity of the oratorio society, especially in New England; and (2) the rise of music teaching in the public schools. The church singing school is generally considered to be the real beginning of music education in the United States.[6]

Some of the early music leaders, also mentioned elsewhere, were Andrew Adgate, Francis Hopkinson, James Lyon, and William Billings. Andrew Adgate (d. 1793) was active in Philadelphia with a school which later, in 1787, was organized as the Uranian Academy. Andrew Law (1748-1821) taught extensively along the Atlantic seaboard from Connecticut to Maryland. He helped in the devising of a "shaped note" system for indicating the *sol-fa* syllables. He also supported the placing of the melody of the

[5]Judge Sewall, b. England, 1652, migrated to New World in childhood; B. A., Harvard, 1671; M. A., 1674; d. Boston, 1730.

[6]For a detailed report on the rise of the singing schools, Nathaniel Duren Gould's *Church Music in America* (Boston: A. N. Johnson, 1853) is valuable.

church songs in the soprano. They had customarily been placed previously in the tenor, for the men to sing; it must not be forgotten that it was believed "the women should keep silence in the church." Andrew Law's *Art of Playing the Organ* (1809) which was reprinted in 1819 is of interest.

Another early musician, Daniel Read (1757-1836), also active in New Haven and Connecticut, is known for the American musical phenomenon, the "fuguin' tune." The fuguing tune, a musical form of early New England colonial days, was descended from the Elizabethan polyphonic motets which were still popular when the colonists left for the New World. It has been thought by some that the motets were remembered from the English Cathedral services by the Virginia and Maryland colonists. But there is another source from which the tunes may also be descended: Goudimel's motet settings of tunes in the French *Psalter*. The Scottish *Psalter* was of course influenced by the contents of the French *Psalter*. In the Scottish *Psalter,* 1625, there is an interesting tune, *Bon Accord,* different from the usual four-voice harmonizations in that it is in the form of an imitative setting. In 1635 the new *Psalter* contained a number of such tunes "in Reports"— a descriptive term derived perhaps from the French *rapporter* meaning to carry back.

The name of William Billings is often connected with the fuguing tunes. He has even been credited as the inventor of them; but this is incorrect. Many of his so-called fuguing tunes were really anthems; and it should also be noted that among the fuguing tunes of the day, his were not always the most popular. The well-known *Adeste Fidelis* in some ways may be said to resemble the structure of the fuguing tune. In this song, the first "O come, let us adore him," should be sung only by the treble voices, the tenors joining in on the repeat of this phrase, all voices singing the phrase together, the third time.

Lyons' *Urania* and William Tans'ur's *Royal Melody* are the earliest American printings of the fuguing tunes. Tans'ur's work, which ran to many editions, is interesting. It was first published in England in 1734 and known as *The Compleat Melody, or Harmony of Zion.* It was again published in 1755 as *The Royal Melody*

Compleat. An edition of it was published in Boston in 1767 by W. M'Alpine.

In 1764 Daniel Bayley (1729-1792), a potter, and organist at St. Paul's Church in Newburyport, Massachusetts, published *A New and Compleat Introduction to the Grounds and Rules of Musick in 2 Books.* In this work Bayley included extracts from William Tans'ur's *Royal Melody.*

Bayley's issue of the first book, released in 1764, contained three fuguing tunes, *St. Luke's,* in four voices, *St. Martin's* and a *Morning Hymn,* in three.

Oliver Holden's *Coronation,* elsewhere mentioned as the oldest American tune still sung generally, was first published in Boston in 1793. Originally, it was intended in this song that the "Bring forth the Royal diadem" would be sung by the male voices alone, to be followed by all voices in the words, "And crown him Lord of all."

Coronation. C. M.
Original.[7]

Edward Perronet
1779-80

Oliver Holden
1792

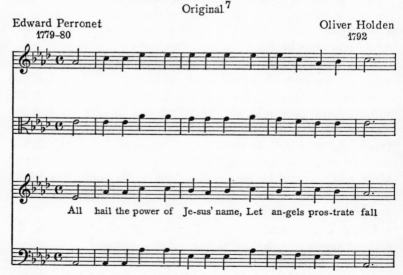

All   hail the power of Je-sus' name, Let an-gels pros-trate fall

---

[7]This is the original arrangement; it appeared in *Union Harmony.* Boston: Isaiah Thomas and Ebenezer, 1793.

Bring forth the roy-al di - a - dem,

And crown Him Lord of

all, Bring forth the roy - al di - a - dem, and

crown Him Lord of all.

223

Fuguing tunes are still used in various regions of the country. They have always been popular in the South. They are to be found in Ely's *Baltimore Collection of Church Music* (1792); William Walker's shaped notes editions of *Southern Harmony* (1835-1854), and Benjamin Franklin White's *Sacred Harp,* including editions still used today. In Boston, in 1916, there were included in the *Golden Sheaf, No. 2,* published by the Advent Christian Publication Society, along with Jeremiah Ingall's *New Jerusalem,* which had been a great nineteenth-century favorite, three other of these peculiarly American "fuguin' tunes."

Another development in eighteenth-century American music was the rise of interest in instrumental music. While this did not at first introduce itself into the churches, it did lead to the use of the pitch pipe in the churches. Eventually, because the bass viol, along with the pitch pipe, were often used in the singing schools, these were introduced into the services of some churches which were immediately recognized as "catgut churches." Because the violin was regarded as an instrument of wicked connections with debauchery, the bass viol, recognized as useful in the singing schools, was known as the "Lord's fiddle." It is reported that it was a custom in some churches to have the bass viol (more likely a 'cello) play the tune before the singing by the congregation or choir. Also, between stanzas, the viol (or 'cello) would play an interlude to provide added grace for the musical service.

In addition to the English settlements, there also sprang up Dutch, German, and Swedish colonies in the vicinity of Philadelphia. As already indicated, many of the Moravian Brethren settled in Bethlehem, Pennsylvania. Their tradition apparently was little affected by the decline in musical virility of the German Lutheran Reformation, for they were noted especially for their good singing which they accompanied with the instruments that they had brought with them. To this day, the community of Bethlehem has a remarkable reputation for its festival of religious song, which people from long distances come to hear.

The influence that came from such religious groups as the Huguenots should not be overlooked. As we already have seen, throughout Protestant Europe during the sixteenth century, except among the Bohemian and Lutheran reformers, singing of metrical arrangements of the Psalms was the only musical exercise permitted in the Protestant churches.

The *Genevan Psalter* already spoken of in other connections reached the shores of the New World even before the old Sternhold and Hopkins book which many feel had to be the one that Sir Francis Drake carried with him on his travels around the world. Francis Fletcher was the chaplain with Drake and he wrote of Drake's putting up for repairs in 1579 just north of what is now San Francisco. In this writing Fletcher also reported on the visits from the Indians who enjoyed the Psalm singing by Drake's men. But it was seventeen years earlier, in 1562, that the earliest Huguenot expeditions reached Florida. Later Huguenot expeditions were settled along the Atlantic seaboard from South Carolina to Massachusetts. The Huguenots of course used the *Genevan Psalter*. In 1566 it was translated into Dutch by Peter Datheen and soon became the official adoption of the Reformed Church. Thus it was that in 1628 the French and Dutch who were settled together in New Amsterdam could sing together, each in his own language, but from the *Genevan Psalter*. The first church of this mixed colonization was the Reformed Protestant Dutch Church. In it the Datheen Psalter was used until Francis Hopkinson in 1767 was appointed to make an English translation of the old texts but in a manner to be set still to the traditional tunes.

It is of interest that a group of Dutch "seceders" took these tunes with them to new settlements in Michigan under the leadership of A. C. Van Raalte. The tunes are still used there in the "Christian Reformed Churches."

There is also a report of a minister, Andreas Sandel, of a non-Puritan background, who, manifesting characteristic serious interest in musical enterprise, imposed a fine of six shillings on certain members of his congregation for "untimely singing." And an excerpt from a letter written by Justus Falckner, minister of the "Old Swedes" Church in Philadelphia, to Heinrich Muhlen of Holstein, indicates the attitude toward music that existed among colonists other than New Englanders. In this letter, Falckner was asking for aid for his church:

. . . I will take occasion to mention that many others besides myself, who know the ways of the land, maintain that music would contribute much towards a good Christian service. It would not only attract and civilize the wild Indians, but it would do much good in spreading the Gospel truths among the sects and others by attracting them. Instrumental music is especially serviceable here. Thus a well-sounding organ would perhaps prove of great profit, to say nothing of the fact that the Indians would come running from far and near to listen to such unknown melody, and upon that account might become willing to accept our language and teaching, and remain with people who had such agreeable things; for they are said to come ever so far to listen to one who plays even a reed-pipe: such an extraordinary love have they for any melodious and ringing sound. Now as the melancholy, saturnine, stingy Quaker spirit has abolished all such music, it would indeed be a novelty here, and tend to attract many of the young people away from the Quakers and sects to attend services where such music was found, even against the wishes of their parents. This would afford a good opportunity to show them the truth and their error.

It should be noted that the German, Dutch, and Swedish settlers had their struggles with the Quakers, who were opposed to any kind of music. To the Quakers, games, recreation, dramatic plays, lotteries, music, and dancing, were all classed alike, and the members were taught not to attend or to participate in any affair where such diversion was offered. The Presbyterians, the Quakers, and the Puritans, who represented the ascetic groups, were opposed not only by the colonists from continental Europe but also by the Church of England. Thus, there arose uniquely in the new world a mixing of the various religious attitudes and systems which would have been very unlikely in Europe and England. This would seem to have given high hope that a synthesis in America would be achieved which could give to the world an authentic Christianity unadulterated with secularism or sectarianism. Actually, this hope has been slow of realization, although the nineteenth-century religious revival (which included the Campbellian-Stone Restoration) made important impacts on religious culture in the United States. And today the great spirit of ecumenicity seems to be sweeping the land.

QUAKER, MENNONITE, MORAVIAN, AND OTHER INFLUENCES

Pennsylvania as a Quaker stronghold gave a refuge to many peoples of central Europe who left there because of persecution in their homeland or for the sake of conscience. These peoples have had a great influence, as it now turns out, not only on Pennsylvania settlements, but upon all the colonies of the New World.

There was the first little band of fifteen Mennonite families which came to Germantown in 1683. Then in 1684, there came from Friesland a group of Labadists who settled in New Castle County. In 1694 Johannes Kelpius came with a group of Pietists known as the Mystics. These Mystics (or "Hermits") settled in what is now the Roxborough section of Philadelphia.[8]

Like the Quakers, the Mennonites and the Dunkards opposed both instrumental and vocal music as commonly encountered in the churches of their time. The Mennonites did permit the singing of a limited number of conservative hymns and, more recently, Mennonite hymnody has become important.

The Kelpius group supported a kind of musical service that was of great interest to many other peoples in their region even though of different creed and nationalities. This group furnished the performers, both choir and instrumentalists, for the ordination of Justus Falckner in 1703, in the *Gloria Dei* or Old Swedes' Church, which still stands on the waterfront in Philadelphia. It was established in 1700. Until 1791, being supplied by competent clergymen from the homeland, the Old Swedes Church maintained the usual high standards of congregational hymnody that have always marked the Swedish Lutheran liturgy.

Conrad Beissel came to Pennsylvania in 1720 to join Kelpius' Hermits. But by this time the group was extinct. Beissel then established a similar group in Ephrata of Lancaster County. By 1770 the group had become one of renown, and was respected by the thoughtful people of other groups as well, for their scholarly in-

---

[8]For further reading see *Church Music and Musical Life in Pennsylvania*, I, II, prepared by the Committee on Historical Research, Pennsylvania Society of the Colonial Dames of America. See also, *Journal of the Musicological Society*, V, 1952, pp. 211-223, Albert G. Hess "Observations on the ms. 'The Lamenting Voice of the Hidden Love.'"

terests. Their schools attracted students from the most influential families of Pennsylvania. Having their own printing press, they published hymnals, and books, tracts, and Bibles. They made much use of antiphonal part-songs for their worship praise songs. Conrad Beissel was a competent composer,[9] teacher, and director of music. Thus it was his work that made music a highly distinctive feature of the Ephrata community. It may be presumed that all the singing of this group was without instrumental accompaniment. They had three women's choirs which sang all four parts, plus men's groups, which also sang in parts. The entire mixed ensemble could produce homophonic music in as much as seven parts; the music was reported to have been in a free rhythmic style taking its movement from the rhythm of the words.

As already indicated, the greatest impact on American music from the settlements in Pennsylvania came by the Moravians who were descendants religiously from John Hus. By the time of Luther, there were Moravian strongholds throughout Bohemia, Moravia, Silesia, and Poland. But they came upon difficult times after the "peace of Westphalia" because they no longer had a prince to represent them. And the famous philosopher and educator, Johann Comenius, was unsuccessful in gaining aid for their cause. Comenius had been invited to become president of Harvard and was instrumental, through his writings, in converting Count Nicholas von Zinzendorf.

Count Zinzendorf gave refuge to fleeing Moravians on his estate in Saxony and the Count's estate became a great center for the movement. Thus in 1735 a small group of the Moravians went to Savannah, Georgia, to work there with the Indians, and in 1740 they established themselves at Nazareth in Pennsylvania. Count Zinzendorf himself came to their settlement in Bethlehem in the winter, a year later. It had become a strong tradition and custom that wherever they went and in whatever activity, the Moravians engaged in singing.

In September, 1745, they held a great love feast in which all who would were welcome to participate. Thus an old German song, *In*

---

[9]Beissel wrote over 400 hymns and some 1,000 pieces of music. He was one of the first important composers in the colonies. A baker by trade, he was also a violinist, much in demand for appropriate social occasions.

Dulci jubilo, was sung in thirteen different languages by participants from all walks of life and from every descent and race of people, including many different representations of Indians. This was in keeping with the Moravian view that the church is universal.

This interest in music led to the founding of the *Collegium Musicum* in 1744 and the growth of a great orchestral program was inaugurated. In the repertory of this group, the works of the great composers of Europe were included. From their own group, composers like John Antes, John Frederick Peter, and John G. Herbst were produced. It is true that Philadelphia, at the close of the eighteenth century, enjoyed a busy concert life, but the quality and quantity of music in Bethlehem could not be excelled. This was so in orchestral, chamber, and also, church music. Quite different from the English colonists, the hymn singing of the Moravians was instrumentally accompanied. Nowhere could be heard the like of the instrumentally accompanied anthems of the Moravians, both as to quality and devotion.

It would not do even in the brevity of this account to pass over the use by the Moravians of the trombone choir as part of their musical usage both secular and religious. With the trombones in four voices, it has ever been the custom (whether in Europe is not clear—but certainly the 26 missionaries to Georgia brought trombones with them) to perform the chorales in full harmony. It is said that this custom served the Moravians well on Christmas morning, 1757, when the sound of their early morning trombone choir so entranced the Indians that they canceled their plans to attack the settlement. For the trombone ensembles, the Moravians worked out a listing of chorale arrangements to serve the respective needs of the people. Hans Leo Hassler's tune for the *Passion chorale* was used to announce the death of a member. Another tune would be used to serve other occasions such as the welcome of distinguished visitors to the community. The trombone quartets were usually played from the belfry of the church. Rufus Grider[10] relates an interesting response to a young minister's question about the propriety of the same in-

---

[10]Rufus A. Grider. *Historical Notes on Music in Bethlehem, Pennsylvania,* from 1741 to 1871. Philadelphia: Pile, 1873.

struments being used for the church service that were used the
night before for an entirely different kind of enterprise: "Will you
use the same mouth to preach with today which you now use in
eating sausage?" came the rejoinder.

FRENCH BACKGROUND

Although not as impressive as the efforts of the English and the
Spanish, the French colonizations in the New World also had an
impact on the developments of church music. The French efforts
were with the help of the Jesuits instead of the Franciscans who
had worked so intensely to establish New Spain. The difficulties
confronting the French came not only from French lack of interest
in colonization but also from the nature of the Indian tribes of the
North regions where the French centered their efforts. The Indians
of the North liked to roam, and thus any continuity of service from
the Jesuit missions was made very difficult.

The Indians loved to hear singing and were always solicitous of
their children's desires. Thus it is reported in the middle of the
17th century that a certain Father Louis André of Green Bay,
Wisconsin, had unusual success with the Indians. He taught their
children songs that included direction for their elders who would
put up with hearing their own behavior berated by the songs
of their children to whom they would ever listen attentively.

It is reported also that a Father Sebastian Rale trained some
forty young Indians of the Abnakis in Maine to sing in a vested
choir for his chapel at Norridgewock. This was about 1700.

Among the Iroquois, a mission was established near Montreal.
This mission was relocated twice within the space of just over a
century. Now at St. Regis, this mission still performs the services in
the Indian tongue instead of the Latin. This privilege, originally
granted by papal consent, is still enjoyed today.

Additional historical mention of Roman Catholic church music
in the North American eastern colonies is infrequent. In 1779, on
July 4th, a Sunday, in commemoration of the Declaration of
Independence, a *Te Deum* was sung to the accompaniment of an
organ "and other kinds of music." This occasion took place in

St. Mary's of Philadelphia and was attended by the President and other members of Congress.

In 1789 John Aitken of Philadelphia published *A Compilation of the Litanies, Vespers, Hymns and Anthems as They Are Sung in the Catholic Church*. This work was published in renewed editions in 1791 and 1814. It also contained treble and bass parts for the "Holy Mass of the Blessed Trinity" and the "Mass for the Dead."

In Boston, a Reverend John Cheverus published in succeeding editions (1803, 1807, and 1823) the *Roman Catholic Manual, or Collection of Prayers, Anthems, Hymns*. Earlier in 1800, he had published a collection of anthems and hymns "usually sung at the Catholic Church in Boston."

Of special interest is the *Masses, Vespers, Litanies . . . for the use of the Catholic Churches in the United States of America*. This publication by Benjamin Carr, dedicated to John Carroll, the first Roman Catholic bishop in the United States, appeared first in 1805 and in a second edition in 1811. The work is notable because it included an original mass and a *Te Deum*. Like Aitken's publication, it also contained some hymns in English which were the same as those sung at the time in Protestant services.

THE CHURCH OF ENGLAND

The Church of England had been well established in Virginia. During the period of the Commonwealth, services in accord with the Book of Common Prayer were not encouraged but with the coming of the new king, the Anglican church of the colonies began once again to flourish in many regions. Of course a hundred years later with the seeds of the American Revolution already taking root, the progress of the Anglican church was again halted. Those of the church who remained loyal to the Crown were forced to escape the anger of the Revolutionists by leaving the colonies, otherwise they suffered great persecution. At the same time it is important to note that most of the signers of the Declaration of Independence were churchmen—among them Washington and Francis Hopkinson.

During the colonial years the services of the Episcopal church were not unlike those of the Puritan churches. However, after the Revolution, the chant, characteristic of the Church of England, was introduced. Andrew Law in his *Rudiments of Music,* 1783, included some chants with directions for singing them. In the early years, communion was commemorated only three or four times a year, and the services were confined almost exclusively to Morning and Evening Prayer.

In 1800 John Cole's *Episcopalian Harmony* published in Baltimore, included some additional settings. It was after the start of the Oxford Movement that the full musical setting for the communion service was provided: *Kyrie, Credo, Sanctus, Agnus Dei,* and *Gloria in Excelsis.*

During the eighteenth century, boys' choirs had been established at Trinity Church, New York, and at St. Michael's of Charleston, South Carolina. In this latter church the municipal orphanage, begun in 1791, was a source of choir-boy recruitment. In 1800 it is reported that the musical program of St. Michael's with its bells, Snetzler organ, and boy choir was the outstanding musical offering of any church in the country.

IMPORTANT MUSICAL PERSONAGES

The history of native religious music in the United States dates from Oliver Holden (1765-1844). There was an important religious musical consciousness in America before this time and there were important, if not refined, native musicians preceding Holden. Holden has a distinction that is enjoyed by no other American composer, having written the earliest tune which has lived from the time of its composition to now and thrived vigorously during all the years. Holden's tune, *Coronation,* is the usual setting for the hymn "All Hail the Power of Jesus' Name." Holden was born in Shirley, Massachusetts, but moved as a boy to Charlestown. In his youth he prepared to be a carpenter but spent his spare time composing; finally he became a singing teacher. In 1792 Holden published a collection called the *American Harmony.* Later he planned to publish a magazine called *The Massachusetts Musical Magazine,* but it seems never to have been published. In a subsequent collection entitled *Union Harmony* (1793) Holden's original tune, *Coronation,* was published. In 1800 and in 1803, he published two additional sacred collections, *Plain Psalmody* and *The Charlestown Collection.*

Since Holden was one of the reputed musicians of his day, on the occasion of George Washington's death, he wrote notable pieces that were widely used in the nation's period of mourning. However, his most important work perhaps was the coediting and compiling of an encyclopedia entitled *The Massachusetts Compiler.*

One of the collaborators in this book was Samuel Holyoke (1762-1820), the son of a minister in Boxford, Massachusetts. Although somewhat meagerly talented in music, Holyoke was active in musical affairs and, in addition to his work with Holden, published on his own account a collection known as *Harmonia Americana.* He is also known for a tune, "Arnheim," which he composed. Among his other works, important in religious development, are *The Columbian Respository of sacred harmony* and *The Christian harmonist.*

A second collaborator with Holden in *The Massachusetts Compiler* was Hans Gram. Gram was noted for his secular compositions and bears the distinction of having published the first orchestral score to be written in the United States. Gram was an excellent musician, and the quality of *The Massachusetts Compiler* is no doubt a result of Gram's superior work in harmonization.

Other men of the day who were active in publishing material for sacred usage were: Jacob French (1754-?); Jacob Kimball (1761-1826); and Timothy Swan (1757-1842).

Of course there were many other important composers in the United States who did not emphasize in any especial way writing for religious service. However, it is important to note the work of Raynor Taylor (1747-1825), who was a teacher of the noted Reinagle. Taylor had been musically well educated in England before coming to America. He was one chosen for the choir which served at the funeral of Handel. While most of his activity was in secular service, he did compose three anthems written and published before he came to America, entitled "Hear My Crying, O God" (Psalm 61), written for two voices; and "Hear, O Lord, and

Consider My Complaint" (Psalm 17), and "I Will Give Thanks Unto the Lord."

At the turn of the eighteenth century, a musician of importance was Oliver Shaw (1779-1848). Blindness, which resulted from complications following yellow fever, in his youth, may have influenced him to exercise his talent for music. He studied organ and clarinet and after achievements of high order became a teacher, employing a little boy to lead him to the homes of his pupils. He also became the organist of the First Congregational Church in Providence. In 1809 he gathered a group of musicians for the purpose of organizing the Psallonian Society. It was the purpose of this group to improve and perfect themselves in the knowledge and practice of sacred music, with emphasis upon improving their taste "in the choice and performance of it." Shaw is known for his tunes "Taunton," "Bristol," and "Weybosset." A sacred song by Shaw which became very popular was "Mary's Tears." He wrote many other melodies which marked the beginning of a trend away from a serious worship style in church music toward the ballad type of church song to come. Shaw compiled several collections of church music, among them *Melodia Sacra.*

The great name in the United States at the beginning of the nineteenth century is that of Lowell Mason (1792-1872). Lowell Mason came upon the musical scene at a time when American hymn writing by the Puritans was showing definite signs of dividing into two distinct channels. The one was to continue in the direction of composing the dignified, refined type of hymn which appears in good hymn collections today. The other took the direction of composing the gospel hymn, used mainly in services at camp meetings and revivals. Lowell Mason was, in the main, identified with the better development. He is known for many hymn-tune settings, among them: "Nearer my God to Thee"; "My Faith Looks Up to Thee"; and "From Greenland's Icy Mountains."

Lowell Mason, one of the few musicians who had a business sense, became a wealthy man. He published many collections of hymns and songs, the royalties from which brought him a handsome fortune. In 1855 he was awarded the first honorary degree in music granted in America, an honor bestowed by New York

University. Along with his service to religious music, and in addition to being a banker, which occupation he early discontinued, he was the founder of musical training in public school education in America.

Many who are aware of his part in the educational history of America are not so well acquainted with his service to the churches.

There were many other important writers contemporary with Mason, one of whom was Thomas Hastings (1784-1872). He compiled several collections of hymns and is known for many tunes, among them, "Toplady," the tune for the song, "Rock of Ages." Hastings often wrote tunes under assumed names because he learned in America that a foreign name was more impressive than one's own. Some of his hymns were composed under the ascription "Kl--f"; the signature "Zol-ffer" may also be a pseudonym used by Hastings.

Another musician, Silvanus Billings Pond (1792-1871), was a piano maker and the principal publisher of Stephen Foster's songs. Pond was a compiler of the hymnbook *United States Psalmody*. He also composed some songs for use in Sunday school.

Charles Zeuner (1795-1857), best known today among hymn singers for his "Missionary Chant," was an eccentric musician who at sixty-two years of age killed himself. He had written an oratorio called *The Feast of Tabernacles* which had been performed in Boston but was a failure from a financial standpoint. Zeuner, losing his temper over this, destroyed all the copies of the music including his original manuscript so that this work, which in spite of its financial failure was received with much favor at the time, was lost.

Henry Kemble Oliver (1800-1885), who ranks in stature with Mason, Hastings, and Webb, is known for the hymn tune "Federal Street" which is the setting for Oliver Wendell Holmes' song "Lord of All Being, Throned Afar." Originally, *Federal Street* was written for a hymn by Anne Steele, "So fades the lovely blooming flower." Oliver published many volumes of hymn tunes.

Another important writer of the period was George James Webb (1803-1887). Among his important compositions is the tune for "Stand Up, Stand Up for Jesus," which is generally known as

"Webb." Webb wrote many sacred songs and cantatas and compiled many collections of hymn tunes. Lowell Mason's son, William, married Webb's daughter, Mary.

Benjamin Franklin Baker (1811-1889) succeeded Mason in the teaching of music in the Boston public schools. He became vice-president of the Handel and Haydn Society and founded a music school in Boston in 1851. Although he was a composer, he is known chiefly for a collection called the *Haydn Collection of Church Music* in which he selected tunes from the masters as settings for his hymns. Also, he is known for his *Classical Chorus Book* in which were included anthems, motets, and hymns taken again from the works of the masters. He wrote, in addition, secular music and also a book on theory called *Thorough Bass and Harmony*.

William Batchelder Bradbury (1816-1868) played an important part in the development of religious music. He is known for his tune "He Leadeth Me," and "Woodworth" ("Just as I Am"), and for "Bradbury" ("Savior, Like a Shepherd Lead Me"), the latter based on a Greek folk tune.

Another of the important writers of this period in the history of American religious music is Isaac Baker Woodbury (1819-1858). Woodbury was a music merchant. He enjoyed great success selling methods for teaching music. He was an advocate of the "learn-music-at-home" idea. He collaborated in the compilation of the *Boston Musical Education Society's Collection of Church Music* (1842) and *The Choral* (1845).

ARTISTIC RELIGIOUS MUSIC IN THE UNITED STATES IN THE LATTER NINETEENTH CENTURY

Religious music is always fairly representative of the output of those groups of people who make up the serious and substantial stock of a nation. Thus one can go confidently to a nation's religious music to learn something about its people. In the latter nineteenth century the secular music of any significance in the United States was, of course, largely the music of artists who came from Europe. These visitors came to a country, reputed to be largely unschooled, with a music that they claimed was artistic. Looking back now, there is good reason to believe that the uninformed American public often was being exploited by these visitors. Of course, in addition, there was the native secular music which served as diversion in the people's weekly "socials," where they would engage in square dances or "singings" or participate in other kinds of entertainment.

However, during the latter nineteenth century the musical consciousness of the people became more discriminating. Although there were no obvious signs, the days of patronizing the European concert artists were already waning as the people's musical intelligence began to improve. But it was still the custom, in fact necessary, for native composers and musical artists to go to Europe to complete their education. It was not until the turn of the twentieth century and later that the practice of being educated musically in the United States instead of Europe was considered to be authentic and acceptable.

Of course, in the latter part of the nineteenth century the War Between the States occurred, from which, even yet, there has not been complete recovery. The cultural and educational development of the country was interrupted by this war, and even musicians of promise who gave themselves to composing during the period began to succumb to a deterioration in standards of art. Stephen Foster is one, and Lowell Mason, another, who, in their later years, wrote both secular and religious music, much of which was nothing more than drivel. Whether it was entirely because of the war or because of the "rough and ready" living on an ever Westward-moving frontier, the artistic consciousness of the United States improved only sporadically. Between times there was an increasing number of retrogressive interferences.

There were many writers of importance during the actual Civil War period who wrote war songs as well as church songs. George Frederick Root (1820-1895) was awarded the Doctor of Music degree from the University of Chicago. He was known for his "Battle Cry of Freedom"; "Tramp, Tramp, Tramp"; "Hazel Dell"; "There's Music in the Air"; and a few sacred songs of the gospel-hymn type: "The Shining Shore," and "When He Comes to Make Up His Jewels." Because of the publicity of Stephen Foster's songs, George Root wanted also to write songs; he had a pupil, the blind Fanny Crosby, whom he assigned to write verses for hymns which he set to music. Root, quite successful financially, is usually regarded as belonging to the Mason, Webb, and Bradbury group.

Henry Clay Worke (1832-1884) was also successful as a popular song writer of the day. Among the many war songs that Worke wrote were: "We're Coming"; "Babylon Is Fallen"; "Wake, Nicodemus"; and "Marching Through Georgia." He was a staunch abolitionist and wrote many songs supporting the temperance movement, one of which was "Father, dear father, come home with me now." He wrote many other songs of which these are examples: "King Bibber's Army"; "The Lost Letter"; and "Grandfather's Clock."

An important group of American composers in the latter part of the nineteenth century is known as "The Boston Group." In this group were: George W. Chadwick (1854-1931); Arthur William Foote (1853-1937); Horatio William Parker (1863-1919); Arthur Batelle Whiting (1861-1936); and Mrs. H. H. A. Beach (1867-1944).

Preceding this Boston group was John Knowles Paine (1839-1906). Paine was a pioneer who succeeded in having music introduced as a curricular subject at Harvard University under the presidency of Charles Eliot. His influence as a teacher and composer at Harvard is still felt. Among his pupils were: Arthur Foote; Louis A. Coerne (1870-1922); Frederick S. Converse (1871-1940), not to be confused with Charles Converse; John Alden Carpenter; and many others. Paine, who in his day was regarded as a great composer, may not be remembered as long as many of his contemporaries would have hoped, but nevertheless his contribution to the arousing of a successful native interest in musical development was significant. Paine had his music performed in this country and abroad by important musical groups of many lands. Among his religious works were his oratorio, *St. Peter,* and a Mass which, before he was thirty years of age, he was invited to conduct at the *Sing Academie* in Berlin.

Chadwick was one of the important composers at the turn of the century who won his reputation not only as a composer but as a theorist. He was a writer of academic books on the subject of music and harmony. He wrote three symphonies and a sinfonietta;

five string quartets; and a piano quintet. He composed several operas and many important choral works. He wrote some music for use in churches, among which are his "Dedication Ode" and his setting of Sidney Lanier's poem, "Ballad of Trees and the Master." Chadwick was at his best in his writing of the ballad style, not the artificially sentimental kind of ballad, but the more profound folklike ballad.

Arthur William Foote graduated from Harvard. He had some music study under Paine and some experience as conductor of the Harvard Glee Club. Although his ambiton had been to go into business, he decided to take some lessons in organ and so on graduation started studying with B. J. Lang, after which he held the position of organist of the First Unitarian Church in Boston from 1878-1910. He was one of the group who founded the American Guild of Organists, but he is known chiefly for his important place as an American composer and musician. While he wrote a great deal for *a cappella* chorus and for church service, he is known better for his composition of a secular kind.

Horatio William Parker, distinguished mostly for his work in choral music, was especially successful in the writing of large works for choruses, of which his oratorio, *Hora Novissima,* is an example. His opera *Mona* is regarded by many as being on a par with such operas as *"Pelléas et Mélisande."* Parker's background was that of the Puritan hymn-singing culture. Strangely enough, as a child he disliked music very much, but at the age of fourteen he suddenly became interested in music and began to study piano with his mother and then with local teachers. Soon he began to compose, and it is reported that in two days' time he set to music 50 poems which he later had published as songs for school children. At sixteen years of age he became a church organist. Later he became a pupil of Chadwick, who had returned from study in Europe. Parker himself went to Europe in 1882 to study. Upon his return, he settled in New York where he served as organist in important churches, and as a teacher in the National Conservatory of Music which was directed by Dvořák. Later, he went to Boston and from there to Yale University to head the Department of Music.

Arthur Batelle Whiting showed definite talent and ability, although he did not compare in output with the others of the Boston group. However, like the others, his influence has affected the American stream in music. Most of these men in the "Boston group" are noted not so much for their religious writings as for their compositions in general, but because they were native Americans whose work had profound effect upon American music, both religious and secular, it is appropriate to include them. Whiting wrote, in addition to other works, a few anthems which have been considered important.

Mrs. H. H. A. Beach was born in New Hampshire, her parents also being of New England colonial descent. She showed marked ability in music very early in life; at the age of seventeen she played the Mendelssohn D Minor Concerto in Boston under Theodore Thomas. At the age of eighteen she married a physician, widely acclaimed as a surgeon and medical authority. After Dr. Beach's death in 1910, Mrs. Beach left her home in Boston and went to Europe, where she stayed for about four years, playing in concert and presenting her own compositions. She has written over 150 songs. Three of these became very popular: "Ah, Love, But a Day," "The Year's at the Spring," and "Ecstasy." However, she is known best to musicians for her instrumental works. She wrote a symphony, a concerto, a sonata for violin and piano, and a quintet for piano and strings, along with many other works. She was very fond of writing church music. Her first important work of a religious nature was a mass for solo voices, chorus, orchestra, and organ.

Contemporary with Paine who so influenced the Boston group was a musician named Dudley Buck. His was among the most respected names in the latter part of the nineteenth century. He was a pioneer composer of choral music for churches. Among his pupils were Harry Rowe Shelley, John Hyatt Brewer, and Frederick Grant Gleason.

Buck was born in Hartford, Connecticut. He was destined to be a businessman—according to the designs of his father—and so was not privileged to have music lessons until he was sixteen years of age although he showed interest in music long before that. He became so diligent in his study of music that his father was won over and permitted his son to become a musician. Dudley went to Leipzig, then to Dresden, and later to Paris to study. When he came back to the United States in 1862, he took the position of organist in Hartford's Park Church. At the end of the Civil War period he published a collection of motets. He later became the director of music at St. Paul's Church in Boston, then moved on to St. Ann's in New York. In 1877 he published a book of directions for choir directors and organists, entitled *Illustration in Choir Accompaniment, with Hints on Registration.* He wrote many other important works, including overtures, sonatas, and cantatas. Among his religious cantatas, "The Coming of the King," "The Story of the Cross," and "Christ the Visitor" are important.

Other writers of the time were: Charles Beach Hawley (1858-1915); and William Harold Neidlinger (1864-1924) who wrote a cantata entitled "Prayer, Promise and Praise." Harry Rowe Shelley (1858-1947) one of Dudley Buck's pupils, was successful as composer of several sacred oratorios and cantatas, among them *The Inheritance Divine, Death and Life,* and *Vexilla Regis.* A long array of writers of anthems and cantatas and other kinds of choral pieces for church use came under Dudley Buck's influence. Among them are: Raymond Huntington Woodman; Homer Newton Bartlett; Lucien Gates Chaffin; Sumner Salter; Hamilton Crawford MacDougall; Peter Christian Lutkin; James Hotchkiss Rogers; and George Waring Stebbins, the son of the famous singing evangelist who wrote the tune commonly used as a setting for the hymn, "Savior, Breathe an Evening Blessing," along with many other successful evangelical tunes. Other United States composers were George Balch Nevin; Charles Whitney Coombs; Louis Raphael Dressler; Clarence Dickinson; Charles Winfred Douglas, a musical leader in the Episcopal church known for his book *Church Music in History and Practice,* as well as for many musical works for religious use; Edwin Shippen Barnes; Eduardo Marzo, a composer of Roman Catholic music; Nicola Aloysius Montani, who wrote much church music including two masses, some motets, and a setting of "Stabat Mater." This list of musicians who have written representative church music which in its own day was regarded as of rather high artistic standard, is by no means complete, but it presents a listing of a few of the more important writers and confirms that the writing of music had become native to the United States by the beginning of the twentieth century.

THE GOSPEL SONG

The "gospel song" has been considered by many to be a religious folk music. More recently it has come to be regarded as the religious counterpart to the sentimental secular balladry which arose in the nineteenth century, a particularly sentimental period in United States history.[11] John Tasker Howard describes it as "lacking in worthy inspiration to worshipers, cheap and tawdry, more suited for use in the dance hall than in the church, its main value being that of emotionally swaying masses of people in 'revival meetings.'"

An opposing view to that of Howard is usually expressed by evangelistic "song leaders." The more thoughtful among them feel that the stately, dignified hymn is rather too impersonal and even too philosophical for the purposes to which the gospel song is directed. They feel that the gospel song has been useful in moving people who had no religious awareness toward a valid, strong, trust in God. However, in general, they, too, decry the gospel song's use in organized worship services. Of importance is Gilbert Chase's recognition that this religious music of the people should be respected as sincere, making a positive contribution to a commendable American culture.

Archibald T. Davison's point in response perhaps would be that sincerity in reference to musical purpose is not the only consideration. He says,

To such an extent, indeed, have we democratized our services, that although we admit the almightiness of God, we behave in His house as though He were a friendly sort of host who, although He is God, would prefer to be treated like one of us. So we build our churches like halls;

---

[11] The Evangelical Movement in England received its impetus from the work of Howell Harris in Wales in the eighteenth century. The movement grew to successively greater proportions under Whitefield, the Wesleys, and John Newton. Whitefield took the movement to the American colonies in the 1740's. Its effects are still felt. Out of it grew the evangelistic movement which must be held distinct from the Evangelical movement. Many influences came together in the United States of the eighteenth century to support the evangelistic movement. One of these was the Young Men's Christian Association which led a revival just prior to and during the Civil War. Among the YMCA leaders was Dwight L. Moody, president of the Chicago Y. Beginning in 1870 he collaborated with Ira D. Sankey; they toured the United States and England in numerous gospel meetings. They compiled six large collections of *Gospel Hymns and Sacred Songs.* In recent years the gospel-song literature has deteriorated in literary, musical, and spiritual quality.

our pulpits like office desks; we must hear modernized versions of the Scriptures which sound vulgar, but which are only stupid; we won't kneel when the minister prays because God, being a democratic God, respects our independence and doesn't ask such servility; we won't intone a service because a man doesn't sing to his father, he talks to him. Whatever may be the merit of such an attitude, it may be stated in behalf of a high standard of church music that no great art has ever issued from any concept of God as the Supreme Benign Rotarian. Or again, what, then, of the lovers of good music? . . . that the church deliberately disregards those worshippers who are weekly thrown into a blasphemous state of mind by the musical inanities of the average service is a truism.[12]

Here, though, is the beginning of a problem: Many of the uncouth types of gospel song may be pathologically, psychologically, and aesthetically damaging beyond calculation. It is doubtful if much good arises out of expressions that are artistically negative.

The gospel hymns were the product of writers from the time of Lowell Mason who not only developed a liking for sentimentality but who also began to write music which served well in rural areas. In such regions the assembly which did not use a choir—the Sunday school class, the camp meeting, and revival tent meeting—could use the gospel hymn to good advantage since it was in the idiom of the popular music of the day.

Among the important gospel hymn writers were Charles Converse (1832-1918), known for "What a Friend We Have in Jesus";[13] William Howard Doane (1832-1915), known for "Saved by the Blood," "My Faith Still Clings"; William Gustavus Fischer (1835-1912), known for "I Love to Tell the Story" and "Whiter than Snow"; Hart Pease Danks (1834-1903), writer of "Not Ashamed of Christ" and a set of *Superior Anthems for Church Choirs* and some 1,300 other compositions of like style.

Thomas Philander Ryder (1836-1887) compiled a collection of hymn tunes, anthems, and chants called *Golden Treasure;* Philip Paul Bliss (1838-1876), a vigorous gospel song leader, is known for his songs "Hold the Fort," "Only an Armor Bearer," "Pull for the

---

[12]From *Protestant Church Music in America*, by Archibald T. Davison, pp. 57, 58. Copyright 1933, 1961, by E. C. Schirmer Music Co., Boston, and used with their permission

[13]In general those referred to in this section are composers of the music for the gospel titles listed. The texts were usually written by an author other than the composer. For example, the text for "What a Friend We Have in Jesus" was written by Joseph Scriven.

Watchman, Tell Us of the Night [14]

(Antiphonal Hymn)

John Bowring   Lowell Mason

PRECENTOR:

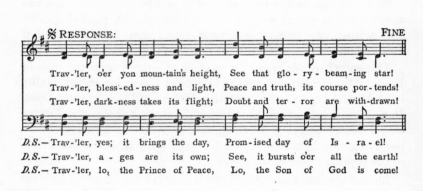

1. Watch-man, tell us of the night, What its signs of prom-ise are:
2. Watch-man, tell us of the night— High-er yet that star as-cends:
3. Watch-man, tell us of the night, For the morn-ing seems to dawn:

RESPONSE: **FINE**

Trav-'ler, o'er yon moun-tain's height, See that glo-ry-beam-ing star!
Trav-'ler, bless-ed-ness and light, Peace and truth, its course por-tends!
Trav-'ler, dark-ness takes its flight; Doubt and ter-ror are with-drawn!

D. S.— Trav-'ler, yes; it brings the day, Prom-ised day of Is-ra-el!
D. S.— Trav-'ler, a-ges are its own; See, it bursts o'er all the earth!
D. S.— Trav-'ler, lo, the Prince of Peace, Lo, the Son of God is come!

PRECENTOR: *D. S.*

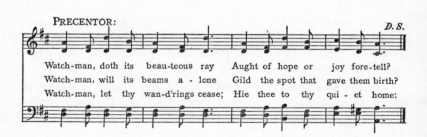

Watch-man, doth its beau-teous ray Aught of hope or joy fore-tell?
Watch-man, will its beams a-lone Gild the spot that gave them birth?
Watch-man, let thy wan-d'rings cease; Hie thee to thy qui-et home:

[14]This arrangement is one sung today, especially in Southern parts of the United States. The Precentor sings his parts, accompanied by piano, organ, or humming chorus; the Response is sung by the assembly, often unaccompanied.

Shore," and "Rescue the Perishing." Hubert Platt Main (1839-1925), a partner in the publishing firm of Bigelow and Main, is known both as a compiler and a writer of religious songs which met with great popular success, among them: "Search me, O Lord," "Our Refuge," and "Wonderful Love."

Another important writer was Ira David Sankey (1840-1908), who was the music partner of Dwight L. Moody (1837-1899), the famous evangelist. "Moody and Sankey songs," while in the eyes of many musicians considered despicable, have a certain moving quality about them which has made them successes through the years in community religious meetings. There is no denying, however, that the tunes are cheap. It is sometimes hard to understand the kind of psychology that made them so successful in their day. Among Moody and Sankey songs are the following: "Shine on, O Star!" "The Ninety and Nine," "A Soldier of the Cross," and "He is Coming." Sankey wrote hundreds of religious songs.

Other composers who succeeded in writing gospel songs were George Frederick Root, George C. Stebbins (1846-1945), and James McGranahan (1840-1907). It is generally thought that the usefulness of the gospel song manifested itself especially in those church groups which fostered Sunday school instruction and "evangelistic efforts." The gospel song served to keep religious emotion alive in the hearts of an emotional people who were living in an emotional age.

WHITE AND NEGRO SPIRITUALS

An interesting musical development in the United States was that of the "White and Negro Spirituals" which arose out of the aftermath of the Civil War when there occurred a breakdown in the established religious institutions of the country. The Baptist church, for instance, broke into numbers of sects. And there were the beginnings of special sects such as the "Shakers" and the "New Light Baptists." The Methodists also found themselves divided. Some of the Methodist groups tried to save the atheistic and the sophisticated religious people of New England; but in general they and the Baptists became strongest in the South. The Presbyterians found themselves divided under the doctrine of New Sidism. Another group, known as the "New Lighters," growing steadily in importance and strength, evidenced an emotional and exacting kind of piety which, rather than building upon an intellectual foundation for religious experience, appealed to the sensuous interests of its membership. Out of all this religious dividing, natural enough in a new nation practicing an extreme democratic technique, there arose an unbridled freedom in religious song.

Religious song always betrays the culture from which it springs, and the religious singing of the period after the Revolutionary War took on those characteristics that perhaps are best described as folk balladry. The results of the rise of this kind of musical literature are still felt. Song texts and their tunes were written specifically to defend doctrinal points of view. For instance, there were songs written to defend the principles of singing as a religious practice; there were songs to teach foot-washing; to teach the "plan of salvation"; and to warn of hell. There were ballads written to tell of the places of woe suggested by the roving preachers; and others which told about eclipses and similar "acts of God." There were even songs written by the Methodists making fun of the Baptists.

Included in this material, the bulk of which had been created by 1830, there were songs sublimating fleshly love for love of God. Their melodies were often taken from the very melodies, some of them vulgar, which had to do especially with the types of people abnormally interested in sexual life. Of interest are the song trends shown among the "Glassites," and the unusual publication entitled *The Christian Harmony* by Jeremiah Ingalls. Of considerable importance also were the collections known as the *Sacred Harp,* which date from 1844. Loyal followers in the "sol-fa" belt of the South still use the *Sacred Harp* on their occasions of official song meetings. From 1830 to the end of the nineteenth century, a period of emotional excitement, songs continued to be written among religious revivalists.

Revivalists, such as "crazy" Lorenzo Dow (1777-1834), a Methodist evangelist, took their American songs back with them across the Atlantic and toured the British Isles. Some in England have not yet recovered from the onslaught, nor have the British brethren shown any inclination to forgive their "pious" American visitors.

In the midnineteenth century, songs for almost any occasion, or imaginable occasion, were written. There were songs about Judgment Day and about the world's end, such as were suggested by William Miller, who prophesied the end of the world. Songs about the second coming of Christ, and about travel through the country have appeared among each of the evangelical groups, even among groups of lesser importance, such as the Shakers.

In the latter part of the nineteenth century, as already suggested in the section on the gospel song, there sprang up, throughout the country, houses that began to publish these tunes or spirituals and to create new ones in imitation of the more or less spontaneous composition evidenced in the genuine tunes. The several publishing houses differed as they set about compiling examples from this literature, because the regional objectives of the Northern compilers were different from those of the Southern compilers, and those of the Boston group were different from those of any other regions in the country. It is from a background such as this that there came what is often referred to by historians as the "folk-socialized religions in America." Important groups in this folk-religion category are those fostered by Elias Smith, James O'Kelly, Abner Jones, and Barton W. Stone. It was groups such as these which gave rise to the musical phenomenon known today as the literature of song spirituals: both Negro and white spirituals.

The white spirituals are sung today in the evangelistic white churches. It is characteristic of these spirituals that they usually are repetitive, with many verses sung to the same tune and followed by a refrain which can be tossed antiphonally back and forth between two or more groups of singers as they wish.

It is interesting that most of the melodies found among the Negro spirituals can be traced back to the ancient tunes of the white people of the British Isles, including Ireland. But in the Negro spirituals there is manifested the natural spiritual fervency of the colored people, their love for the rhythmic and the dramatic. Thus there has been given to the Negro spiritual in spite of its possible white connection a style that is peculiarly Negro. The

Mary, Don't You Weep

NEGRO

O Ma - ry, don't you weep, don't you mourn,

O Ma - ry, don't you weep, don't you mourn; Pha-roah's arm - y got

drown - ded O Ma - ry, don't you weep!

Th' way of e - vil do - ing is— a wide an' fair,

An' man - y, man - y, man - y they who per - ish there!

Negro, evangelized in the United States by many of the sects of the country, learned the songs and the melodies of his white neighbors, and of the white evangelizing visitors from the North who brought to them "gospel preaching." The rhythmic modifying of these songs as they were sung by memory by Negroes and the free whites who were "evangelizing" them, influenced the resident white people in the area also. Thus, perhaps it is not too far from the truth to say the gospel hymns as sung by the evangelistical white churches are directly the product of the Negro and the white spirituals. Countless white and Negro spirituals actually have been compiled and transcribed into the gospel-hymn literature. Many who use this literature are not aware of the interesting socialized spiritual backgrounds involved in the songs which they sing every Sunday morning for worship.

THE RISE OF THE "SHAPED-NOTE" SINGING SCHOOL

With the universalizing of religious singing in the United States among the community assemblies who gathered to worship, there came the need for teaching the worshipers how to sing and for teaching them new songs as the years went by. As already mentioned, singing schools (a cultural institution involving a traveling song leader's coming to a town and establishing, under the auspices of a church group, a short-time program of training) sprang up all over the country; they still continue seasonally throughout the Southeast, the South, and the West.

It was early seen that a method for teaching a person to read music notation and to "sing at sight" involved his being able to identify the successive notes of the melody in keeping with what he knew of scale structure, by looking at the key sign and locating the tonic tone. Then he would have to note the intervals between the successive pairs of notes and, by aid of his musical feeling and his intellectual apprehension of the various note names, to work out the melodic line and sing his tune. It was not long before some enterprising song leaders happened upon the discovery that they could simplify the identification of the various *sol-fas* by giving to each note a shape that would indicate its name. Two systems were started almost at the same time, one by a singing teacher, Andrew

We Praise Thee, O God [15]

Wm. P. Mackay   (Revive Us Again)   J. J. Husband

1. We praise Thee, O God, For the Son of Thy love, For Je - sus who
2. We praise Thee, O God, For Thy Spir - it of light, Who has shown us our
3. All glo - ry and praise To the Lamb that was slain, Who has borne all our
4. All glo - ry and praise To the God of all grace, Who has bought us, and
5. Re - vive us a - gain: Fill each heart with Thy love; May each soul be re-

CHORUS

died, and is now gone a - bove.
Sav - ior, and scat-tered our night.
sins, and has cleansed ev - 'ry stain.   Hal - le - lu - jah! Thine the glo - ry;
sought us, And guid - ed our ways.
kin - dled With fire from a - bove.

Hal - le - lu - jah! A - men! Hal - le - lu - jah! Thine the glo - ry; Re - vive us a - gain.

Law, and the other by two partners in publishing, William Little and William Smith. Many writers have credited Andrew Law as being the earliest inventor of such a system, but it is now thought that William Little and William Smith were the first. Little and Smith devised the plan of using four shapes placed upon the staff as regular notation, while Law devised the system of using four

---

[15]"We Praise Thee, O God" is often used in "gospel meetings." The refrain lends itself to antiphonal singing, that is, to having different sections of the assembled congregation sing in quick succession the short phrases and Hallelujahs. Men and women, girls and boys, "take turns" singing the stanzas. Such group singing has a strange power over the participants. Notice the shaped notes. This song has some of the qualities of the white spiritual.

shapes without the regular staff notations, putting the notations over the words.[16] It was some time later that a system of seven shapes was devised, respectively providing shaped notes for *do, re, mi, fa, sol, la, ti,* and *do.*

Early in the 1830's Lowell Mason compiled a book known as the *Ohio Sacred Harp.* Although he was opposed to the use of shaped notes, his *Ohio Sacred Harp* was at first printed with them; later, it was printed in both shaped and round notes.

The loyal following of singing schools which gave support to the publishing and selling of the singing school books and which advocated publishing in the patent notes, that is, the shaped notes, grew and spread throughout the South and West; and while many musicians have never even heard of the phenomenon and many others have said that the shaped note era of the United States is past, it is common knowledge to many that today tens of thousands of people sing, all over the United States, each Sunday, out of hymnals printed in the shaped notes.[17]

The earliest tune books had been scored with the tenor voice at the top and the treble voice third above the bass. Occasionally in this music a "figured bass" was also indicated but with no separate provision for accompaniment. With Lyon's *Urania,* regular notation but in round or shaped notes was provided.

In publishing songbooks in both round and shaped notes, publishers' awareness of the needs of the churches and the relationships of these to successful merchandising are apparent. It was not long until publishers were learning how to cater to the peculiar preferences of the respective denominations.

It is interesting that in some instances, churches themselves published or compiled anthem collections in manuscript form for their own use.

An important impact was made upon American musical merchandising by Alfred and Vincent Novello of England. They were

---

[16]The English system of placing initials over the words to indicate *do,* d; *re,* r; *etc.,* has not been adopted for use in the United States. It is a very good system, which through an ingenious use of dots and dashes also indicates the rhythm. It saves printing costs of staff notation, and could be easily recorded by a typist.

[17]Just recently some leaders in the Music Educators National Conference have been advocating use of shaped notes in school music. We are disappointed at this; it would be much better to include the already established British system of solfeggio initials. In British choral music, the initials are included over the staff notation.

Sweet By and By[18]

S. F. Bennett

Jos. P. Webster

1. There's a land that is fair - er than day, And by faith we can
2. We shall sing on that beau - ti - ful shore The me - lo - di - ous
3. To our boun - ti - ful Fa - ther a - bove We will of - fer our

see it a - far; For the Fa - ther waits o - ver the way, To pre-
songs of the blest; And our spir - its shall sor - row no more— Not a
trib - ute of praise. For the glo - ri - ous gift of His love, And the

CHORUS

pare us a dwell - ing place there. In the sweet by and
sigh for the bless - ing of rest.
bless - ings that hal - low our days. In the sweet

by, We shall meet on that beau - ti - ful shore; In the
by and by, by and by;

sweet by and by, We shall meet on that beau - ti - ful shore.
In the sweet by and by,

---

[18]The song, "Sweet By and By," is typical of songs to be found in gospel hymnals at the turn of the century. Such songs are still used widely. Note the shaped notes.

brothers, who, in 1844, established *The Musical Times*. It was the custom in this monthly publication for the Novellos to insert an anthem in full score. They also published separately a great number of anthems and oratorios. These were always in full notation including complete notation for the accompanist. (Up to this time it had been the habit for the accompaniment music to be in the form of a "figured bass," which of course was beyond the comprehension of small-town musicians such as in the United States.) Thus the Novellos made a substantial contribution in publishing the music as they did. Even so, the English firm's publications were slow of sale in America until 1894 when the church music publisher, H. W. Gray, became the agent for Novello. The relationship between the H. W. Gray Co., and Novello still stands.

Another interesting publishing innovation was that of the church music periodical which brought to isolated regions, suitable selections of music appropriate to the seasons, occasions, and capabilities of the churches. First among these was *The Parish Choir* which was begun in 1874 and published until 1919. Another influential publisher of church music periodicals has been the E. S. Lorenz Company of Dayton, Ohio. Its publications range in quality from stereotyped material not unlike the gospel song literature, to a more mature music of a quality suitable for more professional type choirs.

RELIGIOUS MUSIC TODAY IN THE UNITED STATES

Several different strains of religious music, deriving from many cultural sources are found in the United States today.[19] Since World War I, a host of late nineteenth-century and twentieth-century names, some European and some native, have become familiar acquaintances in an ever-enlarging circle of music lovers in the United States. Some of these represent a synthesizing of what

---

[19]It is to be noted that in addition to the large well-known church communions there are in the United States many small, obscure groups. Many of these have had a traditionally distinctive kind of music. Mostly, such groups will have transplanted to the United States an "old country" flavored music like that of the Moravian Brethren who settled in Bethlehem, Pennsylvania.

In general, such small groups, whether running counter to or in accord with the *main* New World idioms, have not had much distinctive effect upon the culture of the United States. The provincial characteristics of all small bands seem as they come in contact with the outer world to become neutralized and soon assimilated.

J. L. Neve's book *Churches and Sects of Christendom* (Burlington, Iowa: The Lutheran Literary Board, 1940) is interesting.

has gone before; others are experimenting and questing into the future.

It would be precarious to place value judgments on the work of contemporary musicians, especially in reference to religious implications. Even so, perhaps three or four names representing the new direction and vision should be noted:

Sir Arnold Bax (1883-1953) was a composer known in religious connection for his *Mater Ora Filium* (1921) *This World's Joie* (1922) two motets for unaccompanied choir evidencing a spirit of earnest Christian devotion. Additionally, Bax wrote a work, *To the Name above Every Name,* which is certainly one of the century's important religious works. So far as is known, it has been performed only at the "Worcester (England) Three Choirs Festival" for which it was commissioned in 1923.

Arthur Honegger (1892-1955), one of "Les Six" in the French school will be remembered in religious conection for his *Le Roi David* (1923), an oratorio, and for his *Symphonie Liturgique* (1946).

A third composer who will be of interest to those of religious bent is Olivier Messiaen (1908-   ). Messiaen was a pupil of Paul Dukas and Marcel Dupré; he was influenced also, perhaps, by d'Indy. As Demuth puts it, one thinks also of André Caplet (1878-1925) when he thinks of Messiaen. Both of these men suffered deeply as a result of war experiences, Caplet in World War I, and Messiaen in World War II. Both evidence sensitive devoutness in their religious composition. Messiaen will be remembered for his *La Nativité du Seigneur;* and Caplet will be remembered for his *Le Miroir de Jésus* (1923). A fifth composer is Arthur Shepherd (1880-1958), a native of the United States, born in Idaho, and musically, a descendant of the Boston group. His setting of Sidney Lanier's poem, "Ballad of the Trees and the Master," for unaccompanied choir; and his *Song of the Pilgrims* for large choir and symphony orchestra are important.

In addition to the art music referred to above which is affecting the cultural pattern in the United States, there are the musical patterns to be associated respectively with the several individualistic church groups.

One finds a continuation of the liturgic music of the Anglican Church as well as a continuation of the conservative solemn singing among those groups that have their impetus in the old Puritan movement; one also finds, of course, a continuation of the music of the Roman Catholic tradition although this music is no longer untouched by the "American" influence of its locale. There is, in addition, in the "American" religious scene, a sort of secular concert-offering which embodies string ensembles, wind instrument ensembles, or organ offerings. These are presented by professional groups of high artistic ability. Frequently in religious connection, or on special church occasions, there are offerings of what may not be religious music at all, although they are validated on the basis of giving to the churches the riches of the artistic heritage which church people might not otherwise hear if they were not heard "in church." Similarly, one finds, as common practice, the presenting in concert of "worship music," or, at least, compositions of religious association. Finally, there is the community-song-type service promoted in many church assemblies, some of them choirless, which emphasize congregational singing, sometimes to the extent of completely prohibiting any kind of "special music" such as that performed by quartets or small choruses. In this latter type of church-assembly singing, the music service may include accompaniment by an organ or piano or there may be definite prohibiting of such instrumental usage. The emphasis by the church-assembly groups upon congregational singing is sometimes modified to permit one musical selection, either accompanied or unaccompanied, by a volunteer choir. It may even be permitted that such a group occasionally sing a musical response to a prayer, or a short offertory during the collection, or a musical invocation or closing benediction.

The variations in the musical practices are so numerous that it is perhaps impossible to describe them in any single statement. These variations occur because the United States, a democracy populated by so many different peoples with so many unique and distinct backgrounds, is a land in which are brought *together* into one people the anciently separated heritages of all their forebears.

It is perhaps true that the anthem is characteristic of the musical worship of the majority of American churchgoers. Depending on the quality of the constituency of the respective congregations, the anthem may be a Latin or ancient motet or it may even be, on occasion, a cantata, but, in general, it is a choral piece in three-part form accompanied or unaccompanied by an organ. The church anthem is a composition of merit at times, but more frequently it is likely to be a most ordinary piece produced by commercial writers, offered to an unsuspecting church group by a publisher who specializes in such musical stereotypes.

By far the most important reservoir of religious music in the United States is that of the churches' hymns and songs to be sung by the assembly. The emphasis upon congregational singing is, of course, popular among democratic people. The unique musical result of the democratic principle of life in the United States' religious culture is still the social hymn-singing of the congregation. Strangely enough, the religious music of any group is quite likely to be unrelated, in any conscious way, to secular artistic awareness of the very same people when out of their religious framework. Congregational singing may become wonderfully alive and enthusiastic in a period of great religious fervor or it may decline to a lifeless emptiness in a period of religious decay, all of this, unconnected with the same people's interest in the arts, education, and social development.

During the early Puritan period, whatever its inartistic qualities, the singing of the people was a great and potent force in the unified religious life of the people. Today in the United States, the contemporary Protestant music[20] is what it is, mainly because it allows every individual worshiper to exercise his own individual conscience in reference to worship and religious activity. Because of their democratic individualities, the masses of people often lag behind the higher attainments of the leaders of the period who will shape the culture to come. They sometimes engage in a kind of music which may be bizarre, or tawdry, uninspiring or inartistic, perhaps even vulgar, although perhaps mostly their music is merely sentimental, associating itself with the manifestations of the people in their more mundane concern with earning a living and compensating for the life emergencies of birth, marriage, and death.

However, in recent hymn collections, stronger emphasis has been given to the better works of the many different historical periods, both English and German and French. For example, the tune, "Dundee," derived from the English and Scottish psalters of

[20]Even Roman Catholic music except for its use of the Gregorian chant is thought by some to have diverted greatly from the older Roman Catholic tradition.

the sixteenth and seventeenth centuries is still a powerful tune and is included in the better modern hymnals. It is not at all surprising to find in the United States modern hymnal, a range of songs for congregational use that includes the simple kind of German balladry or German chorales along with an arrangement of a motet of ancient time adapted to congregational assembly-type usage with additional selections from the Gregorian chants. The newer hymnals of better quality today are including good texts and music representative of the better achievements of the different historical periods, nations, and peoples. Generally, compilers of hymnals are giving some attention to eliminating such gross relations as would be caused by including, along with the better selections, the cheap music representative of a more inartistic side of culture. Attention is also being given to including hymn settings composed by recent or contemporary writers who are sensitive not only to the demands of artistic performance, but also to the psychology of group religious participation.[21]

It should be noted that such writers as Dykes, Smart, Barnby, Sulley, and Monk, who originally had their works exclusively in the Anglican service, came half a century ago to being represented in the hymnbooks of the newer nonliturgic groups. Many of the songs of such writers provided a kind of interest that afforded to the congregation using them a considerable spiritual satisfaction. Of course, many of these same tunes were more suitable when presented by special groups performing before a listening audience. Even in the most conservative religious groups, there has been a growing recognition of this value of having some songs sung by a talented group before a listening congregation.

However, with the increasing vitality and discrimination of a few of today's religious groups, Dykes, Barnby, and the other Victorian writers are dropping out of use. But one should keep in mind that even that church music which is ineffective today, may have been in its own cultural setting and time, very beautiful and moving. After all, the popular song of any one generation is its spontaneous mass expression. It should not be overlooked of course

---

[21]A relic of the old German Reformation is being revived in many church groups: namely, having the congregation as a whole sing the hymn tune in unison, but accompanied by a small rehearsed group who sing the harmonic parts. The *Sine Nomine* of Ralph Vaughan Williams, a unison melody (with organ harmonization), is an example to be found in the new *Service Book and Hymnal of the Lutheran Church in America.*

that there has always been a segment in the United States culture which has given itself to a kind of "hill billy" religious music. This group never has bothered itself very much with even the appearance of respectability that usually has been the mark of the Victorian group.

There is a growing optimism on the part of many hymnologists that the quality of congregational music usage is improving. Surely it is true that in the "official" hymnals of some churches, a much finer quality of material over previous years is now being included. And together with the turning away from the Victorian flavor, there is also a turning away from such work as has characterized, for instance, the Boston group. Horatio Parker, for example, represents the spirit of an age gone by; in general, his music is being dropped from church usage. The waning of interest for music of the Boston group perhaps has occurred because their music was too intricate, too chromatic, and at times overly self-conscious, so that it failed after all to represent the simple religious spirit of the people of the United States.

Characteristic of some of the church music of the United States are the rigid and legalistic strictures and attitudes which are loyally adhered to by respective church groups, thus preventing much improvement in the individual patterns.[22] For instance, the Methodist, the Presbyterian, and the "Restoration" churches, along with many others, have found themselves rent asunder over the questions as to how to use their music in worship. This doctrinal struggle over music has appeared notably among the English-speaking people and others under Calvinistic influence.[23] Although some may have regarded it as amusing, to the people involved it has ever been a solemn and desperate conflict. What all too frequently has not been recognized by church leaders is that no religious music of a period can continue on and on as if no religious-secular-cultural changes were occurring. "The old order changeth, yielding place to new."

[22]Such individual provincialism exists, of course, in Europe and elsewhere, but, for the most part, in respective homogeneous geographical areas. However, in the United States, and in England too, such provincialisms find themselves thrown together in the *same* geographical areas. This sometimes engenders strife as each provincialism endeavors to preserve its peculiar individuality in spite of its contact with other idioms.

[23]For a treatment of Roman Catholic church music in the United States, see Erwin Nemmers, *Twenty Centuries of Catholic Church Music*, Milwaukee: The Bruce Publishing Co., 1949.

CONCORDANCE

CONCORDANCE OF MUSICAL TERMS IN THE BIBLE

Ballad Singers
Numbers 21:27

Bagpipe
Daniel 3:5, 7, 10, 15

Castanets
2 Samuel 6:5

Cymbal
1 Corinthians 13:1

Cymbals
2 Samuel 6:5
1 Chronicles 13:8; 15:16, 19, 28;
   16:5, 42; 25:1, 6
2 Chronicles 5:12, 13; 29:25
Ezra 3:10
Nehemiah 12:27
Psalm 150:5

Flute
1 Samuel 10:5
Isaiah 5:12; 30:29
Jeremiah 48:36
Matthew 9:23
1 Corinthians 14:7
Revelation 18:22

Harp
1 Samuel 10:5
Psalms 33:2; 57:8; 71:22; 81:2; 92:3;
   108:2; 144:9; 150:3
Isaiah 5:12; 23:16
Daniel 3:5, 7, 10, 15
Amos 6:5
1 Corinthians 14:7
Revelation 5:8

Harpers
Revelation 14:2; 18:22

Harps
2 Samuel 6:5
1 Kings 10:12
1 Chronicles 13:8; 15:16, 20, 28;
   16:5; 25:1, 6
2 Chronicles 5:12; 9:11; 20:28; 29:25
Nehemiah 12:27
Isaiah 14:11
Amos 5:23
Revelation 14:2; 15:2

Horn
Joshua 6:5
2 Samuel 6:15
1 Chronicles 15:28
Psalms 98:6
Daniel 3:5, 7, 10, 15
Hosea 5:8

Horns
Joshua 6:4, 6, 8, 13
2 Chronicles 15:14

Instrument
Ezekiel 33:32

Instruments
1 Samuel 18:6
1 Chronicles 15:16; 16:42; 23:5
2 Chronicles 5:13; 7:6; 23:13; 29:26,
   27; 34:12
Nehemiah 12:36
Psalms 45:8
Isaiah 38:20
Amos 6:5
Romans 6:13
1 Corinthians 14:7

Lyre
Genesis 4:21; 31:27

1 Samuel 10:5
2 Samuel 6:5
1 Kings 10:12
1 Chronicles 13:8; 15:16, 21, 28; 16:5; 25:1, 6
2 Chronicles 5:12; 9:11; 20:28; 29:25
Nehemiah 12:27
Job 30:31
Psalms 33:2; 49:4; 57:8; 71:22; 81:2; 92:30; 98:5; 108:2; 137:2; 149:3
Isaiah 5:12; 24:8
Daniel 3:5, 7, 10, 15

Melody
Judges 5:3
Psalms 27:6; 33:2; 57:7; 92:3; 98:5; 147:7; 149:3
Isaiah 23:16
Amos 5:23
Ephesians 5:19

Music
1 Samuel 18:6
1 Chronicles 15:22, 27, 28; 16:42; 25:6
2 Chronicles 7:6; 34:12
Psalms 49:4; 92:3
Lamentations 5:14
Ezekial 26:13
Daniel 3:5, 7, 10, 15
Amos 6:5
Luke 15:25

Musical
1 Chronicles 15:16
2 Chronicles 5:13; 23:13
Nehemiah 12:36

Musicians
Judges 5:11

Noise
Exodus 32:17
1 Samuel 4:6
1 Kings 1:40, 45
Psalms 66:1; 95:1, 2; 98:4, 6; 100:1
Isaiah 24:8
Jeremiah 51:55
Ezekial 37:7
Daniel 10:6
Amos 5:23

Noisy
1 Corinthians 13:1

Pipe
Genesis 4:21
Job 21:12; 30:31

Psalms 150:4
Daniel 3:5, 7, 10, 15

Piped
Matthew 11:17
Luke 7:32

Pipes
1 Kings 1:40

Piping
Judges 5:16

Psalm
Psalm 47:7
Acts 13:33, 35

Psalmist
2 Samuel 23:1

Psalms
Luke 20:42; 24:44
Acts 1:20
Ephesians 5:19
Colossians 5:16

Sing
Exodus 15:1, 21
Numbers 21:17
Judges 5:3
1 Samuel 21:11; 29:5
2 Samuel 22:50
1 Chronicles 16:9, 23, 33
2 Chronicles 20:21, 22; 29:30
Job 21:12; 29:13
Psalms 5:11; 7:17; 9:2, 11; 13:6; 18:49; 21:13; 27:6; 30:4; 33:3; 47:6, 7; 51:14; 57:7, 9; 59:16, 17; 61:8; 63:7; 65:13; 66:2, 4; 67:4; 68:4, 32; 71:22, 23; 75:9; 81:1; 84:2; 89:1; 92:1, 4; 95:1; 96:1, 2, 12; 98:1, 4, 5, 8; 101:1; 104:12, 33; 106:12; 108:1, 3; 119:172; 135:3; 137:3, 4; 138:1, 5; 144:9; 145:7; 146:2; 147:1, 7; 149:1, 5
Isaiah 5:1; 12:5, 6; 23:16; 24:14; 26:19; 27:2; 35:6; 38:20; 42:10, 11; 44:23; 49:13; 52:8; 54:1; 65:14
Jeremiah 20:13; 31:7, 12; 33:11; 51:48
Amos 6:5
Zephaniah 3:14
Zechariah 2:10
Romans 15:9
1 Corinthians 14:15
Colossians 3:16
James 5:13
Revelation 4:8; 14:3; 15:3

Singer

1 Chronicles 6:33

Singers

Numbers 21:27
1 Kings 10:12
1 Chronicles 9:33; 15:16, 19, 27
2 Chronicles 5:12, 13; 9:11; 23:13;
    29:28; 35:15
Ezra 2:41, 65, 70; 7:7, 24; 10:24
Nehemiah 7:1, 44, 67, 73; 10:28, 39;
    11:22, 23; 12:28, 29, 42, 45, 46,
    47; 13:5, 10
Psalms 68:25; 87:7
Ecclesiastes 2:8

Singing

Exodus 32:18
1 Samuel 18:6
2 Samuel 19:35
1 Chronicles 25:7
2 Chronicles 23:18; 30:21; 35:25
Nehemiah 12:27
Psalms 26:7; 84:4; 100:2; 105:43
Song of Solomon 2:12
Isaiah 14:7; 24:9; 35:2, 10; 44:23;
    49:13; 51:11; 52:9; 54:1; 55:12
Zephaniah 3:17
Acts 16:25
Ephesians 5:19
Revelation 4:10

Sings

Job 33:27
Proverbs 25:20; 29:6
Ezekial 33:32

Song

Exodus 15:1, 2
Numbers 21:17
Deuteronomy 31:19, 21, 22, 30; 32:
    44
Judges 5:12
2 Samuel 22:1
1 Chronicles 6:31, 32; 13:8; 16:42
2 Chronicles 5:13; 29:27
Job 30:9
Psalms 26:7; 28:7; 33:3; 40:3; 42:8;
    68:4; 69:30; 78:63; 81:2; 96:1;
    98:1, 4; 118:14; 137:4; 144:9;
    147:1; 149:1
Ecclesiastes 75; 12:4
Song of Solomon 1:1
Isaiah 5:1; 12:2; 23:15, 16; 25:5;
    26:1; 30:29; 42:10; 51:3
Micah 2:4
Revelation 5:9; 14:3; 15:3

Songs

Genesis 31:27
1 Samuel 18:6
2 Samuel 6:5
1 Kings 4:32
Nehemiah 12:8, 46
Job 35:10
Psalms 42:4; 47:1; 69:12; 95:2;
    107:22; 119:54; 137:3
Proverbs 25:20
Isaiah 16:10; 24:16
Jeremiah 30:19
Lamentations 3:14, 63
Ezekial 26:13; 33:32
Amos 5:23; 6:5; 8:3, 10
Ephesians 5:19
Colossians 3:16

Sound

Exodus 19:19; 32:18
Joshua 6:5, 20
Judges 5:11
2 Samuel 6:15; 15:10
1 Kings 1:41
1 Chronicles 15:19, 28; 16:5
2 Chronicles 13:12
Ezra 3:13
Nehemiah 4:20
Job 21:12; 39:24
Psalms 5:2; 47:5; 66:8; 81:2; 98:5,
    6; 150:3
Isaiah 14:11; 30:29, 32
Jeremiah 4:19, 21; 6:17; 42:14;
    49:21; 50:42
Ezekial 23:42; 26:13; 33:4, 5
Daniel 3:5, 7, 10, 15; 10:6
Amos 2:2; 6:5
Zechariah 9:14
Matthew 6:2
Acts 2:2, 6
1 Corinthians 14:8; 15:52
1 Thessalonians 4:16
Hebrews 12:19
Revelation 14:2; 18:22

Sounded

Judges 3:27; 6:34
2 Chronicles 7:6; 29:28
Nehemiah 4:18
Revelation 10:7

Sounding

Psalm 150:5

Sounds

Exodus 19:13
1 Chronicles 15:16
Job 39:25

Stringed
Psalms 45:8; 144:9

Strings
Psalms 33:2, 3; 150:4

Tambourine
Genesis 31:27
1 Samuel 10:5
Job 21:12

Tambourines
2 Samuel 6:5
1 Chronicles 13:8

Timbrel
1 Samuel 18:6
Psalms 149:3; 150:4
Isaiah 5:12; 24:8

Trigon
Daniel 3:5, 7, 10, 15

Trumpet
Exodus 19:13, 16, 19; 20:18
Leviticus 25:9
Joshua 6:5, 20
Judges 3:27; 6:34; 7:18
1 Samuel 13:3
2 Samuel 2:28; 15:10; 18:16; 20:1, 22
1 Kings 1:34, 39, 41
2 Kings 9:13
Nehemiah 4:18, 20
Job 39:24, 25
Psalms 47:5; 81:3; 150:3
Isaiah 18:3; 27:13; 58:1
Jeremiah 4:5, 19, 21; 6:1, 17; 42:14; 51:27
Ezekiel 7:14; 33:3, 4, 5, 6
Hosea 5:8, 8:1
Joel 2:1, 15
Amos 2:2; 3:6
Zephaniah 1:16
Zechariah 9:14

Matthew 6:2; 24:31
1 Corinthians 15:52
1 Thessalonians 4:16
Hebrews 12:19
Revelation 1:10; 4:1; 8:7, 8, 10, 12; 9:1, 13, 14; 10:7; 11:15

Trumpeters
2 Kings 11:14
2 Chronicles 5:12, 13; 23:13; 29:28
Revelation 18:22

Trumpets
Leviticus 23:24
Numbers 10:2, 8, 9, 10; 29:1; 31:6
Joshua 6:4, 6, 8, 9, 13, 16, 20
Judges 7:8, 16, 18, 19, 20, 22
2 Kings 11:14; 12:13
1 Chronicles 13:8; 15:24, 28; 16:6, 42
2 Chronicles 5:13; 7:6; 13:12, 14; 15:14; 20:28; 23:13; 29:26, 27
Ezra 3:10
Nehemiah 12:33, 41
Psalm 98:6
Revelation 8:2, 6, 13

Voice
2 Samuel 19:35
Job 30:31
Isaiah 51:3; 58:1
Jeremiah 7:34; 16:9; 25:10; 31:15; 33:11
Ezekiel 33:32
Jonah 2:9
Micah 6:1
Matthew 2:18
Revelation 1:10; 5:12

Voices
Isaiah 24:14
Jeremiah 30:19; 33:11
Acts 4:24; 14:11
Revelation 11:15

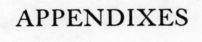

APPENDIXES

APPENDIX I

A NOTE ON *PSALLO*

(See page 43)

(A listing of commonly encountered points of view, not necessarily those of the author.)

1. If *psallo* in the New Testament is correctly translated in the English word "sing," then *psallo* perhaps has no bearing on use or nonuse of an instrument of music.

2. Some have considered that both singing in the heart and making melody in the heart (Eph. 5:19) are satisfied only by *inward* spiritual exercise and that neither audible vocalization nor audible instrumental performance are scripturally authorized. (See Pambo, quoted p. 43)

3. If *psallo* prohibits use of musical instruments in formal church services, then it prohibits use of musical instruments in any religious service (see Basil, Jerome, *et al.*); indeed it prohibits instruments altogether for either religious or secular usage. (See Basil, Jerome, *etc., etc.*) This is the case because the New Testament passages in question are passages applicable mainly in a general way to Christians' day-to-day living.

4. The use or nonuse of instruments of music for church services is not to be clearly argued by any reference to *psallo*. Generally the basis for non-use of instruments in those present-day churches which abstain from in-strumental usage is established in the assumption that the earliest churches did not use them and that the Scriptures do not authorize them since they do not mention them. However, if Moffatt's translations of *Ephesians* 5:19 and *Colossians* 3:16 are correct (he uses the inclusive word, "music"), then so far as those passages are concerned, instrumental usage would be definitely authorized except that knowledge of the precedent of instrumental usage by the earliest churches is lacking.

5. It has to be shown, by holders of the view that church music is to be restricted to noninstrumentally accompanied singing, that nonuse of the instruments by the early church was a consideration of doctrinal legality and not merely one of contemporary custom or abstinence because of abhorence of sensual associations of the day.

    (a) It has to be shown also that practice or nonpractice by the early Christians of some specific (such as the using of one cup for all who are assembled at an appointed hour for the eucharistic communion) whether embraced or not embraced in scriptural direction is a con-sideration of doctrinal legality and therefore binding upon Christians today.

6. As early as A.D. 190, there was mention of instruments being used for Christians' religious service. Some investigators have seen great difficulty in explaining how Clement could have written such a teaching, therefore doubt that he wrote the passage or else declare that he contra-dicted himself or else assert that he was using the names of instruments symbolically. (Kurfees, M. C. *Instrumental Music in the Worship,* Nash-ville: McQuiddy Printing Co. 1911. pp. 124-134.) Yet such explanations seem to be overlaborious. There is another view set forth by M. C.

Kurfees to the effect that *psallo* when referring to singing in Old Testament writings might include the notion of instrumental music. (*Originally* the word had reference to plucking a string, such as a carpenter's string; in the New Testament, Paul uses the word in reference to touching the strings of the heart.) Kurfees goes on to defend a view that *psallo* later lost this meaning and that in the New Testament it refers to pure vocalization in song. He refers to Thayer's *Greek Lexicon* in which it is pointed out that in the New Testament the word refers to singing. That is to say that it does not refer to carpenters' processes, in the New Testament. Kurfees erringly asserts that Thayer meant that *psallo* by New Testament time had lost any reference to instrumental music and thus could only specify vocally pure, noninstrumentally adorned, singing.

7. A song is a sequence of worded ideas set to music. So far as the word "song" is concerned the setting may be vocal, instrumental, or a combination of both. The Old Testament psalms were always set musically; sometimes they were sung without instrumental setting, sometimes with. Scholars believe that in the apostolic period, the musical settings were purely vocal in Christian religious usage. This belief is probably true; however, there is no demonstrative proof. It may be said further that while the word *"song"* might at times refer only to words set in a vocal melody, the view that the music of a song may be only vocal, never otherwise, is to misapply the term.[1] In the word "song" the idea of musical setting (vocal or instrumental) is always inherent. Exactly what apostolic song usage was, will have to be determined when more facts from history are available.

8. As Reese says (see p. 46), Clement tolerated the lyra and kithara because David was said to have used them, but he disapproved of instruments generally because he feared that they might bring to the ears of the Christian listeners echoes of pagan festivity and stage obscenity.

After Clement, Grecian asceticism continued to increase among the people of the church (see pp. 42-48.) By the time of Eusebius, writers in general vehemently denounced instruments of music. This fact makes it improbable that any writers of this later time interpolated approval of instruments into Clement's earlier writing in order to find support for instrumental usage, since the antipathy toward religious use of instruments was more vigorous and general by all of the clergy of the later periods, i.e., fourth, fifth, and sixth centuries, than previously.

---

[1]There is the interesting collection of short pieces by Mendelssohn, entitled "Songs without Words." Here the word "song" is being used very loosely to indicate harmonized melodies to be performed instrumentally.

APPENDIX II

IMPORTANT HYMN-WRITERS IN ENGLISH HYMNODY

Adams, Sarah Flower, 1805-1848. A great friend of Robert Browning, she is thought to be the inspiration of his poem entitled, "Pauline." One of her important hymns[1] includes the lines "He sendeth sun, He sendeth shower, Alike they're needful for the flower." She wrote "Nearer, My God, to Thee" and "Part in Peace."

Addison, Joseph, 1672-1719. This important literary man of eighteenth-century English letters is known for *The Spectator.* He was an honored, trusted, man of affairs, a member of Parliament. He wrote "The Spacious Firmament on High," and "When All Thy Mercies, O My God."

Alford, Dean Henry, 1810-1871. He is known for "Come, Ye Thankful People, Come."

Alexander, Cecil Frances, 1818-1895. This Anglican high church representative wrote "There Is a Green Hill Far Away," and "Once in Royal David's City."

Baring-Gould, Sabine, 1834-1924. This distinguished parish rector began his work with the underprivileged people at Horbury. He published eighty-five books, never employed a secretary; had time for romance and happy marriage. He is popular for his "Onward, Christian Soldiers," and "Now the Day Is Over."

Baxter, Richard, 1615-1691. He was a well-educated nonconformist who dared to write "hymns of my own." His life was tempestuous, steering an honest and courageous course amidst the fierce sectarianism of his day, he took favor from none and extended approval to whomever was deserving. He wrote "Lord, It Belongs Not to My Care." For almost nineteen years he was preacher in Kidderminster where there now stands a monument to his life which transformed the town.

Bunyan, John, 1628-1688. Bunyan was an independent Baptist who earned his livelihood as a tinker. He spent about twelve years in jail during which he wrote nine books. That his writings are known by English-speaking peoples is attested on every hand; that they are not read very much is clear, else the tyranny over freedom that is cropping up again would not be so bold. He wrote "He Who Would Valiant Be."

---

[1]It should be noted again that the term "hymn" refers to the poem; "hymn tune" refers to the music. In recent years the need for clarity at this point has become more apparent. Since the middle of the last century, in the United States, confusion has arisen because church people more and more choose their hymns not so much for their content as for the tune to which they are set.

"Nearer, My God, to Thee" is by Sarah Flower Adams; its usual musical setting is by Lowell Mason.

Cennick, John, 1718-1755. After a misspent youth, he became guilt-conscious. After several months of spiritual self-examination he was converted. First he associated with John Wesley, then with Whitefield, and then later he became one of the Moravian Brethren. Cennick is known for his songs, "Children of the Heavenly King"; "Lo! He Comes with Clouds Descending"; and then two songs, one to be sung before eating, entitled "Be Present at Our Table, Lord," and the second after repast, entitled "We Bless Thee, Lord, for This Our Food." He is known also for his composing of "dialogue songs."

Cowper, William, 1731-1800. From boyhood he was subject to attacks of depression. These occurred frequently and although he fought against their bad effects, oftentimes they were very acute and painful. On occasions he attempted to take his life. When he was free from the attacks of moroseness and depression, he was an unusually sensitive and happy person. He was a poet of distinction. He, like Bishop Ken, was born at Berkhampstead. His mother died when he was six. He was educated at the Westminster School. He was a companion of Warren Hastings, who was being accused far and wide of being an oppressor of India. Upon leaving Westminster School, he took a position as a clerk in a solicitor's office. He is reported to have one day said to his fellow clerk, the future Lord Thurlow, "Thurlow, I am nobody, and shall always be nobody, and you will be Lord Chancellor. You shall provide for me when you are!" to which Thurlow answered, "I surely will!" When the future Lord Thurlow received his title, he forgot his promise to Cowper. When little over thirty years of age, Cowper was offered an appointment to the clerkship of the House of Lords, but his fear of the examination involved brought on his first attack of insanity. Among his hymns (which, perhaps are more melancholy than they would have been if Cowper had associated with people of Wesley's spiritual temper rather than with a disciplinarian personality such as Newton's) are "Sometimes a Light Surprises"; "Far from the World, O Lord, I Flee"; O for a Closer Walk with God!"; "Hark, My Soul! It Is the Lord."

Dix, William Chatterton, 1837-1898. He was a high church layman who wrote a number of overly sentimental hymns. Of lasting value is his "As with Gladness Men of Old."

Doddridge, Philip, 1702-1751. Doddridge was born at London, the twentieth child, laid aside at birth as being stillborn. In spite of his being offered the opportunity by the Duchess of Bedford to train in the University and to prepare for the ministry in the Church of England, Doddridge, like Isaac Watts, decided to cast his lot with the "dissenters." He received many calls to take up the Presbyterian ministry, but he decided to become a minister of the Independent church in Northampton. He was a man of great personal consecration. He is known for the hymns, "Ye Servants of the Lord"; "O Happy Day, That Fixed My Choice"; and "Fountain of Comfort, Source of Love."

Elliott, Charlotte, 1789-1871. She wrote the hymn, "Just as I Am." She is known for two other important hymns: "My God and Father, While I Stray" and "Christian, Seek Not Yet Repose." Miss Elliott was an invalid from childhood until the age of eighty-two. In spite of her physical weakness she manifested a desire to do a great quantity of work. She had a strong will and a strong faith. Miss Elliott was the granddaughter of Henry Venn, a minister, the author of *The Complete Duty of Man.* She was profoundly influenced during a period of forty years by the Genevan evangelist, Cesar Malan.

Grant, Sir Robert, 1785-1838. Grant achieved governmental and political success; from 1834 until his death in 1838, he was lieutenant-governor of Bombay. Among the texts which he wrote is the very famous, "O Worship the King."

Hankey, Arabella Katherine, 1834-1911. She is known for "I Love to Tell the Story."

Havergal, Frances Ridley, 1836-1879. She wrote "Lord Speak to Me That I May Speak"; "Take My Life and Let It Be."

Heber, Reginald, 1783-1826. Heber was an Oxford student, a contemporary and associate of young Walter Scott. He won the prize for a poem which he entitled "Palestine," a poem that still lives. In 1807 he became the vicar of Hodnet where he established himself as being a deeply sympathetic minister to the needy and the unhappy. He had fine literary gifts. Heber was a contributor to the *Quarterly* and edited the works of Jeremy Taylor. He was appointed to be Bampton Lecturer in 1815. In 1823 he became the Bishop of Calcutta. His bishopship included India, Ceylon, and Australia. He died three years after this appointment. He is known especially for his hymn, "Holy, Holy, Holy"; also, "Lord of Mercy and of Might"; and "The Son of God Goes Forth to War."

Herbert, George, 1593-1632. Herbert distinguished himself as an Oxford scholar. He numbered among his friends, James I and Lord Bacon. Taking Holy Orders, he became rector of Bemerton. His life was characterized by a sincere, kindly, continuous generosity to the poor. He was author of "Let All the World in Every Corner Sing"; and "Teach Me, My God, and King."

How, William Walsham, 1823-1897. He is known for "We Give Thee but Thine Own."

Keble, John, 1792-1866. The son of a clergyman in Gloucestershire, he studied with great success at Oxford and was an intimate of Lord Coleridge and of Newman. He was an unassuming, shy individual, a fact the more astonishing because he was known as "the first man in Oxford." In 1831 he became Professor of Poetry at Oxford. He delivered his lectures in Latin. Upon his father's death he became Vicar of Hursley. He kept this position for the rest of his life. He married an untitled woman, whom he styled as being "his conscience, his memory, and his common sense." She died six weeks after he died. Keble is known for the songs "Sun of My Soul"; "New Every Morning Is the Love"; "Hail! Gladdening Light"; and "Lord, in Thy Name Thy Servants Plead." Keble published in 1827, a volume entitled *The Christian Year.* This is a book of poetry which was designed to be a companion to the English prayer book. It was a very successful book, the profits of which Keble used to restore the church at Hursley.

Ken, Thomas, 1637-1711. Ken was born at Berkhampstead; he is known for his hymn, "Awake, My Soul, and with the Sun" and, "Glory to Thee, My God this Night," and the doxology, "Praise God from Whom All Blessings Flow." He was in favor with King Charles II. He was a courageous, honest soul and when King Charles II came to Winchester, where Ken was Bishop, the king requested that he give up his home for Nell Gwynne. This the Bishop refused to do. King Charles respected him for this. He would, at times, go to visit the Bishop in order to hear "little Ken tell him of his faults." When James II became king, Bishop Ken refused to read the Declaration of Indulgence, for which refusal he was sent to the tower. He was later released. When William III was king, Ken refused to take the oath of allegiance and, as a result, he lost his bishopric.

Lyte, Henry Francis, 1793-1847. Lyte was born in Ednam, Scotland, but of English parentage. He was schooled in Ireland but entered the ministry of the Church of England. He was a minister during most of his life, in Lower Brixham, a fishing village on the Devonshire coast. It was here that William of Orange landed in 1688. He suffered from chronic ill health. In September, 1847, before leaving for a winter in Nice, in spite of his failing health, he determined to preach to his people one more time although his family tried to prevent him. He preached a stirring sermon on the Holy Communion. On the evening of that day he gave to a close relative the little hymn entitled "Abide with Me." He never returned from Nice. He died and was buried there. Among song-text arrangements for which he is known are: "O that the Lord's Salvation" founded on Psalm 14; "God of Mercy, God of Grace," founded on Psalm 67; and "Sweet Is the Solemn Voice That Calls," founded on Psalm 127. His song, "Jesus, I My Cross Have Taken," was sung for ten years before it was known that it was his.

Marriott, John, 1780-1825. He studied with the Dean of Christ Church. Later, after distinguishing himself as a student, he became a tutor in the family of the Duke of Buccleuch. Here he became acquainted with Sir Walter Scott. It is to him that Sir Walter Scott dedicated the second canto of *Marmion.* He is known for a stirring missionary hymn, "Thou Whose Almighty Word."

Montgomery, James, 1771-1854. Montgomery was born at Irvine. His father was a Moravian minister. In 1783 his parents went as missionaries to the West Indies where they died. They had left their son at a Moravian school in Yorkshire. At school James began to compose secular poetry, even though both secular poetry and fiction were banned at this institution. The Brethren were not satisfied with him as a scholar and sent him off to be an apprentice to a baker. He ran away. Soon he took a job in the office of a Sheffield newspaper, of which he later became head and proprietor. He was twice put in prison—once for publishing a poem about the fall of the Bastille. He became well known for his poetry, although he never took himself seriously as a poet. He expected none of his poetry to live but thought that, perhaps, a few of his hymns were important. Among his hymns are "Hail to the Lord's Anointed"; "Forever with the Lord"; and "Pour Out Thy Spirit from on High."

Newman, John Henry, 1801-1890. At first an Anglican minister, Newman later became a Roman Catholic cardinal (1879). He is known for his "Lead, Kindly Light." Cardinal Newman had great influence on the world of his time, both as a churchman and as a tract writer. He was one of the group that had to do with the founding of the Oxford Movement. He was one of the most important thinkers of his age. He was extremely influential, as educator, writer, and preacher.

Newton, John, 1725-1807.

JOHN NEWTON

CLERK

ONCE AN INFIDEL AND LIBERTINE

A SERVANT OF SLAVES IN AFRICA

WAS

BY THE RICH MERCY OF OUR LORD AND SAVIOUR

JESUS CHRIST

PRESERVED, RESTORED, PARDONED

AND APPOINTED TO PREACH THE FAITH

HE HAD LONG LABOURED TO DESTROY.

These words were written by Newton himself and placed on his tombstone.

Two women had great influence upon his life: his mother who, although she died when he was seven, had taught him to pray, and Mary Catlett, who became his wife. At eleven years of age he went with his father to sea. He served both in the merchant marine and Royal Navy. He deserted and upon capture was flogged and demoted to rank of common sailor. Even as a sailor he was a student, who read Horace and Euclid. He never was wholly indifferent to religion but at one time, influenced by a companion and his reading, he became an utter skeptic. Later, having studied Thomas a Kempis' "Imitation" and having experienced near-death at sea, he was converted. After his conversion he followed the profession of a slaver, not seeming to feel that this conflicted with his religion. He came, later, under the influence of Wesley and Whitefield and decided to take up the ministry. After some dubiety on the part of the Archbishop of York because of his previous record, Newton was, nevertheless, ordained by the Bishop of Lincoln as the curate of Olney, Bucks. He held this position for eighteen years, a period in which he wrote many hymns. The closing years of his life were spent in the position of rector of St. Mary Woolnoth, London. His hymns are deeply earnest and anxious, seldom are they joyous. Among them are the songs, "How Sweet the Name of Jesus Sounds" and "Why Should I Fear the Darkest Hour?"

Oxenham, John, 185?-1941. Oxenham was a novelist and poet of most unusual success. His *Hymns for Men at the Front* circulated 8,000,000 copies. He was an earnest crusader against sectarianism and denominationalism. He wrote "In Christ There Is No East or West."

Perronet, Edward, 1726-1792. Perronet is best known for his song "All Hail the Power of Jesus' Name." He took a very active part in the evangelical revival of the eighteenth century. He worked for a time with John Wesley but was so self-willed that he finally left that work to become a minister of the Countess of Huntingdon's "connection." His final appointment was as pastor of a small Congregational church in Canterbury.

Pierpont, Folliett Sandford, 1835-1917. He is remembered for his "For the Beauty of the Earth."

Steele, Anne, 1716-1778. One of the most popular writers in her day, following closely after Watts and Doddridge, she was a Baptist "dissenter." Her work showed the greatest reverence for the "infallible Bible," which in the English mind had taken the place of the "infallible church," headed at Rome, and against which the English had revolted. Of the 144 hymns she wrote, one still lives: "Father of Mercies, in Thy Word."

Stone, Samuel John, 1839-1900. He is remembered for his essay, "The Soliloquy of a Rationalistic Chicken." He wrote fifty-five hymns of which one is well known: "The Church's One Foundation."

Tennyson, Alfred Lord, 1809-1892. Tennyson, Poet Laureate, felt inadequate for hymn writing, but there are three of his poems which have been accepted as part of the English hymn literature: "Strong Son of God, Immortal Love"; "Sunset and Evening Star"; "In Memoriam."

Toplady, Augustus Montague, 1740-1778. He wrote "Rock of Ages," perhaps the most widely known and one of the best loved hymns in the English language. This hymn owes its popularity to its spiritual qualities rather than to its artistic or literary value.

Waring, Anna Laetitia, 1820-1910. She is known for "In Heavenly Love Abiding."

Wesley, Charles, 1707-1788; *Wesley, John,* 1703-1791. (See footnote, p. 134.) The two brothers are usually considered together, although Charles is more noted for his writing than John. John's contributions were mainly in the translating of hymns and compiling of them into collections for public worship.

Charles is credited with having written more than 6,000 hymns. Charles, with John, collaborated in the publishing of some fifty collections of hymns. He wrote a number of very remarkable hymns treating of the Lord's Supper. It is marvelous that, having written so much, he also wrote so well. Some of his compositions are poor enough but, on the whole, his songs represent a highly dignified attainment in the business of "admonishing with hymns." The brothers were born at Epworth, where their father was rector of the church. Their mother was a disciplinarian with inexhaustible patience. She taught her children to "cry softly." Her husband complained that she had told her children the same thing twenty times, to which she replied that if she had told them the same thing for only nineteen times she would not have succeeded. Charles was educated at the Westminster School. He made friends with William Murray of Scone who, after becoming Earl Mansfield and Chief Justice of England, never forgot Wesley who had befriended him when he was in school where his strange Scotch dialect had made him the butt of schoolmates. From Westminster, Charles went to Christ Church, where he met with a band of serious students, including Whitefield, who gathered about for the study of the Greek Testament, for the observance of weekly communion, for private devotion at appointed hours, and for the visiting of the sick and the teaching of neglected children. Because of the pious way in which this group of students under the tutelage of Charles and John organized this association of students, they were ridiculed by others and called "religious methodists," from which the name was taken for the church which has sprung from this earlier association. Both John and Charles owed much of their religious as well as poetical development to the influence of two members of the Moravian brotherhood, Count Zinzendorf and Peter Bohler. Henry Ward Beecher said that Wesley's hymns were really "Moravian hymns resung." This does not mean that Charles Wesley, who was unable to translate Greek, took the Moravian hymns and re-arranged them, rather, he took the spirit of the Moravian hymns as inspiration for the writing of his own. Among the many hymns of Charles Wesley these are highly important: "Hark! the Herald Angels Sing"; "Come, Thou Long-Expected Jesus"; "Gentle Jesus, Meek and Mild"; "Jesus, Lover of My Soul." Henry Ward Beecher said of this latter hymn, "I would rather have written that hymn than to have the fame of all the kings that ever sat upon the earth!"

Whiting, William, 1825-1878. Whiting was Master of the Winchester College Choristers' School. He wrote "Eternal Father, Strong to Save," a hymn which has been a favorite for years, and is an appointed hymn of the United States Naval Academy.

Williams, William, 1717-1791. He was ordained to be a deacon of the Church of England but was not held in high favor by the authorities of that church because of his association with Whitefield and other revivalists. He worked mostly with Calvinistic Methodists of Wales. He compiled a small hymnbook for the use of Whitefield's Orphan Homes in America in which appeared, among others of his most famous songs, "Guide Me, O Thou Great Jehovah!"

Wordsworth, Christopher, 1807-1885. Bishop in the Anglican Church, he wrote "O Day of Rest and Gladness"; "O Lord of Heaven and Earth and Sea"; and others.

ENGLISH COMPOSERS

Arne, Thomas Augustine, 1710-1778. Arne, one of the important English composers of his day received the degree, Doctor of Music, from Oxford in 1759. He was composer for the Drury Lane Theatre. His wife, a singer often performed for Handel in his productions. The hymn tune ARLINGTON is by Arne.

Bambridge, William S., 1842-1923. He was born in New Zealand, later he migrated to England, where he spent fifty-nine years. He is known for his tune ST. ASAPH.

Barnby, Joseph, 1838-1896. Barnby is known as a conductor, composer, editor, and organist. He composed hundreds of hymn tunes, among which LAUDES DOMINI is representative.

Calkin, John Baptiste, 1827-1905. Calkin was a distinguished church musician, especially noted for WALTHAM, which serves well as a processional.

Croft, William, 1678-1727. He composed the earliest English psalm tunes distinct in idiom from the Genevan. Croft composed thirty anthems, and perhaps influenced Handel's oratorio writing; he received his Doctorate in Music in 1713.

Dykes, John Bacchus, 1823-1876. The composer of 300 hymn tunes along with many other writings, was one of several to contribute to the formalization of the tasteful English hymn.

Elvey, George J., 1816-1893. A highly successful church musician and organist, Elvey is known for ST. GEORGE'S, WINDSOR.

Gower, John Henry, 1855-1922. During early years he was organist and college professor at Trent College, Nottingham. He came to the United States and interested himself in mining, maintaining, however, his interest in music and organ playing. He is known for his tune MEDITATION, the usual setting for "There Is a Green Hill Far Away."

Hopkins, Edward J., 1818-1901. An organist and crusader for heightening standards in church music, he composed many organ pieces and anthems, edited several hymn collections. He wrote the well-liked tune, ELLERS.

Horsley, William, 1774-1858. An English organist, friend of Mendelssohn, he was a composer of some note, having produced a number of hymn-tune settings, songs, and sonatas.

Maker, Frederick C., 1844-1927. Maker was an organist in Bristol, composer of a cantata, and contributor to *The Bristol Tune Book.*

Mann, Arthur H., 1850-1929. Mann was famous as organist and musical editor *(The Church of England Hymnal)*; an authority on Handel. He composed a considerable quantity of important church music. He wrote the tunes, VALOUR and ANGEL'S STORY.

Peace, Albert L., 1844-1912. A child prodigy as an organist, in later life he was a distinguished organist in important offices, such as the Glasgow Cathedral. He is famous for his Lux Beata, used as a setting for "Immortal Love Within Whose Righteous Will"; and his St. Margaret, setting for "O Love That Wilt Not Let Me Go."

Smart, Henry, 1813-1879. A self-taught organist and composer, he is known for many important musical works of high order. His *Service in F* is a superb work. His hymn-tune setting, Regent Square, is well-known.

Stainer, Sir John, 1840-1901. Stainer was a great and popular organist. His compositions were well liked and still remain in high favor. He was a fellow choir boy with the famous Sullivan; they remained lifelong friends. His harmonization of In Dulci Jubilo, his cantata, *The Crucifixion,* and his Sevenfold Amen are well known.

Sullivan, Sir Arthur Seymour, 1842-1900. The famed composer of *H. M. S. Pinafore,* also wrote the setting used for "Onward, Christian Soldiers," and the song, "The Lost Chord." He was a professor of composition, and an organist of distinction.

Wesley, Samuel, 1810-1876. He was a grandson of Charles Wesley. He published a collection of hymn tunes, performed as an organist in many churches and cathedrals of England. He was renowned as an improviser at the organ.

Williams, Ralph Vaughan, 1872-1961. Ralph Vaughan Williams, a contemporary composer, musical editor, was distinguished for his dignified, restrained, although stimulating modern style in religious composition. His Sine Nomine is a fine example of his simpler work.

SCOTTISH HYMNISTS

Bonar, Horatius, 1809-1889. This descendant of a long line of Scottish ministers aligned himself with the Scottish Free Church. He was a scholarly biblical student, educated at Edinburgh, who became Scotland's greatest hymnist. He wrote nearly 600 hymns of which a few are still held in high regard: "Go, Labor On: Spend and Be Spent"; "I Heard the Voice of Jesus Say"; "Here, O My Lord, I See Thee Face to Face."

Clephane, Elizabeth Cecilia Douglas, 1830-1869. She is best known for "Beneath the Cross of Jesus."

Matheson, George, 1842-1906. Matheson is known for "O Love That Wilt Not Let Me Go."

IMPORTANT ENGLISH WRITERS OF CHILDREN'S SACRED SONGS OF YESTERYEAR

Among the women:

Duncan, Mary Lundie, 1814-1840. Her best-known song is "Jesus, Tender Shepherd, Hear Me." This song was included in a tiny book which she published entitled *Rhymes for My Children.*

Havergal, Frances Ridley, 1836-1879. She wrote a version of the Lord's Prayer that is very useful for children; also, the song, "God Will Take Care of You," which is to be sung *to* children rather than to be sung *by* children.

Leeson, Jane E., 1807-1882. She wrote a collection of verses for children, published in 1842, entitled *Hymns and Scenes of Childhood.*

Shepherd, Anne, 1809-1857. She compiled a book entitled *Hymns adapted for the Comprehension of Young Minds.*

Strafford, Elizabeth, 1828-1868. She wrote one hymn which became very popular for children, "Once to Our World There Came."

Taylor, Ann and *Jane.* They are known for *Hymns for Infant Minds.*

Thrupp, Dorothy Ann, 1779-1847. She is known for one excellent children's song, "A Little Ship Was on the Sea."

Among the men who wrote for children were:

Burton, John, 1803-1877. He wrote "Savior, While My Heart Is Tender." Another author of the same name (1773-1822) wrote "Holy Bible, Book Divine."

Edmeston, James, 1791-1867. He wrote "Little Travelers Zionward."

Henley, John, 1800-1842. He wrote "Children of Jerusalem."

Young, Andrew, 1807-1889. He wrote "There Is a Happy Land, Where Care's Unknown."

Among additional writers who wrote for children:

Baring-Gould, Sabine, 1834-1924. He was author of "Onward, Christian Soldiers" and "Now the Day Is Over."

Betham-Edwards, Matilda Barbara, 1836-1919. She was author of two well-known hymns:

> God make my life a little light
>   Within the world to glow;
> A little flame that burneth bright,
>   Wherever I may go.

> God make my life a little flower,
>   That giveth joy to all,
> Content to bloom in native bower,
>   Although the place be small.

> The little birds now seek their nest;
> The baby sleeps on mother's breast;
> Thou givest all Thy children rest,
>   God of the weary.

Hawkins, Hester P. She published the collection, *The Home Hymn Book* in 1885.

How, William Walsham, 1823-1897. He wrote:

> It is a thing most wonderful,
> Almost too wonderful to be,
> That God's own Son should come from heaven,
> And die to save a child like me.

Luke, Jemima, 1813-1906. She wrote "I Think When I Read that Sweet Story of Old."

Midlane, Albert, 1825-1909. He was the author of "There's a Friend for Little Children."

Palgrave, Francis Turner, 1824-1897. Palgrave wrote "Thou that Once, on Mother's Knee" and "O God, Who When the Night Was Deep."

Threlfall, Jeanette, 1821-1880. She wrote "Hosanna! Loud Hosanna!" one of the finest hymns for children.

Waugh, Benjamin, 1839-1908. He compiled a book called *Sunday Evenings with My Children.*

The song writers listed above were, in the main, English writers. There were several American writers who composed successfully for children, among them:

Bliss, Philip Paul, 1838-1876. He was born at Clearfield, Pennsylvania. He wrote the song:

> I am so glad that our Father in heaven
> Tells of His love in the Book He has given:
> Wonderful things in the Bible I see,
> This is the dearest—that Jesus loves me.

Cooper, George, 1840-1927. He wrote:

> There are lonely hearts to cherish
>   While the days are going by.
> There are weary souls who perish
>   While the days are going by.
>   Up! then, trusty hearts and true,
> Though the day comes, night comes, too;
>   Oh, the good we all may do
> While the days are going by!

Crosby, Fanny (Mrs. Frances Jane Van Alstyne), 1823-1915. She wrote "Jesus the Water of Life Has Given"; "Safe in the Arms of Jesus"; "Rescue the Perishing"; "Pass Me Not"; "Blessed Assurance"; "What a Gathering." Typical of her lifelong faith is the refrain:

> Close to Thee, close to Thee;
> All along my pilgrim journey,
> Savior let me walk with Thee.

All in all she wrote 6,000 texts. Only Isaac Watts and Charles Wesley have rivaled her influence in modern times.

She was born at South East, New York, and became blind at six weeks because of the application of too hot a poultice to her eyes. At thirty-eight years of age she married a musician, also blind, a student in the New York Institution for the Blind, where she was teaching.

Cushing, William O., 1823-1902. He wrote a hymn that has gone around the world, "When He Cometh, When He Cometh, to Make Up His Jewels," set to a tune by George F. Root.

Palmer, Horatio Richmond, 1834-1907. He was author of:

> Yield not to temptation,
> For yielding is sin;
> Each victory will help you
> Some other to win.
>
> Fight manfully onward,
> Dark passions subdue;
> Look ever to Jesus,
> He will carry you through.

Riley, Mary Louise (Mrs. Albert Smith), 1842-1927. She was author of:

> Let us gather up the sunbeams
> Lying all along our path;
> Let us keep the wheat and roses,
> Casting out the thorns and chaff.

GERMAN—BOHEMIAN—AUSTRIAN—DANISH HYMNISTS

Claudius, Mátthias, 1740-1815. He is known for his "We Plough the Fields and Scatter."

Gerhardt, Paul, 1607-1676. He was a German hymnist who has outstripped Luther in influence. His hymns were of great influence upon the Wesleys. John Wesley translated his "Jesus, Thy Boundless Love to Me."

Herbert, Peter, ? -1571. Herbert was born in Moravia; later, he became a disciple of John Huss (1369-1415). The Bohemians and Moravians had been "converted to Christianity" under the Eastern Church. When by conquest, they came into the jurisdiction of the Roman church, they vigorously opposed Catholicism. John Huss, their earlier champion who founded the "Bohemian Brethren," was burned at the stake. Herbert, much later, through his hymn writing, did much to strengthen the "brotherhood." He wrote the hymn now translated, "Now God Be with Us, for the Night Is Closing."

Ingemann, Bernhard Severin, 1789-1862. Ingemann was a Dane, known for his "Through the Night of Doubt and Sorrow," translated by Sabine Baring-Gould.

Mahlmann, Siegfried Augustus, 1771-1826. He is known for his "God Bless Our Native Land!"

Mohr, Josef, 1792-1848. An Austrian, Mohr is famous for his "Silent Night, Holy Night."

Neander, Joachim, 1650-1680. Neander was an intemperate student in his early days at Bremen, but he was converted when he visited St. Martin's Church and heard Under-Eyck preach. Neander came to be a most influential hymnist. He wrote 19 important poems, one of which is the magnificent, "Praise to the Lord, the Almighty, the King of Creation." He was a tune composer also.

Nicolai, Philipp, 1556-1608. He was a Lutheran minister who boldly opposed Catholicism and Calvinism. He wrote the hymn translated "How Brightly Beams the Morning Star!"

Tersteegen, Gerhard, 1697-1769. Tersteegen's uneven success in business and his spiritual despondency were relieved by his conversion to Jesus. He wrote with his own blood a covenant with God. Wesley translated his "God Himself Is Present: Let Us Now Adore Him."

Von Canitz: Ludwig, Friedrich Rudolph, Freiherr von Canitz, 1654-1699. He was a consecrated, well-educated nobleman who wrote twenty-four hymns. Familiar today is his "Come, My Soul Thou Must Be Waking."

Von Zinzendorf: Ludwig, Nicolaus, Count von Zinzendorf, 1700-1760. He was a precocious student, educated at Halle to become a Pietist. At the age of twenty-two he became sympathetic to the Moravian Brethren; he attempted to set up a "true Church" uninfluenced by State Lutheranism. He wrote hymns all his life; was a considerable influence upon John Wesley, who translated his "O Thou to Whose All-searching Sight." He also wrote "Jesus, Lead the Way."

GERMAN COMPOSERS[2]

Gruber, Franz, 1789-1863. He is well known for the setting of "Silent Night, Holy Night."

Kocher, Conrad, 1786-1872. He composed oratorios, operas, and sonatas; founded a school of sacred music which was the pattern for many more later established throughout Württemberg. He is known for the tune, DIX.

Mendelssohn, Felix, 1809-1847. This famous composer had considerable influence on the composition of hymn tunes and their harmonizations. Although he was of Jewish parentage, he was a Lutheran.

Schulz, Johann A. P., 1747-1800. Schulz is known for his setting of "We Plow the Fields and Scatter" by Claudius.

Crüger, Johann, 1598-1662. Crüger was a distinguished educator and choir director; composer of many musical works. He is known mostly for his religious chorales.

Pleyel, Ignaz Joseph, 1757-1831. He was a prolific composer; a pupil of of Haydn. His tune, GRACE CHURCH, is an adaptation from one of his string quartets.

---

[2]These are among those who have become well known to American church musicians. It is interesting to note that original hymn settings or adaptations from their works are commonly included from the masters, among whom are Beethoven, Gounod, Handel, Haydn, Mozart, Schumann, Sibelius, and Weber.

SWISS COMPOSERS

Malan, Henri A. Cesar, 1787-1864. He was a composer in the Calvinistic school. However, he was an evangelist and as such was always welcome in the British Isles. He was nearly as influential as Watts and Wesley. His tune, HENDON, is representative; widely used in the United States.

Nägeli, Hans G., 1768-1836. Nägeli was a music educator who had considerable influence upon Lowell Mason; he resided most of his life in the vicinity of Zurich. He composed the music which was later arranged by Mason in the tune known today as DENNIS.

UNITED STATES HYMNISTS

Bates, Katherine Lee, 1859-1929. She wrote "O Beautiful for Spacious Skies."

Brooks, Phillips, 1835-1893. He was revered by all of Boston; he wrote "O Little Town of Bethlehem."

Doan, George Washington, 1799-1859. Doan was a scholarly clergyman who became Bishop of New Jersey. He was in deep sympathy with the Oxford movement. He wrote, "Softly Now the Light of Day"; "Fling Out the Banner, Let It Float."

Duffield, George, Jr., 1818-1888. He wrote "Stand Up, Stand Up for Jesus." He was an American Presbyterian.

Dwight, Timothy, 1752-1817. Dwight was an American Congregationalist, President of Yale University, an important religious revivalist. He wrote, "I Love Thy Kingdom Lord."

Gilmore, Joseph Henry, 1834-1918. He is known for "He Leadeth Me! O Blessed Thought."

Gladden, Washington, 1838-1918. He wrote "O Master, Let Me Walk with Thee."

Hawks, Annie Sherwood, 1835-1918. She wrote "I Need Thee Every Hour."

Holmes, Oliver Wendell, 1809-1894. "Lord of All Being, Throned Afar," is representative of this great man of letters.

Hopper, Edward, 1818-1888. He wrote "Jesus, Savior, Pilot Me."

Lathbury, Mary Artemesia, 1841-1913. She is known for "Day Is Dying in the West"; "Break Thou the Bread of Life."

Longfellow, Samuel, 1819-1892. "Holy Spirit, Truth Divine," is representative of his work.

Palmer, Ray, 1808-1887. Palmer was a Rhode Islander Congregationalist who wrote 38 hymns. Among them is "My Faith Looks Up to Thee."

Phelps, Sylvanus Dryden, 1816-1895. Phelps, an American Baptist is known for "Saviour, Thy Dying Love."

Prentiss, Elizabeth Payson, 1818-1878. Mrs. Prentiss was a lifelong invalid, native of Maine, wife of Dr. George L. Prentiss, professor at Union. She is known for "More Love to Thee, O Christ."

Rankin, Jeremiah, Eames, 1828-1904. He wrote "God Be with You Till We Meet Again."

Roberts, Daniel Crane, 1841-1907. He wrote "God of Our Fathers, Whose Almighty Hand."

Sears, Edmund Hamilton, 1810-1876. He is remembered for "It Came Upon the Midnight Clear."

Smith, Samuel Francis, 1808-1895. He was an American Baptist known for "My Country! 'Tis of Thee"; and "The Morning Light Is Breaking."

Whittier, John Greenleaf, 1807-1892. A Quaker of New England whose spiritual insight makes him the greatest of United States hymnists. Among his hymns are "Dear Lord and Father of Mankind."

UNITED STATES COMPOSERS[3]

Gottschalk, Louis M., 1829-1869. He was a composer of some merit but known mostly as a pianist. He was popular as a traveling artist in Spanish America. The tune, MERCY, is an adaptation from one of his piano pieces.

Gould, John E., 1822-1875. A Philadelphian, son of a sea captain, he did much to elevate the level of music in the United States. He is known for PILOT, a setting for "Jesus, Saviour, Pilot Me." This song is one of the few of the gospel-song literature to take an important place in church hymnology.

Redner, Lewis H., 1831-1908. Redner was a Philadelphia organist and Sunday school teacher. He composed the setting for "O Little Town of Bethlehem."

Sherwin, William F., 1826-1888. He was a pupil of Lowell Mason, later a singing teacher at the New England Conservatory. For years he was director of music at Chautauqua. He wrote the tune, EVENING PRAISE, for "Day Is Dying in the West" and also the tune setting for "Break Thou the Bread of Life."

Taylor, Virgil Corydon, 1817-1891. Much influenced by Lowell Mason and Thomas Hastings, he was a director of singing schools. He composed the tune, LOUVAN, which is a setting for Oliver Wendell Holmes' "Lord of All Being, Throned Afar."

Walter, William H., 1825-1893. He was an organist at Columbia University; and composer of FESTAL SONG for "Rise Up, O Men of God."

---

[3]For U.S. Catholic composers, see Nemmers, E. E. *Twenty Centuries of Catholic Church Music.* Milwaukee: The Bruce Publishing Co., 1949.

Ward, Samuel A., 1847-1903. Ward was a music merchant and patron of music in Newark, New Jersey. He wrote MATERNA, setting for "America the Beautiful."

Warren, George William, 1828-1902. He was a self-taught organist who played at churches in Albany, where he was born. He wrote many hymn settings and compiled a hymnal. He is known for ECCE AGNUS.

Willis, Richard S., 1819-1900. Yale educated, friend of Mendelssohn in Germany, author of *Our Church Music,* he is known for his setting of "It Came Upon the Midnight Clear."

BIBLIOGRAPHY

BIBLIOGRAPHY

1. *Anthologies*

   Bach, Johann Sebastian, *371 Harmonized Chorales and 69 Chorale Melodies with Figured Bass,* ed. by Albert Riemenschneider. New York: G. Schirmer, Inc., 1941.

   Davison, Archibald T. and Willi Apel, eds., *Historical Anthology of Music.* Cambridge: Harvard Univ. Press, 1946-1950. Vol. I. Oriental, Medieval and Renaissance Music; Vol. II. Baroque, Rococo and Pre-classical Music.

   Geiringer, Karl, ed., *Music of the Bach Family; An Anthology.* Cambridge: Harvard Univ. Press, 1955.

   Gilbert, Henry F. and others, eds., *The Art of Music.* New York: The National Society of Music, 1916. Vol. XIII, Book I. Musical Examples from History.

   Gleason, Harold, ed., *Examples of Music Before 1400.* New York: Appleton-Century-Crofts, 1945.

   Orthodox Eastern Church, *The Hymns of the Hirmologium* (Part I) transcribed by Aglaia Ayoutanti and Maria Stöhr. Copenhagen: Einar Munksgaard, 1952.

   Orthodox Eastern Church, *The Hymn of the Octoechus* (Part I) transcribed by H. J. W. Tillyard. Copenhagen: Einar Munksgaard, 1940.

   Parrish, Carl G. and John G. Ohl, eds., *Masterpieces of Music Before 1750.* New York: W. W. Norton & Co., 1951.

   Schering, Arnold, ed., *History of Music in Examples.* New York: Broude Bros., 1950.

   Soderlund, Gustave Fredric, comp., *Examples of Gregorian Chant and Works by Orlandus Lassus and Giovanni Pierluigi Palestrina.* Rochester, N. Y.: Eastman School of Music of the University of Rochester, 1937.

   Tudor Church Music. London: Oxford Univ. Press, 1923-1929. 10 vols.

2. *Bibliography and Source Readings*

   Coover, James B., *A Bibliography of Music Dictionaries.* Denver: Denver Public Library, 1952.

   Darrell, R. D., comp., *Schirmer's Guide to Books on Music and Musicians; a Practical Bibliography.* New York: G. Schirmer, Inc., 1951.

   Krohn, Ernst C., comp., *The History of Music; an Index to the Literature Available in a Selected Group of Musicological Publications.* St. Louis: Washington University, 1952.

   Nettl, Paul, *The Book of Musical Documents.* New York: Philosophical Library, 1948.

   Strunk, Oliver, ed., *Source Readings in Music History; from Classical Antiquity through the Romantic Era.* New York: W. W. Norton & Co., Inc., 1950.

3. *Criticism, Interpretation and Theory*

Apel, Willi, *The Notation of Polyphonic Music, 900-1600*. Cambridge, Mass.: Mediaeval Academy of America, 1942.

Benade, Arthur H., *Horns, Strings and Harmony*. Columbus, Ohio: Wesleyan University Press, 1960.

Demuth, Norman, comp., *An Anthology of Musical Criticism*. London: Eyre & Spottiswoode, 1948.

——, *Musical Trends in the 20th Century*. London, Rockliff Publishing Corp.; New York: Macmillan Co., 1952.

Dolmetsch, Arnold, *The Interpretation of the Music of the XVIIth and XVIIIth Centuries Revealed by Contemporary Evidence*. London: Novello and Company, 1915.

Helmholtz, Herman L., *On the Sensations of Tone as a Physiological Basis for the Theory of Music*. 2nd English ed. New York: Dover Publications, Inc., 1954.

Nettl, Paul, *Luther and Music*. Philadelphia: Muhlenberg Press, 1948.

Schweitzer, Albert, *J. S. Bach*. London: A. & C. Black Ltd.; New York: Macmillan Co., 1935. 2 vols.

4. *Church of England*

The Book of Common Prayer.

Fellowes, Edmund H., *English Cathedral Music from Edward VI to Edward VII*. London: Methuen & Co., Ltd., 1945.

Gardner, George and Sydney H. Nicholson, eds., *A Manual of English Church Music*. London: Society for Promoting Christian Knowledge, 1936.

Goodrich, Wallace and Charles Winfred Douglas, *The Choral Service*. London: Novello and Company, 1927.

Merbecke, John, *The Office of the Holy Communion as Set by the Author*. London and New York: Oxford Univ. Press, 1949.

Shaw, Martin, *The Principles of English Church Music Composition*. London: Musical Opinion, 1921.

5. *Dictionaries and Encyclopedias*

The Catholic Encyclopedia. New York: The Encyclopedia Press, 1907-1914. 15 vols.

A Dictionary of Hymnology, ed. by John Julian. London: John Murray, 1925.

Grove's Dictionary of Music and Musicians, ed. by Eric Blom. New York: St. Martin's Press; London: Macmillan, Ltd., 5th rev. ed., 1954. 9 vols.

Harvard Dictionary of Music, ed. by Willi Apel. Cambridge: Harvard Univ. Press, 1944.

The International Cyclopedia of Music and Musicians, ed. by Oscar Thompson, rev. and enl. under the editorial direction of Nicolas Slonimsky. New York: Dodd, Mead and Co., 8th ed., rev., 1958.

The Jewish Encyclopedia. New York: Funk & Wagnalls Co., 1901-1906. 12 vols.

6. *Hymnal Handbooks*

Covert, William C. and Calvin W. Laufer, eds., *Handbook to the Hymnal*. Philadelphia: Presbyterian Board of Christian Education, 1935.

Haeussler, Armin, *The Story of Our Hymns; the Handbook to the Hymnal of the Evangelical and Reformed Church*. St. Louis: Eden Publishing Co., 1952.

Hostetler, Lester, *Handbook to the Mennonite Hymnary.* Newton, Kansas: General Conference of the Mennonite Church of North America, 1949.

The Hymnal 1940 Companion, prepared by the Joint Commission on the Revision of the Hymnal of the Protestant Episcopal Church. New York: The Church Pension Fund, 1949.

Lutheran Church in America, *Service Book and Hymnal.* Minneapolis: Augsburg Publishing House, 1958.

Polack, W. G., comp., *Handbook to The Lutheran Hymnal.* St. Louis: Concordia Publishing House, 1942.

7. *History*

Allen, Warren Dwight, *Philosophies of Music History.* New York: American Book Co., 1939.

Bukofzer, Manfred F., *Music in the Baroque Era, from Monteverdi to Bach.* New York: W. W. Norton & Co., 1947.

——, *Studies in Medieval & Renaissance Music.* New York: W. W. Norton & Co., 1950.

Burney, Charles, *General History of Music from the Earliest Ages to the Present Period (1789).* New York: Harcourt, Brace and Co., 1935. 2 vols.

Dickinson, Edward, *Music in the History of the Western Church.* New York: Charles Scribner's Sons, 1902.

Douglas, Charles Winfred, *Church Music in History and Practice.* New York: Charles Scribner's Sons, 1937.

Ferguson, Donald N., *A History of Musical Thought.* New York: Appleton-Century-Crofts Co., Inc., 1948.

Grout, Donald Jay, *A History of Western Music.* New York: W. W. Norton & Co., 1960.

Làng, Paul Henry, *Music in Western Civilization.* New York: W. W. Norton & Co., 1941.

Leichtentritt, Hugo, *Music, History, and Ideas.* Cambridge: Harvard Univ. Press, 1938.

Migne, Jacques Paul, ed., *Patrologiae Cursus Completus.* (Music index, Latin series, vol. CCXXI)

Reese, Gustave, *Music in the Middle Ages.* New York: W. W. Norton & Co., 1940.

——, *Music in the Renaissance.* New York: W. W. Norton & Co., 1954.

Sachs, Curt, *The Rise of Music in the Ancient World, East and West.* New York: W. W. Norton & Co., 1943.

——, *A World History of the Dance.* New York: W. W. Norton & Co., 1937.

Schaff, Philip, *History of the Christian Church.* New York: Charles Scribner's Sons, 1882-1888.

Wellesz, Egon, *A History of Byzantine Music and Hymnography.* Oxford: Clarendon Press, 1949.

8. *Hymns, Hymnology, and Psalmody*

Bailey, Albert Edward, *The Gospel in Hymns.* New York: Charles Scribner's Sons, 1950.

Benson, Louis F., *The Hymnody of the Christian Church.* Richmond: John Knox Press, 1956.

Brown, Ray F., ed., *The Oxford American Psalter.* New York: Oxford Univ. Press, 1949.

Dearmer, Percy, ed., *Songs of Praise Discussed*. London: Oxford Univ. Press, 1933.
Douglas, Charles Winfred, *A Brief Commentary on Selected Hymns and Carols*. Evanston, Ill.: Northwestern University, 1936.
Duffield, Samuel Willoughby, *English Hymns: Their Authors and History*. New York: Funk & Wagnalls Co., 1886.
Fraser, Duncan, *The Passing of the Precentor*. Edinburgh: John Knox's House, 1905.
Isaac, Heinrich, *Choralis Constantinus*. Book III, Transcribed from the Formschneider first edition by Louise Cuyler. Ann Arbor: Univ. of Michigan Press, 1950.
Messenger, Ruth Ellis, *The Medieval Latin Hymn*. Washington: Capital Press, 1953.
Neale, J. M., *Hymns of the Eastern Church*. London: Hayes, 1862.
——, *Mediaeval Hymns and Sequences*. London: J. Masters, 1851, 1861, 1863.
Patrick, Millar, *Four Centuries of Scottish Psalmody*. London: Oxford Univ. Press, 1949.
Pratt, Waldo Selden, *The Music of the French Psalter of 1562*. New York: Columbia Univ. Press, 1939.
Walpole, A. S., ed., *Early Latin Hymns*. Cambridge: Harvard Univ. Press, 1922.

9. *Jewish Music*

Box, G. H., *Judaism in the Greek Period*. New York: Oxford Univ. Press, 1932.
Idelsohn, Abraham Z., *Jewish Music in Its Historical Development*. New York: Tudor Publishing Co., 1944.
Werner, E., "The Conflict between Hellenism and Judaism in the Music of Early Christianity" in *Hebrew Union College Annual*, 1947.

10. *Musical Instruments*

Galpin, Francis W., *Old English Instruments of Music, Their History and Character*. London: Methuen & Co., Ltd., 1910.
——, *A Textbook of European Musical Instruments, Their Origin, History and Character*. New York: John de Graff, Inc., 1956.
Sachs, Curt, *The History of Musical Instruments*. New York: W. W. Norton & Co., 1940.

11. *Organ*

Apel, Willi, *Masters of the Keyboard*. Cambridge: Harvard Univ. Press, 1947.
Barnes, William H., *The Contemporary American Organ; Its Evolution, Design and Construction*. New York: J. Fischer & Brother, 1952.
Farmer, Henry G., *The Organ of the Ancients from Eastern Sources (Hebrew, Syriac and Arabic)*. New York: E. P. Dutton & Co., 1931.
Klein, John, ed., *The First Four Centuries of Music for the Organ*. New York: Associated Music Press, 1948.
Praetorius, Michael, *Syntagmatis Musici Michaelis Praetorii C. Tomus Secundus De Organographia*. Gedrucktzu Wolffenbüttel, 1619; facsimile edition. Kassel: Bärenreiter-verlag, 1929.
Schweiger, Hertha, ed., *A Brief Compendium of Early Organ Music*. New York: G. Schirmer, Inc., 1943.
Sumner, William L., *The Organ*. New York: Philosophical Library, 1952.

12. *Plainsong*

Apel, Willi, *Gregorian Chant*. Bloomington: Indiana University Press, 1958.

Gajard, Joseph, *The Rhythm of Plainsong According to the Solesmes School*, translated by Aldhelm Dean. New York: J. Fischer & Brother, 1945.

Nicholson, Sydney H., ed., *A Plainsong Hymnbook*. London: William Clowes & Sons, Ltd., 1932.

Sceats, Godfrey, *Plainchant and Faburden*. London: The Faith Press, 1937.

Wellesz, Egon J., *Eastern Elements in Western Chant; Studies in the Early History of Ecclesiastical Music*. Boston: Byzantine Institute, 1947.

13. *Roman Catholic Church Music*

Cabrol, Fernand, *Mass, Its Doctrine and History; the Story of the Mass in Pen and Picture*. New York: P. J. Kenedy & Sons, 1931.

Catholic Church. Liturgy and Ritual, *Delectus Missarum e Graduali Romano*. New York: J. Fischer & Brother, 1928.

Goodchild, Sister Mary Antonine, comp., *Gregorian Chant for Church and School*. Boston: Ginn & Co., 1944.

Johner, Dominicus, *A New School of Gregorian Chant*. Ratisbon and New York: F. Pustet, Typographer, 1906.

La Messe et l'Office des Benedictines de Solesmes. Paris: Societé de Saint Jean L'Evangeliste, 1936.

Liber Usualis Missae et Officii pro Dominicis et Festis . . . Tournai: Desclée & Cie., 1934.

Nemmers, Erwin Esser, *Twenty Centuries of Catholic Church Music*. Milwaukee: Bruce Publishing Co., 1949.

Pius X, Pope, *Sacred Music, Motu Proprio*. Washington, D. C.: The Catholic Education Press, 1928.

Weinmann, Karl, *History of Church Music*. Boston: McLaughlin and Reilly, 1948.

14. *The United States*

Britton, Allen P., "The Musical Idiom in Early American Tunebooks," *The Journal of the American Musicological Society*, III, 1950, p. 286.

Chase, Gilbert, *America's Music*. New York: McGraw-Hill Book Co., 1955.

Davison, Archibald T., *Protestant Church Music in America*. Boston: E. C. Schirmer Co., 1945.

Ellinwood, Leonard, *The History of American Church Music*. New York: Morehouse-Gorham Co., 1953.

Foote, Henry Wilder, *Three Centuries of American Hymnody*. Cambridge: Harvard Univ. Press, 1940.

Gould, Nathaniel D., *Church Music in America*. Boston: A. N. Johnson, 1853.

Grider, Rufus A., *Historical Notes on Music in Bethlehem, Pennsylvania. From 1741-1871*. Philadelphia: Printed for J. H. Martin by J. L. Pile, 1873.

Hood, George, *A History of Music in New England: with Biographical Sketches of Reformers and Psalmists*. Boston: Wilkins, Carter & Co., 1846.

Howard, John Tasker, *Our American Music; Three Hundred Years of It*. New York: Thomas Y. Crowell Co., 1936.

Jackson, George Pullen, ed., *Another Sheaf of White Spirituals*. Gainesville: University of Florida Press, 1952.
——, *The Story of the Sacred Harp, 1844-1944*. Nashville: Vanderbilt University Press, 1944.
MacDougall, Hamilton C., *Early New England Psalmody*. Brattleboro, Vermont: Stephen Daye Press, 1940.
Metcalf, Frank J., comp., *American Psalmody; or Titles of Books Containing Tunes Printed in America from 1721-1820*. New York: C. F. Heartman, 1917.
National Society of the Colonial Dames of America, Pennsylvania. Committee on Historical Research. *Church Music and Musical Life in Pennsylvania in the Eighteenth Century*. Philadelphia: Printed for the Society, 1926-1947.
Paine, J. K., and others, *Famous Composers and Their Works*. Vol. II, "Music in America." Boston: J. B. Millet and Co., 1901.
Ritter, Frédérick Louis, *Music in America*. New York: Charles Scribner's Sons, 1884.
Scholes, Percy, *The Puritans and Music; in England and New England*. London: Oxford Univ. Press, 1934.
Stevenson, Arthur L., *The Story of Southern Hymnology*. Roanoke: Stone Printing and Manufacturing Co., 1931.
Warrington, James, *Short Titles of Books Relating to or Illustrating the History and Practice of Psalmody in the United States, 1620-1820*. Philadelphia: Privately printed, 1898.

15. *Worship Considerations*

Ashton, Joseph Nickerson, *Music in Worship*. Boston: The Pilgrim Press, 1943.
Clokey, Joseph W., *In Every Corner Sing; an Outline of Church Music for the Layman*. New York: Morehouse-Gorham Co., 1945.
Davies, H. Walford and Harvey Grace, *Music and Worship*. London: Eyre and Spottiswoode, 1948.
Phillips, C. Henry, *The Singing Church*. London: Faber and Faber, Ltd., 1945.
Whitley, W. T., *Congregational Hymn-Singing*. London: J. M. Dent & Sons, 1933.

INDEX

INDEX

A

Aachen, 178
Aaron, 20
Abbey, organ builder, 203
Abijah, 20
Abingdon, Abbot of, 196
Abnakis, 230
"Abstract" music, 72
A cappella, 88, 92, 102, 103, 104, 105, 127, 145, 147, 154, 156, 159, 189
Accent rhythm, 32
Acoustical considerations, 190
Acousticians, 195
Acquincum, 177
Act of Uniformity, 142
Acts (4:24), 34
Acts (15:22-29), 50
Adah, 14
Additional musical forms and devices, 110
Adeste Fidelis, 221
Adgate, Andrew, 220
Adrian le Roy, 129
Advent Christian Publication Society, 224
Aegidus, Johannes, 180
Aeolian-Skinner Co., 209, 210
Aesthetic abstraction, 105
Aeterne rerum conditor, 55, 56
"Age of the Netherlanders," 82
Agnus Dei, 69, 70, 144
Agricola, Martin, 117
Aguilera, Sebastian, 149
"Ah, Love but a Day," Mrs. H. H. A. Beach, 240
Ahle, J. R., 114
Ainsworth Psalter, 214
Aitken, John, 231
Alabados, 212
Alexandria, 14, 174
Alexandrian Invasions, 32
Algonquin, 213
"All Hail the Power of Jesus' Name," 232
Allegorical music, 44
"Alleluia," 40, 68, 72
Allison, Richard, 130
Altenburg, 151
Ambo, 62, 64
Ambrose of Milan, 36, 40, 46, 47, 53, 55, 57, 63, 66, 75, 131
Ambrosian chant, 55, 57, 58, 59, 70
Ambrosian hymn, 56
Ambrosian liturgy, 57
America, 125, 135, 164, 199, 214, 226, 233, 234, 235, 251
American churches, 208
American churchgoers, 255
American colonies, 217
American Guild of Organists, 239
American Harmony, Oliver Holden, 232
American Revolution, 215, 231
Amiens, Cathedral at, 182
Ammerbach, Elias, 188
Amos, 18, 19, 42
Amos (6:5), 19
Amos (5:22-23), 19
Amsterdam, 193, 214
Anastasius, 174, 175
Ancient beginnings,, 172
André, Father Louis, 230
Anglican, 140, 163, 165, 257
Anglican church, 138, 139, 144, 168, 169, 197, 231, 255
Anglican church leaders, 142
Anglican church music, 143
Anglican revolt, 100
Anhalt-Cöthen, 193
Antegnati Family, 191
Ante-Nicene, 37, 39
Antes, John, 229
Anthem, 98, 107
Anthem, Anglican, 144, 145
Ant-hymn, 145
Anti-Catholic feeling, 197
Anti-Christ, 164
Antico, Andrea da Mantona, 188
Antigonus, 22, 23
"Anti-instrumentalists," 19
Antiphon, 70
Antiphonal chanting, 63
Antiphonal choirs, 91
Antiphonal Psalm singing, 48
Antiphonal singing, 40, 57, 168
Antiphonal singing, "gospel songs," 250
Antiphonale, 61, 78
Antiphonally, 52
Antiphonary, 61
Antiphons, classic, 150
Antwerp, 94
Apollo, 32
Apollonius, 176
Apology, Justin Martyr, 37, 60
"Apostle to the Indians," 213
Apostles, 21, 36, 37, 39, 43
Apostolic, 44
Apostolic age, close of, 64
"Apostolic" Christianity, 180
Apostolic Confessions, 60
Apostolic Period, the, 32
Apostolic period, 32, 34
Apostolic simplicity, Puritan, 168
Aquitaine, Guillaume de, 109
Arabians, 47
Arabic manuscripts, 173
Arabic scholars, 176
Aratic, 65

Arcadelt, Jacob, 94
Arch of Titus, 26
Archimedes, 176
Arezzo, 78, 158
Aria, baroque, 147
Aria, Italian, 121
Aristotle, 29, 43
Aristoxenus, 29
Arithmetic, 16
Ark, 17
Ark's loss, 21
Armenian, 65
Armenian chant, 55
Arnaut, Henri, 181
Arnerio, Felice, 157
"Arnheim," Samuel Holyoke, 233
Ars antiqua, 85
Ars nova, 83, 84, 85
Ars nova—fourteenth century, 83
Ars Novae Musical, 111
Ars sacra, 160
Art and science, 44
Art, church, 104
Art form, 14
Art, Gothic, 84
Art, medieval, 85
Art of Playing the Organ, Andrew Law,
    208, 221
Art, religious means of teaching, 103
Art, secular, 104, 105
Artist, church, 105
Artistic, 74, 81
Artistic advancement, 104
Artistic communication, 217
Artistic culture, 105
Artistic decoration, 67
Artistic demands, 82
Artistic musical composition, 51
Artistic musical development, 81
Artistic purpose, 14
Artistic religious music in the United
    States in the latter nineteenth cen-
    tury, 236
Artistic song, 40
Artistry, 70
Ascetic, 48, 70, 108
Asceticism, 44, 48, 52, 53, 93
Asceticism, Calvinistic, 164
Asceticism, Grecian, 49
Asceticism, Puritan, 168
Asia Minor, 55
Assyrian, 16
Athanasius, 46
Athletics, 29
Atlantic, 246
Atlantic City, 210
Atlantic seaboard, 225
Atonement, Day of, 22
Augsburg, 94
Augsburg, Bishop of, 95
Augustine, 47, 55, 66, 115, 164
Aus tiefer Noth Schrei ich zu dir, 116
Austria, 95, 186
Authentic, 76
Authentic modes, 75
Authentic tones, 63
Ave Maria, 87
Ave Maria, Schubert, 155
Ave, Verum Corpus, Josquin des Prés, 89
A very plaine and easy introduction to
    the whole Art of Singing Psalm
    Tunes, Tufts, 218
Avignon, 110
Avilac, 122

B

Babylon, 21, 22, 28
"Babylon is Fallen," Henry Clay Worke,
    238
Babylonian, 16, 20
Babylonian captivity, 20
Babylonian exile, 21
Babylonian Jewish Pentateuch Melody, 60
Bach, Johann Christopher, 192
Bach, Johann Sebastian, 86, 118, 119,
    121, 123, 125, 126, 134, 139, 146,
    148, 151, 160, 188, 192, 193, 194,
    195, 201, 202, 206, 209
Bach, Karl Philipp Emanuel, 150, 151
Bacchus, 36, 43
Baeumker, 116
Bagpipe, 173, 177
Bailleul, 84
Baini, Giuseppe, 102, 156
Baker, Benjamin Franklin, 236
Balkan cultures, 54
Ballad (English), 15
"Ballad of Trees and the Master," Geo.
    Chadwick; Sidney Lanier, 239
"Ballad of the Trees and the Master,"
    Sidney Lanier, Arthur Shepherd, 254
Ballads, 246
Ballet, 105, 149
Baltimore, 208, 232
Baltimore Collection of Church Music,
    Ely, 224
Baptist church, 129, 245
Baptists, 246
Baptized, 37
Barahona, Juan de Esquivel, 149
Barak, 15
Barbarian cultures, 36, 37
Bardi, Giovanni, 106
Bards, 15
Barnby, Sir Joseph, 45, 257
Barnes, Edwin Shippen, 241
Baroque, 107, 146, 163, 181
Baroque organ, 194
Baroque period, 147, 149, 160, 191, 196
Barrel organs, 176
Bartlett, Homer Newton, 241
Basel, 94
Basil, 46, 47, 53, 84
Bass, 106
Bass drum, 13
Bassoons, 14
Bass viol, 224
Battle, 22
Bavaria, 162
Bavaria, Court of, 186
Bax, Sir Arnold, 254
Baxter, Richard, 132
Bayley, Daniel, 222
Bay Psalm Book, 213, 214
Beach, Mrs. H.H.A., 238, 240
Beasts, fatted, 19
"Beautiful breathing instruments of
    music," 38
Beautiful, pursuit of, 151
Beauty, 32, 43, 67
Bedos, Dom Francois, 203
Beethoven, Ludwig van, 145, 150, 154,
    155, 194
Beginnings of modern notation and
    theory, 74
Beginnings of multi-voiced music, 69
Beissel, Conrad, 227, 228
Belgium, 82, 85, 92
Bellermann, Heinrich, 156
Benedicite, 65

Benedicite, Anglican, 142, 144
Benedictines of Solesmes, 156, 157, 158, 159
"Benedictus," 34, 61, 68, 96
Benedictus, Anglican, 142, 144
Benequi Venit, Anglican, 144
Bennet, John, 130
Bennett, William Sterndale, 145
Benoît, Pierre, 161
Berchem, Jachet de, 92
Berlin, 156, 159, 160, 192, 238
Berlioz, Hector, 155
Besançon, 98
Best, W.T., 205
Bethlehem, Penna., 220, 224, 229, 253
Béthune, Conon de, 94, 109
Beza, Theodore, 128
Bible, 124, 147
Bible, Indian, 213
Biblicism, 60, 61
Bigelow and Main, 243
Billings, William, 220, 221
Binchois, Gilles, 85, 188
Blair Atholl Castle, 186
Blancks, Edmund, 130
Bliss, Philip Paul, 243
Blois, Chateau de, 182
"Bloody Mary," 163
Blow, John, 146, 148, 149, 200
B Minor Mass, Bach, J.S., 154
Boccaccio, Giovanni, 83
Bohemia, 95, 134
Bohemian reformers, 225
Bohm, Georg, 192
Bon Accord, 221
Bonn, 192
Book of Common Prayer, 140, 142, 144, 231
"The Booke of Common Praier Noted," John Merbecke, 142, 143, 198
Books of songs, 33
Borel, engineer, 203
Born, Bertrand de, 109
Bornelh, Giraut de, 109
Bortnyansky, Dmitry Stepanovich, 162
Boston, 208, 209, 219, 220, 222, 224, 231, 239
"Boston Group, The," 238, 240, 247, 254, 258
Boston Orchestra, 209
Boston public schools, 236
Bourbourg, 84
Bourgeois, Louis, 128, 166, 170
Bowring, John, 244
Boxford, Massachusetts, 233
Boyce, William, 145
Boyden, 86
Brabant, 187
Bradbury, William Batchelder, 236, 238
Brahms, Johannes, 155, 161, 188
Brattle, Thomas, 207, 208
Brattle street church, 207
Bread and wine, 67
Breitkopf and Hartel, 116
Brescia, 191
Breviary, 61
Brewer, John Hyatt, 240
Bridge, 145
Brightling church, 176
Brimle, Richard, 129
"Bristol," Oliver Shaw, 234
Britain, 54, 129, 138, 139
British Brethren, 246
British Colonies, 128
British Isles, 110, 247
British Museum, 57

Brittany, 200
Browne, Simon, 132
Brucker, Anton, 155, 163
Bruges, 187
Bruhns, Nikolaus, 192
Buchner, Johannes, 188
Buck, Dudley, 240, 241
Budapest, 177
Bugle, 25
Bull, 48
Bull, John, 197
Bunyan, 180
Burgos, 94
Burgundian, 94
Burgundian School, 86
Burgundy, 186
Burgundy, Court of, 85
Burgundy, Duke of, 181
Burney, Charles, 37, 39
Busnois, Antoine, 86
Buttelstadt, 151
Butts, Thomas, 135
Buttstadt, Franz Vollrath, 151
Buus, Jacob, 92
Buxheim, 188
Buxheim Organ Book, 188
Buxheimer Orgelbuch, 187
Buxtehude, Dietrich, 123, 146, 192
Byrd, William, 86, 97, 122, 143, 148, 197
Byrom, John, 134
Bythynia, 40
Byzantine chant, 54
Byzantine Greeks, organ builders, 175
Byzantium, 51, 180

C

Cabezon, Antonio de, 94, 149
Caccia, 83
Caccini, Guilio, 106
Caesarea, 47
Cain, 14
Calabria, Duke of, 211
Caldara, Antonio, 147
Calf (golden), 15
California, 212, 213
Callinet, Louis; organ builder, 203
Calvin, John, 114, 117, 128, 129, 142, 164, 165, 166, 169
Calvinistic, 34, 54, 163, 165, 258
Calvinistic music, 138
Calvinistic revolt, 100
Calvinists, 115, 168
Cambridge, 197, 198
"Camerata," 106, 107
Campbellian Restoration, 199
Campbellian—Stone Restoration, 226
Canon, 21, 81, 83
Canon (59th), Council of Laodicea, 61
Canon of the Mass, 68
Canonic, 89
Cantata, 120
Cantata, baroque, 147
Cantata, German, 121, 123, 124
Cantata, Italian, 124
Cantata, sacred, 107
"Cantata mass," 147
Cantate Domino (Psalm 98), Anglican, 142, 144
Canterbury, 122
Canticles, Anglican, 144
Cantillation, 16, 17, 22, 35, 40, 52
Cantor, 22, 62
Cantus firmi, 95, 114

Cantus firmus, 74, 81, 87, 96, 99, 110, 111, 149, 189
Caplet, André, 254
Cappella Giulia, St. Peter's, 99, 100
Capucin monastery, 190
Carazzoni, Marco Antonio da Bologna, 188
Cardinals, 99
Carey, Henry, 131
Carissimi, Giacomo, 122, 124
Carlsruhe, 154
Carpenter, John Alden, 238
Carr, Benjamin, 231
Carroll, John, 231
Carthage, 176
Carvalho, Faustino, 195
Castille, 186
Catch, 83
Cathedrals, English, 196
Cathedral mode, 140
Catherine de Medici, 166
Causton, Thomas, 129
Cavaillé-Coll, Aristide, 195, 203, 204, 206
Cavaillé-Coll, Vincent, 204
Cavalieri, Emilio de, 121, 123
Cecilian movement, 156, 158
Cecilianism, 157, 159
Celestine I, 57, 63
'Cello, 224
Celsus, 37
Cennick, John, 138
Certaine notes set forth in foure and three parts, John Day, 144
Chace, 83
Chadwick, George W., 238, 239
Chaffin, Lucien Gates, 241
Chalice, 69
Chamberlain, Deacon, 216
Chanson, 95, 96, 97, 103
Chant, 63, 71 (See Plainsong)
Chant, Ambrosian, 55, 57, 58, 59, 70
Chant, Anglican, 143
Chant, Armenian, 55
Chant, Coptic, 55
Chant, eastern, 65
Chant, Ethiopian, 55
Chant, Gallican, 58
Chant, Gregorian, 55, 57, 58, 59, 60, 63, 112, 143, 156, 157, 256
Chant, Gregorian, unaccompanied, 159
Chant, Medieval, 70
Chant, Mozarabic, 55, 58, 59
Chant, Roman, 53, 58, 63
Chant, Russian, 55
Chant, Spanish, 55, 58
Chant Unison, 69
Chant, Visigothic, 55
Chanter, medieval, 71, 76
Chanting, 16, 22, 52
Chanting, antiphonal, 63
Chanting, liturigal, 82
Chantings, lyrical, 52
Chant motifs, 84
Chants, 76
Chants, body of, 64
Chants, four western, 58, 59
Chants, sacred, 84
Chapel, in the mode of, *a cappella,* 88
Chapel Royal, 98, 148
Charlemagne, 58, 178
Charles I, 163
Charles IX, 166
Charleston, 232
Charleston Collection, The, Oliver Holden, 233
Charleston, Massachussetts, 232

Charwoman, 201
Chase, Gilbert, 242
Chaucer, Geoffrey, 83
Cherubini, Luigi, 154
Chesterfield, 133
Chethubbeth (4:6), 27
Cheverus, Rev. John, 231
Chicago, 242
Chinese, 173
Choir of the Sistine Chapel, 99
Chor-Gesang-buch, 116
Choral, The, Isaac Baker Woodbury, 236
Choral Mode, Anglican service, 140, 141
Choral Music and the Organ, 189
Choral Music, glorious age, church, 88
Choral Music, instrumentally accompanied, 70
Choral Music in the Medieval Period, 81
Choral Music, medieval, 82
Choral Music, unaccompanied, 70
Choral parts "doubled," 88
Choral tunes, 114, 123
Chorales, German, 257
Chorallieder, 114
Chordal (progressions), 72, 74, 87
Christe, eleison, 68
"Christ the Visitor," Dudley Buck, 241
Christian Harmonist, The, Samuel Holyoke, 233
Christian Harmony, The, Jeremiah Ingalls, 246
Christian Reformed Churches, 225
Christians at Alexandria, 46
Christians, communally joined, 49
Christians, early, 34, 51, 52
Christians, Jewish, 49
Christians, Maronite, 65
Christians, Medieval, 51
Christians, postapostolic, 43
Christmas, 102
Christmas morning, 229
Christmas Oratorio, Saint-Saëns, 161
Christ's College, 198
Christus am Ölberge, Beethoven, 161
Christus, oratorio, Liszt, 160
Chromatic, 30, 101
"Chromatic" church music, 158
1 Chronicles (9:33), 17
1 Chronicles (15:16-23), 16
1 Chronicles (15:, 16:, 23:, 25:), 17
1 Chronicles (25:), 16
2 Chronicles (5:1), 16
2 Chronicles (5:7), 18
2 Chronicles (5:7; 7:3), 19
2 Chronicles (7:1-7), 16
2 Chronicles (8:14), 18
2 Chronicles (13:12), 18
2 Chronicles (20:19-21), 18
2 Chronicles (29:), 20
2 Chronicles (36:16), 21
Chrysostom, St. John, 46, 47
Church art, 104
Church, early, 41, 62
Church, Eastern Orthodox, 51, 66, 67
"Church Fathers," 39, 53
Church government, two centers, 51
Church leaders, 61, 62, 64
Church meetings, public, 52
Church modes, 109
Church music, baroque, 146
Church Music in History and Practice, Winfred C. Douglas, 241
Church Music of the Future, Liszt, 160, 161

Church of England, 124, 134, 138, 139, 140, 163, 169, 205, 207, 219, 226, 231, 232
Church of England, post-reformation, 131
Church of Holland, 128
Church of St. Baron, Haarlem, 202
Church of St. John the Lateran, 158
Church, Roman Catholic, 51, 60, 61, 63, 66, 67, 69, 74, 78 88, 93, 94
Church, Syrian, 65
Church, western, 64, 69
Church worship, public, 53
Circumcision, 50
Cithara (kithara), 26, 44, 46, 48, 180
Civil War, 198, 241, 242, 245
Clarinets, 14
Clarke, Adam, 19
Classic, 160
Classic antiquity, 29, 32
Classic Greek drama, 106
Classic period, 150
Classical Chorus Book, Benj. Franklin Baker, 236
Classicist, 145
Claudin le Jeune, 129
Clavichord, 13
Clefs, 78
Clemens, Jacob, 94
Clement of Alexandria, 38, 39, 42, 43, 46, 47, 48, 60, 64, 180
Clement XIV, 155
Clemm, John, 208
Clergy, 64, 78, 100
Clergy, Roman, 93
Clergy, secular minded, 93
Cléve, Johannes de, 94
Cleveland, Ohio, 210
Cleves, 94
Climacus, 80
Cliquot, Francois Henry, 203, 206
Clivis, 80
Cobbold, William, 130
Coclico, Adrien Petit, 92
Coerne, Louis A., 238
Cole, John, 232
Collection of Church Music, Boston Musical Education Society, Isaac Baker Woodbury, 236
Collection of Hymn Tunes, Francis Hopkinson, 219
Collectio Operum Musicorum Batavorum, 156
Collegium Musicum, 229
Cologne, 156
Colonial Days, 213 ff
Colonies, 208
Colossians, 27, 35
Colossians (3:16), 34, 36, 43
Columbian Repository of Sacred Harmony, The, Samuel Holyoke, 233
Columbus, 211
Come, Let Us Join Our Cheerful Songs, 133
Comedia de Adan y Eva, pageant, 212
Comenius, Johann, 228
Comes, Juan Battista, 149
"Coming of the King, The," Dudley Buck, 241
Commentary, Adam Clarke, 19
Commer, Franz, 150
Commonwealth, British, 197, 200
Common of the Saints, 61, 62
Communion, 21, 67
Community song-type service, 255
Como, 191
Compenius, 192
Compiègne, 178

A Compilation of the Litanies As They Are Sung in the Catholic Church, John Aitken, 231
The Compleat Melody, or Harmony of Zion, William Tans'ur, 221
Composition, algebraic calculation, 82
Composition, choral, 97
Composition, contrapuntal, 87
Compositional experimenting, 81
Concert hall, 202
Concert organist, 208
Concertato, 88
Concerto, 88
"Concordance of the Bible in English," Marbeck, 198
Condé, 86
Conductus, 72
Congregational singing, 151, 168, 255, 256
Congregational style, 22
Connecticut, 220, 221
Consonance, 102
Constantine, 40, 41, 42, 52
Constantine Capronymus VI, 178
Constantinople, 68, 175, 178
Conte di Vernio, 106
Contrapuntal composition, 87, 92
Contrapuntal polyphonic music, 105
Contrary motion, 72, 81
Contratenor, 87
Convention Hall, Atlantic City, 210
Converse, Charles, 238, 243
Converse, Frederick S., 238
Conybeare, W. J., 36
Cooke, Captain Henry, 148
Coombs, Charles W., 241
Cooper, George, 205
Copenhagen, 92, 192
Coptic, 55, 65
Coptic chant, 55
Corinthians, 36
1 Corinthians (14), 35
1 Corinthians (14), 37
1 Corinthians (14:7-8, 15), 35
1 Corinthians (14:26), 34
Cornets, 14
Coronation, Oliver Holden, 222, 232, 233
Corpus Christi, 72
Cortēz, Hernando, 211
Cosmos, 66
Cosyn, John, 130
Cotton Mather, 219
Cotton, Reverend John, 215
Council of Laodicea, 61
Council of Laodicea, 13th Canon, 64
Council of Toledo, 58
Council of Trent, 72, 95, 99, 100, 103
Count Elwin, 179
Counter Reformation, 94, 100
The Counter Reformation as Part of the Roman Catholic Reform, 93
Counterpoint, 74, 81
Couperin, Francois, 192
Couplings, 185
Coussemaker, Charles Edmund Henri de, 84
Cowen, Sir Frederic, 162
Cramner, Bishop, 142
Creation, Josef Haydn, 150
Credo, 61, 62, 68
Credo, Anglican service, 141, 142
Cremona, 102, 107, 191
Crequillon, Thomas, 94
Croce, Giovanni, 97, 98

Cromwell, Oliver, 142, 165, 180, 196, 198
Cromwellian revolt, 88, 152
Crosby, Fanny, 238
Crotch, William, 145
Crucifixion, John Stainer, 161
Crüger, Johann, 114
Crusades, 84
Crystal Palace, 205, 206
Ctesibius, 14, 174, 176
Cultures, admixture of, 37
Cultus dei, 117
Cup and the bread, 69
Cured, 38
Curtis Institute, 186
Custom, Jewish, 50
Cybele, 43
Cylinder, organ, air pressurized, 175
Cylindrical drum, 176
Cymbals, 24, 27, 43
Cypriano de Rore, 92, 94
Cyrrhus, Bishop of, 48

D

Daily Hours of Divine Service, 61
Dallam, Robert, 200
Dallam, Thomas, 199
Dallery, Louis Paul, organ builder, 203
Damasus I, 63
Damon, William, 130
"Dance forms," 72
Dance Movements, 48
Dances, 44
Dancing, 13, 53
Dandrieu, Jean Francois, 192
Daniel (3:5,7,10,15), 178
Daniel (3:5), Sambuke, Sackbut, 25
Danks, Hart Pease, 243
Dante, Alighieri, 83, 102
Daquin, Louis Claude, 193
Das Paradies und die Peri, Robert Schumann, 161
Datheen, Peter, 225
Davalos, Diego López, 212
David, 16, 17, 18, 19, 38, 97
"David, Psalm of," 16, 215
Davison, Archibald T., 242
Duy, John, 129, 130, 144
Day of Atonement, 22
Dayton, Ohio, 253
"De tous instruments le roi," 180
"Death and Life," Harry Rowe Shelley, 241
Deborah (Judges V), 15
Decad, 43
"Decently and in order," 37
Declamation musical, 107
Declaration of Independence, 230, 231
"Dedication Ode," George Chadwick, 239
Democracy, 62
Democratic Homogeneity, earlier Christianity, 64
Demuth, Norman, 254
Denmark, 192, 209
Der Tod Jesu, Karl Heinrich Graun, 151
Descant, 87
Descant "away from the tenor," 182
Des Prés, Josquin, 86, 92
Design, modern musical, 87
Deus Creator omnium, Ambrosian, 55
Deus Miseratur, (Psalm 67), Anglican, 142, 144
Deutsches Requiem, Brahms, 161
Development of the pedal, 189

Developments in the keyboard, 183
Diaphony, 71, 72
Diatonic, 30, 75, 101, 103, 183
Dickinson, Clarence, 241
Dickinson, Edward, 35, 101
Diderot, Denis, 150
Dido and Aeneas, Henry Purcell, 149
Dies Irae, 62, 69, 72
d'Indy, Vincent, 254
Dijon, 85
Diptych, 174, 176
Discant, 72, 74, 81
Dissenters, 129
Dissolution of the Monasteries, 197
Dissonance, 81, 102
"Divers Arts," 183
Divine Musical Miscellany, George Whitefield, 138
Dixmude, 94
Dixon, Lt. Col. George, 206
Doane, William Howard, 243
Dolmetsch, Arnold, 176
Dominant, 101
"Dominant chromatic" progressions, 101
Domine, 79
Dominus ac Redemptor noster, 155
Dorian, 38, 76
Douai, 94
"Double chant" Anglican, 143
Doubling, voice, instrument, 98
Douglas, Charles Winfred, 241
Dow, "crazy" Lorenzo, 246
Dowland, John, 130
"Doxology," 166, 214
Draghi, Giovanni Battista, 148
Drake, Sir Francis, 214, 225
Drama, 29
Drama, church, 106
Drama, Greek, 106
Drama, liturgical, 72
Drama, music, 107
Dramatic spectacles, 44
Dream of Gerontius, Sir Edward Elgar, 162
Dresden, 122, 241
Dressler, Louis Raphael, 241
Drinking-songs, 36, 114
Drum, 13, 15
Dubois, Francois Clement, 204
Dufay, Guillaume, 85, 86, 94, 159, 188
Dukas, Paul, 254
Duke d'Anjou, 166
"Dundee," 257
Dunkards, 227
Dunstable, John, 85, 159, 188
Duple measure, 83
Duplum melody, 72
Dupré, Marcel, 254
Durán, Padre, 212, 213
Durante, Francesco, 146, 149, 162
Dutch, 214, 224, 225
Dutch "Seceders," 225
Dutch settlers, 226
Dvorak, Antonin, 239
Dykes, John, 257

E

Early Hebrew music, 14
Early postapostolic period, the 36
Easter, 72
Easter Mass, 106
Easter Sepulchre Play, 106
Eastern Catholic Communion, 53
Eastern chant, 53, 65

Eastern church, 47, 54, 56, 66, 67
Eastern faiths, 65
Eastern Orthodox church, 51
Eastern Patriarchs, 64
Eccard Johannes. 114
Ecce Dominus reniet, 70
Ecclesiastes, (2:8), 18
Ecclesiastical tonalities, 86
"Ecstasy," Mrs. H. H. A. Beach, 240
Ecstatic states, 62
Editio Medicea, Cecilian, 157, 159
Edward, Richard, 130
Edward VI, 143, 163
Edwards, Jonathan, 219
Egypt, 16
Egyptian abbot, 48
Egyptian bondage, 15
Egyptian cymbals, 24
Egyptians, 18, 23, 47
Eighteenth century, 104, 121, 136, 145, 146, 151, 152, 165, 202, 217, 219, 229, 232, 234
Eighth century, B.C., 20
Eighth century, 58, 66, 178
Ein 'feste Burg, 116, 117, 118, 119
Eisenach, 192, 193
Eisleben, 114
Eleventh century, 66, 70, 82, 109, 180, 183, 184, 196, 205
Elgar, Sir Edward, 123
Elijah, Felix Mendelssohn, 161
Eliot, Charles, 238
Elizabeth I, 142, 197, 198, 199
Elizabethan polyphonic motets, 221
Elphege, Bishop, 179
Embellishment, florid, 77
Embellishment, free, 77
Embellishment, spontaneous, 77
Empress Justina, 55
England, 65, 85, 88, 111, 115, 128, 129, 131, 132, 135, 143, 146, 148, 150, 151, 152, 163, 164, 176, 180, 186, 189, 195, 196, 200, 203, 205, 206, 208, 210, 217, 221, 233
England, home of oratorio, 162
Englanders, New, 214
English, 65, 97, 101, 140, 149, 224, 257
English ballad, 15
English Cathedral services, 221
English Cathedrals, 196
English church, 196
English church history, 139
English colonies, 207
English colonizations, 230
English liturgy, 142
English period, 110
English-speaking, 258
"Enlightenment," 150, 152, 153, 155, 156
Ephesian, 27, 35
Ephesians (5:14), 34
Ephesians (5:19), 34, 36, 43
Ephraem, 54, 64, 65
Ephrata, 227, 228
Episcopal Church, 232, 241
Episcopalian Harmony, John Cole, 232
Epitaph of Seikilos, 59, 60
Equal temperament, 126, 127
Equalizing voices, 87
Érard, Pierre, organ builder, 203
Erasmus, Desiderius, 180
Erfurt, 151, 193
Essex, 122
Established church, Scotland, 199
Este, Thomas, 130
Ethiopic, 65

Ethos 31, 32
"Eucharist," 67, 143
Euridice, 121
Europe, 55, 82, 106, 125, 145, 153, 196, 202, 210, 211, 226, 227, 229, 236, 239, 240
European, 84
European Renaissance, 54
Eusebius, 39, 41, 46, 47, 53
Euterpe, 33
Evangelistic white churches, 247
Evelyn, John, 198, 200
Evensong, 140
Evolutional development, 32
Exeter, 186
"Exhortation to the Heathen," 39
Exodus, 15, 28, 65
Exodus (12:21), 60
Exodus (15:1-21), 14
Exodus (15:20-21), 15
Exodus (32:17-19), 17
Exodus (32:18), 15
Exotic dancing, 17
Experimentation, 17
Expostulation, 17
Ezra, 21

F

Faber, Jacobus, 166
Faber, Nicholas, 185, 189
"Faith, order of the" (in liturgy), 61
Faith, propagating of, 47
Falckner, Justus, 225, 227
Faleiro, Antonio Padro, 195
"False bas," 110, 111
"Familiar style," 100, 101
Fanfare, 17
Farmer, H. G., 173
Farmer, John, 130
Farnaby, Giles, 130
"Father, dear Father, come Home with me now;" Henry Clay Worke, 238
"Father, Son, Holy Spirit," 68
"Father Willis," 210
Fathers (Christian), 43
Fatted beasts, 19
Faux bourdon, 110, 188
Fawkes, Guy, 213
Feast of the Tabernacles, Charles Zeuner, 235
Feast of Trumpets, 15
Feasts, 36, 47, 63
"Federal Street," George J. Webb, 235
Ferrara, Duke of, 92, 186
Festivals, 64
Festivals, dramatic and orgiastic, 49
Festivities, vulgar, 48
Festivity, 17
Fiesole, 183
Fifteenth century, 81, 85, 87, 101, 110, 114, 181, 183, 185, 189
Fifth century, 65, 81, 85, 87, 101, 110, 114, 181, 183, 185, 189
Firenze, 187
First century, 22, 55
First Prayer Book of Edward VI, 143
Fischer, Johann Kasper Ferd., 193
Fischer, William Gustavus, 243
Flagellants, 114
Flanders, 86, 186
Flemish. 92, 94
Flemish influence, 92
Flemish school, 189
Fletcher, Francis, 225

Florence, 106, 121, 148, 183, 187
Florid embellishment, 77
Florid plainsong, 71
Florida, 213, 225
Flute, 42, 46
Flute players, 27
Folk background among the English-speaking people, 163
Folk nature, 35
"Folk-socialized religion," 247
Foote, Arthur William, 238, 239
Foster, Stephen, 235
The *Foundery Tune Book,* Charles Wesley, 134, 135
Four gospels, Heinrich Schütz, 123
Four Western chants, 59
Fourteenth century, 51, 58, 81, 82, 83, 84, 85, 91, 100, 109, 113, 114, 181, 183, 185
Fourth century, 42, 60, 61, 64, 180
Franc, Guillaume, 128, 166
France, 79, 83, 85, 108, 109, 128, 129, 138, 139, 147, 150, 158, 159, 161, 163, 165, 178, 181, 191, 192, 194, 200, 203, 205
Francesco Landini, 83
Francis I, 165
Franciscan Missions of California, 212
Franck, César, 162, 203, 204
Francois des Oliviers, 192
Francois I, 117
Frauenkirche, 187
Frankish monk, 63
Franklin, Benjamin, 219
Franklin's Printing Press, 219
Franks, 58
Frauenlob, 109
Frederick III, 186
Frederiksborg Castle, 192
Free art, 82
Free Church, 199
Free embellishment, 77
"Free will," 65
Freer organum, 73
Freiburg, 188
French, 94, 117, 230, 257
French church service, 158
French colonizations, 230
French court, 148
French, Jacob, 233
French Lutherans, 166
French Protestants, 166
French Protestantism, 117
French Revolution, 203
Frescobaldi, Girolamo, 98, 191, 193
Friesland, 227
The *Friends at the Grave of the Saviour,* Schmittbauer, 154
Fritsche, 192
Froberger, Johann Jakob, 193
"From Greenland's Icy Mountains," Lowell Mason, 234
Fuenllana, Miguel de, 149
Fugal Music, 147
"Fugue," 81
"Fuguin' tune," 221
Fuguing tune, 221, 224
Fulness of wine, 36
Fundamentum Organisandi, Conrad Paumann, 186
Funeral service, 23, 27
Fux, Johann, 147, 158

G

Gabrieli, Giovanni, 123, 146
Gabrielis, Andrea and Giovanni, 86, 92, 98
Gallican chant, 58
Gante, Father Pedro de, 211
Garrett, George, 145
Gascogne, de la, marcabru, 109
Gaudentios, 43
Gaukler, 108
Genesis, 65
Genesis (4:21), 15
Genesis (4:23-24), 14
Genesis (31-27), 15
Geneva, 117, 128, 166, 167
Genevan Psalter, 165, 166, 170, 225
Gentiles, 36, 37, 43, 49, 50, 65
Geometry, 16
Georgia, 219, 228, 229
German, 88, 94, 97, 117, 224, 257
German cantata, 145
German chorales, 135
German church, 139
German church concertos, 148
German Lutheran Reformation, 224
German music, 128
German princes, 148
German Protestant church, 124, 126, 146, 153, 154
German Protestant groups, 138
German settlers, 226
German town, 227
Germans, 113
Germany, 95, 102, 108, 109, 114, 115, 116, 121, 128, 129, 132, 134, 139, 146, 147, 151, 156, 179, 186, 189, 190, 191, 192, 193, 194, 200, 201, 202, 205, 206, 208
Gesang-buch der Germeine in Herrnhut, Count Zinzendorf, 219
Ghent, 94
Gibbons, Orlando, 122, 143, 198
Gigault, Nicholas, 193
Gigout, Eugène, 204
Giulio del Monte, Cardinal, 99
"Glassites," 246
Gleason, Frederick Grant, 240
Gleemen, 110
Gloria, 61, 62, 142
Gloria Dei church, 227
Gloria in excelsis Deo, 65, 68, 141, 144
Gloria Patri, 65
"Glossolalia," 35
Gloucester, 208
God, 18, 19, 21, 23, 28, 34, 37, 41, 46, 103, 165
Godward, 18
Golden Age of Greece, 29
Golden Calf, 15
Golden Sheaf, 224
Golden Treasure, Thomes Philander Ryder, 243
Gomberto, Nicolas, 93
"Good," 43
Gospel, 68
Gospel hymns, 249
Gospel hymns, Moody and Sankey, 242
Gospel of John, 69
"Gospel preaching," 249
Gospel song, 242, 243, 245, 247
Gospels, 40
Goss, Sir John, 145, 162
Gothic, 181
Gothic art, 84

Goudimel, Claude, 98, 129, 142, 162, 166, 221
Graduale, 61, 62, 68
Gradus, 62
Gradus ad Parnassum, Johann Fux, 158
Gräff, Joachim, 116
Gram, Hans, 233
"Grandfather's Clock," Henry Clay Worke, 238
Grand jury, Savannah, 219
Graun, Karl Heinrich, 151
Gray Co., H. W., 252
Great Awakening, 219
Great Rebellion, 131
Greco-Roman music, 59
Greece, 29
Grecian background, 29
Grecian cultures, 36
Grecian music, 27, 35
Grecian philosophy, influences of, 46, 48
Grecian thinking, 35
Greek, 30, 31, 54, 64, 65, 77
Greek Christian Poets, 66
Greek Christians, 36
Greek Cithare, 44
Greek composer, 32
Greek culture, 29, 178
Greek drama, 106
Greek hymnody, iconoclastic, 66
Greek modes, 76
Greek music, 32, 37
Greek musical theory, 32
Greek philosophers, 39
Greek pipes, 45
Greek scale, 30
Greek scale system, 75
Greek spiritual meanings, 31
Greek theatre, 180
Greek tympanon, 45
Greek writings, 173, 176
Greeks, 28, 36, 37, 42, 48, 49, 106, 177
Greeks, organ builders, 175
Greeks, pagan, 48
Green Bay, 230
Greenwich, 97
Grëfenroda, 151
Gregorian, 85
Gregorian antiphon *(Hosanna Filio David)*, 60
Gregorian chant, 55, 57, 58, 59, 60, 63, 70, 116
Gregorian modality, 105
Gregorian modes, 75
Gregorian plainsong, 71
Gregory, the Great, 40, 53, 55, 63, 66, 75, 78, 115
Gregory XIII, 157
Grider, Rufus, 229
Grigny, Nicholas de, 193
Grell, Edouard, 156
The Grounds and Rules of Music Explained, Thos. Walter, 218
"Guardrobes, Inventory of," 186
Guéranger, Abbott, 156
Guerrero, Francisco, 149
Guido d'Arezzo, 77, 78, 79, 81
Guidonian "hand," 79, 80
Guilmant, Alexandre, 203, 204, 206, 207

H

Hadrian, 60
Hake, Edward, 129
Halberstadt, 185, 189
Halle, 193
Halle, de la, Adam, 109

Hamburg, 123, 125, 192, 193
Hammerschmidt, Andreas, 114
Hampton Court, 198
Handclapping, 17, 48
"Hand," Guidonian, 79
Handel, George Frederick, 77, 135, 145, 146, 151, 160, 161, 162, 193, 233
Handel and Haydn Society, 236
Hannah's song, 34
Hanover Square, 201
Hanseatic League, 193
Harmonia Americana, Sam'l Holyoke, 233
Harmonia Sacra, Thomas Butts, 135
Harmonic, 87
Harmonic flexibility, 104
Harmonic idiom, 101
Harmonic system, 101
Harmonie Universelle, Marin Mersenne, 191
Harmonious arrangement, 38
Harmonized melody, 105
Harmony, 74, 101
Harmony (of whole Christian people), 46
Harper, 38
Harp, 13, 15, 19, 38, 42, 43, 46, 110
"Harp, pipe and temple", 38
Harpsichord, 13
Harris, Howell, 242
Harris, Renatus, 200, 201
Harris, Thomas, 200
Harrison, G. Donald, 210
Harrison organ, 210
Hartford, Conn., 240, 241
Harvard, 207, 228, 238, 239
Harvard Glee Club, 239
Hasmoneans, 22
Hasse, 149
Hassler, Hans Leo, 98, 114, 229
Hastings, Thomas, 162, 235
Haweis, Thomas, 133
Hawley, Charles Beach, 241
Haydn Collection of Church Music, Benj. Franklin Baker, 236
Haydn, Joseph, 150, 154, 194
Hayes, Phillip, 131, 145
"He is Coming," Moody and Sankey, 245
"He Leadeth Me," William Batchelder Bradbury, 236
"Hear My Crying, O God," Raynor Taylor, 233
"Hear, O Lord, and Consider My Complaint," Raynor Taylor, 234
Heathen, 36, 47
Heathen feasts, 36
Hebrew, 15, 20, 23, 24, 30, 54
Hebrew cantillations, 35
Hebrew Christmas, 36
Hebrew cultures, 36
Hebrew cymbals, 27
Hebrew horn and trumpets, 24
Hebrew institutional music, 15
Hebrew institutions, 21
Hebrew king, 42
Hebrew language, 22
Hebrew music, 17, 20, 21, 27, 32, 35, 59
Hebrew nation, 20
Hebrew people, 28
Hebrews, 14, 16, 17, 22, 35, 39, 42
Heidelberg, 102, 190, 192
Hellenic culture, 173
Hellenistic culture, 60
Hellenistic Judaism, 44

Hellenistic odes, 60
Helmholtz, Herman, 191, 192
Helsingborg, 123
Henry VIII, 97, 142, 186
Herbert, George, 132
Herbst, John G., 229
Hereditary, 17
Heresy, 64, 65
Heretical, 61
Hermits, Kelpius, 227
Hero, 176, 177
Herod, 21, 23, 41, 42, 49, 175
Herod's temple, 21, 22, 28
Hexachord, 78
Hezekiah, 20
Hic est dies Dei, 57
Hierarchical institutionalism, 64
Hilary, 66
"Hill billy" music, 258
Hinaut, 86
Hinault, 92
Hirsch, Paul, 190
"His own image," 38
Hodie nobis coelorum rex, 102
Hofhaimer, Paul, 180, 187
Holborn, 200
"Hold the Fort," P. P. Bliss, 243
Holden, Oliver, 222, 232, 233
Holdich, George Maydwell, 201
Holland, 82, 129, 202, 205, 214
Hollowed log, 13
Holstein, 225
Holtkamp, H., Organ builder, 210
Holy Catholic Church, 138
Holy Communion, 140
Holy Ghost, 46, 48, 63
"Holy League," 166
"Holy Mass of the Blessed Trinity,"
   John Aitken, 231
Holyoke, Samuel, 233
Holyrood, 199
Holy of Holies, 21
Holy rites, 66
Holy Sacrifice of the Mass, 69
Holy See, 138
Holy Spirit, 38
Holy Week, 61
Homophonic, 104
Homophonic composition, 105
Honegger, Arthur, 254
Hood, George, 217
Hook and Hastings, American builders,
   209
Hooker, Richard, 168
Hooper, Edmund, 130
Hope-Jones, Robert, 206
Hopkins, John, 129, 145
Hopkinson, Francis, 219, 220, 225, 231
Hora Novissima, Horatio William Parker,
   239
Hosanna Filio David, 59, 60
Host, 69
Horns, blaring of, 17
Horse races, 44
Hour Service, 61, 63
Hours, striking the, 17
Howard, John Tasker, 242
Howe, John (Father), 197
Howson, J. S., 36
Hucbald, 77, 81
Huguenots, 98, 117, 120, 224, 225
Huguenot massacre, 129
Huguenot party, 166
Humfrey, Pelham, 148
Hundred Years War, 85

Hungary, 95, 187
Hus, John, 134, 228
Husband, J. J., 250
Hutchings and Roosevelt, organ builders,
   209
H W. Gray Co., 252
Hyde Park, 205
Hydraulic organ, 14, 174
Hydraulus, 174, 175, 176, 177
Hymn, 37, 107, 112
Hymn, congregational, Anglican, 143
Hymn singing, modern English, 134
Hymn singing, Puritan, 239
Hymn to Apollo, 32
Hymn to St. John the Baptist, 79
Hymn tunes, 101
Hymn writing, American Puritan, 234
Hymnal compilers, Northern, 247
Hymnal compilers, Southern, 247
Hymnals, modern, 257
Hymnody, English, 131, 132, 138
Hymnody, folk like, 61
Hymnody, Greek iconoclastic, 66
Hymnody, Lutheran, 120
The hymnody of Calvin and Watts, 128
Hymnody of Luther, 112
Hymns, 19, 34, 39, 48, 64, 65, 67
Hymns, Eastern, 64
Hymns, Isaac Watts, 132
Hymns, Latin, classic, 151
Hymns, Luther, 132
Hymns and Poems, 35, 36
Hymns and Psalms of David Imitated,
   Isaac Watts, 219
Hymns and Sacred Poems, Charles Wes-
   ley, 134
Hymns, none in public worship, 131
Hymns of the Medieval Period, 64
*Hymns on the Great Festivals and other
   Occasions*, 135
Hymns, original, 34
Hymns, unmetrical, 65
Hymns, unscriptural," 132
Hymn-settings, classic, 150
Hypodorian, 76
Hypoionian, 76
Hypolydian, 76
Hypomixolydian, 76
Hypophrygian, 76

I

Iam surgit hora tertia, 55
Iconoclastic, 66
Idolatry, 67
Idols, 38
"I know that my Redeemer Liveth,"
   George Handel, 77
Ileborgh, Adam, 186
"I Love to Tell the Story," William G.
   Fischer, 243
*Illustration in Choir Accompaniment,
   with Hints on Registration*, 241
Imitation, 81
Important musical personages, 232
Improvisation, 14, 62, 71
Indian Bible, 213
Indian tongues, 212
Indians, 207, 213, 225, 226, 228, 229, 230
In Dulci Jubilo, 229
Informal group singing, congregational, 64
Ingalls, Jeremiah, 224, 246
Ingegoneri, Marc Antonio, 102
"Inheritance Divine, The," Harry Rowe
   Shelley, 241
Innovations, 85

Innsbruck, 187
Inscription of seikilos, 33
Institutional, 15
Institution, church, 22
Instrument, 14, 22, 30, 38, 42
Instrument families, 13
Instrumental accompaniment, 29, 30, 104
Instrumental accompaniment, Bach, 148
Instrumental accompaniment, Palestrina, 148
Instrumental accompaniment required, 145
Instrumental combinations, 102
Instrumental, groups, 18, 107
Instrumental music, 14, 19, 29, 47, 52, 66, 224, 226
Instrumental music, "an abomination unto the Lord," 197
Instrumental music banned, 159
Instrumental music, baroque, increased use in churches, 146
Instrumental music, Christian opposition to, 175
Instrumental music, English opposition to in religious service, 196
Instrumental music in the early postapostolic period, 41
Instrumental music, German church, 126
Instrumental music, Jews' antipathy for, 175
Instrumental, pure music, 105
Instrumental solo, 107
Instrumental usage, 91
Instrumentally unaccompanied, 22, 88
Instruments, 17, 19, 53, 70
Instruments, "doubling" choral parts, 88
Instruments, musical, 95
Instruments, orchestra, 107
Introit, 68
Ionian, 76
Ireland, 247
Iroquois, 230
Isaac, Heinrich, 187
Isidore of Seville, 77
Israel, delivery of, 14
Israel, music of, 16
Israelites, 27
Israelites in the Wilderness, Bach, K. P. E., 150
Italian, 91, 97, 185
Italian opera, 82
Italo-Flemish, 92
Italy, 15, 58, 83, 92, 93, 107, 122, 123, 146, 147, 158, 162, 186, 189, 191, 205
"I will give thanks unto the Lord," Raynor Taylor, 234

J

Jacob, 27
Jacques de Liége, 82, 111
James (5:13), 35, 36
James I, 163
Jamestown, 214
Jean Cotton, 82
Jean de Muris, 111
Jehoiakim, 20
Jehovah, 19
Jeptha, 122
Jerome, 47, 48, 53
Jerusalem, 20, 21, 22, 34, 36, 50, 63
Jesuit Order, 95
Jesuits, 155, 230
Jesus, 22, 27, 32, 34
Jesus Christus unser Heiland, 115
Jesus, Lover of My Soul, 137

Jew, orthodox, 18, 49
Jewish, 21, 23, 27, 62
Jewish Christians, 49
Jewish music, 27, 32
Jews, 16, 21, 23, 28, 41, 43, 48, 49, 56
Jingling, 15
Job, 23
Job (21:11-12)
Job (30:31), 23
Job, Hubert Parry, 161, 162
John, 34
John (13: 20-35), 68
John XXII, 82, 84, 85
John, Gospel of, 69
John of Damascus, 66
John of Salisbury, 111
Johnson, Edward, 130
Johnson, Thomas, 208
Jones, Abner, 247
Jongleurs, 108
Jordan, Abraham, 201
Joseph, 27
Joseph, ruin of, 19
Josephus (Lib. 33, Cap 4), 18
Josquin des Prés, 86, 87, 88, 89, 92, 93, 97, 114, 159
Jousseline, 197
Jubal, 14, 38
Jubilate, Anglican, 142, 144
Jubilation, year of, 22
Judaeus, 16
Judges (chapter 5), 15
Judgment Day, 247
Judith, Hubert Parry, 162
"Just As I Am," William Batchelder Bradbury, 236
Justin, *Apology* of, 60
Justin, Liturgical plan of, 60
Justin Martyr, 37
Justina, 55
Justus ut palma, 60

K

Keach, Benjamin, 131
Keiser, Reinhard, 123
Kellner, Johann Peter, 151
Kelpius, Johannes, 227
Kerle, Jacob van, 94, 95
Kerll, Johann Kasper, 193
Kettle drum, 13
Kimball, Jacob, 233
"King Bibber's Army," Henry Clay Worke, 238
King David, 46
King Ladislaus, 187
King Saul, Hubert Parry, 162
King of Britain, 139
"King of Judaea," 23
The Kingdom, Sir Edward Elgar, 161
King's Chapel, 208
I Kings (4:32), 18
King's College, 198
Kinnor, 26
Kirbye, George, 130
"Kiss of Peace," 61
Kleber, Leonhard, 188
Kleuzberg, 146
"KL__f," 235
Klopstock, Friedrich Gottlieb, 153
Knightly minstrelsy, 84
Konigsberg, 192
Kostrich, Saxony, 122
Kotter, Hans, 188

Krebs, Johann Ludwig, 151
Kyriale, 61
Kyrie, 60, 62, 65, 68, 113, 142, 144, 153

L

Labadists, 227
Laeta, 48
Laity, 64
Lamech, 14
La Messe du XIII siécle, 84
Lampe, John Frederick, 135
La Nativité du Seigneur, Oliver Messi-
    aen, 254
Lancaster County, 227
Landini and the organetto, 183
Landini, Francesco, 91, 183
Lang, B. J., 239
Láng, Paul Henry, 86, 97, 102, 160
Lanier, Sydney, 239, 254
Laodicea, Council of, 61
La Rappresentazi- óne di'Anima e di
    Córpo, 122
L'Art du facteur d'orgnes, 203
L'Arte organica, 191
Lasso, 97
Lasso, Orlando di, 94
Lassus, Orlandus (Roland de) (Orlando
    de Lasso), 86, 92, 94, 96, 97, 98,
    103, 159
The Last Judgment, Louis Spohr, 161
Last Supper, 67
Later periods of medieval chant, 58
Latin, 34, 79, 83, 84, 101, 113, 140
Latin (for Indians), 230
Latin masses, 116
Latin motet, 144, 145, 256
Latin music, 120
Latin plainsong as used in Italian can-
    tata, 124
Latinized, 67
Lauda Sion, Mendelssohn, 161
Lauda Sion Salvatorem, 72
Laurentius, 174
Law, Andrew, 208, 220, 221, 232, 249,
    250
Lawmaking, 21
"Lead part," 81
"Lead voice," 81
Leading tone, 78
"Learning music at home," Isaac Baker
    Woodbury, 236
"Lectors," 62
Leicestershire, 97
Leipzig, 116, 162, 193, 241
Le Jeune, Claude, 142
Le Miroir de Jésus, André Caplet, 254
Le Roi David, Arthur Honegger, 254
Lessing, Gotthold E., 150
"Les Six," 254
Levi, tribe of, 17
"L'Homme Armé Mass," 103
Leonardo (da Vinci), 86
Levites, 16, 17, 18, 20
Leviticus (25:8-10), 22
Leyden, 129
Liber Usualis, 61
Libyans, 47
Lichfield Cathedral, 201
L'Enfance du Christ, Hector Berlioz,
    160, 161
Leo XIII, 158
Les Béatitudes, Cesar Franck, 161
Leslie, William, 192
Lesselier, Guillaume, 192

Life and Letters of Erasmus, 179
Lifeless instruments, 38
Lima, 212
Lincoln, 198
Lincolnshire, 122
"Lining out," 214, 216
Liszt, Franz, 155, 159, 160, 161, 163
Litanies, 140
Litanies, classic, 150
Literature, early Christian, 64
Little, William, 250
Liturgical, 74
Liturgical chanting, 82
Liturgical drama, 72
Liturgical legacy, 153
Liturgical music, 64
Liturgical music drama, 121
Liturgical musical services, 63
Liturgical plan, Justin, 60
Liturgical purpose, 71
Liturgical requirements, 36
Liturgy, 47, 53, 54, 60, 61, 62, 63, 72,
    85, 95, 150
Liturgy, Anglican, 144
Liturgy, broken down in Protestantism
    of classic period, 151
Liturgy, final establishment, 51
Liturgy, Roman Catholic, 67, 68, 153,
    157
Liturgy, Swedish Lutheran, 227
Liverpool, 205, 206
"Living psaltery," 46
Lobwasser, Ambrosius, 128
Locke, John, 150, 200
Logos, 64
Lohengrin, Richard Wagner, 160
London, 85, 134, 162, 193, 197, 204
London Bridge, 201
Long Island, 210
Loosemore, John, 186
Lord, 18, 19, 21, 23, 38
Lord Jesus Christ, 36
"Lord's fiddle," 224
Lord's song, 20
Lord's Supper, 168
Lorenz Co., E. S., 253
"Lost letter, The," Henry Clay Worke,
    238
Louis IV, 82
Love songs, 114
Love themes, 83
Low Countries, 95, 181, 189
Loyola, Ignatius, 95, 122
Lübeck, 123, 192, 193
Lübeck, Vincent, 193
Lucretius, 173
Ludovisi Villa, 174
Ludwigsburg, 209
Luke (1:46-55), 34
Luke (1:68-79), 34
Luke (2:14), 34
Luke (2:29-32), 34
Luke (22:14-23), 68
Lully, Jean Baptiste, 148, 149
Lüneberg, 151, 192
Lute, 19
Luther, Martin, 86, 94, 114, 115, 116,
    117, 118, 119, 129, 131, 134, 228
Lutheran, 54
Lutheran Chorale, 116, 163
Lutheran Church, 138
Lutheran Music, classic, 151
Lutheran order of service, 115
Lutheran people, 167
Lutheran Reformation, 93, 100, 112, 114
Lutheran Reformers, 225

Lutherans, 120
Lutkin, Peter Christian, 241
Lydian, 38, 70, 76
Lyon, John, 219, 220
Lyons, 98, 128, 129, 221
Lyre, 13, 15, 20, 23, 26, 27, 29, 36, 38, 42, 46, 48, 180
Lyric songs 64
Lyrical chanting, 52

M

Mechelen, 94
Medici, Giovanni de, 187
Medici, Lorenzo de, 187
Medici, Pietro de, 187
Medieval art, 85
Medieval chant, 70
Medieval choral music, 82
Medieval Christianity, 51
Medieval Church, 66, 76, 77
Medieval church notation, 77
Medieval history, 54
Medieval modal patterns, 76
Medieval modes, 75
Medieval music, 51
Medieval period, early, 42
Medieval polyphonic music, 104
Medieval Roman chant, 53
Medieval secular music, 84
Mediterranean, 36
Meissen, Heinrich von, 109
Meistersinger, 109, 110
Melancthon, Philipp, 117
Melisma, 56
Melismatic, 71
Melodia Sacra, Oliver Shaw, 234
Melody of the heart, 36
Melody, principal, 73
Melody, single line, 106
Memory aids, 75
Mendelssohn, d minor concerto of, 240
Mendelssohn, Felix, 150, 155, 201, 202
Mendham, 216
Mennonite, 227
Merbecke, John (See Marbeck)
Merseberg, 151
Mersenne, Marin, 191
Mese, 31
Mesomedes of Crete, 43
Mesopotamia, 177
"Messengers of God," 21
Messiaen, Oliver, 254
Meter, double, triple, 109
Methodist Church, 129, 134, 135, 258
Methodist Collaborators, 132
Methodist Hymnody, 134, 165
Methodist Movement, 134, 138
Methodists, 169, 245, 246
Methuen Hall, 209
Metz, 98
Mexico, 211
Mexico City, 207, 212
Michigan, 225
Micomachos, 43
Middle Ages, 105, 108
Midmer-Losh, Inc., 210
Migne, 63, 178
Milan, 57, 191
Milan, Bishop of, 55
Milanese liturgy, 57
Millennium, first, 71
Miller, William, 247
Milton, John, 132, 167, 180
Minnesinger, 84, 109, 110
Minstrel entertainers, 108

Minstrels, 110
Minstrelsy, 84
Miracle plays, 72
Miriam, 14, 15
Misa de Catluñ, Padre Narciso Durán, 212
Miserere, Jean Baptiste Lully, 149
Mishnah, 22
Missa Brevis, Palestrina, 148
Missa Solemnis, Beethoven, 150, 154
Missal, 61
Mission Music Collection, San Jose, 212
"Missionary Chant," Charles Zeuner, 235
"Mit ganczen Willen," 186
Mixed mode, Anglican service, 140, 141
Mixed solo, 70
Mixolydian, 76
Modal church style, 103
Modal patterns, 75
Modal System, 75
Modality, 104
Modality, Gregorian, 105
Modern period, 52
"Modes," 75
Modes, church, 109
Modes, Gregorian, 75
Modestus, 177
Modulatory, 101, 102
M'Alpine, William, 222
I and II Maccabees, 22, 23
MacDougall, Hamilton Crawford, 241
Mace, Thomas, 198
McClintock and Strong Cyclopedia, 46
McGranahan, James, 245
Machaut, Guillaume de, 83, 84, 85, 86, 180
Mackay, William P., 250
Mackenzie, Sir Alexander, 145, 162
Madrid, 94, 122
Madrigal, 83, 91
Maestro compositore (Palestrina), 100
Magadizing, 30, 40
Magdalen College, 198
Magdeburg, 184
Magical Music, 44
Magister puerorum, Palestrina, 99
Magnificat, 34, 65
Magnificat, Goudimel, 98
Magnificat (Mary's song), Anglican, 142, 144
Main, Hubert Platt, 243
Maine, Abnakis in, 230
Mainz, 189
Major and minor modes, 75, 188
Malaga, 94
Mantua, 191
Manual keyboard, 189
Manzoni, Alessandro, 162
Marbeck, John, 142, 143, 198
Marblehead, 208
Marcellinus, 175
"Marching through Georgia," Henry Clay Worke, 238
Margaret, sister of Francois I, 117
Mark (14:17-26), 68
Mark Anthony, 22, 23
Marlow, Isaac, 131
Maronite Christians, 65
Marot, Clement, 128, 131, 165, 166
Mar Saba Monastery, 66
Marsh, Simeon B., 137
Martin, Sir George, 145
Martyn, 137
Martyrism, 61
"Mary, Don't You Weep," Negro, 248
Mary, Queen of England, 198

Maryland, 220, 221
Mary's Song, 34
Marzo, Eduardo, 241
Mason, John, 132
Mason, William, 234, 235, 236, 238, 243, 244, 251
Mass, 61, 62, 63, 67, 68, 69, 180
Mass, Easter, 106
"Mass for the Dead," John Aitken, 231
Mass in F minor, Anton Bruckner, 161
Mass of Pope Marcellus, Palestrina, 99, 100
Mass, Ordinary of, 61, 62, 84, 85, 161, 212
Mass, Proper of, 61, 85 (See Proper of the Saints, of the Season).
Mass, Roman Catholic medieval, 104
Massachusetts, 218, 222, 225, 232
Massachusetts Bay Colony, 214
Massachusetts Compiler, The, Oliver Holden, 233
Massachusetts Musical Magazine, Oliver Holden, 232
Massacre, Huguenot, 129
Massacre, St. Bartholomew's Night, 166
Massenet, Jules, 162
Masses, 69, 96
Masses, Vespers, Litanies . . . Catholic Churches . . . United States, Benjamin Carr, 231
Mater Ora Filium, Sir Arnold Bax, 254
Mating, 13
Matins
Matteis, Nicola, 148
Matthew, 27
Matthew (9:23), 23
Matthew (21:9), 34
Matthew (26:20-30), 68
Maximillian I, 187
Measured rhythm, 32
Mechanical orchestra, 202
Moffatt, James, 19
Moller, from Denmark, 209
Mona, Horatio William Parker, 239
Monasteries, Dissolution of, 197
Monastery, 48, 83
Monastic, 70, 82
Monk(s), 48, 74, 145, 257
Monodic style, 106, 107
"Monotonous congregational singing," Lutheran Church, 148
Montani, Nicola Aloysius, 241
Monte Cassino, 58
Monte, Philippe de, 94
"Monterey," 213
Motetus, 72
Monteverdi, 92, 98, 102, 107
Montfort, Hugovon, 109
Montreal, 230
Moody, Dwight L., 242, 245
"Moody and Sankey" Songs, 245
Moors, 58, 59
Morales, Cristóbal, 94, 149, 211
Moravia, 228
Moravian Brethren, 135, 220, 224, 253
Moravians, 219, 228, 229
Mores, 35
Morgan, George W., 208, 209
Morley, Thomas, 97, 130, 218
"Morning Hymn," fuguing tune, 222
Morungen, Heinrich von, 109
Mosaic law, 23
Moses, 14, 15, 16, 97, 174
Moshroquitha, 177
Motets, 91, 98
Motets, classic, 150

Motets, Elizabethan polyphonic, 221
Motets, Palestrinian era, 100
Motu Proprio, 158
Mount (Sinai), 15
Mozarabic chant, 55, 58, 59
Mozart, Wolfgang Amadeus, 97, 150, 154, 194
Muffat, Georg, 193
Muhlen, Heinrich, 225
Müller, Christian, 202
Multivoiced, 74
Munich, 94, 98, 187, 188, 190, 193
Muristus, 176
Music, accompanied, 105
Musica Enchiriadis, 73
*Music, Christian, 62
Music, church-style, 105
Music, "classic," 150
Music, concert, classic, church, 151
Music, drama, 107, 160
Music, earlier Christian, 64
Music, Eastern stagnation of, 66
Music Educators National Conference, 251
Music for funerals, 27
Music, fugal, 147
Music, German church, 125, 126
Music, Greek, 7
Music, ideal sacred, 70
Music, instrumental, 66, 105
Music, Italian sixteenth century, 122, 123
Music, liturgical, 64
Music, liturgical, drama, 121
Music, medieval polyphonic, 104
Music, medieval secular, 84
Music, modern harmonized, 70
Music, Passion, 125
Music, pleasures of, 47
Music, poetic vehicle, 31, 107
Music, Protestant, 129
Music, pure instrumental, 105
Music, religious connection, 155
Music, Roman, 36, 37, 94, 102, 129
Music, romantic choral, 155
Music, romantic oratorio, 155
Music, symbolistic, 39, 46
Music, synagogue, 22
Music, temple, 20, 22
Music, vocal, 66
Music, written, 82
Music Hall, Boston, 209
Music in the Church of England
Music in the Reformation, 112
Music notation, 17, 51, 74, 75, 77, 78, 79
Music notational development, 82
Music of the Middle Ages, 75
"Music of the stage," 44
Music of the temple and synagague, 20
Music tablature, 186
Musica reservata, 92, 93
Musica Sacra, Commer, 150
Musical activity, 18
Musical composition, forms of, 51
Musical expression, classic period of the people, deteriorated, 152
Musical custom, freedom in (second century), 50
Musical development, artistic, 81
Musical idiom, 47
Musical instruments, 28, 35
Musical instruments, aversion to, 48
"Musical instruments in worship," 41

*For a kind of music, e.g., Anglican church music, see Anglican, etc.

Musical literature, 91
Musical, modern design, 87
Musical notation, 92
Musical outlook, 83
Musical services, liturgical, 63
Musical Times, The, Novello, 253
Musicians, 16, 17, 23, 63
Musicians, church, 87
Musicians, temple, 20
Musick's Monument, 198
"My Faith Looks Up to Thee,"
    Lowell Mason, 234
"My Faith Still Clings," William Doane,
    243
Mystery, 67
Mystery plays, 72
"Mystery, adorable," 69
Mystic services, 41
Mystics, Kelpius, 227
Mysticism, 93

N

Nachtgall, Ottomar, 188
Naked dancing, 17
Nanini, Giovanni, 102
Naples, 122
Napoleonic period, 161
National Conservatory of Music, 239
"National" religion, 41
Nations, 20
Natural science, 29
Navarro, Juan, 212
Nazareth, Pennsylvania, 228
Neapolitan school, 149
Neale, J. M., 65
"Nearer My God to Thee," Lowell
    Mason, 234
Nebuchadnezzar, 20
Negro, 249
Negro spirituals, 245, 247, 249
Negroes (southern), 15
Nehemiah, 21
Neidlinger, William Harold, 241
Nemming bei Sierck, 174
Nero, 174
Nesle, Blondel de, 109
Netherland(ers), 82, 92, 94, 123, 138,
    139, 149, 166, 190
Neumes, 58, 77, 78, 81
Nevin, George Balch, 241
*A New and Compleat Introduction to
    the Grounds and Rules of Musick*,
    Daniel Bayley, 222
Newburyport, 208, 222
New Castle County, 227
New England(ers), 207, 214, 220, 221,
    225, 240, 245
New Hampshire, 208, 240
New Haven, 221
New Jersey, 216
New Jerusalem, J. Ingalls, 224
"New Light" Baptists, 245
"New Lighters," 246
"New Sidism," 246
New song, 38
New Spain, 230
New Testament, 33, 34, 60, 77, 106, 140,
    215
"New Testament Christians," 43
New Testament Gospels, 65
New World, 152, 207, 212, 214, 221,
    227, 230
New World idioms, 253
New York, 220, 232, 239
New York University, 234

Newton, Isaac, 150, 200
Newton, John, 242
Nicene Creed, 144
Nietsche, 150
Nineteenth century, 136, 145, 156, 162,
    176, 202, 203, 205, 207, 236, 238,
    247, 253
"The Ninety and Nine," Moody and
    Sankey, 245
Ninth century, 66, 72, 113, 176, 178,
    179
Nisibis, 64
Noise, 19, 27
Non-Christian culture, 44
Nonconformers, 129, 134, 139
Non moriar sed vivam, 116
Non-parallel progressions, 72
Normandy, 186
Norridgewock, 230
North Africa, 55
North America, 128, 164, 214
North American eastern colonies, 230
North American Puritan, 213
Northern France, 82
Northern Germany, 189
Northern Protestants, 161
"Not Ashamed of Christ," Hart Pease
    Danks, 243
Notation, music, 17, 32, 54, 74, 77, 78,
    79, 82, 92
A Note on Baroque Music, 146
A note on Classic music, 150
A note on Romantic music, 154
Notre Dame, 203, 204
Novellos, Alfred Vincent, 251, 253
Numbers (21:27), 15
Numbers (29:1), 15
Nunc dimittis (Simeon's Song), Angli-
    can, 34, 142, 144
Nuremberg, 186, 190, 193

O

O Bone Jesu, 102
Obrecht, Jacob, 86
Occasional offices, 140
"*O come, let us adore him*," 221
Ockeghem, Johannes, 86
Octavean, 23
Odes, 35
Oelred, Abbot of Riverby, 82
"Office" books, 76
Officium Maioris Hebdomadae, 61
Oblation of the Host, 68
Ohio Sacred Harp, Lowell Mason, 251
Ohl, John G., 88
O'Kelly, James, 247
Old Hundreth, 166, 170, 214
"The old order changeth, yielding place
    to new," Alfred, Lord Tennyson,
    258
"Old Swedes" Church, 225, 227
Old Testament, 14, 15, 16, 17, 18, 21,
    33, 34, 60, 106, 122, 140
Old Testament canon 21
Old Testament Psalms, 34, 165
Old world provincialisms, 211
Oliver, Henry Kemble, 235
Olivers, Thomas, 138
On freudt verzer ich manchentag, Paul
    Hofhaimer, 188
"Only an Armor Bearer," P. B. Bliss,
    243
Opera, 105, 106, 107, 125, 135, 194, 202
Opera composition, classic, 153
Opera, French, 148

Opera, Italian, 82
Operatic form, Italian, 121
Optatianus, Publilius, 175
Oratorio, 107, 120, 121, 149
Oratorio, baroque, 147
Oratorio, classic, 150
Oratorio, "The Feast of the Tabernacles," Charles Zeuner, 235
Oratorio, German, 123
Oratorios, Handel, 151
Oratorio, *Hora Novissima,* Horatio William Parker, 239
Oratorio, *St. Peter,* John K. Paine, 238
Oratorio society, 220
Orchestra, 22, 107, 202
Orchestra composition, classic, 153
Ordination, 140
Organ, 15, 83, 88, 91, 98, 107, 120, 172, 180
Organ, anti-organ feeling, 199
Organ, Arabian, 178
The organ as a factor in worship, 179
Organ, baroque and symphony orchestra, 196
Organ "beaters," 184
Organ, bell chimes, harp, psaltery, 178
Organ, British, 196, 206
Organ, choir, 200, 201
Organ, Continental, 201
Organ couplers 204
Organ, "deaf to sound of," 48
Organ, descant pipes, 182
Organ, drones, 182
Organ, "drone pipes," 179
Organ, electric, 210
Organ, English, 180, 205
Organ, for Roman Catholic service, 205
Organ, French, 201, 202, 205
Organ, "full-organ," 184
Organ, German, 181, 195, 202, 205
Organ, German baroque, 196
Organ, German pedals, 201
Organ, "great" manual, 201
Organ, historical contributions, 172
Organ, in Christendom, 172
The organ in the new world, 207
Organ, its History and Construction, The Edward Rimbault, 177
Organ, "keys," 184
Organ, mutation ranks of pipes, 204
Organ, mutation stops, 206
Organ, pallets, 202
Organ, pedal clavier, 189, 201
Organ, pedal point, 182
Organ, pedals, 189, 196
Organ, pipe, 174, 210
Organ playing, baroque manner, 204
Organ, pneumatic, 175, 176, 177
Organ, portative, 183, 185
Organ, positives, 181, 183, 185, 200
Organ, regals, 186
Organ repertoire: orchestral transcriptions, English, American, 206
Organ, John Snetzler, 232
Organ, stop cock,
Organ, Spanish, 201
Organ, swell, 195, 196, 201, 205
Organ, synthetic, 210
Organ, technical developments, 172
Organ, "trackers," 195
Organ, varied air pressures, 204
Organ, Walcker, Eberhard Friedrich, 209
Organ, Winchester, 179, 180
Organ works, French, 203
The organ's effects upon music composition, 186

Organs, medieval, no stops, 190
Organum, 71, 72, 73, 77, 85
Orient, 16, 77
Origen, 37
Orthodox Calvinistic church, 34
Otto, Cardinal Truchsess, Bishop of Augsburg, 95
Oudenarde, 86
"Our Refuge," Main, H. P., 245
Overture to William Tell, Rossini, 209
Oxford, 122, 198
Oxford movement, 232
Oxyrhynchos hymn, 39, 60

P

Pachelbel, Johann, 193
Padro de Gante, 207
Pagan, 23, 37, 48, 215
Pagan customs, 14, 41
Pagan festivities, 28, 29, 46, 49
Pagan literature, 37
Paganism, 39, 47
Paine, John Knowles, 209, 238, 239
Painting, 67, 102
Paleographie Musicale, 157
Palermo, 122, 147
Palestrina, Bishop of, 99
Palestrina, Giovanni Pierluigi, 86, 88, 92, 95, 97, 98, 99, 100, 101, 102, 103, 122, 127, 139, 143, 148, 156, 157, 159, 188, 214
Palestine, 23, 39
Palestinians, 47
Palotta, Matteo, 147
Pambo, 48
Pamplona, 109
Pan, 173
"Pandean Pipe," 173
Pan's, 85, 94, 123, 129, 148, 192, 193, 203, 204, 241
Pan's pipes, 45
Papacy, Papists, 66, 93, 95, 218
Parallel melodic lines, 71
Parallel motion, 81
Parallel organum, 73
Parallel progressions, 72
Paris, synod of, 15, 59, 117
Parish Choir, The, 253
Parker, Horatio William, 238, 239, 258
Parliament, 198, 207
Parma, 94
Parochial mode, Anglican service, 140, 141
Parrish, Carl G., 88
Parry, Sir Charles Hastings Hubert, 162
Parsifal, Richard Wagner, 160
Parsons, William, 129
Pasquini, Bernardo, 193
Passau, 193
Passion music, 121, 122
Passion chorale, Hans Leo Hassler, 229
Passion, four narratives; Navarro, Juan, 212
Passions, four, Schütz unaccompanied, 147
Patriarchs, eastern, 64
Patrologia cursus completus, Migne, 178
Paul, the apostle, 34, 35, 37
Paul the Deacon, 79
Paul III, 95, 120
Paul IV, 99
Pauline, 27, 65
Paumann, Conrad, 186
"Peace of Westphalia," 228

Pelléas et Mélisande, Horatio William Paker, 239
Pennsylvania, 220, 227, 228, 253,
Pentecost, 72
Pepin, 178
Percussion instruments, 13
Pergolesi, Giovanni Battista, 146
Peri, Jacopo, 106, 121
Perotinus, 85
Perronet, Edward, 222
Persians, 64
Pesaro, 123
Peter, John Frederick, 229
Peter, King of Cyprus, 183
Peter and John, 34
Petrarch, Francesco di, 183
Pforzheim, 188
Philadelphia, 186, 219, 220, 224, 225, 227, 229, 231
Philippe de Vitry, 83
Philo, Judaeus, 16, 39, 44, 176
Philosophy, of music for worship, 54
Phoenicians, 47
Phonograph recordings, 28, Appendix III
Phrygian, 76
Physics of sound, 30
Pierluigi, 99
Pilgrims, 213, 214, 216
Pipe, 15, 23, 25, 27, 38, 48, 202
Pipes of Pan, 45
Pirro, André, 207
Pitches, 17, 78, 224
Pius IV, 95
Pius VI, 134
Pius, VII, 155
Pius, IX, 158
Pius X, 158, 159
Pisari, Pasquale, 147
Plagal modes, 75, 76
Plagal tones, 63
Plain Psalmody, Oliver Holden, 233
Plaine and Easie Introduction to Practicall Musicke, Thomas Morley, 97, 218
Plainsong, 70, 72, 74, 81, 185 (see Chant)
Plainsong, *florid,* 71
Plainsong, Gregorian, 71
Plainsong, Latin, 143
Plainsong, Roman, 63
Plainsong, *simple,* 71
Plato, 29, 43
Plays for Puritans, George Bernard Shaw, 180
Plan, liturgical of Justin, 60
Pliny the Younger, 39
Plotinus, 43
Plymouth, 214, 215
Po, 186
Podatus, 80
Poetry, poets, poems, and hymns, 13, 30, 31, 32, 33, 35, 39, 64, 66, 108, 110
Poland, 95, 185, 228
Polyphonic, 74, 81, 83, 84, 87, 92, 95, 104, 105, 106, 148, 189
Pompey, 23
Pomposa, 77
Pond, Silvanus Billings, 235
Pope, 95, 150, 186
Pope, Alexander, 132
Pope John XIX
Pope John XXII, 110
Pope Pius X *Motu Proprio,* 163
Pope Sixtus, 100
Pope Stephen IX, 58

Pope Vitalian, 180
"Popery," 167, 168
Popes, Western, 64
Popular religious song, 72, 114
Porphyry, 43
Porrectus, 80
Portsmouth, 208
Postapostolic, 35, 36, 43, 44
Praetorius, Michael, 98, 121, 146, 181, 191, 192, 193, 194, 207
Prague, 94
Praxiteles, 29
Prayer Book, Anglican, 142, 144
Precentor, 77, 79, 214
Predestination, 164
Prés, des, Josquin (see Josquin)
Presbyterians, 129, 226, 245, 258
Presbyterian Church, First, Mendham, 216
Priest(s), 17, 18, 19, 20, 49, 68, 69
Primitive peoples and origins, 13
Prince Henry, 165
"Prince of Music" Palestrina, 99
Princes of Europe, 82
Private masses, 69
Probus, 177
Processionarium, 60
Procilus, 44
Progressions, chordal, 74, 87
Proper of the Saints, 61, 63
Proper of the Season, 61, 62
Proprium Missae, 85
Prophecies, fulfillment of, 49
"Prophets, schools of," 14, 16
Protestant, 92, 93, 95, 163, 225
Protestant church music, 113, 125, 151, 152, 256
Protestant Europe, 224
Protestant faiths, 65
Protestant Reformation, 95, 166
Protestant services, 124, 231
Protestantism, 116, 162
Protestantism, lack of liturgy, 156
Provénce, 108
Providence, 234
Psallo, 43, 52
Psallonian Society, 234
Psalm 42 (43KJV), 68
Psalm 46, 116
Psalm 90, 16
Psalm 100, 130
Psalm 130, 116, 166
Psalm 134, 166
Psalm 137, 16
Psalm (137:1-5), 20
Psalm and hymn singing, 40
Psalm settings, classic, 150
"Psalmtones," 65
Psalm tunes, 176, 219
Psalm singing, antiphonal, 40, 48
Psalmodia Christiana, Bernardino de Sagahún, 212
Psalmody, 42
Psalmody, Calvinistic, 167
Psalmody, Frencj, 128
Psalmody, Netherlands, 128
Psalmody, Puritan, 216
Psalmes of David, 215
Psalms, Anglican, 144
Psalms of David, 16
Psalm(s), 18, 33, 35, 36, 43, 140,
Psalms (33:1-3), 43
"Psalms, hymns, and spiritual songs," 42
Psalms in the Form of Motets, Claude Goudimel, 98
Psalms, into English verse, 129

Psalms, Mendelssohn, 161
Psalms, metrical setting of, 128, 129, 131
Psalter, French, 221
Psalter, Guillaume Franc, 128
Psalter, The Ravenscroft, 131, 214
Psalter, Scottish, 221
Psalter, Sternhold and Hopkins, 214
Psalter, Thomas Este, 130
Psaltery, 25, 42
"Psaltery, living," 46
Psaltery, ten-stringed, 42, 43, 46
Psychology, of music for worship, 54
Ptolemy II, of Alexandria, 174
Puberty, 13
Public church meetings, 52, 53
Public games, 23, 28, 29
Public school education, America, 235
Pujol, Juan, 149
"Pull for the Shore," P. B. Bliss, 243
Punctum, 80
Purcell, Henry, 145, 146, 148, 149, 200
"Pure" instrumental music, 105
"Pure" music, 72
"Pure singing," 22, 28
Pure temperament, 128
Purist, 108
Puritan(s)(ism), 35, 115, 139, 163, 164, 165, 167, 168, 197, 214, 217, 226, 255, 256
Puritan churches, 167, 232
Puritan England, 213
Puritan hymn-singing culture, 239
Puritan reformation (revolt), 131, 152, 196, 197, 207
Pustet et Ratisbon, 159
Pythagoras, 29, 30

Q

Quaker(s), 218, 226, 227
Queen Elizabeth I, 163
Quilisma, 80

R

Rabbi Joshua ben Hananiah, 22
Radstadt, 187
Raison, André, 193
Rale, Father Sebastian, 230
Ram's horn, 22
Raphael, 86
Rapporter, French, 221
Rastatt, 193
Ravenscroft, Thomas, 130, 214
Read, Daniel, 221
Real Presence, 67
"Recesses of the soul," 107
Recitative, Italian, 121
Recklinghausen, 207
Red Sea, 14
Redford, John, 197
Reed, 14
Reedless instruments, 14
Reed pipes, 185
Rese: *Music in the Middle Ages*, 46
Reese, Gustave, 48
Reform, Roman Catholic, 95, 100
Reformation, 93, 114, 115, 120
Reformation, European continent, 139
Reformation, German,* 117, 120, 121, 257
Reformation in England, 139
Reformation, Lutheran,* 113
Reformation, Protestant,* 95
Reformation, Roman Catholic,* 103

Reformed church, Dutch New World, 225
"Reformed churches," 128
Reformed churches of Switzerland, France, and the Netherlands, 167
Reformed Protestant Dutch Church, 225
Reformers, 114
Regal, 185
Reger, Max, 162
Regnart, Jacob, 94
Reinagle, Joseph, 233
Reinken, Johann Adam, 193
Religious art music, 120
Religious music in the United States of America, 211
Religious music, not church, 146
Religious nature, 15
Religious outlook, 83
Religious revival, nineteenth century, in U.S.A., 226
Religious rites, 42, 43
Religious songs, 114
Renaissance, 51, 54, 72, 74, 85, 86, 91, 181
Reuenthal, Neidhart von, 109
Requiem mass, 62, 72, 161
Requiem Mass, Mozart, 150
Requiem Mass, Verdi, 162
Requier, Giraut, 109
"Rescue the Perishing," P. B. Bliss, 243
Responsive song, 35, 52, 57, 67
Restoration, 200
Restoration, Campellian-Stone, 226
"Restoration" churches, 258
The Resurrection, Bach, K.P.E., 150
Revelation (4:11) (5:9-13) (11:15-18) (15:3-4), 34
"Revival meeting," 134
"Revive Us Again," J. J. Husband, 250
Revolt, 62
Revolt, Anglican, 100
Revolt, Calvinistic, 100
Revolt, Lutheran, 100
Revolution, American, 215, 246
Rheims, 83
Rheinberger, Josef, 162
Rhythm, 17, 29, 32, 82, 83, 84, 109
Rhythmic accompaniment, 42
Rhythmic arrangement (patterned trope), 71
Rhythms, duple, triple, syncopated, 84
Richards, Senator Emerson, 210
Rigabello, 185
Rimbault, Edward, 176
Rimini, 148
Rinck, Johann, 205
Rite, Roman, 63
Rites, 64
Ritter, Frederic, 188
Ritual, 15, 49, 71
Riverby, Abbot of, 82
Robert of France, 82
Robinson, John, 201
"Rock of Ages," 235
Rogers, James Hotchkiss, 241
Rohrau, 154
Roman Catholic Church, 51, 54, 60, 61, 63, 66, 67, 69, 74, 78, 88, 93, 94, 107, 129, 134, 138, 147, 153, 168, 207, 230
Roman Catholic church music, 102, 108, 112, 113, 120, 125, 147, 156, 161, 241
Roman Catholic doctrine, 155
Roman Catholic liturgy, familiar value of, 157

*See under this topic also.

Roman Catholic Manual, Rev. John Cheverus, 231
Roman Catholic Reform, 93, 95, 100
Roman Catholic tradition, 102, 197, 255
Roman chant, 53, 58, 63
Roman Christendom, 116
Roman cultures, 36
Roman Empire, 66
Roman Latin Masses, 142
Roman liturgy, 66, 67, 68, 160
Roman music, 36, 37
Roman plain-song, 63
Roman Senate, 23
Roman school, 101, 103, 104
Roman theatre, 180
Romanos, 54
Romans, 21, 28, 36, 37
Romantic movement period, 83, 145, 154, 155, 156, 158, 160, 161
Rome, 23, 51, 57, 59, 60, 63, 69, 86, 88, 99, 102, 106, ·21, 122, 138, 147, 149, 174, 193
Rome, fall of, 51
Rome, Imperial, 14
Root, George Frederick, 238, 245
Rore, Cypriano de, 92
Rossini, Gioacchino Antonio, 123, 155, 203, 209
Rotenburg, 151
Rouen, Cathedral at, 182, 193
"Round," 81
Roxborough, Philadelphia, 227
Roxbury, 218
Royal Albert Hall, 204
Royal Chapel of Madrid, 211
Royal Melody, Wm. Tans'ur, 221, 222
Royal minstrelsy, 84
Rudiments of Music, Andrew Law, 232
Rules, music, 110
Russian chant, 55
Ryder, Thomas Philander, 243

S

Sackbut, 177
"Sacrament," 67
Sacred Harmony, Charles Wesley, 138
Sacred Harp, 246
Sacred Harp, Benjamin Franklin White, 224
Sacred Melody, Charles Wesley, 135, 136, 138
Sacred Songs, Moody and Sankey, 242
Sacrifice, 16, 18
Sagahún, Bernardino de, 212
St. Andrews Church, 200
St. Ann's Church, New York, 241
St. Bartholomew's night, 166
St. Bees, 206
Saint Bonaventura, 195
St. Cornelius, Compiègne, 178
St. Denis church, 203, 204
St. Dunstan, 178, 196
Saint Elizabeth, oratorio, Liszt, 160
St. Ethelwold, 178, 196
St. George, Windsor, 143
St. George's Cathedral, 206
St. George's Hall, 205
St. George's Chapel, 198
St. John's Church, 208
St. Godric, 110
St. Jakobi church, 192
St. James, 65
St. John the Baptist, 78
St. John's, 100
St. Leander, 58

St. Luke's, fuguing tune, Daniel Bayley, 222
St. Magnus' Church, 201
St. Mailduf, 178
St. Mark's, 65, 91, 98, 146
St. Martin's, fuguing tune, 222
St. Mary's, Philadelphia, *Te Deum,* 230
St. Michael's, Charleston, 232
St. Michael's Episcopal Church, 208
St. Nicholas Church, Brussels, 189
St. Paul (the apostle), 179
St. Paul's Cathedral, 197, 198, 201, 204, 205
St. Paul's Church, Boston, 241
St. Paul's church, Newburyport, 208, 222
Saint Paul, oratorio, Felix Mendelssohn, 161
St. Paul's Episcopal Church, 208
St. Peter, oratorio, John K. Paine, 238
St. Peter's, Rome, 99
St. Regis, 230
Saint-Saëns, 204
St. Sebald, Neuremberg, 189
St. Stephens, Cathedral, 187
St. Sulpice church, 204
St. Thomas, cathedral, 188
Saints, 61
Sale, Francois, 94
Salt Lake City, 210
Salter, Sumner, 241
Salzburg, 154, 187
Sambuke, 25
Samuel, Book of, 17
I Samuel (2:1-10), 34
II Samuel (6:14-23), 17
Sancte Johannes, 78
Sanctus, 61, 68, 141, 142, 144
Sandel, Andreas, 225
San Diego, 212
San Francisco, 225
San José Mission, 212
Sankey, Ira D., 242, 245
Santa Maria Maggiore, 99, 100
Saragossa, 58
Sarto, Patriarch, 158
Saul, 17, 38
Sausage, 230
Savannah, 219, 228
"Saved by the Blood," William Doane, 243
"Saviour, Breathe an Evening Blessing," George Waring Stebbins, 241
"Saviour, Like a Shepherd Lead Me," William Batchelder Bradbury, 236
"Saviour of Church Music," (Kerle) 95, 98
Saxony, 128, 190, 228
Scale pattern, 75
Scandicus, 80
Scarlatti, Alessandro, 122, 149, 162
Scheidermann, Heinrich, 193
Scheidt, Samuel, 193
Scherer family, 192
Schering, Arnold, 88
Schlick, Arnold, 187, 190
Schmid, Bernhard, 188
Schmidt, W., 177
Schmittbauer, Joseph Alois, 154
Schnitger, Arp, 192, 194, 203, 204
Schola cantorum, 158, 159
School, Burgundian, 85, 86
School, French, 161, 254
School of the Netherlands, 82
School, Roman, 101, 103, 104, 146, 158
School, Venetian, 91, 101, 103, 146, 158
School, Milan, 158

School, Neapolitan, 147
"Schools of the prophets," 16
Schubert, Franz, 145, 154, 155
Schuedt, 151
Schütz, Heinrich, 98, 121, 122, 123, 124, 125, 146
Schulz, Johann, 151
Schulze, Edmund, 206
Schumann, Robert, 145
Schweitzer, Albert, 205, 206
Scops, 110
Scotland, 115, 128, 129, 186, 199, 217
Scott, Dr. John, 135
Scottish culture, 82, 173, 257
Sculptures, 67
Seagrave, Robert, 134
"Search Me, O Lord," Main, H. P., 245
Second century, 37, 47, 50, 52
Secular, 14, 83, 95, 96
Secular living, 105
Secular-minded clergy, 93
Secular music, 66, 84, 86, 99, 108, 236
"Select Hymns with Tunes Annext," Charles Wesley, 135
Senfl, Ludwig, 94, 114, 117
Sensations of Sound, Herman Helmholtz, 192
Sentences, 22
Sequence, 68, 71, 72
Sergios, 54
Sermisy, Claude de, 94
Serra Junipero, 212
Seventeenth century, 74, 75, 79, 105, 106, 107, 120, 121, 125, 126, 128, 130, 132, 142, 145, 146, 148, 165, 191, 193, 194, 196, 199, 257
Seventh century, 51, 62, 63, 74
Seville, 58, 94
Seville, Cathedral at, 195
Sewall, Samuel, 220
Shakers, 245
"Shaped-notes," 220, 250
Shaw, George Bernard, 180
Shaw, Oliver, 234
Shelley, Harry Rowe, 240, 241
Sheng, 173
Shepherd, Arthur, 254
Shew bread, 26
"Shine on, O star," Moody and Sankey, 245
Shirley, Massachusetts, 232
Shofar, 22, 25
Shouting, 17
Sicily, 66
Sigismund, Archduke, 187
Sign, 77
Silbermann brothers, 194, 203, 207
Silesia, 228
Simeon's song, 34
Sine nomine, 96
Sing Academie, Berlin, 238
Singing, English appreciation for, 196
Singing of Psalmes, a Gospel Ordinance, 215
Singing schools, 63, 220, 249
Sistine chapel, 88, 99, 100, 102
Sixth century, 175, 178
Sixteenth century, 70, 74, 86, 93, 97, 101, 103, 104, 105, 109, 123, 128, 130, 142, 143, 146, 165, 180, 186, 189, 197, 199, 211, 257
Skilled workers, 15
Smart, Henry, 145, 205, 257
Smith, Elias, 247
Smith, "Father" Bernard, 200
Smith, William, 250

Snare drum, 13
Snetzler organ, 232
Socrates, 29
"A Soldier of the Cross," Moody and Sankey, 245
Solfeggio, 78, 220, 249
Solfeggio initials, British system, 251
Solmization, 78, 79
Solomon, 16, 18
Solomon's Temple, 17, 18, 20, 21, 28
Son of Herod, 23
Song, office of, 64
Song Leader, 77
Song of the Pilgrims, Arthur Shepherd, 254
Song of the Three Children, (Benedicite), 65
Songs, drinking, 36
Songs, noise of, 19
"Songs of Praise," New World Spanish folk, 212
Songs, to defend doctrinal points of view, 246
Sotah (VII: 7,8), 22
Sorbonne, 166
South Carolina, 225, 232
Southern Harmony, William Walker, 224
Spain(ish), 58, 93, 94, 149, 157, 181, 195, 211, 230
Spanish chant, 55, 58
"Speaking with(in) tongues," 35, 37
Spectator, 201
Speculum Musicaae, 111
Spencer (Chethubbeth), 27
Spirituals, Negro, 245, 247, 249
Spirituals, White, 245, 247, 249
"Spiritual songs," 34, 35, 43, 151
"Spiritual trance," 104
Spofforth, Samuel, 201
Spoleto, 122
Spontaneous, spontaneity, 14, 15, 35, 64, 71, 77
Spurgeon, Charles, 131
"Stabat Mater," Nicola Aloysius Montani, 241
Stage spectacles, 46
Stainer, Sir John, 145, 205
"Stand Up, Stand Up, for Jesus," George J. Webb, 235
Stebbins, George C., 245
Stebbins, George Waring, 241
Stanford, Sir Charles, 162
Stendhall, 186
"Step songs," 62
Stephanus, 178
Sternhold, Thomas, 129
Sternhold and Hopkins, 225
Stevenson, Robert Louis, 213
Stile Antico, 147, 149
Stile famigliari, 101
Stile moderno, 147
Stile misto, 147
Stone, Barton W., 247
"Story of the Cross, The," Dudley Buck, 241
Strasbourg, 166
String instruments, 13
Stubbs, Simon, 130
Sulley, 257
Sullivan, Sir Arthur, 145
Sultan, Mohamed III, 199
Sumner, William L., 194, 195, 202
Superior Anthems for Church Choirs, Hart Pease Danks, 243
Suriano, Francesco, 157
Sussex, 176

Swan, Timothy, 233
Swedish Settlers, 224, 226
Sweelinck, Jan Pieterzoon, 193
Switzerland, 115, 128, 138, 139, 163
Symbolic representations, 44, 67, 82
Symmes, Reverend Thomas, 218
Symphonie Liturgique, Arthur Honegger, 254
Synagogue, 20, 21, 22, 28, 32, 33, 41, 47, 49, 50, 62, 63
Synagogue tradition, 47
Synagogue worship, 49
Synesius, 64
Syrians, 23, 47, 48, 55, 64, 65
Syrian chant, 54
Syrians, organ builders, 175
Syrinx, 173

T

Table of Neumes, 80
Tabernacle (Old Testament), 15
Tabernacle organ, Salt Lake, 210
Tabulaturen etlicher Lobegesang, Arnold Schlick, 190
Tabut, 43
Tallis, Thomas, 97, 98, 129, 130, 143
Talmud, 27
Tambourine, 15, 23
Tans'ur, William, 131, 221, 222
"Taunton," Oliver Shaw, 234
Taylor, Raynor, 208, 233
Teaching, 22
Te Deum, 65, 230
Te Deum, Anglican, 142, 144
Te Deum, Berlioz, 161
Te Deum, John Carrol, 231
Te Deum, Lully, 143
Telemann, George Phillip, 193
Temperament, equal; pure, 127, 128
Temple, 16, 17, 18, 21, 22, 32, 38, 42, 43, 49
Temple Levitical Choir, 22
Temple music and offices, 16, 20, 21
Temple worship, Greek, 39
Temple worship, Roman, 39
Temple, destruction of, 21
Temple of Herod, 21
Temple of Solomon, 21
Temple, Zerrubabel's, 21, 29
"Temples of Reason" (Notre Dame), 203
Ten-stringed psaltery, 46
Tenth century, 66, 71, 77, 106, 179, 196
Ter Sanctus, 65
Tertullian, 62, 175
Tetrachords, 30, 31
Tewkesbury Abbey, 198
Texcoco, 211
"Thanksgiving," 67
Dr. Thatcher, 208
Thebans, 47
Theophilus, 182, 183
Theodoret, 48
Therapeutae, 39
Thibout IV, 109
Thibout, Justus, 102, 156
Third century, 52
Third century B.C., 14
Third century Christians, 37
Thirteenth century, 72, 81, 83, 84, 97, 106, 109, 180, 181
Thirty Years War, 93, 147, 194
This World's Joie, Sir Arnold Bax, 254

Thomas, Theodore, 240
Thorn, 185
Thorough Bass and Harmony, Benjamin Franklin Baker, 236
Thracian music, 38
"Through-composed," 87
Thuringia, 146
Timbrel, 24, 42
Timothy, Lewis, 219
I Timothy (3:16), 34
I Timothy (4:3-4), 43
II Timothy (2:11), 34
Tinel, Edgar, 161
Titelouze, Jean, 193
Tivoli, 102
To the Name above Every Name, Sir Arnold Bax, 254
Toledo, 58, 59, 211
Toledo, Council of, 58
Tonality, tonal relations, 72, 75, 101, 105, 126, 127
Tone pyramiding, 194
Tones, Georgian, 144
"Toplady," Thomas Hastings, 235
Torculus, 80
"Total depravity," 164
Toulouse, University of, 203
Tours, 86, 145
Tractus, 68
Traditionalism, 16, 48, 155
Trajan, 39
Traxdorff, 189
Tremont Temple, 208
Trent, Council of, 72, 95
Trinity, 82
Trinity Church, New York, 208, 232
Trombone choir, 229
Trombones, 14
Tropes, 71, 72
Troubadours, 84, 108, 109
Trouvéres, 84, 108, 109
Troyes, 109
Trumpets, 17, 22, 25, 26, 42
Tufts, John, 218
Tunder, Franz, 193
Twelfth century, 53, 74, 81, 82, 109, 180
Twentieth century, 159, 163, 253
Tye, Christopher, 143
Tympanon, 45
Tyrol, Duke of, 187
Tyrrhenia, Julia, tomb, 174

U

Unaccompanied anthems, 145
Unaccompanied choral music, 70
Unaccompanied motets, 145
Unaccompanied music, 88
Unaccompanied Passions, Schutz, 147
Union Harmony, Oliver Holden, 222, 233
Unison chant, 69, 70
United Presbyterian Church, 199
United States, 15, 54, 65, 134, 152, 208, 209, 212, 213, 220, 231, 232, 233, 234, 236, 241, 242, 249, 251, 254, 256, 257, 258
United States, Puritan thinking, 197
United States Psalmody, Silvanus Pond, 235
United States universities, 210
Unity, 32, 82, 87
"Universal Church," 140
Universities, United States, 210
Unmetrical, 35

Urania, or a Choice Collection of Psalm Tunes, etc.; John Lyon, 219, 221, 251
Uranian Academy, 220
Utile Dulci, or Joco-Serious Dialogue, Rev. Thos. Symmes, 218
Utrecht Psalter, 175

V

Valbeke, Ludwig van, 189
Valencia, 211
Valentinian, boy emperor, 55
Valentinian medallion, 174
Van Raalte, A. C., 225
Venetian madrigal, 91
Venetian school, the, 88, 91, 98, 101, 102, 103
Veni redemptor gentium, 55
Veni sancte Spiritus, 72
Venice, 97, 98, 102, 107, 123, 146, 188
Venite, Anglican, 142
Ventadour, Bernard de, 109
Venus, 36
Verdi, Giuseppe, 155, 162
Verona, 102
Versification, 39
Vesperale, 61
"Vexilla Regis," Harry Rowe Shelley, 241
Viatorinus, Gaius Julius, 177
Victimae paschali, 72
Victoria, Tomás Luis, 122
Victorian group, 257, 258
Vienna, 92, 94, 147, 154, 187, 193
Vierne, 203
Violin, 13
Virga, 80
Virgil, 173
Virgin Mary, 113, 140
Virginia, 221, 231
Visigothic chant, 55
Vita Mosis, 16
Vitalian, Pope, 180
Vittori, Loredo, 122
Vocal music, 14, 43, 66, 88
Vogelweide, Walther von der, 109
Voice, 27, 87, 88
Voltaire, 150

W

Wackermagel, 113
Wagner, Joachim, 194
Wagner, Richard, 155, 160, 161
Wahrenbrück, 151
Wainwright, Richard, 131
"Wake, Nicodemus," Henry Clay Worke, 238
Walcker, Eberhard Friedrich, 207
Wales, 115, 128, 242
Walker, William, 224
Walmisley, Thomas Attwood, 162
Walter, Thomas, 218
Waltham Abbey, 97
Walther, Johann, 114, 116, 117, 146, 193
War between the States, 220
Washington, George, 231
"Watchman, Tell Us of the Night," John Bowring, 244
"Water organ," 174
Watts, Isaac, 131, 132, 133, 165, 168, 219
"Watt's whims," 132
Webb, George James, 235, 238
Webb, Mary, 236
Webster's Dictionary, 202
Weckman, Matthias, 193

Weerbecke, Gaspar van, 86
Weimar, 193
Weissenfels, 123
Well-tempered clavier, Bach, 128
"We Praise Thee, O God," Wm. P. Mackay, 250
"We're Coming," Henry Clay Worke, 238
Wesley, Charles, 132, 134, 135, 137, 138, 206
Wesley, Charles and John, 219
Wesley, John, 132, 134
Wesley, Samuel, 134, 206
Wesley, Samuel Jr., 132
Wesley, Samuel Sebastian, 206
Wesleys, the, 242
Wesleyan, 54
Wesleyan movement, 168
Western chants, four, 59
Western church, 58, 63, 64, 66, 69, 174, 180
Western Europe, 176, 178
"Weybosset," Oliver Shaw, 234
"What a Friend We Have in Jesus," C. C. Converse, 243
White Spirituals, 245, 247, 249, 250
Whitefield, George, 138, 219, 242
"Whiter than Snow," William G. Fischer, 243
Whiting, Arthur Battelle, 238, 240
The Whole Booke of Psalms, Ravenscroft, 129, 130
Whyte, Robert, 143
Widor, Charles M., 203, 204, 205
Willaert, Adriaan, 91, 92, 93, 97, 98
William Tell, Overture to, Rossini, 209
Willis Co., 210
Willis, Henry, 195, 204, 206
Winchester, 106, 143
Winchester, Bishop of, 196
Winchester Organ, 179, 180, 183
Wind horns, 14
Windsor, 79
Wine, fulness of, 36
Wir glauben all' an einem Gott, 115
Wisconsin, 230
Wolfenbüttel, 146, 193
Women, 18, 22
"Wonderful Love," H. P. Main, 245
Woodbury, Isaac Baker, 236
Woodman, Raymond Huntington, 241
"Woodworth," William Batchelder Bradbury, 236
Worcester, 123, 216
Worcester Musical Convention, 220
"Worcester Three Choirs Festival," 254
Word texts, 65, 95, 105
Worgan, Dr. J., 138
Worke, Henry Clay, 238
World War I, 253, 254
World War II, 254
Worship service, 15, 16, 17, 18, 21, 22, 49, 62, 64, 71, 95, 98, 104
Wulstan, Deacon, 179
Wurlitzer, 206
Wren, Christopher, 200
"Wrestling Jacob," 132

Y

Yale University, 239
"The Year's at the Spring," Mrs. H. H. A. Beach, 240
Year of Jubilation, 22
Yomah (VII:1), 22
Yonge, C. D., 16

York, 198
York Minster, 198, 205
Young Men's Christian Association, 242
Ypres, 94

Z

Zachariah's song, 144
Zechariah, 34
Zerubbabel, 17, 21

Zeuner, Charles, 235
Zillah, 14
Zinzendorf, Count Nicholas von, 219, 228
Zion, 19, 20
Zither, 13
"Zol-ffer," 235
Zur Geschichte des Orgelspiels, Paul Hof-
    haimer, 188
Zurich, 94, 134
Zwingli, Huldreich, 115, 134, 181

This scholarly, concise compilation is planned to help ministers, church musicians, and students who find available information on introductory church music too scattered and overly pointed toward the particular needs of certain religious sects to be practical.

Russel N. Squire writes with a compelling narrative vigor, creating an absorbing and authentic panorama of religious music history to interest and stimulate the reader. Tirelessly and with singular expertness he has searched out important details to compose this book—a revelation of facts and insights.

Musical history quickens to life as his thesis traces its ebb and flow across the centuries from primitive origin to modern times. Ancient Hebrew history is painted with a broad sweep, beginning with the spontaneous songs the people sang during Moses' leadership to the more advanced music of the early Christians.

To complete his topic's full spectrum the author continues his discourse by examining the music of Western medieval Christians and the European reformers, concluding with a penetrating summation about the results of all this activity on the North American continent.

Of unusual value is the distribution throughout the book of music representative of historical periods and places. A bibliography and complete concordance of musical subjects and terms referred to in the Bible make up the final pages.